Learning to <u>Teach</u>

. . . not just for beginners

By Linda Shalaway

Doris Dillon, Consultant

SCHOLASTIC
PROFESSIONAL BOOKS

New York • Toronto • London • Auckland • Sydney

ACKNOWLEDGMENTS

This book results from the support, encouragement, and guidance of many people.

Dr. Judith Lanier, dean of Michigan State University's College of Education, has greatly influenced my ideas and attitudes about teaching. Under her tutelage at the Institute for Research on Teaching, I learned and wrote about many different aspects of teaching and research. The conversations we had as we pored over manuscripts—discussions of professionalism, the wisdom of practice, the growing knowledge base, and the never-ending challenge of learning to teach—are reflected throughout this book. Judy's vision of professional teachers as thinkers and decision-makers has inspired my efforts and the work of many others.

Leanna Landsmann, former editor-in-chief and publisher of Instructor publications, is this book's *raison d'être*. Realizing the need for such a resource book, she initiated this effort and offered her support and special insights throughout. I thank her for her faith in me, and for her commitment to teachers in general.

Doris Dillon, primary grade teacher and teacher mentor, faithfully read every page of my first draft and offered insightful comments and suggestions. Doris has more than 20 years of classroom experience, and I greatly valued and appreciated her input. Doris also put me in touch with many of the other teachers who contributed to this book. The general consensus among those of us who know Doris is that she's "the best."

Editor and former teacher Jane Schall improved my manuscript with her careful readings and insights. Editor Christine Van Huysse worked long and hard to see this book through production, and I appreciate her patient yet persistent efforts.

Thanks, too, to all the teachers and researchers I have ever worked with and learned from. They are too numerous to mention.

Special thanks to my husband, Scott, who is my constant support and inspiration. And I'd like to acknowledge my daughter, Nora, who is now in kindergarten. She's the main reason I care so much about good teaching.

ISBN 0-590-49037-0

FOREWORD

Learning to Teach is a gem, a beautifully designed and crafted volume that speaks clearly to both new and veteran teachers about the essential topics of instruction: those critical first days of the year, organization and management, planning, subject-matter teaching, relating to parents, mentoring and being mentored. Most of all, the book celebrates the challenge of learning *by* teachers. A school is a community of learners, and no one is entitled or obligated to learn more continuously, reflectively and joyfully than teachers themselves. *Learning by teachers* is the essential theme of this book, and Linda Shalaway carries it off with the skill of someone who has herself been engaged in learning about teaching for many years.

Learning to Teach is unique in the ways in which it draws its lessons equally well from the two main sources of educational understanding, research and experience. Neither is given primacy; each is offered its due consideration in turn. The findings of educational research are presented accurately and always embedded in a context of usefulness to the learning teacher. Moreover, I sense that the readers will grasp the emerging character of educational research, the ways in which its findings and recommendations are always evolving and becoming reformulated.

The reader should also sense that research on teaching is not a laboratory science, not a program of inquiry that conducts its investigations in isolated hothouses and then attempts to plant its seedlings in the real world of classrooms and schools. Indeed, research on teaching takes place in the vibrant, busy and complex arena of those real classrooms themselves. The scholar's laboratory is the classroom, not the test tube or isolation chamber. Researchers on teaching gain their understanding through the study of practice. They observe and interview able teachers, attempting to discern the insights and accomplishments of veterans and novices alike. Research thereby becomes a vehicle for detecting the wisdoms of practice, refining and elaborating those insights, and then sharing those understandings with practitioners from whose work they derive. *Learning to Teach* captures the excitement and the fruitfulness of that shared activity in which researchers and practitioners jointly produce the wisdom that can guide future practice.

I commend this book to you with the assurance that you will find it valuable whatever your role in education and however long you have practiced. I invite you to share with its other readers, and with the many teachers and researchers who contributed to its contents, the boundless excitement of learning to teach.

—Lee S. Shulman
Director
Teacher Assessment Project
Stanford University
Stanford, California

USING THIS BOOK

To write this book, I read and reviewed hundreds of research reports and interviewed many different teachers and researchers nationwide. I also drew from my own long experience as an education writer and my involvement with research on teaching. My statements about teaching represent findings replicated in numerous studies, not personal opinion. Because these well-documented findings are widely accepted, I have not cited them in the text (it woud be unfair to include only one or two studies, and cumbersome, if not impossible, to list them all). But you will find ample support for these findings in the publications listed at the end of each chapter.

I have also listed at the end of Chapter 8 the names and adresses of the federally funded research centers and educational laboratories where much of the research on teaching originates. (These labs and centers provide a wealth of information for teachers, as I stress in Chapter 8.)

Designed as a working resource book, *Learning to Teach* is an unfinished product. Missing are the comments, suggestions, insights, and activities you can contribute as you continue learning to teach. Use the wide margins throughout the text to record your thoughts, helpful tips from colleagues, your own adaptations of activities, ideas gleaned from professional publications—anything that helps you improve your teaching. Use the blank pages after each chapter's resource list to add the resources and references you discover as you grow professionally.

My best wishes to you as you learn to teach!

Linda Shalaway

Cameron, West Virginia
February 1989

C O N T E N T S

Knowledge is Power

"These recruits that face teaching as a life work are ready to learn to teach, and they are ready, though they know it not, to be formed by teaching."

Educator Willard Walter Waller's statement about novices just entering the ranks of teachers is as true today as it was when he made it more than 50 years ago. For beginners and experienced teachers alike, teaching is a continual learning process. Good teaching demands constant refinement and fine-tuning.

Okay. But tell that to the beginning teacher fresh out of college who has just received her assignment and begins full-time teaching in three days. Or to the retired biologist just embarking on a new career as a middle-school teacher. Or to the five-year veteran who has been reassigned to a grade and subject area totally unfamiliar to him. These *beginners* are just trying to survive.

Estimates are that before the end of this century, half the nation's teachers will be beginners. And unless conditions continue to change, most of these new teachers will enter the profession just like those before them—left on their own to sink or swim.

Survival skills must come first: learning to manage a classroom, learning to organize instruction—and yourself. But it is not enough simply to survive the first few years.

"Future professional growth can be limited by teachers' reluctance to give up the very practices that helped them get through their first year," writes Sharon Feiman-Nemser of the Institute for Research on Teaching.

Research and practice show that experiences during the first year set the tone for a teacher's career. They may even determine whether or not a teacher will remain in the profession.

So first you learn to survive. Then you begin to think about specific teaching strategies and developing your own style. Still later, you seek to refine and improve the strategies you adopt. It is this third step in the learning-to-teach process—striving to improve—that continues throughout a good teacher's career.

What do educational researchers and experienced teachers know that could help you? Most experts agree that new teachers are beginners for at least three years. This book is intended as a guide and map through those years and beyond. And like a map, it can point

you in the right direction, but you have to get there yourself. There are no recipes in teaching that guarantee specific results. Effective practice depends on skilled decision-makers matching what to teach, and how, with dfferent students in many situations.

This is a book about teaching. The first three chapters concentrate on setting the stage for effective instruction to occur. They mirror the needs and concerns of the new teacher: interested and involved students, organized days, and stimulating classrooms. And rightly so. Good teachers must develop good classroom management.

But it doesn't stop there. Teachers of today must be reflective, autonomous professionals set apart by special knowledge and skills. This is the science of teaching. *Learning to Teach* combines knowledge about teaching and learning to teach with practical insights on how to apply that knowledge. It is a blending of the practical wisdom of experienced teachers with insights gleaned from research.

Also included is a well-deserved measure of moral support. As in any profession, beginning teachers—all teachers—need the continued support and encouragement of their peers.

In the most general sense, this is a book about professional growth and development: forming partnerships with colleagues, learning to reflect on one's practice, sharing insights with others, and understanding the research and knowledge base.

It is meant to be read and reread many times. Not from cover to cover, but in bits and pieces, choosing the sections that address your needs.

If possible, read at least the first two chapters before school starts. These chapters and the ones that follow reflect major areas of teacher concern. And within each are topics, strategies, and activities. What happens when a behavior problem erupts in January? Refer to the corresponding section in Chapter 3. Could you use some rejuvenating by the end of winter? Chapter 8 can help. And what about

Surviving the First Year

Have fun in your classroom, be prepared to learn from your inevitable mistakes, think positively, and keep in mind Kevin Ryan's ten rules for surviving the first year of teaching (*The Induction of New Teachers*, Bloomington, IN: Phi Delta Kappa Educational Foundation, 1986):

1. Before you begin the first year of teaching, decide to teach a second year.
2. If you are not organized, get organized.
3. Do not look for love in the classroom. Look for respect. Look for student achievement. . . . The new teacher who is looking for love is vulnerable and erodes the authority needed to lead a class.
4. Love thy school secretary.
5. Focus on learning.
6. Become a member of the faculty. . . . Colleagues can provide a great source of satisfaction and professional learning.
7. Pay your body its dues.
8. Come to terms with your authority.
9. Do not get married the week before school starts.
10. Find a mentor — an experienced, older teacher who is willing to act as a guide and confidant through the first year.

involving parents at critical points throughout the year? See Chapter 6. As a professional, you will combine these guidelines in a personal way to achieve your special instructional blend.

That's what good teaching is all about.

Each chapter also includes suggestions for additional resources and readings. Space has been left for you to add your own references and notes—a place to keep them organized by topic. Use *Learning to Teach* as a career-long resource, continually updated by your own practical insights.

So have fun in your classroom, be prepared to learn from your inevitable mistakes, and think positively. Good luck! Good Reading!

First things first

The first day and before

"New teachers can read about teaching, they can watch other teachers, but it is only by teaching that they become teachers."

—*Susan Audap*
veteran teacher

Welcome to the ranks of professional teacher. There's no easing into it, so just forge ahead. Right from the beginning you have the same duties and responsibilities as the most experienced veteran. As a beginner, you may have had four or more years of college to prepare for this moment, a one-year graduate course, or just six weeks of emergency training. No matter how long or how much, it's never enough.

Oh, you're familiar with classrooms, you say. For at least sixteen years you sat in them. Yet, somehow the scene is strangely unfamiliar from the other side of the teacher's desk. As all those eager faces stare back at you, the great expectations you held about teaching seem to melt away.

If this is your first year, you may suffer from a case of the beginner's blues. Whether you are fresh out of college, changing careers, or assigned to a radically different group or subject, you may experience such beginning symptoms as nervous apprehension, sweaty palms, sleeplessness, feelings of inadequacy, and nightmares about those 25 faces waiting for your words of wisdom while you have nothing to say.

Take heart. If misery loves company, you've got plenty of it. Every teacher goes through this.

What can you do?

Take a deep breath, count to ten, and tackle each task one step at a time. Put your (justifiable) anxiety to work for you as a positive, creative force; it means you really care about doing well. And that says a lot for you as a professional. Besides, anxiety can sure get the old adrenaline pumping. And you may need it in the days ahead.

This chapter offers a step-by-step plan to help you get ready to set the stage for an efficient, well-run classroom. And if you don't already know, you will learn that some of the most important work takes place before the first day of school.

Before the Beginning

First impressions do count. The attitudes and expectations students develop as early as the first few hours of school affect their behavior and learning all year. So get off to a good start before students ever set foot in the classroom. Even if you received your assignment late and have only a day or two to get ready, you can accomplish many of the most important preparations.

Important beginnings for beginners

Most of the suggestions and activities offered in this chapter apply to experienced teachers as well as beginners. But if you are a new teacher or new to a school you need to remember to:
• Read the school policy manual and become acquainted with the rules and procedures, attendance policies, fire-safety regulations, and medical services.
• Begin to get to know your colleagues and don't hesitate to ask them for help.
• Become familiar with schoolwide objectives as you plan your instructional objectives.
• Get to know the principal. Ask about special policies and procedures so you can get an idea of the kind of support you can expect. (For example, should you expect the principal to visit your classroom during the first day? What other visits or observations should you know about and plan for? Does the school have a

send-home for parents that lists policies and procedures, or will you need to make your own?)

• Get to know your building: locate exits, bathrooms, special classrooms, the principal's office, and so on.

• Write out a detailed first-day schedule and realize you must remain flexible enough to respond to the unexpected.

• Purchase business cards (inexpensively, from one of the large mail-order catalogs).

Cultivating your allies

It takes the talents and hard work of many people to make schools function. Secretaries, custodians, teachers, principals, aides, librarians, counselors, cooks, specialists, and nurses are your allies. As co-workers, they'll be able to help and inform you. Get to know them before school begins.

Perhaps a helpful colleague will introduce you to the building staff. If not, don't wait for people to come to you. Take the first step. Introduce yourself as a new teacher and explain that you are trying to learn the proper procedures. They'll appreciate your effort and be much more inclined to help.

Aside from learning names, preferred titles, and responsibilities, here's what veteran teacher Sally Hudson of Cedar Falls, Iowa[1], says you need to find out from school staff members:

Custodians. Learn how and when you may call on their services to help with special events or accidents. Ask what procedures they'd appreciate that you follow (chairs up on the desk at the end of the day) and find out what types of equipment they have available for your use (ladder, hammer and nails, cleaning aids, and so forth).

Secretaries. Find out what office machines are available to you and when you may use them; how you acquire classroom supplies (chalk, paper, pencils); where the faculty mailboxes are located; how you should handle attendance, and what records you must keep for office purposes; and how you can make and receive phone calls during the school day.

Kitchen staff. Ask what responsibilities teachers have in the cafeteria and what lunches are available to them at what price. Find out whether the cafeteria and kitchen are available for class projects and how you can schedule their use. Explore the possibilities of having food service staff offer workshops on diet or nutrition to your class.

Librarians and media specialists. How are books organized and classified? Ask about reference materials and media equipment, and how you reserve or order them. Find out if teachers may help make book, magazine, and other media selections. Ask about procedures for visiting the media center—how and when students may come individually or as a class, and how they check out materials. Are there special services the librarians will provide, such as book talks, reading contests, or compiling bibliographies? Can they arrange to borrow professional journals or books from university libraries?

Special teachers. Most schools have at least some specialists, including those for reading, math, gifted or learning-disabled children, Chapter I, ESL (English as a Second Language), art, music, or band. Find out if the specialists have classrooms, how you refer a student for their services, what their schedules are, and whether or not you can help decide scheduling (to keep classroom disruptions at a minimum). Also, let them know they have your support and express an interest in being kept informed of your students' progress.

Counselors. Find out where student records are kept, who has access to them, and how. Ask how you might refer a student for counseling. What types of tests—county, state, or national—are given to students, and how does the school use the scores?

The principal. You've already met the principal, of course. But stop by before school to get better acquainted and learn more about what's expected of you. Find out what responsibilities you have outside of class (hall or lunchroom duty, for example). What annual activities should you know about—spring fair, field trips, talent show? How are assemblies and other programs planned and announced? Are there established procedures for involving parents or community members in the school? How will you be evaluated, and when? Find out when faculty meetings are held. And ask about the standardized tests used in your district.

The physical environment

Warm, well-run classrooms begin with the room's physical layout. Attractive, usable classrooms encourage students to like school; they help create the positive first impression that's so critical. Easily accessible materials and supplies can eliminate delays, disruptions, and confusion as students prepare for activities. In poorly arranged classrooms, students spend a lot of time waiting—waiting in line, waiting for help, waiting to begin.

Here are two musts:

• Make sure there are enough desks and chairs. Find out how to get more in case new students are added at the last minute.

• Decorate your classroom with attractive bulletin boards. (*Blockbuster Bulletin Boards* is a good source.)

Additional musts:

• Arrange files and curriculum materials so you can find things quickly.

• Secure enough textbooks.

• Make sure students have the supplies they need to get started—paper, pencils, crayons.

• Plan seating and furniture arrangements with instructional goals and activities in mind.

• Tell yourself you're going to be flexible.
Don't hesitate to give the room your

Bulletin boards

Here are three ideas that involve students in designing the boards. These double as get-acquainted and opening exercises on the first day.

A. Write *Welcome Back!* on a long strip of butcher paper and tack it to a bulletin board. Ask students to *sign in* with broad felt-tipped pens as they arrive. Encourage them to embellish the greeting with bright borders and personal touches and personal good wishes. (Suggested by Janet Anderson)

B. Cover a bulletin board with bright paper and write *Hats off to you!* in bold letters at the top. As students arrive, have them get right to work making a paper hat that illustrates their hobbies or career aspirations—baseball cap, nurse's hat, astronaut's helmet, etc. When all the students have finished, have them take turns introducing themselves and explaining why they made the hats they did. (Adapted from an idea by Ruth Dale)

C. Caption a bulletin board, *How do you fit in?* Then take a large piece of poster board and cut it into jigsaw pieces corresponding to the number of students. (Number the pieces before cutting them.) As students arrive, hand them puzzle pieces and ask them to write their names and draw pictures of themselves. Then begin calling the numbers of the puzzle pieces; ask each child to introduce him- or herself and fit his/her piece into the larger puzzle. The message to make clear is that while we all have a few rough edges, everyone fits in. (Adapted from an idea by Gail Pucci)

---

personal touch with plants, art, rugs, or posters, and add some cozy pillows for the reading corner. Also, keep basic safety precautions in mind. Ask yourself if your room is arranged so that:

• High traffic areas (pencil sharpener, sink, and so forth) are free of congestion.
• Desks, chairs, and other furniture are positioned where students won't trip over them.
• Students' desks are always visible.

• Storage space and materials are readily accessible so students don't have to wait in long lines. (Frequently-used items such as scissors and paste should be located in several different areas.)
• Art and science supplies—especially anything toxic—are stored safely.
• Students can easily see instructional displays and presentations from their desks.
• Desks are arranged to correspond to a temporary seating chart. Make name tags for

Room appearance

Temperature, lighting, noise level, furniture arrangements—these environmental factors and others affect each of us in different ways. In their research on individual learning styles, Rita Dunn, director of the Center for Learning, St. John's University, and Kenneth Dunn, of Queens College, New York, found that when teachers adjusted various environmental factors to students' preferences, the students performed better academically and were better behaved. The authors recommend that teachers:

• Create both well-lit and dimly-lit areas in the classroom by using bookcases, screens, plants, and other furniture. Some children learn best in bright light, but others do significantly better in low light. Dunn and Dunn found that bright light actually makes some students restless and hyperactive. They suggest allowing students to sit where they feel most comfortable. Also, try placing fidgety children in low-light areas and listless children in brighter areas.

• Provide opportunities for children to move around while visiting learning stations. Another myth is that children learn best when sitting still. Dunn and Dunn report that 50 percent of the seventh graders in one study needed extensive mobility while learning. These children achieved significantly more when they moved from one area to another to learn new information.

• Establish informal furniture arrangements where students can sit on soft chairs or pillows, or lounge on the carpet. Children do not always learn best when sitting up straight in hard chairs. The researchers stress, *While sitting in a hard chair, 75 percent of the total body weight is supported on only four square inches of bone, resulting in stress on the tissues of the buttocks that causes fatigue, discomfort, and the need for frequent changes in posture for people who are not padded well.* They found that many students pay better attention and achieve higher grades in more comfortable settings.

• Establish listening stations with headsets for children who need sound, as well as quiet study areas for those who work best in silence. Many children disprove another commonly-held conception—that silence helps kids concentrate better.

• Help students to be aware of their individual temperature preferences and encourage them to dress accordingly. Temperature preferences vary dramatically, and most children can't concentrate when they're either too cool or too warm.

the children and put them at their assigned seats, or have the children make their own. (This is a good opening-day activity—see the reproducible on p. 32.)
• Students have space to store their belongings.
• Electrical outlets are available for the tape recorder, computer, record player. (Make sure there are no frayed cords or other dangerous electrical hazards.)
• Window and door exits are unobstructed.
• Your name is written clearly on the board.
• Your name, class, and room number are posted on the classroom door, where parents and students can easily see them.
• A prominent *Welcome* sign is displayed.
• The room's overall appearance is attractive and inviting.

Routines and procedures

Another before-school-begins task: Decide on the routines and procedures that will help you operate your classroom efficiently. Children need specific ways of doing things— sharpening pencils, using the lavatory, receiving and turning in materials and supplies, handing in homework assignments, cleaning up, and using classroom space and facilities, among other things.

Use the checklist on p. 29 to decide which procedures you should plan first. Circle those you want to teach on the first day of school. Obviously, you won't use them all.

If you are comfortable with these, designate signals (hands, bells, flicking lights) for following certain procedures. For example, the *T-sign* could indicate that a student should get back on task.

General rules of conduct

In addition to procedures, you will need to establish general rules of conduct. Here are a few possibilities to consider in developing them. Remember, your students—especially the older ones—will respect rules more if they've had a hand in creating them. Come up with a list of what you consider the bare

Classroom rules

The following list is a starting point for rules for your classroom. Use these rules as guidelines. Vary them according to your students' age level (less formal for younger children, for example).

1. Treat others as you would like to be treated.

2. Respect other people's property and person (no hitting or stealing, for example).

3. Laugh with anyone, but laugh at no one.

4. You are responsible for your own learning.

5. Come to class and hand in assignments on time.

6. Do not disturb people who are working.

essentials, then keep in mind the additional items that you and the students can negotiate.

Select only a few rules—those that contribute to successful learning and an orderly environment. (No one can remember a long list.) Make them as clear and specific as possible. Finally, decide with the class's help the consequences for breaking these rules.

Teach these rules as you would a regular lesson. (Indeed, the veterans say it should be your first lesson.) Discuss each one individually, explaining the rationale behind the rule and ask for examples of how they could be broken. With examples, explain that rules help make everyone's time in school more enjoyable. (For an interesting early-year activity ask students to write and share their opinions of why rules are necessary.) It's a good idea to post the rules as a reminder and send a copy home with each child. Older students might write their own copies of the rules; just the act of writing the rules helps children remember them.

Start on the right foot with parents

First impressions count with parents, too. Good public relations at the beginning of the year can make the difference in parental support. Experienced teachers suggest it is a good idea to contact parents even before school starts.

While this book devotes Chapter 6 to home-school relations, there are things you can do initially to set a positive tone. One good idea: mail a back-to-school kit to each child's parents. Include such things as:

• A welcome letter to parents and a separate one for the student. Tell parents they are welcome to make an appointment to discuss any special concerns or to observe the classroom. Explain how important it is to get off to a good start, and suggest that appointments will help you avoid interruptions during those critical first few days. Tell parents you will spend the first weeks teaching rules and standard operating procedures. Urge them to schedule children's medical appointments for after school or weekends whenever possible.

• A form to return that lists home and office telephone numbers, emergency numbers, and the best times for you to reach them by telephone.

• A request for room parents and volunteers (see the reproducible on p. 34).

• A form for writing out special instructions for their child regarding medical or other considerations.

• A copy of the rules and regulations for the school and your classroom, with a request that parents support and help you in enforcing these rules.

• A list of supplies students should bring the first day. And for younger children, suggestions for show-and-tell. This demonstrates to both parents and students that you mean to get down to the business of learning right away.

Get serious about safety

Set the stage for a safe school year by recognizing and guarding against common hazards.

First, read and become familiar with basic first aid. For information, contact the American Red Cross or a local health agency or hospital. Post a tip sheet somewhere in your classroom where you—and your students, aides, or substitutes—can find it immediately. And make sure you fill in emergency phone numbers.

Next, find out if school regulations stipulate that only a school nurse treat an ill or injured child. (Even so, teachers need to administer aid in cases where the situation is life-threatening and immediate action is required.)

Familiarize yourself with these procedures for a medical emergency:

• Stay calm.

• Quickly assess the nature of the illness or injury so you'll know exactly what to report when you call for an ambulance or rescue squad.

• Send a responsible student to call for help while you administer first aid. (Exception: If a child has been poisoned, contact a poison-control center before aiding.)

• Don't move an injured child. Cover him or

Back-to-school kits

Mail a back-to-school kit to each child's parents. Include:

• A welcome letter to the parents and a separate one for the student

• A form to return that lists home and office telephone numbers.

• A request for room parents and volunteers.

• A form for special instructions for their child.

• A copy of the rules and regulations for the school and your classroom.

• A list of student supplies.

her with your coat or something else to prevent shock.

• Have someone notify the injured child's parents immediately.

• Fill out an accident report as soon as possible, while the details are still clear.

It's also a good idea to check with the school nurse and parents to find out which students have special health problems—conditions such as asthma, epilepsy, or diabetes. Request that asthmatic children keep a supply of medicine in the office in case of an attack. And you might take a Cardiopulmonary Resuscitation (CPR) course offered by the Red Cross or other health and service organizations. Most CPR courses also teach the Heimlich maneuver, the method for helping someone who is choking.

More before-school business

If you haven't already, now is the time to start an idea file or scavenge for supplies. On p. 35, there are some great ideas for things to start collecting and what you can do with them. A *Must-Do List* is on p. 28.

The First Day of School

It's here! Get off to a great start by making the first day much more than a chance to recount summer vacations or get acquainted.

The first day is the most critical point in the critical first few weeks. This is the first time students will see you in action. And what they see will color their perceptions for the whole year. Your role as teacher and classroom manager will be much easier if you create a positive first impression.

Students can detect your attitude, expectations and demands within the first few hours. If classroom activities flow smoothly, students will expect that's how things should go; if things are terribly disorganized, they will think chaos is the norm— and will behave accordingly.

It's a form of role modeling, really. Be organized and prepared if you expect the same from your students. And be work-oriented and business-like if you expect students to be serious about learning.

Pretty overwhelming, isn't it? Here you are with a bad case of the first-year jitters, and now you learn that your first day must run smoothly or you risk setting a bad tone for the year. But keep your chin up. Kids and classrooms are resilient, just as you have to be. And there are some proven ideas and strategies for successfully conducting that first day.

Most important is the immediate emphasis on rules and routines. Effective teachers introduce rules, routines, and procedures on the very first day, and continue to stress them throughout the first weeks. (See section on routines in Chapter 2, p. 39.)

Again, students must know right from the start how they are expected to act and behave. Routines offer security. Students can't really get down to the serious business of learning until they feel secure in class—how to get help, how to line up or turn in their work, how to properly participate in group activities, and so on.

Don't assume they will know all this on their own. You must actually teach routines and let kids practice until they understand what's expected. This is easier to do if you plan mostly whole-group activities for the first day or so.

It all sounds so serious. And yes, teaching and learning are serious endeavors. But don't think you must heed the advice, *Don't smile until Christmas.* On the contrary, be warm and friendly while still remaining firm and in control. The more pleasant the classroom climate, the more relaxed and secure your students and you will feel.

Your first day can be a good and productive one. There are bound to be the usual distractions—interruptions by school staff or the intercom; late-arriving students and parents; missing books and supplies. But effective teachers anticipate these distractions and just keep going. They actually plan for interruptions.

Tips for the first day

1. Arrive early so you can greet your colleagues and be in the room before any of the students are.
2. Greet students with a smile and a pleasant *Good morning.*
3. Write your name on the board so the students can learn it immediately.
4. Ask students to be seated when they arrive. They can wait to sharpen pencils, recount their summer, or ask questions. This helps you create a good working climate as soon as possible.

On the First Day

On the first day of each new school year, veteran Betty Forney reads *Ira Sleeps Over,* by Bernard Waber (Houghton Mifflin, 1972). She's found that the story works well at all grade levels.

Here's a summary: Six-year-old Ira is invited to spend the night at his friend Reggie's house, but he's not sure his teddy bear is invited, too. He's afraid to leave the teddy bear behind, but he's also afraid of looking like a baby. Bravely, he decides to go alone. When it's time to go to bed at Reggie's house, Ira discovers Reggie has a teddy bear, too.

"Kids often fear the unfamiliar turf they face at the beginning of a school year," says Forney. "I always tell them to 'take along a teddy bear.'

Fifth graders understand the symbolic meaning of this story and enjoy discussing what kinds of 'teddy bears' are suitable for kids their age. From lucky hats to big smiles to old friends—they suggest things they can take along to help themselves feel comfortable in strange settings."

For suggestions on great read-aloud books and ones that work best with kids of a certain age, see Jim Trelease's *The Read-Aloud Handbook* (Penguin Books, 1982).

---

5. Start the first day on time with an activity. If you anticipate a delay until all the students arrive, begin with a simple, fun drawing or writing activity. (Use, for example, one of the three interactive bulletin board ideas on p. 47. Or use the reproducibles on pp. 32-33 and ask students to create a nameplate or map out their new classroom.) Class should start on time and be smoothly under way as late-comers arrive.
6. Check attendance.
7. Conduct a get-acquainted exercise (this could be combined with roll call.) Judith Rio suggests creating a class dictionary. Begin by asking each child to write a three-part definition of himself or herself: physical characteristics, personality traits, and favorite hobbies or interests. Definitions should also include a pronunciation key to last names. Don't forget to do one for yourself. Finally, compile the definitions in a book.
8. Create a pleasant mood and ease kids' fears and anxieties by enjoying a good story and a good laugh together.
9. Introduce the important features of the room and the school.
10. Present the classroom routines and procedures in a positive way, as you would a regular lesson. Explain, discuss, and give students a chance to practice such routines as beginning- and end-of-the-day exercises.
11. Work with the students to develop classroom rules. Post the rules. (Older students can copy them.) Don't forget to discuss the consequences for disobeying rules.
12. Post a general schedule for lunch, music, physical education, recess, and classwork. Emphasize and teach the routines that will help students move into these periods quickly and efficiently. (Remember, they won't learn it all in a day. Continue to emphasize and practice classroom routines for the first few weeks.)

13. Begin to teach students how to follow oral and written directions. In the reproducible found on p. 30, teachers Joan Seifert and Fredrick Fedorko offer many activities for practicing following directions.
14. Begin simple academic activities—short reviews that guarantee a high success rate. This will boost confidence and ease fears. Compliment them on doing such a good job.
15. Monitor, watch, and maintain constant contact with students. Don't spend time on clerical work the first day. Try not to leave the room while the students are there.
16. Deal promptly with behavior problems.
17. Tease students with exciting new topics you plan to begin later in the week.
18. Issue books and discuss their care.
19. Give a brief writing assignment or put questions on the board for children to answer as a quick way to begin assessing abilities.

In general, make a good impression and keep enthusiasm high with first-day activities that involve students; provide success for all, maintain a whole-group focus, establish yourself as leader, provide a variety and change of pace, focus on content, and communicate a little about who you are and your positive expectations.

What the Veterans Say

What can you expect those first days or weeks or years in the classroom? Your experienced colleagues can paint an accurate picture. They've been there, and they're anxious to alert you to the joys and challenges ahead. Sure, you'll learn from your experience and mistakes. But you can learn from theirs, too.

Look at teaching through their eyes for a moment, and you may recognize many of your own fears and concerns. You're not the only one who's ever experienced the simultaneous exhilaration and panic of beginning to teach, many others have. Just listen to their comments:

What nobody really can prepare you for during teacher training are the inevitable ups and downs of teaching. The dreams I had at night were my first surprise. I dreamed I couldn't find my room, that the students had locked me in a locker, that my seventh graders had gotten control of the class. What I didn't know then was that struggling, coping, experimenting, and dreaming are the norms—the mark of a growing adult, not signs of personal failure or inadequate preparation.

—Karen Kepler Zumwalt

I was so happy—but scared and anxious. Everything was so new and there were so many unknowns—how much to plan, hours of planning, routines to establish, names to learn, behaviors to deal with, how to keep them all productively busy. I was exhausted every day for almost a year.

—Jean Medick

I had a very real high from teaching. However, I came home totally shot. I often went to sleep at 6 p.m.

—Dale Buboltz

I remind [beginning teachers] of common cycles of elation and despair. For instance, practically everyone cries during the fifth and sixth week, just before Christmas. I say, I know you don't want to be like everyone else, but I want you to know that everyone else is having a rough time. Somehow, just knowing that fact makes most new teachers feel better.

—Susan Audap

Teaching tips

- Prepare twice as much material as you think you'll need.
- Don't listen to the other teachers' evaluations of students in your classroom.
- Find another first-year teacher and have monthly seminars.
- Ask questions.
- Don't think of yourself as a finished product.
- Be aware of the personal feelings, moods, and attitudes you bring into the class.
- Have your most exciting units between Christmas and Easter.
- Try not to overreact.
- Encourage laughter in your class.

These veterans and millions like them met the challenges of beginning teaching. And you can, too. Share their joys and triumphs and anticipate your own. Pay attention to the advice they offer. And always remember that good teachers never stop learning—especially from each other.

Words of Wisdom

What have the veterans learned that could make your entry into teaching a little smoother? Most stress that you just can't do everything at once, no matter how much you want to. Accepting that fact will make your first year much easier. Here is their heartfelt advice based on hard-earned experience:

For your first year of teaching, concentrate on your job. Don't try to be super-wife, super-mom, or super-anything. Just do your best. And pat yourself on the back for a job well done; don't wait for someone else to do it.
—Debbie Frain

Work hard every day to do a good job while realizing that learning to teach well is a long-term process. Don't criticize yourself. If something doesn't work, try something else. Maintain a healthy life of your own—exercise, have fun, pursue personal friendships and interests. And develop personal relationships with your students. This takes time and sincere interest, but the payoff is tremendous.   —Jean Medick

Teaching is never monotonous. There are always new beginnings. Each year you can become rekindled and make a fresh start.
—Doris Dillon

Don't try to do everything! Set priorities—you can't do everything the first year. You will feel failure some days and with some children and yet there will be successful days and gains for some children.
—Pamela Shannon

Teacher success is directly related to joy in the classroom—joy in learning, joy in shared humor, joy in each other. That joy needs to be built into lessons—and can be!
—Jane Schall

Establish goals and work to accomplish these goals systematically and not all at once. Maintain a sense of humor and don't take yourself too seriously. Enjoy the students. I feel they're the best part about teaching.
—Barbara Diamond

Don't take advice from too many people. Trust in your own feelings. Remember that the outstanding teacher is a good leader. Our teacher training schools spend very little time on leadership skills, and that's what a new teacher needs the most.
—Dale Buboltz

Set realistic short-term goals. Enforce a classroom management scheme from the first day. Be prepared. Know as much about the district, the curriculum, and so on as you can. Find a buddy to confide in. And decide you will give it at least two years—no matter what!
—Jan Whitlack

Here's more good advice from veteran Glen Walter, author of *So Where's My Apple?: Diary of a First Year Teacher*. Walter admits that while his first year of teaching was a rewarding and productive one, it was also one of the toughest times in his life. He shares some lessons he learned the hard way:
• Prepare twice as much material as you think you'll need. Otherwise, you may finish your lesson 20 minutes ahead of time and will have to go on and try to teach the next day's material without having read it.
• Don't listen to the other teachers' evaluations of students in your classroom. Evaluate your students yourself.
• Find one of the best teachers in the school and seek out his or her advice during the first year.
• Find another first-year teacher and have monthly seminars. It's always nice to find out that someone else needs a 4 p.m. nap after a day at school.
• You're not a finished product, so don't think of yourself as one. You're still learning your art. Don't be afraid to make mistakes or admit that you've made them.
• Be aware of the personal feelings, moods, and attitudes you bring into the class and how they will affect your students.

• Don't be afraid to ask questions.
• Have your most exciting units between Christmas and Easter; you'll need them.
• Try not to overreact when students lie, when parents complain, or when the principal calls you on the carpet for something that wasn't your fault. Overreaction is common in first-year teachers.
• Encourage laughter in your class. Sometimes, the class clown can be the first-year teacher's best friend.

The Intangibles

Teaching is a people profession. Despite the many teacher-tested and research-based strategies contributing to a bona-fide "science of teaching," there are personal qualities each teacher brings to the classroom. Patience, flexibility, affection, humor—these are the intangibles that lead to happy, successful careers.

Your patience, acceptance, and persistence communicate to your students that it's okay if everything isn't perfect right away. They will be encouraged to keep trying.
—Jane Bluestein

Accept your place at the front of the room. The newly born teacher must be sprightly, vivacious. Possess enthusiasm and success will be yours.
—Maureen Robinson

Do and say everything with love. Be centered as persons, uncomplicated in behavior with each other, and clear in your vision of the job to be done.
—Ruth Donnelly

Remember the ancient Chinese saying: Be like bamboo; bend with the breeze . . .
—Susie Hochenberg

As you believe, so you'll teach. Will the climate of your place be love, respect, and caring? Will your time be hallowed by the real basics: imagination, curiosity, enthusiasm, celebration? I wish you courage, brains, and heart on your journey.
—Mimi Brodsky Chenfeld

Good luck! And happy teaching!

[1] This book has a wealth of teaching ideas, concepts, and data, drawn from many sources—teachers, surveys, and reseach. The first time an individual is mentioned, his or her affiliation and/or location, when known, is mentioned. On subsequent quotes or contributions by the same individual, the name is only given.

Chapter 1—Read more about it

1. "Effective Classroom Management at the Beginning of the School Year." Edmund T. Emmer, Carolyn M. Everston, and Linda M. Anderson. *Elementary School Journal* (1980), pp. 218-28.

2. *What's Noteworthy on School Improvement*, Summer 1981. Aurora, CO: The Mid-continent Regional Educational Laboratory.

3. *Teacher Planning in the First Weeks of School.* Christopher Clark and Jan Elmore. Research Series No. 56, Institute for Research on Teaching.

4. *Classroom Organization and Management* (Occasional Paper No. 54). Jere Brophy. East Lansing, MI: Institute for Research on Teaching, 1982. Also in *Elementary School Journal*, 1983, 83, 265-85.

5. *Don't Smile Until Christmas: Accounts of the First Year of Teaching.* Kevin Ryan (ed.). Chicago: University of Chicago Press, 1970.

6. Beginning Teacher's Resource Book. Jane Bluestein. Fearon, 1988.

7. *100 Ways to Enhance Self-Esteem.* Jack Canfield and Harold C. Wells. Englewood Cliffs, NJ: Prentice Hall, 1976.

8. *The Sociology of Teaching.* W. Waller. New York: John Wiley and Sons, 1932.

9. *Teacher Savers II.* Jane Schall. Cleveland: Instructor Books, 1985.

10. *Big Book of Absolutely Everything.* Rosemary Alexander (ed.). Cleveland: Instructor Books, 1986.

11. *The Induction of New Teachers.* Kevin Ryan. Bloomington, IN: Phi Delta Kappa Educational Foundation, 1986.

N O T E S

NOTES

✔ Must-Do List
Before the first day...

_____ Make bulletin board decisions: where to post announcements, menu, and calendar; what kind of welcome-back display to make; which boards will be for subject area stress; where to display children's work; which boards you will let students design

_____ Set up learning centers

_____ Make signs for room

_____ Prepare class rolls and permanent records

_____ Make class list to post on door

_____ Put your name outside the door

_____ Make student name tags for desks or have them make their own

_____ Find out schedules for lunch, gym, art, music, library

_____ Obtain supplies
     _____ plan books
     _____ attendance materials
     _____ paper clips
     _____ duplicating paper and masters
     _____ construction paper
     _____ manila folders
     _____ different kinds of tape
     _____ extra writing paper
     _____ grade book
     _____ rubber bands
     _____ stapler and staples
     _____ thermal masters
     _____ handwriting paper
     _____ receipt book
     _____ straight pins
     _____ spare pencils/pens
     _____ tissues

_____
_____
_____
_____
_____

_____ Prepare packets for students to take home the first day. Include:
     _____ emergency forms
     _____ school rules
     _____ supplies
     _____ bus or transportation rules
     _____ note to parents/request for room parents

_____
_____
_____

_____ Tentatively group students by reading levels using reading or permanent records

_____ Check to see which students may be going to special classes (Locate testing and psychological files)

_____ Get textbooks from book room; do paperwork needed to issue them

_____ Secure materials that accompany texts

_____ Gather appropriate supplementary materials

_____ Check out library books

_____ Set up a folder for a substitute to use in case of emergency
     _____ daily schedule (fill in as soon as possible)
     _____ seating chart (fill in as soon as possible)
     _____ reproducible activities (change monthly)

_____
_____
_____

_____ Prepare a file for correspondence from parents

_____ Prepare a file for faculty bulletins

_____ Write tentative lesson plans for the coming week

_____ Duplicate materials needed the first few days

_____ Write your name and other important information on the board

_____ Make a checklist for returned forms (can be used later for report cards and other items)

_____ Other

Developed by Rhoda London, original appeared in INSTRUCTOR, August 1984.

Beginning the School Year Checklist

The following is an adaptation of a checklist developed by the Mid-continent Regional Educational Laboratory, 12500 East Iliff Street, Suite 201; Aurora, Colorado 80014. Write them for the complete list or use these categories as guidelines to create your checklist.

Beginning Class

_____ A. Roll call, absentees
_____ B. Tardy students
_____ C. Get-ready routines
_____ D. Distributing materials
_____ E. _____
_____ F. _____

Work Requirements

_____ A. Heading papers
_____ B. Use of pen or pencil
_____ C. Writing on back of paper
_____ D. Neatness, legibility
_____ E. Incomplete work
_____ F. _____
_____ G. _____

Instructional Activities

_____ A. Signals for students' attention
_____ B. Signals for teacher's attention
_____ C. Student talk during seatwork
_____ D. Activities to do when work is done
_____ E. Student movement in and out of small group
_____ F. Bringing materials to group
_____ G. Expected behavior in group
_____ H. Expected behavior of students not in group
_____ I. _____
_____ J. _____

Ending Class

_____ A. Putting away supplies, equipment
_____ B. Cleaning up
_____ C. Dismissing class
_____ D. _____
_____ E. _____

Interruptions

_____ A. Rules
_____ B. Talk among students
_____ C. Turning in work
_____ D. Handing back assignments
_____ E. Getting back assignments
_____ F. Out-of-seat policies
_____ G. _____
_____ H. _____

Other Procedures

_____ A. Lunch procedures
_____ B. Student helpers
_____ C. _____
_____ D. _____

Room/School Areas

_____ A. Shared materials
_____ B. Teacher's desk
_____ C. Water fountain, bathroom, pencil sharpener
_____ D. Student desks
_____ E. Learning centers, stations
_____ F. Playground
_____ G. Lunchroom
_____ H. _____
_____ I. _____

Communicating Assignments

_____ A. Returning assignments
_____ B. Homework assignments
_____ C. _____
_____ D. _____

Checking Assignments in Class

_____ A. Students exchanging papers
_____ B. Marking and grading assignments
_____ C. Turning in assignments
_____ D. _____
_____ E. _____

Grading Procedures

_____ A. Recording grades
_____ B. Grading criteria
_____ C. Contracting with students for grades
_____ D. _____
_____ E. _____

Academic Feedback

_____ A. Rewards and incentives
_____ B. Posting student work
_____ C. Communicating with parents
_____ D. Students' record of grades
_____ E. Written comments on assignments
_____ F. _____
_____ G. _____

Excerpted from a list developed by the Mid-continent Educational Research Laboratory, 12500 East Iliff, Suite 201, Aurora, Colorado 80014.

Following directions:
as simple and basic as A-B-C

Developed by Jean Seifert and Frederick Fedorko, original appeared in INSTRUCTOR, February 1978.

Skill with oral directions

1. Have children identify and manipulate parts of the body. Give directions, such as:

"Touch your nose."

"Show me your left hand."

"Shake your left foot."

2. Give the children a set of oral directions. Have them carry out the entire set of directions after hearing them only once. For example:

"Come to my desk, pick up a book, and walk back to your seat."

"Stand up, touch your desk and your knee, turn around from right to left, say your name and address, then sit down and close your eyes."

3. Hand each child three blocks or objects of different colors, e.g. red, blue, and yellow. Then give specific directions:

"Pick up the red block."

"Put the red block beside the blue block."

"Lift the blue block over the red block and put it in front of the yellow block."

4. Cut 3″ x 5″ pieces of paper of different colors. On each piece, write with felt pen a number from one to ten, and give one card at random to each child. Then have them listen for these directions:

"Blue numbers, stand and take a big step forward."

"All even numbers, turn around."

"All red 3s, close your eyes and touch your right elbow."

5. Tell the children to write the numbers from one to ten at the top of their paper, then do the following:

"Put a box around the fifth number."

"Underline all the odd numbers."

"Put a circle around the sum of two and four."

6. Give each child a set of cards containing different geometric forms. When the children can identify each shape, give commands similar to the following:

"Hold up the circle."

"Hold up the diamond in your left hand."

"Hold up the triangle and rectangle and shake them."

7. Ask the children to draw a three-inch square. Tell them to divide it in three parts horizontally, divide it in half vertically, divide the four corners in half diagonally, then color each area they have created.

8. Have the children take out paper, pencil, and crayons. Read them a set of directions, and suggest they listen carefully, because the directions will not be repeated. Give commands similar to the following, pausing between each one:

"Draw three two-inch squares."

"Number them 1, 2, and 3."

"Write your name in square 1."

"Divide square 2 into two equal parts with a line going from top to bottom."

"In square 3, color the left half red."

Skill with written directions

1. Develop a set of flashcards with a single action on each, such as:

"Find something with a point on it."

"Jump in the air."

"Touch your left knee with your right hand."

The class can then be divided into teams. The teacher holds up the cards and the members of the teams do what is asked.

2. Place the following words on the chalkboard: *housekeeper, paperboy, doctor, animal trainer*. Students arrange them in alphabetical order.

3. Select a simple game and write directions on the board for playing it. Do not give any oral directions or explanation. Children read the directions and play the game.

4. Write a sentence, and have the children copy it. Put the following directions on the chalkboard:

"Underline the third word in this sentence."

"Circle the last word."

"Put a check over each word with a double letter."

5. Have the children construct an outline map of their neighborhood. Then have them write directions for getting from one place to another.

6. Cards are passed out to the children with directions asking them to perform a pantomime. After his pantomime is over, the child reads his directions orally, and the other children check to see if the directions were followed correctly.

7. Have pupils read and follow specific written directions similar to the following:

"Make an X on the fourth line from the bottom of your paper."

"Make three O's on the third line from the top of your paper."

"Draw a line connecting the X with each O."

8. Call on three children at a time to come to the front of the room. Give one child a noun written on a slip of paper and each of the other two children an adjective. Ask the first child to make a sentence using his word. Tell the second child to repeat the sentence, and add his word to the sentence. Tell the third child to repeat the second child's sentence and add his word to it. For example:

First Child—"I have an *apple*."

Second Child—"I have a *red apple*."

Third Child—"I have a *big, red apple*."

9. Give children written directions which require them to follow a process, such as constructing a pinhole camera. Children may follow the directions in groups or individually.

10. Conduct a "silent lesson." All directions for the lesson and any questions from the students are in writing.

11. Duplicate directions from old examinations to teach students how to do better on exams. Show them how to attend to such words as *list, define, summarize,* and *best choice*.

12. Give a "brain twister" for following directions. Once students can follow yours, ask them to write their own. Examples:

"Draw a straight, vertical line about two inches long. Beside it, at the right, draw a parallel dotted line of equal length."

"Here are names of five states: California, Maine, Iowa, Nevada, New Mexico. Print the names in a column, one below the other, in descending order according to length, as indicated by the number of letters in each name. In a column at the left of each name, write the number of letters in the column. Add the numbers in the column and write the sum underneath. If the total is less than 55, circle the sum. If the total is greater than 55, underline the sum."

"Draw a horizontal line about two inches long. Just below the line, make four small circles. Just above the line, make four small squares. Select the vowels from the word *suspicion* and write one in each circle in the order in which the vowels appear in the word. Next select the consonants from the word *supreme* and write one in each square in reverse order in which they appear in the word."

13. Give the children a complex set of directions based on one idea. Allow them only a certain amount of time, and permit no questions after work begins. For example:

"Write in a line the letters of the word *pleasure*. If the first letter in the line is the sixteenth letter in the alphabet, change it to the sixth letter of the alphabet. Change the first s to the twentieth letter in the alphabet. If there are more than 3 *e's*, change the r to the second letter in the line. Change the fourth letter from the left to the fifth letter of the alphabet. Change the last three letters to *ing*. Read the new word you have created (*fleeting*)!"

The Lineup!

57 ways to get kids in a row

LINE UP IF YOU CAN TELL ME . . .

1. what you would wish if you had one wish
2. something people don't like: being late, sour milk, flies, noise . . .
3. something people do like: rainbows, picnics, hugs, good movies . . .
4. a safety rule for home or school: don't play with matches . . .
5. a health rule for home or school: cover coughs and sneezes
6. the name of a television character or show title
7. the name of a state: Missouri, Kansas, Colorado, New Mexico . . .
8. where your father works, mother's occupation
9. the name of a city: New York, Boston, Detroit, Chicago . . .
10. the name of a country: Scotland, Canada, India, Italy . . .
11. what you would like to be when you grow up: an engineer, a news reporter, a pilot, a movie producer . . .
12. your favorite subject in school
13. your favorite place to visit: the woods, the ocean, the park, the gym . . .
14. a book title, author, character, or illustrator
15. a kind of fruit: banana, plum, grape . . .
16. a kind of vegetable: lettuce, beans, corn, cabbage, carrots . . .
17. a type of tree: oak, maple, weeping willow, elm, lilac . . .
18. a type of flower: rose, tulip, daisy, iris, marigold . . .
19. the name of a movie star, singer, or rock group
20. your favorite cereal: Cocoa Puffs, Rice Krispies, Raisin Bran, Sugar Smacks . . .
21. a hobby or collection: gardening, stickers, stamps, dolls, biking, shells . . .
22. an animal in the zoo: ostrich, panda, monkey, rattlesnake, polar bear . . .
23. an animal on a farm: rooster, goat, pig, cow, hen, duck . . .
24. where your family went on vacation
25. the name of a school worker: Mr. Manors, the cook; Ms. May, the principal . . .
26. your address, phone number, birthday
27. what you would do with a million dollars
28. one thing you learned in school this week

LINE UP IF YOU HAVE . . .

1. a tooth missing, two teeth, three, four . . .
2. aqua as your favorite color, violet, maroon, peach . . .
3. a T-shirt on, short sleeves, long sleeves
4. a ribbon in your hair, a watch on your left hand, a ring, a necklace . . .
5. a "z" in your name, a "b," an "f," a "q" . . .
6. a short vowel in your name, a long vowel
7. a birthday in January, February, March . . .
8. been to the circus, a rodeo, the zoo . . .
9. sneakers on, boots, loafers . . .
10. two persons in your family, three, four . . .
11. a pet dog, cat, bird, fish, turtle, horse . . .
12. seen the movie *Star Wars, Pinocchio, E.T.* . . .
13. striped socks on, pink socks, brown socks . . .
14. taken lessons in dance, judo, swimming, voice, piano, guitar, flute . . .
15. visited other states: California, Florida, Texas, Utah, Arizona . . .
16. participated in a wedding as a bridesmaid, flower girl, ring bearer . . .
17. flown in an airplane, a helicopter, an air balloon, sailed, motorcycled . . .
18. gone snow-skiing, water-skiing, snorkeling . . .
19. cooked: hotdogs, hamburgers, grilled cheese sandwiches, cookies, cakes . . .
20. helped parents mow grass, wash the car, clean the kitchen . . .
21. performed in a recital, play, sports activity for an audience . . .
22. moved to a new country, state, city, town, neighborhood . . .
23. brought back your library books today, yesterday or will bring them back tomorrow
24. walked to school, ridden the bus, the subway, driven with a parent or friend
25. been polite to a friend, teacher, parent today
26. blue eyes, brown, hazel, black . . .
27. been to a hospital for tonsils, broken bones or to visit a friend
28. written a poem, story, song, play . . .
29. stood on your head, played tag, skipped rope, hung on the monkey bar, raced . . .

Developed by Glenda Stroup Smithers. Originally appeared in INSTRUCTOR, August 1984.

All about <u>you!</u>

Kids, don't be a whosit or a whatchamacallit! Tell the world who you are with your very own nameplate. It's easy to make. Just cut along the solid lines. Then write your name on one side and decorate the other side with words, photos, and pictures that tell about YOU--your hobbies, your interests, your likes and your dislikes. Next, fold along the dotted lines to make a pyramid. Tuck the little flap inside and tape it. Put your new nameplate on top of your desk.

Tuck this flap inside

your name

your picture here

All about me!

Tape here

Welcome aboard, Buccaneers!

Yo, ho, ho! Pirates, ahoy! Let's make a treasure map of our room. Draw and label the landmarks listed below on your map. Then draw your desk on the map and place a big X on it. Why? Every pirate knows that X marks your spot!

Find and draw:

the door(s)	the windows
the chalkboard	the art supplies
the coat closet	the wastebasket
the pencil sharpener	the students' desks
the teacher's desk	the bulletin board(s)

Finished so soon? Draw a pirate's treasure map of our school on the back.

HELP WANTED

Dear _____ ,

As we start the new school year, I am sure you would like to know how you can help your child at home. Here are some ideas you might try. They'll improve your child's communication skills while they demonstrate how school's activities are related to everyday living. If you have any questions, please don't hesitate to call me at _____ . By working together, we'll ensure that your child enjoys success in school!

Sincerely,

_____

P.S. We need parents to help at school, too! If you are interested in becoming a parent volunteer, please let me know.

Talk with your child. By initiating conversations with your child and drawing him or her into family discussions, you'll help your child's language development. Don't hesitate to use words you feel your child may not know. You'll increase his or her vocabulary by using new words frequently.

Read together. Reading is a skill, and like all skills, requires practice. Encourage your child to read to you, and read to your child from a variety of materials—newspapers, magazines, and children's books. Get your child a library card and check out new books regularly. Most important of all, let your child see you reading. If you enjoy reading, chances are your child will, too.

Let children help in the kitchen. Reading recipes, making measurements, and listening carefully to directions are all important skills your children can practice while enjoying a pleasurable afternoon cooking with you.

Go shopping together. Going to the grocery store and discussing prices, bargains, and buying decisions with your child help him or her practice math while learning the value of money. For example, ask your child to compare prices by weight, to count your change on the way home, and so on. Teach good nutrition, too, by explaining how you select foods to make a balanced meal for your family.

Watch television selectively. Watch programs together and discuss them. Ask your child, "If you had been that character, what would you have done?"

After a news program, pull out an atlas of the world or look at a globe and show your child where news events are taking place.

Encourage children to write. Let them write shopping lists, stories, and movie reviews. Catch up on your correspondence by dictating letters to them while you do the ironing or other chores.

Discuss papers and projects your child brings home. Let your child know you're proud of his or her efforts and accomplishments. When the going gets tough, offer help and encouragement. This will give your child the confidence needed to persevere.

Appeared in INSTRUCTOR, August 1982.

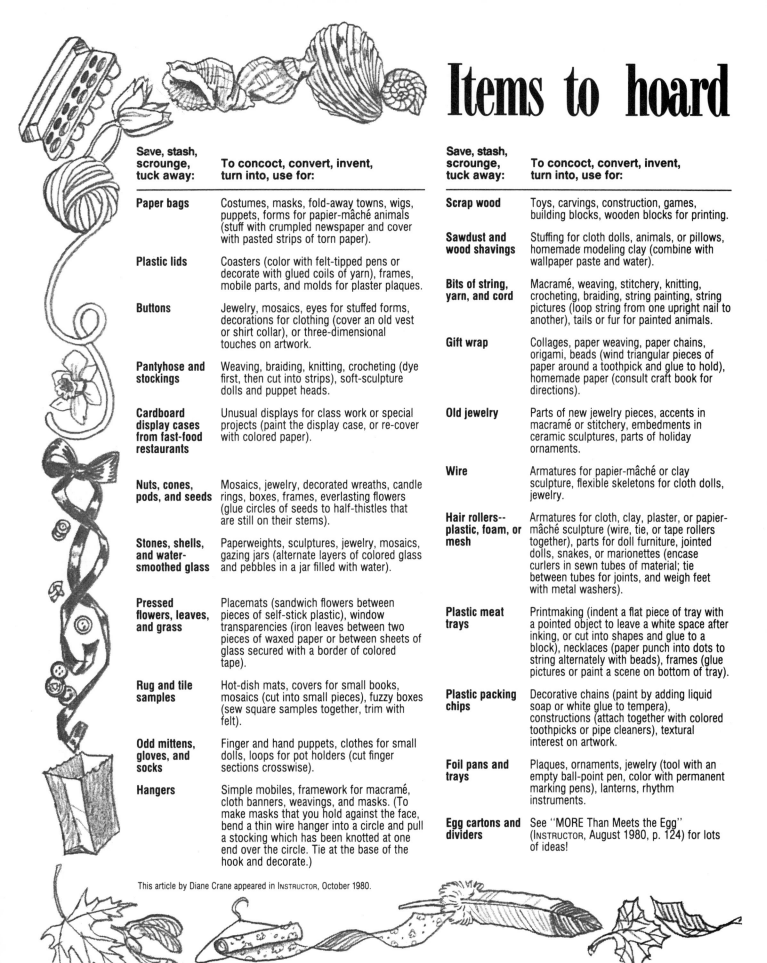

Items to hoard

Save, stash, scrounge, tuck away:	To concoct, convert, invent, turn into, use for:
Paper bags	Costumes, masks, fold-away towns, wigs, puppets, forms for papier-mâché animals (stuff with crumpled newspaper and cover with pasted strips of torn paper).
Plastic lids	Coasters (color with felt-tipped pens or decorate with glued coils of yarn), frames, mobile parts, and molds for plaster plaques.
Buttons	Jewelry, mosaics, eyes for stuffed forms, decorations for clothing (cover an old vest or shirt collar), or three-dimensional touches on artwork.
Pantyhose and stockings	Weaving, braiding, knitting, crocheting (dye first, then cut into strips), soft-sculpture dolls and puppet heads.
Cardboard display cases from fast-food restaurants	Unusual displays for class work or special projects (paint the display case, or re-cover with colored paper).
Nuts, cones, pods, and seeds	Mosaics, jewelry, decorated wreaths, candle rings, boxes, frames, everlasting flowers (glue circles of seeds to half-thistles that are still on their stems).
Stones, shells, and water-smoothed glass	Paperweights, sculptures, jewelry, mosaics, gazing jars (alternate layers of colored glass and pebbles in a jar filled with water).
Pressed flowers, leaves, and grass	Placemats (sandwich flowers between pieces of self-stick plastic), window transparencies (iron leaves between two pieces of waxed paper or between sheets of glass secured with a border of colored tape).
Rug and tile samples	Hot-dish mats, covers for small books, mosaics (cut into small pieces), fuzzy boxes (sew square samples together, trim with felt).
Odd mittens, gloves, and socks	Finger and hand puppets, clothes for small dolls, loops for pot holders (cut finger sections crosswise).
Hangers	Simple mobiles, framework for macramé, cloth banners, weavings, and masks. (To make masks that you hold against the face, bend a thin wire hanger into a circle and pull a stocking which has been knotted at one end over the circle. Tie at the base of the hook and decorate.)

This article by Diane Crane appeared in INSTRUCTOR, October 1980.

Save, stash, scrounge, tuck away:	To concoct, convert, invent, turn into, use for:
Scrap wood	Toys, carvings, construction, games, building blocks, wooden blocks for printing.
Sawdust and wood shavings	Stuffing for cloth dolls, animals, or pillows, homemade modeling clay (combine with wallpaper paste and water).
Bits of string, yarn, and cord	Macramé, weaving, stitchery, knitting, crocheting, braiding, string painting, string pictures (loop string from one upright nail to another), tails or fur for painted animals.
Gift wrap	Collages, paper weaving, paper chains, origami, beads (wind triangular pieces of paper around a toothpick and glue to hold), homemade paper (consult craft book for directions).
Old jewelry	Parts of new jewelry pieces, accents in macramé or stitchery, embedments in ceramic sculptures, parts of holiday ornaments.
Wire	Armatures for papier-mâché or clay sculpture, flexible skeletons for cloth dolls, jewelry.
Hair rollers-- plastic, foam, or mesh	Armatures for cloth, clay, plaster, or papier-mâché sculpture (wire, tie, or tape rollers together), parts for doll furniture, jointed dolls, snakes, or marionettes (encase curlers in sewn tubes of material; tie between tubes for joints, and weigh feet with metal washers).
Plastic meat trays	Printmaking (indent a flat piece of tray with a pointed object to leave a white space after inking, or cut into shapes and glue to a block), necklaces (paper punch into dots to string alternately with beads), frames (glue pictures or paint a scene on bottom of tray).
Plastic packing chips	Decorative chains (paint by adding liquid soap or white glue to tempera), constructions (attach together with colored toothpicks or pipe cleaners), textural interest on artwork.
Foil pans and trays	Plaques, ornaments, jewelry (tool with an empty ball-point pen, color with permanent marking pens), lanterns, rhythm instruments.
Egg cartons and dividers	See "MORE Than Meets the Egg" (INSTRUCTOR, August 1980, p. 124) for lots of ideas!

All-Purpose Chart

Don't Be Afraid To Fail

You've failed
many times,
although you may not
remember.
You fell down
the first time
you tried to walk.
You almost drowned
the first time
you tried to
swim, didn't you?
Did you hit the
ball the first time
you swung a bat?
Heavy hitters,
the ones who hit the
most home runs,
also strike
out a lot.
R. H. Macy
failed seven
times before his
store in New York
caught on.
English novelist
John Creasey got
753 rejection slips
before he published
564 books.
Babe Ruth struck out
1,330 times,
but he also hit
714 home runs.
Don't worry about
failure.
Worry about the
chances you miss
when you don't
even try.

A message as published in the *Wall Street Journal* by United Technologies Corporation, Hartford, Connecticut 06101.

Getting organized

—classroom organization and management

❝I could see that things were not going well. Children were out of their seats, voices were at a roar, [the teacher] was yelling across the room for quiet. A tap dancing bear and a juggler would have made the scene complete. My heart went out to this new teacher because we've all been there.**❞**

—anonymous
The Mentor Teacher Casebook

The first day proceeded smoothly enough. You were well-prepared, and the students were polite and cooperative as you sized each other up. But now the honeymoon is over. Your task in the weeks and months ahead will be to establish the classroom control necessary for doing your job—for actually teaching! This is the time to establish good work habits and behavior patterns that will persist throughout the year.

Good management skills are critical for all aspects of teaching, whether you are instructing the whole class, working with small groups, using learning centers, giving individualized assignments, or holding student conferences. Popularity or talent won't assure a well-managed classroom. Only hard work and careful planning can.

Discipline is only a small aspect of classroom management. The concept is much larger, including all activities that lead to and support effective instruction.

What happens in a well-managed classroom?

The Northwest Regional Educational Laboratory in Portland, Oregon, analyzed the results of numerous studies on effective schooling practices and identified these characteristics:

• Students are highly involved.
• Students know what is expected of them, and they are given frequent opportunities to succeed.
• There is little wasted time, confusion, or disruption.
• The climate is work-oriented but relaxed.

Student behavior is an important component of classroom management. (Read about behavior in Chapter 3.) Classroom management often is equated with discipline, yet discipline is only a small aspect of it. The concept of management is much broader; it encompasses all the routines and procedures of daily classroom life. It includes the physical arrangement of both classroom and students.

It involves time management, record-keeping, lesson planning, grading—all those activities that lead to and support effective instruction.

Successful classroom management establishes the right conditions for teaching and learning and, in the process, prevents problems before they occur. Effective teachers differ from those who are less effective not in how well they handle disruptive students, but in how they establish and manage classroom routines.

Teaching techniques also contribute to good management and problem prevention—techniques such as lesson-pacing, keeping students on task, and matching instruction with ability levels. (See Chapter 4.) But here the focus is on setting the stage for good teaching. This chapter addresses the major aspects of classroom management and includes research-based suggestions and teacher-tested activities.

Management continues to be the number one concern of beginning teachers, sometimes through their second or third year. And rightly so. Management skills take time to learn and perfect. If you can't keep kids occupied in meaningful learning tasks for a large percentage of the school day, chances are you won't be able to teach them much.

But as important as management is, don't lose sight of your larger goals. As Susan Audap, director of the Park Avenue Teachers' Center in Los Angeles, puts it:

"When new teachers get sidetracked into thinking that teaching is management and control, someone needs to remind them that these skills only set the stage so that teaching and learning can happen more often and with more joy."

The Same Old Routine

Consider these two classrooms:

In the first, the teacher is trying to start a math lesson. She raises her voice for attention and gestures frantically as students jump out of their seats to sharpen pencils, get scratch paper, or ask their friends for help. Cries of

What are we supposed to be doing? fill the air. The time this teacher has allotted for math is half over before the textbooks are passed out and the lesson begins.

Meanwhile, just across the hall . . .

A reading period progresses smoothly. Circulating among small reading groups, the teacher works with some students while continuing to monitor those doing seatwork. As they complete workbook assignments, the students carry their papers to the teacher's desk, then return to take out their library books, as previously instructed.

Routines. One teacher established and enforced them, the other did not. It's obvious which is which.

Routines are the backbone of daily classroom life. They facilitate teaching and learning. That's the bottom line. Routines don't just make your life easier, they save valuable classroom time. And what's more important, efficient routines and procedures make it easier for students to learn and achieve more.

That's not to say that teaching and learning can be routinized. Never! But procedures for turning in seatwork assignments, talking in class, lining up for lunch, using the pencil sharpener, passing out materials, and getting assistance must be. (If you aren't sure about how to handle these procedures, talk to colleagues and find out what works well for them.)

Routines are critical, says David Berliner, of Arizona State University. Berliner views teachers as executives who each day make more important decisions affecting the lives of others than some chief executive officers make in a month or a year. The only way teachers can do that, he explains, is to manage by routine. Many decisions become automatic as they transform patterns of activities into smooth routines.

Routines differ from teacher to teacher and class to class. The important thing is that there are routines which are consistent and which students know.

One fifth-grade teacher in Michigan, for example, has an elaborate system of color-coded cards, a bell, and light signals to indicate which activities and rules students should follow. While most of us would operate more subtly, this highly successful teacher finds that his system works well and the results justify the extra time it takes to teach it.

Academic routines help kids learn better. University of Pittsburgh researcher Gaea Leinhardt studied mathematics teaching in elementary classrooms and found that the major difference between expert and novice teachers was in the use of well-practiced routines.

Leinhardt tells of an expert teacher who gave students guided practice after a lesson by assigning two problems and asking the children to stand when they finished. This way, the teacher could readily see who needed help, which she would offer during the next round of problems.

This routine enabled the teacher to pace the practice and give rapid feedback on performance to all of the children, Leinhardt explains.

For new and seasoned professionals alike, the beginning of the school year is the time to teach and reteach classroom routines. It usually takes several weeks for these to become firmly entrenched. But the initial time invested in teaching and firmly reinforcing routines pays huge dividends later in the year.

Take it from Texas teacher Michelle Baker. After a five-year leave from teaching, Baker returned to the classroom to find things had radically changed during her absence. She felt like a beginner again—with all of a beginner's classroom management problems.

"By Christmas I knew there was a problem in my room," says Baker. "The off-task behavior was getting out of control, and teaching effectively was becoming increasingly difficult. A slow change began within me. I started having tension headaches daily. Clock-watching became habitual. In the mornings I would lie in bed dreading going to school in fear of what the day would be like."

That first year back Baker characterizes as a "devastating failure." But the very next year was "a rewarding and enriching experience"—a complete success!

What happened? Baker learned to establish rules and routines. And more importantly, she took time to teach them to her students.

"For the first two weeks of school, I committed myself to teaching the rules to my children," Baker reports. "I spent a great deal of time modeling what I expected from the children. I used children to role-play each time a special direction was given. Those first two weeks of school resurrected me from a disastrous year and laid the foundation for a successful one. Always before, I took for granted that my students understood what I expected."

After teaching the rules and routines, you must consistently enforce them. What you are doing is establishing good discipline. By dealing quickly and consistently with misbehavior, you can prevent small problems from becoming larger ones later. Good managers are "authority figures." This does not mean ruling with an iron hand, but rather, providing leadership and a strong example of how to behave.

During the first few weeks, students are learning how to learn. And you must teach them.

Planning

My principal wants weekly lesson plans, and I don't even know what I am doing after lunch.

Beginning teachers commonly express such concerns. Planning lessons, weekly units, and a productive school year is a big task for any teacher, let alone a new one.

Good planning takes practice. It's the key to professionalism. When you plan, you use your professional judgment to match ideas, activities, and materials with students' interests and abilities. It is not simply a matter of making a *To Do* list. Planning is deciding

when, where, why, and how a certain lesson is taught.

Couldn't a good teacher just "wing it"?

No way. A plan offers direction, confidence, and security. And plans help you use classroom time more efficiently by reducing confusion and wasted time. Generally, the more thoroughly you plan an activity, the less time it takes to complete it.

Despite the demonstrated benefits, many beginners feel uncertain about planning: *How can I plan something I've never done before?*

The First Few Weeks

- Make a list of important rules and routines.
- Be firm, fair, and predictable in enforcing rules.
- Make sure students understand the consequences of breaking rules.
- Always have materials and activities ready.
- Reinforce good behavior by noting or commenting on it.
- Use student helpers.
- Closely monitor students, give clear instructions and directions.
- Be calm.
- Make sure students know what to bring to class.
- Teach academic routines as well as "housekeeping" routines.
- Hold students accountable for their work.
- Eat lunch with students during the first week or two.
- Try not to leave the classroom when students are there.
- Communicate instructional objectives and the minimum standards you expect.
- Make sure parents understand your goals and objectives.

That's the question many veterans remember having as rookies. "Beginners don't know enough to know if a plan will work," says Susan Audap. As an advisor to new teachers, Audap tells beginners that planning, like teaching itself, is something you can only learn by doing. "The extent to which you reflect and think about it later is how much is learned," Audup stresses.

The research shows . . .

Take a look at what the experts do. In studies of teacher planning, Clark found that experienced teachers plan around specific activities, not learning objectives. They generally use a four-step process when deciding whether to use an activity:

1. Understand the total activity.
2. Imagine using it in the classroom.
3. Think of ways to avoid foreseen problems and modify the activity accordingly.
4. Create a mental image of the revised version.

Researcher Christopher Clark at the Institute for Research on Teaching advises beginners to think of their plans as "flexible frameworks for action, as devices for getting started in the right direction, and as something to depart from or elaborate on, rather than as rigid scripts."

Effective teachers also:
• plan for interruptions and unexpected events, thus maintaining order and minimizing disruptions when they occur.
• plan transitions from one activity to another. This minimizes wasted time, confusion, and behavior problems.
• communicate the plan to students.
• find out what students already know about a particular topic with a formal or informal pretest before planning lessons and units.
• set aside a regular time for planning.
• make their daily and weekly plans fit into larger units and yearly plans.

Tips from the experts

There are other planning practices that distinguish successful teachers. In 1975, teacher Ruth Tschudin took a year's leave to identify extraordinary teachers across the country and determine just what makes them different from others. In terms of planning, she found, successful teachers make long-term plans, are less likely to rely on commercial plan books, involve students in their planning, and are flexible enough to take advantage of those unplanned "teachable moments."

Here are some practiced planning ideas and activities from extraordinary teachers:
• Use a large section of white shelf paper or butcher paper to map out the entire year. Include content to be covered, major concepts, resources and materials, and activities. Posting this long-term plan not only shows you the year at a glance and keeps you on track, it demonstrates an important skill to students.
• Use the summer months to order films and materials that are related to topics which will be studied the coming year.
• Solicit lesson ideas from students. Asking students from time to time what they would like to study can give you some good ideas they are guaranteed to like. By matching their ideas to the concepts and skills you want to teach, you can tailor your lessons to student interests.
• Teach your students how to plan. For example, have students write down what they plan to do each day, including the requirements as well as their individual desires. They can review the plan at the end of the day and evaluate their accomplishments. Have older students plan and teach single lessons to their classmates. This would include selecting a topic, researching the topic, preparing lesson plans, gathering materials, teaching the lesson, and helping to evaluate its success.
• Don't ignore the "teachable moments." Veterans reflecting back on their first few years of teaching report that they were slaves to

their plans. While it is important to develop and follow instructional plans, don't be so rigid that you pass up unexpected opportunities.

Suppose, for example, that a migrating flock of Canada geese lands briefly in a field outside your window. The students are excited. Where are they going? Where did they come from? What are they eating? In response to the students' questions and enthusiasm, why not fly with a science unit on birds and migration?

One first-grade teacher turned the noisy disturbance of a nearby building demolition into an exciting class discussion. Her class learned about the machines being used, what the buildings are made of, and also the people who had lived there. Another teacher used an incident of student littering on the playground to involve her students in an extended

ecology, conservation, and recycling unit. Teachable moments crop up often, especially if you stay alert for ways to build on students' interests, needs, and moods.

Plan ahead

Here are some things you can do at the beginning of the school year to save yourself planning time later on:
• Block in all the givens in your lesson plan book—the activities you will be doing each week at the same time, such as library visits, physical education, music, art, lunch, recess, and so on. If you are using your own weekly lesson plan forms instead of a commercial plan book, make duplicate copies after blocking in the givens so you don't have to rewrite them each week.
• Mark in holidays, vacations, parent conferences, teacher in-service days, and other times you won't have classes.
• Decide how much time you will spend—and when—on reading, math, science, and other subjects. (Some of these times are fixed in many schools.) List these times on a weekly schedule and paste it in the front of your plan

Mark in personal and professional commitments as far in advance as possible.
• Determine the blocks of time in your weekly schedule that are not filled with required activities. These are the times you might try to schedule movies and guest speakers.
• Establish priorities for field trips. If you can only take three, what will they be? Tentatively schedule them.
• Do you have ideas for special events or projects? List them in back of your plan book and schedule them as time permits.
• Remember your notes and lessons aren't carved in stone. Feel free to amend them as your needs change.

Planning for the unexpected

Always try to be prepared.

Most of the time you will be, thanks to your careful plans and well-thought-out lessons. But what about those times you are unexpectedly absent from the classroom, or a situation demands your immediate time and attention?

Once again, planning comes to the rescue. With advance planning, you can be prepared for the unpredictable.

Build a file of emergency activities, time-fillers, and sponges to soak up time lost to interruptions or unexpected situations (a child gets sick in class, a parent knocks on the classroom door, the assembly is scheduled to start ten minutes late). By planning meaningful "instant" activities, you can turn lost time into learning time.

Start your emergency activity file with the ten-minute think sessions suggested on pp. 62-63 by teacher Susan Petreshene. Or use the sponge activities suggested on p. 159.

Also plan for those times when you must be absent from the classroom by developing a file for substitute teachers. Here's what your substitute file might include, suggest teachers Peggy Hlavinka and Sharon Shea from Bryan, Texas:
• A letter to students. For unexpected absences such as illness, file a letter explaining the situation and encouraging students' good behavior. Word it something like this: *Dear students, I cannot be at school today. You are very special to me, and I am leaving you in good hands with a substitute. I know you'll be helpful and cooperative. Please put your best foot forward and make the sub's day a great one.*
• Forget-me-nots. Prepare a sheet that familiarizes substitutes with required daily procedures, such as lunch counts, attendance counts, and other duties. Also include a list of names and schedules for aides, special-area teachers, and students in pull-out programs. Explain emergency procedures, where to get materials and equipment, and the names of helpful students, teachers, and school staff. And don't forget to define clearly your daily classroom routines and discipline procedures.
• Seating charts. Whole-class and small-group seating charts are a must. Your sub will sink without them.
• A daily schedule. Write out your general school schedule—when school begins and ends, when lunch is served, and recess.
• Lesson plans. Most substitutes can and want to undertake genuine teaching responsibilities, so don't insult them and bore students with piles of busywork or filmstrip fillers. Leave lesson plans when possible and give your substitutes the freedom to teach.
• Sub starters. While you want to give substitutes the opportunity to teach, it's a good idea to prepare a few reproducible activity sheets and suggest other activities they can use in spare moments. (For ideas, see "Shorts for Subs" on p. 64.) Again, ask your colleagues for ideas they've used. And why not file away a book you know your students will love the substitute to read to them? Reading aloud is a pleasurable activity, and students will be impressed by a substitute who knows their interests.
• Sub notes. Don't hesitate to ask the substitute to give you a complete report of the day. Use the report form on p. 65 or develop your own. Remind subs to list both the pleasures and the problems.

Don't forget to prepare your class. Discuss with your students the conduct you expect from them when you are absent and how they can help the substitute. Their involvement is important.

Finally, thank the substitutes who do a good job in your classroom. Call them or write a note. Let the principal know you were pleased, and ask for them again.

Seatwork Can Work

Seatwork—the tasks and assignments students complete while working independently at their desks—is an important classroom management tool. Children learn at different rates, and you can't be everything to everyone all the time. So seatwork helps you keep the class engaged in meaningful learning tasks while you work with individual students or small groups.

In many classrooms, students spend as much as 70 percent of their instructional time doing independent seatwork. Unfortunately, students doing seatwork are not always accomplishing what we think they are. They often develop strategies for completing the work with no idea of what they're doing or why.

One first grader's comment about seatwork was typical: "I don't know what it means—but I did it."

Working with first graders in different classrooms, Linda Anderson of Michigan State University's Institute for Research on Teaching discovered that most students cared only about completing their assignments. When assignments were too difficult or didn't make sense, they completed them as best they could—by copying answers from friends, guessing at answers, selecting randomly from choices, leaving blanks, and so on. By completing their work, many fooled their teachers into thinking they were learning more than they were.

Anderson suggests that the emphasis on *staying busy* combined with tasks that are too tough, "may lead students to define successful seatwork in terms of task completion and the appearance of working hard, instead of understanding content." She adds that lower achievers learn to expect school tasks not to make sense and give up trying to understand.

In the study, few students had any idea of the reasons for or goals of their seatwork assignments, or of how the skills they were learning (reading skills, in this case) fit together. One first grader's comment about seatwork was typical among his classmates: "I don't know what it means, but I did it!"

Though there are many problems with seatwork, you can't just stop assigning it, at least not until your class numbers five or fewer students. What you can do is make seatwork effective.

Anderson and the teachers she and her colleagues worked with offer specific strategies for selecting, presenting, monitoring, and evaluating seatwork. These strategies are based on reading instruction, but they could apply to other content areas as well.

Selecting seatwork
• Consider whether each assignment contributes to your larger purpose.
• Match the task to the student's ability. Whole-class assignments are more likely to cause problems than tasks assigned by ability level.

Presenting assignments:
• Emphasize the assignment's purpose and the strategy for completing it. For example: *This seatwork is to help you practice the words we learned yesterday. Say each word to yourself as you read it, then see if you can use it in a sentence.* Or: *This will help you practice the new rules about sounding out words with 'ou' in the middle, so you can get faster at doing that and read more new words on your own.*
• Model through think-aloud techniques with one or two examples of each assignment, especially for low achievers.

Monitoring seatwork

• After assigning seatwork, spend five minutes circulating among students to make sure they all have gotten started before you begin working with a small group.

• Between groups, take another few minutes to troubleshoot. Circulate among students; concentrate on those who most often have problems. If you detect a pattern of errors in a child's seatwork, give a quick re-explanation, modify the assignment, or tell him/her to go on to something else until you can give more help.

• When troubleshooting, occasionally (but regularly) ask students to explain how they got an answer (correct or incorrect). This forces students to think about what they're doing and shows them you value their thought processes, not just the answers they write on their papers.

• Establish routines for seeking help. This reduces wasted time and interruptions. Buddy systems are one way—but carefully teach students that helping someone does not mean giving the answers. Some teachers use "help cards" that children prop on their desks to signal the teacher. (Here, students must learn to go on to another item or assignment until you can help.) Others use hand signals. When a student approaches them while they work with a group, they either signal, *Come whisper your question to me,* or *I can't stop now, but I know that you need help, so please go back to your seat.*

• Take the time at the beginning of the year to teach students to recognize when they don't understand; to seek help appropriately; to articulate processes for getting answers; and, the differences between appropriate and overly dependent help-seeking.

Evaluating seatwork assignments

• Check seatwork in a predictable, routine way, even if it means having students check their own or each other's work.

• Emphasize understanding, not just neatness and accuracy.

• Let students know you value comprehension as well as persistence, effort, and independence.

• Use monitoring routines to evaluate students' thinking processes (for example, ask them to explain how they got certain answers.)

• When the class visits learning centers or plays instructional games, use the time to talk to students who need extra help and feedback.

Add to this list of strategies two more tips offered by Jere Brophy of the Institute for Research on Teaching. Based on his studies and others, Brophy suggests you:

• Tailor assignments to ability levels, at least in certain subject areas.

• Select seatwork that is easy enough to allow all students a 95 percent success rate.

Use seatwork that allows all students a 95% success rate.

Yes, you read it right. In situations where students must progress independently, such as seatwork and homework, students need to succeed at least 95 percent of the time. As Brophy explains, skills must be "mastered to the point of overlearning if they are going to be retained and applied to still more complex material. Confusion about what to do or lack of even a single important concept or skill," Brophy says, "will frustrate students' progress and lead to management and learning problems."

He says that teachers should strive to select seatwork that is easy enough to allow all students to succeed, yet difficult or different enough from previous work to challenge students. This requires different assignments for different students.

Of course, it's not always possible to offer differentiated assignments. When it is, select assignments that match students' abilities—math worksheets varying in difficulty, guided free choice on books to read, and so on. It requires practice and skill. And part of that is helping kids understand their abilities while encouraging them to reach ever higher.

Learning Centers

By arranging desks, storage space, and bulletin boards before school started, you prepared a functional physical environment for instruction. Now you can enhance that environment by creating learning centers.

What is a learning center? It is any part of the classroom designated for independent learning; for example:

• A full-length mirror where kindergartners try on costumes, masks, hats, or silly glasses. Here, they role-play or learn about themselves and their friends by observing and creating their own mirror games.

• A *Book Box* on a table filled with books and materials about a certain subject or theme.

• An *Art Cart* with materials and instructions for making mobiles, puppets, dioramas, cartoon strips, crayon rubbings, and friendship cards.

• A *Math Path*, where students find math games and activities stored in a large box.

• A *Spare Chair*, a corner designated for independent reading. Many students love the challenge and the change of pace that working in a center promotes. Learning centers allow them to explore, apply newly learned skills, feel independent, be creative, and interact with peers.

What's in it for you?

Plenty. When you want to work with small groups of individuals, learning centers are an exciting alternative to assigning seatwork. You can use centers as rewards and places for extra help and practice. Use them to encourage kids to cooperate or work independently. Pare down your paperwork by developing center activities that are self-checking. Students can use individual folders to save their work and record their progress. Learning centers are also a great way to involve parents as classroom helpers.

How to go about it

Arizona teacher Alice Rice points out that in learning centers, students learn more than

A potpourri of ideas for Learning Centers

Doris Dillon, a 22-year veteran, and Jane Schall, teacher-turned-writer, offer these ideas for learning centers to set up early in the year:

1. Penmanship and calligraphy: Have felt-tip calligraphy pens and lettering books available to help kids learn to write in new ways. For example, on a butcher-paper scroll, students practice their penmanship by copying the Preamble to the Constitution.

2. Math Manipulatives, including graphing, cubes, and measurements.

3. Fun Print Art Center, where students use stamp pads and felt-tip pens to create their own art.

4. A typewriter, where all types of fun learning activities are possible.

5. Collections of puzzles.

6. A *Book Bin* reading center.

7. Alphabet Center (for younger children)—finding letters in magazines, cutting them out and pasting them in sequence on a page.

8. Poetry Place: Stock this center with poetry books and activities for children to choose to help them learn and enjoy poems.

9. Rainbow World: Build a colorful center around the colors of the rainbow. Kids can mix paints to form these colors, as well as study the physical properties of rainbows. Utilize other subject areas; ask students to read and write about legends and tales about rainbows.

10. Wishful thinking: Set up a special quiet area where kids can work on their journals. Provide journal-starter ideas to provoke imaginations.

academic content. They learn decision-making skills, record keeping, filing, time management, and interpersonal skills.

Rice has developed many learning centers herself and employs them extensively in her classroom. Each center generally has one theme with four activities, she explains. The purpose of an activity may be to teach, enrich, remediate, have children apply a new skill, or test. She suggests that each learning center activity include these six features:

1. The objective.
2. Simple directions.
3. A sample, when appropriate.
4. Materials in a self-contained box, folder, or area.
5. A self-checking or proofreading system, if possible.
6. Follow-up or recognition by the teacher.

Be creative. Learning centers are limited only by your imagination. They are as simple or complex as you care to make them. Set aside a whole table or countertop for a center, or file the activities in a box or drawer to be completed at students' desks. Stock the centers with easily obtained supplies and materials. Use one or two centers and rotate students, or develop enough centers and activities to engage the whole class.

Here are Rice's tips for organizing and maintaining learning centers:
• Organize centers around topics such as art, creative writing, language, math, and independent reading.
• Give centers catchy titles such as Art Cart, Math Path, Think Tank, and Spare Chair.
• Designate a monthly theme to tie together activities and learning centers. Rice's third graders used the following schedule:

September—Friendship
October—Sports and Hobbies
November—The Five Senses and
  Thanksgiving
December—Celebrations Around the World
January—Jobs and Careers
February—Patriotism

March—Space
April—Ecology
May—Review

• Plan the year with another teacher who is interested in rotating themes and sharing materials.
• Solicit help from volunteers. Parents can help collect materials, make the activities, set up the centers, and assist students. This is an opportunity for them to participate in the classroom. Keep a schedule of volunteers and a substitute they can call if they are not available. Also, make sure parents understand the purpose of the learning centers.
• Give students active opportunities to draw, color, cut, glue, match, list, write, play games, sequence items, talk, listen, fasten or connect, tie, select, compare, classify, outline, rearrange, assemble, and so on, as they learn academic content.
• Set a time schedule for using the centers. Rice and her team teacher schedule two 40-minute periods back to back each morning. During each period, half of the students are in learning centers while the other half are in reading groups.
• Supply the necessary materials for each activity. It doesn't work to have students sharing materials for different activities.
• Give the students a record sheet listing the activities, and have them record the ones they complete. They can keep the record sheet and the papers and products they produce in their own 8½ x 11-inch folder.
• Periodically review student folders and decide how much catch-up or review is necessary, if any.

Paperwork, Paperwork (Making a Molehill Out of a Mountain)

"When I was going to college, I was never told how much grading and record-keeping there'd be. As a student teacher, I wrote the lesson plans and my supporting teacher did all the grading. I was just never exposed to all the paperwork. If you're not on top of it daily, you'll be swamped!"

—Lisa Roe, first-year teacher,
San Jose, Calif.

Doris Dillon reports that the first-year teachers working with her team of mentors in San Jose consistently rank paperwork and grading as the most overwhelming aspect of teaching. And they're not alone.

New teachers and veterans are besieged daily with what seems like a never-ending stream of paper. There are daily attendance records, lunch counts, lesson plans, subject-area testing, report cards, homework and seatwork to check and record, information to gather for emergencies, records for parent conferences, students in special pull-out programs to keep track of, and much more.

These are tasks you can't just ignore. You need to keep records on students to assess their progress, diagnose problems, assign them to ability groups, plan appropriate instruction, and communicate with parents. Homework and seatwork assignments deserve your serious attention if you expect students to take them seriously.

Help! What can you do short of hiring a secretary or working 24 hours a day? Here are some strategies experienced teachers use for putting paperwork in its place.

Basic record-keeping forms
• Duplicated or photocopied master lists. Add your students' names to the all-purpose chart on p. 36 and make a stack of copies for daily use.
• Index cards. These are quick and handy and can be used in many ways, especially for anecdotal records or telephone calls. Have children write their names, addresses, and telephone numbers on a large card. Record telephone calls or notes to parents, including the gist of the communication. Major problems can also be noted.
• File folders. Manila folders have simplified many aspects of record-keeping. Children can

easily handle these folders and thus help with many routine record-keeping tasks. For example, ask students to put papers to be checked or recorded into appropriate folders each day. Have them put the corrected papers into a going-home folder marked with their names. At the end of the week, just staple and send the whole batch home. Also, keep individual file folders on each child. Use them to record your observations and notes.
• Loose-leaf notebooks. Use these notebooks for recording schedules, procedures, and curriculum guides. Or use them for a handy two-page spread charting students' progress through different subjects. In reading and math, for example, make a master list of skills for the class range of achievement levels. Put one skills list for each child into a notebook with a facing page for conference notes, special assignments, and books read.

Contracts as record-keeping tools
Record-keeping in any classroom is challenge enough. But if your class includes highly diverse children, such as mainstreamed, gifted, and physically-challenged students, record-keeping poses monumental problems. Before you panic, consider learning contracts.

Individual learning contracts record the

Writing a contract

To write a contract:

1. Define the student's needs.

2. Plan activities to meet those needs.

3. Decide how to determine successful completion.

Don't forget to have students help to write the contracts; this encourages them to learn to define topics and plan steps to complete a task.

activities assigned to a student, completion of the activities, and the level of success achieved. Contracts can chart daily or weekly work. In succession, they record progress over time. Two samples are included on pp. 66, 114.

Paring down paperwork

"Teachers should work smarter, not harder," says educator Madeline Hunter, who suggests the following ways to cut paperwork to a minimum.

Seatwork and homework

• Instead of developing and duplicating practice pages, have students make their own practice problems. Some samples are:
1. List ten words in your reader that are objects you can touch (boy, ball) and ten words you cannot touch (in, new, the).
2. Using the same facts as those in the story problem in your text (or on the chalkboard), write a question that requires you to add to find the answer, one that requires you to subtract, one to multiply, and one to divide.
3. Make up five questions to test whether someone understood this chapter. Star the question you think is best. (This lets you examine just one question, reserving the others for verification if you doubt the student's understanding. Also, get double mileage here by choosing several of the best questions to give to the rest of the class.)

• Instead of correcting every homework assignment, give quick quizzes to assess what's been learned. The quiz should include one or two questions from the assignment and one or two different questions of the same type. Collect and grade them on some days, and on others, give students the answers to evaluate their own quizzes. (Keep them guessing so they will always be motivated to learn from the homework.)

Testing and diagnosis

• Measure student achievement formally by preparing short quizzes that test specific skills and concepts. These are easy to correct, and they give information you can use immediately.

• Informally diagnose by having kids sign or signal answers. A simple head shake, raised hand, or hand signal can indicate answers to your questions. Deviant signals stand out. If you suspect they are copying, ask students to close their eyes and signal their answers.

• Verbal responses, individual or in chorus, are another way to diagnose learning. *Tell your neighbor* exercises give each student the chance to respond, and the neighbors will usually correct wrong responses.

Checking assignments

Homework and in-class assignments serve specific purposes. Students need practice with new skills or concepts, or they need to brush up on old ones. Perhaps the assignment calls for an expression of student creativity. Or maybe it's an opportunity for children to learn to work together. At any rate, these are activities you want students to take seriously. And they will, if you do. They don't always have to be graded. But show them that you value their efforts. Here's how:

• On worksheets, mark a circle near each of the problems students answer incorrectly. When they correct their mistakes, simply add a *K* beside the original circle to give the children a positive *OK* on the end product.

• Use the all-purpose chart on p. 36 to keep track of completed assignments on a daily basis. Indicate only those students who have not completed an assignment. This will be much faster than marking all of the completed assignments, and you will be able to see at a glance who is regularly missing assignments. (Remember to keep this list for your eyes only!)

• Ask students to mark their own or each other's papers when possible.

• Have students help you collect papers.

• Use a pen of one color to record work that is handed in on time, and another for work that comes in late.

A Timely Topic: Time Management

Teaching takes time. And in school, as elsewhere, there's never enough of it. Like any executive responsible for the efforts of others, you will find that managing time—yours and the students'—is one of your biggest challenges.

Time management is the thread running through almost all aspects of teaching— organizing the day,

Like any executive, you will find that managing time is your greatest challenge.

organizing the classroom, deciding how long and how often to teach various subjects, recording student progress, keeping time-consuming behavior problems to a minimum, and so on. Students only have so much time to learn in your classroom and you only have so much time to teach them.

Effective use of school time begins with efficient classroom organization and management—and vice versa. Almost every topic covered up to this point has involved time management in some way: paring down paperwork; planning to save time; routines that eliminate wasted time and confusion; transition times between lessons and activities; using learning centers, independent assignments, and seatwork to give you time to work with small groups; and classroom arrangements that allow students and activities to proceed smoothly.

This section features timely tips for organizing and managing the classroom; for example, the use of volunteers to handle time-consuming tasks, tutors to extend instructional and learning time, and tips for managing your own time.

Other chapters feature additional aspects of time management, including instructional techniques that save time and suggestions for improving students' engaged time (Chapters 4 and 5), and time-saving techniques for working together with fellow teachers and administrators (Chapter 6) and parents (Chapter 7).

Increase teaching time

You may have less time to teach than you think. Lunch, recess, breaks, down-time between lessons or activities, moving from one classroom to another, interruptions, and other periods of noninstructional time account for at least 27 percent of an elementary school day. In many classrooms, that figure climbs beyond 40 percent. Incredible as these statistics may sound, they have been confirmed by separate studies at the Far West Laboratory for Educational Research and Development and the Institute for Research on Teaching.

Sure, lunch, recess, and restroom breaks are important. But too much teaching time is often lost. Add to that the time students stare out the window or are disengaged during instruction and you get the point. (This is a story saved for Chapter 4.)

Here are some ways beginners and veterans alike can substantially increase teaching time:
• Decrease the time allotted for breaks and social activities. Contrary to popular belief, students do not need a lot of break time to refresh themselves. In fact, the research shows that long or frequent breaks may actually lower their involvement with academic work.
• Find out which aspects of school time you can control. In some schools, teachers discover they can change the scheduling of class periods, pull-out programs, lunch breaks, extracurricular activities, planning time, and outside interruptions. Ask your principal to help you control time-wasters such as unexpected visitors and frequent intercom announcements.
• Schedule solid blocks of teaching time for each day. You might hang a *Do Not Disturb* sign outside your door during those times. Also, secure your principal's help in scheduling student pull-out programs around your scheduled teaching blocks. And inform parents of these times so they don't plan a classroom visit or schedule medical or dental appointments then.
• Plan for smooth transitions between lessons,

Record-keeping ideas

Though these hints may seem overwhelming, they will prove invaluable. Remember you don't have to do everything at once. Start building in strategies, one at a time, and soon each one will seem natural and comfortable.

- Make *To Do* lists of your paperwork tasks and prioritize them.

- Beg, borrow, or steal a file cabinet. You can't live without one. A cardboard box will do if you can't get the real thing.

- Purchase a box of manila folders and start to make files, not piles. Label folders for: each student, each subject area, holidays, specific assignments, leftover duplicating papers, sources for free materials, newspaper or magazine articles, and so on. Organize major categories; alphabetize or file chronologically.

- Track progress through individual subjects by having students file current assignments and worksheets for math or reading in a manila folder (one per child). Staple a sheet to record conferences, activities, and quiz scores inside the back cover.

- Label a basket or folder *to be filed* for temporary placement of the items you collect.

- Raise your right hand and promise, *I will file papers at least once a week.*

- Assign a certain part of the day to your routine paperwork tasks (15 minutes at the close of the school day, for example).

- At the beginning of the school year, form impressions of students before reading their previous records. When you do study earlier records, don't accept subjective reports unquestioningly.

- Keep a folder (some prefer index cards) on each child and record your observations as well as grades. Anecdotal records are important, and they help you communicate more accurately with parents.

- Number the student files instead of using actual names. This way, you can use the files from year to year.

- Label folders for each child to use for storing completed work to send home.

- Send classwork home on a regular basis to let parents know what their children are doing. Use folders or large envelopes as mail pouches. Ask parents to sign their names and date the envelope each time papers are sent home.

- Tape a paper pocket near or on the class door for daily attendance slips going to the office.

- Note absences on a chart (use the all-purpose chart on p. 36) and tape it to your desk or plan book. This way you can assess attendance at a glance.

- Let students help you with record-keeping tasks. This not only saves you time, but gives students a sense of pride and responsibility. The helper role can be a reward for good behavior or performance.

- Date everything! This helps you detect trends and patterns. (A rubber stamp with movable dates is useful.)

- Have a rubber stamp made with your name on it. Also have stamps made with "Parent Signature," "Rough Draft," and "Under Construction."

- For a student with a behavior problem, keep a small checklist handy on your desk to remind you of appropriate intervention techniques. Record all incidents with date, time of day, place, action you took, and other pertinent details. (Develop a form for including this information and keep multiple copies handy.) Also keep copies of all communication with parents and other personnel, daily contracts, and conference records. Records document the need for special help.

and always try to have materials ready for each lesson or activity.

• Assign homework to extend practice time. Homework should allow students to practice skills they have already learned.

• Take a critical look at how you schedule restroom breaks.

Delegate, Delegate

Good managers know how to delegate. Aides, volunteers, and older students can handle many classroom tasks and save you enormous amounts of time. Following are ideas on how to put these individuals to work productively.

Aides

If you are one of the lucky ones, you have an aide assigned either full- or part-time to your classroom. Chances are this individual is trained. He or she may even be a new or former teacher. Communicate your expectations to the aide and listen to his or hers. Make sure you both agree on and understand the responsibilities. Discuss school and classroom rules; children's names; location of supplies, equipment, records, and files; discipline procedures; and students' special needs or problems.

How can aides help? Some of the ways are listed below. And you and your aide can think of others. Don't hesitate to draw on your aide's special strengths and abilities.

1. *Instructional activities.* Aides can work with small groups or tutor individuals. They can make instructional games and resources, keep bulletin boards current, monitor seatwork and learning centers, read stories to the class, and assist you in testing.

2. *Clerical services.* An aide can provide these time-saving services: correct papers, type, mimeograph or photocopy, record test results, file, and keep records.

3. *Housekeeping.* While aides should help keep the classroom neat and organized, don't expect them to assume student responsibilities. Teach students to clean

---

Student absences

Student absences are another factor affecting teaching and learning time. While absences are usually outside your control, there are ways you can help improve student attendance.

• Teach an actual lesson on the importance of good attendance.

• Use classroom participation as one criterion of grading, and inform both students and parents of this.

• Stress the importance of regular attendance in parent newsletters and conferences.

• Urge parents to schedule medical and dental appointments after school.

• Award certificates for good attendance, if your school doesn't.

• Allow perfect attenders a special treat or reward on the last day of school. (Remember to be lenient here. There may have been times of emergency or hardship when a child was absent, such as attending a funeral, that shouldn't damage his/her record.)

• Identify attendance problems early on and notify administrative or counseling staff.

---

their areas, put away supplies, and so on.

4. *Additional services.* Aides can assist with special programs, class parties, field trips; they can operate audio-visual equipment, and help organize student tutors and volunteers. Try to build in ways your aides can grow in responsibility and classroom involvement.

Volunteers

Volunteers generally can do anything aides do—with your supervision and guidance, of course. By involving parents, relatives of students, and other community members in your classroom, you receive well-deserved help. But that's not all. Volunteer programs can improve home-school relations. Parents and other volunteers become sympathetic to the problems facing schools, and supportive of better budgets and improved opportunities. And they learn to play an active role in educating their children. It's a winning proposition for everyone.

Following are some methods of securing volunteers. You may not have the time or be organized enough to try these in your first year. But keep them in mind for other years.

• Parents and relatives of students are your best bet.

1. Have a recruitment flier ready on the first day of school. Hand it to parents when they bring their children, or send it home with students. List the volunteer opportunities available, and be sure to mention that Grandma and Grandpa are welcome, too!

2. Solicit volunteers at school functions such as a school play, an art or music festival, or an open house. Talk to the attendees and ask them to fill out a volunteer application.

3. Ask your students' teachers from the previous year for the names of parents who volunteered. Many parents want to move along with their children. (See Chapter 6 for more ideas on involving parents.)

Senior citizen organizations are often good sources for volunteers. Service-minded groups such as the Retired Seniors Volunteer Program and the American Association of Retired Persons look for projects in which their members can participate. Attend various community-group meetings and ask to be included on the agenda. You can take a few minutes to describe the wide range of services that would benefit your class and school.

• Don't forget districtwide volunteer programs, such as the PTA or parent clubs. These groups sometimes are staffed by people experienced in recruiting and supervising volunteers.

• High school and college students can help, too. For college-age volunteers, get permission to post recruitment information around campus or the community. Check with the college's volunteer bureau, or talk to the instructors of education courses and ask them to nominate some likely student volunteers or make announcements in their classes. At the local high school, check with the Future Teachers of America or similar organizations. These students can contribute in many ways, such as after-school tutoring.

Cross-age tutors

One underused but potentially valuable time-saver is the use of cross-age tutors. Here, older children help younger ones to read, write, and do math. Consider the experiences of Jacki Lamb, a resource teacher from Missoula, Montana. Jacki offers remediation for low-achieving students. She hadn't intended to set up cross-age tutoring. But when her first and second graders were hard-pressed to finish their writing assignment, she enlisted the help of her fifth graders. Here's what happened:

"I listened to the fifth grader who had the worst handwriting and spelling of all the older students in the resources room encourage in a positive manner his young charge to write clearly and legibly, saying, 'You are doing a good job of keeping the words on the line, but look at your spacing. Use your finger between words so they don't run together. I can't understand what you're saying otherwise. Check to see how you are holding your pencil. That's important, you know.' A few minutes later, I was amused to hear him say, 'Let's look at this word. Do you really think this is how to spell "because"?' That was the same boy who could not spell 'because' himself! He continued to tutor his student in the merits of good handwriting and

When possible, select tutors who are low-achieving readers. They can benefit from what they learn, are likely to be sympathetic, and the responsibility can give them more confidence.

correct spelling, and they both felt successful when the young writer was finished."

Lamb continues, "My attention was drawn to the shy fifth-grade boy who usually was reluctant to participate either in the resource room or in his classroom. In his gentle manner, he was involved with his student by reading aloud what the second grader had written. 'Tell me if you like what you hear.' Together they made the necessary changes until the second grader was satisfied.

"I was excited by what was happening. The fifth graders were moving from student to student, helping each one until the young author was pleased with the final product. The older students exhibited patience, motivation, and, surprisingly, knowledge of writing skills. The primary students gave the older students an opportunity to share their individual writing skills, limited as those skills may seem."

Jacki Lamb had experienced one of the big pluses of cross-age tutoring. It helps the tutor as well as the tutee. Cross-age tutoring resembles a real-life or family situation of older children helping the younger. (Peer tutoring, on the other hand, involves students in the same class or grade helping each other. This strategy is discussed on p. 171 of Chapter 5.)

To initiate your own cross-age tutoring program in reading:
• Work with a teacher from a different grade level—higher if you want tutors for your students, lower if you want to give your students the opportunity to be tutors.
• Help the tutors to be sympathetic and nonjudgmental.
• When possible, select tutors who are low-achieving readers. They can benefit from what they learn about proper reading behavior; they are most likely to be sympathetic to others having difficulty; and the responsibility of helping others gives them more confidence.
• Use tutoring as an alternative to silent reading or enrichment activities, not to replace a student's free time or your instruction.

• Celebrate each success, such as an advance in reading level.

• Teach tutors the three-step Pause, Prompt, Praise system. This method, suggested by Kevin Wheldall and Paul Mettem of the University of Birmingham, England, is compatible with current theories of reading acquisition. And what's more important, it really works. Students whose tutors used this method soon read at a much higher level and with greater accuracy than students who read alone or had untrained tutors. And they corrected their own errors more frequently. Here's how to teach the three-step technique to tutors:

The first step, *pause*, requires the tutor to delay attention to a reader's error for at least five seconds, or until the end of a sentence. This encourages the reader to self-correct more often, which, in turn, increases overall accuracy and comprehension. If tutors correct errors immediately, readers may lose the meaning of the prose. Also, they fail to learn self-correcting behavior.

Second, tutors should offer *prompts* or clues instead of correcting an error outright. If the reader still can't correct an error, the tutor must model the use of clues to predict words and meanings.

The third step is *praise*. Praise is important. Tutors should praise when readers correct their own mistakes. And they should praise for general effort and progress.

• Teach this technique to tutors by modeling it yourself. Then let them practice it with you playing the role of the tutee. Later they can practice on each other. In one study, a group of high school students with low reading ability learned the Pause, Prompt, Praise technique in just two 30-minute sessions.

Managing Your Own Time

Don't forget to make time for yourself, too. The following time management tips are gleaned from several sources, including ideas shared by Michigan State Department of Education staff development specialists Janice Hammond and Dennis Sparks, and Barbara Samuels of the University of Calgary.

• Set goals, both personal and professional. Write your goals, review them periodically, and make them realistic. (See the reproducible on p. 67 for a simple exercise on goal-setting.)

• Make a *To Do* list every day, including only items that are not part of your daily routine.

• Do your toughest task early in the day, if possible, so you don't spend time worrying about it throughout the day.

• Know your personal time needs and learn to work within them. This means knowing your daily periods of highest productivity, learning just how much sleep you need, and determining the amount of exercise that will keep you healthy and happy. When is your mind most alert—in the morning, afternoon, or at night? Schedule your workload accordingly. Could you accomplish more by arriving at school a half hour earlier each day than by working an hour or two after school?

• Learn to say no to committee work, volunteer work, or social functions you just don't have time for.

• Learn to concentrate. Everyone needs quiet work space and uninterrupted work time.

• Avoid procrastinating.

• Avoid perfectionism. The extra hours you spend making that slide show just a little bit better may not be worth it. Teachers can fall into this defeating habit as easily as students do.

• Put to use the time you spend waiting. Write letters, develop lesson plans, read, or make tomorrow's *To Do* list while you wait for meetings or parent conferences to begin, commute on the bus or train, or sit in the dentist's office. If you drive or walk to school, use this quiet time to think about new lessons or activities.

• Set time limits for tasks. Remember Parkinson's Law: Work expands to fill the time available for its completion.

• Set deadlines for yourself and your class and stick to them.

• Never do anything a student can do just as

well. Students can take lunch count, run errands in school, decorate bulletin boards, clean the classroom, file completed assignments, and so on. Not only are they helping you save time, they're getting a good dose of responsibility and self-esteem in the process.

• Decorate the classroom walls with students' work instead of your own time-consuming masterpieces. It will be more meaningful anyway.

• You don't have to correct every paper yourself. Your students can correct many of their own or each other's papers. Aides, volunteers, and older students can also do much of the paper-correcting for you.

• Use support systems available in your school. Other teachers, secretaries, principals, aides, students and parents can all be called on for help.

• Team up with other teachers for special projects and events.

• Handle each piece of mail only once. Do you have an ever-growing stack of school mail on your desk that you occasionally read or reread, and then still have to hunt through when you want a specific item? Instead, try skimming each item as you pull it from the box and immediately toss into the wastebasket those that require no response. Those that do, attend to immediately.

• Enhance your workspace. If your desk is in full view of the door, perhaps it's too easy for people who pass by to pop in for a chat when you're working. Move the desk or close the door when you need serious work time. Organize your materials so you don't waste precious time looking for things you need or become distracted by extraneous items.

• Make telephone calls in groups, rather than one at a time. And keep a list of student telephone numbers and addresses close. (Index cards are handy for this purpose.)

• Energize during break periods. Take a walk, read the newspaper, or chat with a colleague between long work sessions. A brief change of pace can increase concentration and efficiency.

• Reward yourself for making better use of your time. Treat yourself to a dinner out, an evening with a great novel, or a good long walk. You'll relax and function even better the next day.

• Take time to play. Everyone needs regular exercise, recreational activities, and social events. Renew yourself and become more effective in the classroom!

Time can be your enemy or your ally. If you learn to use it effectively, the payoffs will be big—for you and your students. Time management is not an easy skill to master. It takes time. But it's time well spent.

Chapter 2—Read more about it

1. *Research on Teacher Planning: An Inventory of the Knowledge Base.* (Research Series No. 142.) Christopher M. Clark. East Lansing, MI: Institute for Research on Teaching, 1984.

2. *The Hidden World of Teaching: Implications of Research on Teacher Planning.* (Research Series No. 77.) Christopher M. Clark and Robert J. Yinger. East Lansing, MI: Institute for Research on Teaching, 1980.

3. *Teaching is Tough.* Donald Cruickshank and Associates. Englewood Cliffs, NJ: Prentice Hall, 1980.

4. *The Induction of Teachers.* Kevin Ryan. Bloomington, IN: Phi Delta Kappa, Educational Foundation, 1986.

5. *Classroom Management in the Elementary Grades* (Research Series No. 329). Jere Brophy and Joyce Putnam. East Lansing, MI: Institute for Research on Teaching, 1978. Also in D. Duke (ed.), *Classroom Management* (the 78th Yearbook of the National Society for the Study of Education, Part III). Chicago: University of Chicago Press, 1979.

6. *Classroom Organization and Management* (Occasional Paper No. 54). Jere Brophy. East Lansing, MI: Institute for Research on Teaching, 1982. Also in *Elementary School Journal*, 1983, Vol. 83 No. 4, pp. 265-285.

7. *Classroom Management Training.* Carol S. Cruz and John Mahaffty. Portland, OR: Northwest Regional Educational Laboratory, 1985.

8. *Making Seatwork Work* (Research Series No. 142) Linda Anderson, Nancy Brubaker, Janet Alleman-Brooks, and Gerald Duffy. East Lansing, MI: Institute for Research on Teaching, 1984.

9. "A qualitative study of seatwork in first-grade classrooms." Linda Anderson, Nancy Brubaker, Janet Alleman-Brooks, and Gerald Duffy. *Elementary School Journal*, Nov. 1985 vol. 86 no. 2, pp. 86, 123-140.

10. "The Cognitive Skill of Teaching." Gaea Leinhardt and James G. Greeno. *Journal of Educational Psychology*, 1986, Vol. 78, No. 2, 75-95.

11. "Classroom Management Techniques." Jere Brophy. *Educational and Urban Society*, 1986, pp. 18, 182-194.

12. *Application of Classroom Management Research Findings* (Research Series No. 154). Joyce Putnam and Henrietta Barnes. East Lansing, MI: Institute for Research on Teaching, 1985.

13. *Classroom Management.* Walter Doyle. West Lafayette, IN: Kappa Delta Pi, 1980.

14. "Synthesis of Research on Classroom Management." E.T. Emmer and C.M. Evertson. *Educational Leadership*, Jan. 1981, pp. 342-347.

NOTES

N O T E S

RULES OF THE ROAD

Nothing worthwhile is ever easy—especially teaching.
Things sometimes go wrong despite our best efforts and carefully organized plans.
Prepare yourself for the inevitable calamities by posting
and remembering these "Rules of the Road."

Murphy's Law

Nothing is as easy as it looks; everything takes longer than you expect; and if anything can go wrong, it will—and at the worst possible moment.

Weiler's Law

Nothing is impossible for the person who doesn't have to do it.

Finagle's Law

Once a job is fouled up, anything done to improve it makes it worse.

Chisolm's Law

Anytime things appear to be going better, you have overlooked something.

Man's Law

No matter what happens, someone knew it would.

Donsen's Law

The specialist learns more and more about less and less until he knows everything about nothing, while the generalist learns less and less about more and more until he knows nothing about everything.

Gumperson's Law

The probability of anything happening is in inverse proportion to its desirability.

Douglass' Law

Clutter tends to expand to fill the space available.

Zimmerman's Law

Regardless of whether a mission expands or contracts, administration overhead continues to grow at a steady rate.

Ten-minute **Think** Sessions

These activities not only fill extra minutes,
they help sharpen all kinds of thinking processes—organizing, imagining, observing,
patterning, questioning. They'll also help you show children
how much you value their original thinking.

Here's to more than one "right" answer! (Grades K-6)

Read each of the following questions and have students think of as many logical answers as possible. It is important to stress that there is no one right answer to any of these. Encourage a variety of responses by showing your amazement at diverse and unusual thinking. In this activity and many of the ones to follow, you will be able to expand and extend the examples, and so will your class!

Suggested Questions:

1. How could you know someone had a fire in a fireplace if you hadn't been there at the time? (fireplace still warm, wood pile lower, things that were in the fireplace to be burned are no longer there . . .)
2. In a hardware store, nails are usually sorted and kept together according to size. What other things are usually sorted in some way and then kept together? (books in the library, clothes in a drawer or closet, food in the grocery store . . .)
3. "It's important you don't lose these," said Kenny to Carl as they left on a week's backpacking trip. What might Kenny have handed Carl? (maps, matches, food . . .)
4. What sounds could you recognize without seeing what made the noise? (cat's meow, honk of a horn, ring of a telephone . . .)
5. If a new city was going to be built, what types of buildings would be needed? (library, post office, police station, grocery store, bank . . .)
6. Some words name numbers: three, ten, twenty. Other words do not directly tell you a number, but when you hear them, you often think of a number. For instance, week and the number seven seem to go together. What other words make you think of numbers? (duet—two; triangle—three; dozen—12; century—100; shutout—zero . . .)
7. "There must be an accident on the highway," said Mrs. West. What might have caused her to say this? (traffic backed up, police car just sped by, flashing red lights ahead . . .)

I'll give you the answer/you give me the question (Grades K-6)

For each of these answers you read to your students, there will be many possible questions. For example, if the answer is "the Dodgers," the question might have been:
Who won the game?
What's your favorite baseball team?

What's the name of the major league baseball team in Los Angeles? Give several examples before starting the activity so students can get used to thinking in "reverse."

1. A: Under the bed. Q: Where are your shoes? Where did that sound come from? Where does the cat hide?
2. A: In a minute. Q: When will we be leaving? When is the bell going to ring? When will you be ready?
3. A: I think we should go investigate! Q: I wonder what that noise was. What's that smell? I wonder why our dog is whimpering.
4. A: Yes! Q: Would you like to go to the movies with me? Would you like an ice-cream cone? Is he coming over?
5. A: Fish. Q: What could you catch in a river? What swims in a bowl? What did you eat for dinner last night?
6. A: My dad. Q: Who taught you to play the trumpet? Who drove you to school today? Who likes popcorn better than anyone you know?
7. A: In the park. Q: Where did you fall down? Where did you find that dollar bill? Where did you play marbles yesterday?
8. A: In the morning. Q: When is your house busiest? When do you eat a meal by yourself? When are you the grumpiest?
9. A: Beside the house. Q: Where did you leave your bike? Where did you find the garbage can? Where are those daisies growing?

"Adverbially" speaking (Grades 2-6)

Name a verb and ask students to give you an adverb that "goes with" the verb. For instance, if you said "cried" a student might say "hysterically." Say the phrase back to them as a whole to emphasize a word picture. Although there are many adverbs that can accompany each verb, ask for only one answer and specify that adverbs cannot be repeated. (A list might be helpful so repetitions can easily be spotted.) The activity becomes more and more difficult as it progresses because the more common adverbs quickly become eliminated and students are forced to search for unusual but appropriate words. Suggested verbs: slept, dropped, tiptoed, played, stood, stopped, sailed, waved, touched, yelled, zig-zagged, whispered, flew, carried, banged, disappeared, drove, wrote, walked, worked, paced, leaned, maneuvered, stared, coughed, floated, giggled.

1,001 uses for ... (Grades K-6)

This is an activity that calls for practical responses to the question: How many ways can you use a . . . ? (As a part of this activity, you might ask students to explain their responses. Hearing the reasoning can give the whole class insight and add to the kind of thinking that creates more possibilities. You'll also gain more understanding about each student's reasoning skills.) Occasionally you may want to remind students that you are interested in practical, not humorous, answers. At the same time, encourage them to think of uses they have never thought of before. How many ways can you think of to use a cup, light bulb, buttons, bird cage, a plain piece of paper . . . ? Take turns suggesting new items.

Codes (Grades 3-6)

Write the alphabet on the board and pair each letter with a number from 1 through 26. (The difficulty of this activity can be increased by not sequencing the numbers or using larger numbers.) You may want students to copy this code chart. Write a word on the board and ask students to determine its "value" by looking at the chart to see what each letter is worth and then adding up the total. To provide multiplication practice, have them first add up the value of a word, then multiply the sum by the value of the last letter.

Math Magic (Grades 4-6)

Here's a "magic trick" that provides practice with adding, subtracting, and multiplying by 5 and 10. Read the following directions to your students.
1. Select a secret number between 1 and 99; write it on your paper.
2. Multiply your number by 10.
3. Add 57.
4. Double your new number.
5. Subtract 91.
6. Multiply by 5.
7. Add 100.
8. Tell me your answer and I will tell you your original number. (To determine the secret number, mentally drop the last two digits off the student's answer. Then subtract 2 and you have the secret number!) After telling several students their secret number, try teaching them the "answer formula" so they can try the trick with others.

For another math trick, have students work this series of calculations several times, each starting with a different number. Regardless of what number is used in the beginning, their answer will always be three. Read the following directions:
1. Select any number and write it on your paper.
2. Add 9 to your number
3. Double your new number.
4. Subtract 12.
5. Divide by 2.
6. Subtract the number you originally selected.

Tell students not to give their answers away, then have them select a new number and repeat the same steps. Let them do this a few times and then verbally compare answers for an interesting surprise!

Is that a fact? (Grades 1-6)

Prepare a list of simple statements. Read a few to your class and discuss whether they are facts or opinions. After children understand the concept, tell them to stand if they think the statement is a fact, remain seated if it is an opinion, or cross their arms if they are uncertain. Allow time to think before you call for a response. Indicate with a hand signal when to begin.

Close your eyes (Grades 1-6)

The object of this activity is to follow a series of directions with eyes closed. With younger children you may want to stop after the first few instructions. After all instructions have been given, have the children "freeze," open their eyes, and listen to the description of the position they should be in.
1. Close your eyes.
2. Fold your arms.
3. Turn your head to the right.
4. Shrug your shoulders five times.
5. Make your pointing fingers touch.
6. Flap your elbows three times.
7. Stretch your feet out in front of you.
8. Wiggle your feet.
9. Put both your hands behind your neck.
10. Now put your right hand on your left elbow.
(If you stop here, the position should be: feet stretched out in front, left hand behind neck, right hand on left elbow, and head turned to the right.)
11. Put your right hand between your shoulder blades.
12. Place your right foot flat on the floor.
13. Grab your right shoe with your left hand.
14. Next, rest your head on your left shoulder.
15. Lean to your left.
(Position: left foot stretched out in front, right foot flat on the floor, left hand grabbing right shoe, right hand between shoulder blades, head resting on left shoulder, and body leaning to the left.)
This activity is fun for students to lead (and keep track of). It will be very helpful if the leader writes down the directions he or she wants to give, as well as what the final body position should be, before beginning to speak.

This article by Susan Petreshene is adapted from *Mind Joggers: 5- to 15-Minute Activities that Make Kids Think!* (Published by the Center for Applied Research, Inc., West Englewood, N.J., 1985.)

Shorts for Subs

Math

★ **Number Search** Draw a 12-squared grid on the chalkboard. Fill each space with either an addition, subtraction, or multiplication problem (without answer), making sure that some have the same answers. Ask children to examine the grid and find two examples, when worked, that give the same answer.

★ **Auction Math** Collect pictures of items (refrigerators, TVs, cassette recorders, toys, cars, books, clothes, and so on) from magazines. Cut them out and paste each item on a 3 x 5 inch card. Underneath each, write its monetary value.

Then hold an afternoon auction. Give each student $5,000 in pretend money to spend. Display the auction items 10 minutes before auction time. Hand out pencils and paper and begin. Caution your buyers to start bidding at a lower price than each expects to finally pay. After each purchase, buyers subtract cost from their allotted $5,000. Also, they can make as many purchases as they want while their money lasts. Compute monies left over at the close of the sale.

★ **Secret Codes** Have pupils make up their own secret codes, using numbers instead of letters. For example, number 1 for A, 2 for B, 3 for C, and so on. Start the ball rolling with this message: 14 / 15   19 / 3 / 8 / 15 / 15 / 12 20 / 15 / 13 / 15 / 18 / 18 / 15 / 23 (No school tomorrow). Ask the kids to make up secret messages.

★ **Math Bingo** Give each child an 8½-by-11-inch sheet of paper, fold it into 16 squares, and copy one math example from the board (6 × 4, 10 + 8, 3 − 2, and so on) in each square. When paper boards are finished, call out the answer to one problem, giving kids time to find the example that fits the answer and place a marker on it. The first child to cover a horizontal or vertical row wins. To check, repeat the answers and compare them with the winner's examples.

★ **Story Math** Read a story containing multiple problems, events, or characters. Children participate by solving mental arithmetic problems the story poses. For example, in "The Three Pigs" pose this problem: "Two of the pigs decided to go to the market before they built their homes. How many pigs were left?" Or, "The wolf huffed and puffed . . . . How many times did he huff and puff?"

★ **Telephone Exchange** Make up a telephone number and write it on the board. Challenge kids to write as many different numbers as they can using the same digits.

★ **Geometric Designs** Have students draw and color a design using circles, squares, and triangles. Or make people-pictures using those forms. Let older students do this with cubes, pyramids, and spheres.

★ **What's My Name?** Write a number on the board, such as 12 or 28. Ask children to think of other ways to express the number. For example, 12 can be expressed as 10 + 2, 12 + 0, 6 × 2, and so on.

★ **Let's Go Shopping** Make a list of priced grocery-store items on the board. Tell pupils they each have $20 to spend at the store-board. On a piece of paper, have them total the cost of the items purchased. When called upon, each gives a list of purchases, indicating cost and leftover change.

★ **Clock Math** Use the classroom clock for fun with addition, subtraction, and multiplication. Add the numbers covering a quarter of an hour $(12 + 1 + 2 + 3 = 18)$, one half hour $(12 + 1 + 2 + 3 + 4 + 5 + 6 = 33)$, three-quarters of an hour $(12 + 1 + 2 + 3 + 4 + 5 + 6 + 7 + 8 + 9 = 57)$, and one hour (add numbers from 12 to 11). Then subtract three quarters of an hour, one half hour, and one quarter of an hour from the total amount. Start again and multiply the numbers.

Reading

✓ **How to Make It** Write directions on the board for children to follow for either a simple folded toy or a game. Children must read and follow the directions to complete their project.

✓ **Picture This** Write the following sentences on the board. Have everyone read them, and then draw a picture showing their interpretation.

> Time was running out.
> He followed his nose.
> She had a nightmare.
> There's a rainbow tree in my yard.
> I saw a giraffe-cat!
> There are dog willows on the pussy willow tree.
> The tulips are dancing and singing.

✓ **Word Scramble** Using a list of reading or spelling words, mix up each word's letters. For example, the word *tree* may look like *eetr*. Write scrambled words on the board, and challenge the class to unscramble them.

✓ **Picture Stories** Display action pictures cut from magazines and newspapers. Ask children to write a three- or four-line story about one.

✓ **Story Fill-ins** Make up or shorten a favorite story. Write it on the board. Omit words which describe or name colors, and list these words next to the story. As children read the story, they fill in the blanks from the word list.

✓ **Now Hear This!** Let kids make up a written advertisement for a favorite book, toy, record album, or piece of clothing. Invite them to illustrate ads if they wish.

✓ **And They Lived Happily Ever After** Ask children to write a different ending to their favorite story, illustrating it with cut out or drawn pictures.

✓ **Spelling Bingo** Decide on 16 to 20 words and write them on the board. Have children fold an 8½-by-11-inch paper so that when it is opened there are 12 squares. Everyone copies 12 words in any order onto their game papers, one word per square. Using markers cut from scraps of paper, kids cover corresponding words as they are given. Play bingo in the ususal way.

✓ **On the Road** Using state maps, take imaginary trips. Read route signs, names of cities, and points of interest along the way.

This list was adapted from ideas by Dorothy Zjawin. The original article appeared in INSTRUCTOR, February 1978.

Substitute report

Some information to assist you in knowing about our day.

Notes received _____

_____

These children were particularly helpful _____

_____

These children needed some extra assistance _____

_____

Reading _____

_____

Math _____

_____

Language/Handwriting _____

_____

Social Studies _____

_____

Science _____

_____

P.E. _____

_____

Other areas _____

_____

Comments _____

_____

_____

_____

A Step at a Time!

I will try harder in this subject: ——————————

I will start by ——————————

My plan of action is ——————————

——————————

——————————

——————————

——————————

——————————

This contract will last for —— weeks.

Pupil ——————————

Teacher ——————————

66

Simple **Goal-setting** Exercise

1. Take three minutes to list lifetime goals. (For example, a loving family, good health, a job that provides autonomy and satisfaction, and so forth.)

_____

_____

_____

_____

2. Take three minutes to list goals you would like to accomplish during the next five years. (For example, promotion to a new job in your district, helping your child through college, learning a new language.)

_____

_____

_____

_____

3. Take three minutes to list things you would want to do if you had only six more months to live. (For example, spend time with loved ones, travel, read the great philosophers.)

_____

_____

_____

_____

4. Review your three lists, then make a master list of your most important goals.

_____

_____

_____

_____

5. Jot down an activity to do in the next week or two that will help you, even in a small way, to achieve each of these goals. Make this part of your weekly "to do" list.

_____

_____

_____

_____

Adapt this exercise to setting goals for your classroom or individual students. It's also a good exercise to use with older children in teaching goal-setting behavior.

Adapted from an article by Alan Lakein which appeared in INSTRUCTOR, August 1981.

Best behaviors

"As a teacher I feel I have a moral obligation to help the children in my classroom grow toward becoming full human beings and to feel successful. Teaching cognitive skills is not enough. A child who can read, write, and do arithmetic, but who is fearful and lonely, cannot resolve conflicts effectively, conforms, or is hostile or withdrawn is not going to be able to cope with the world satisfactorily, much less find fulfillment or happiness in life."

—*Jean Medick*
Teacher, East Lansing, MI

This chapter is about behavior—yours and the students'. Behavior problems, poor expectations, prejudices based on cultural, racial, gender, or socioeconomic stereotypes, and student apathy all have negative effects on teaching and learning. Addressing these social and emotional factors has become an increasingly important part of teaching.

Is Your Behavior at its Best?

Student behavior is closely linked to our own. As teachers, our actions, attitudes, and expectations greatly influence how students act. There are many things teachers can do to increase the odds that students will be on their best behavior.

What is it you want students to do? How do you want them to behave? Answering these questions is the first step in establishing discipline.

Classroom research shows that effective teachers spend very little time dealing with student misconduct. It's not that they ignore behavior problems; they have established strategies for preventing problems in the first place.

As discussed in Chapter 2, you can significantly reduce student misconduct with good classroom management—routines, consistent enforcement of rules, adequate lesson planning, smooth transitions between lessons, challenging seatwork, and so on.

"Always be prepared," stresses Carol Wary of Pennsylvania, who's taught for 26 years. "Ninety-nine percent of discipline problems can be prevented if you know what you're doing and have all materials ready."

Time and other teachers will tell you that Wary is right.

Good teachers also address children's emotional needs by raising their self-esteem, teaching them to be responsible and fair, and motivating them to learn (see corresponding sections in this chapter).

Further, there are ways teachers can act to nip problems in the bud. Researcher Jacob Kounin found that the experts share these behavioral qualities:

First, they are *"with it."* They let their students know that they are aware of what is happening at all times. They regularly monitor and scan the classroom and position themselves where they can see all students.

Good classroom managers can also *overlap their activities.* That is, they can do more than one thing at a time without disrupting the class as a whole. They can work with individuals or a small group and still, almost unnoticed, deal with other students who have questions. For example, if a student approaches you while you're working with a reading group, you might use hand signals that mean either, "Come whisper your question to me" or "I can't stop now; please go back to your seat and I'll be there soon." (Here again, you are teaching routines—teaching students various hand signals and teaching them to discern which questions warrant your immediate attention.)

Maintaining the momentum in teaching a lesson is another quality the experts share. They keep attention focused on the lesson—and not on misbehaving students—by avoiding extended reprimands or overreactions. They ignore minor inattention. And more serious misbehavior they promptly attend to in nondisruptive ways—eye contact, a brief comment, a question directed to the offender. But lesson momentum is possible only if a teacher is well-prepared. False starts, backtracking, and confusion can destroy a lesson.

Other qualities associated with good discipline were identified by Jere Brophy and Joyce Putnam in their extensive review of classroom research. They include:
• *Ego strength and self-confidence.* These qualities enable a teacher to hear student complaints without becoming authoritarian or defensive.

• *Positive attitude.* Students respond well to and are motivated by teachers who like and respect them. Veterans strongly recommend getting to know students, communicating a sincere interest in their lives, and establishing good rapport. First, "tune in" to kids' interests by listening to what they say. Then "make the bridge" by expressing your interest. Finally, demonstrate your sincerity by "incorporating their interests into the curriculum."

• *High expectations.* When teachers help students perceive themselves as able and responsible, the students act that way.

• *Authoritative leadership.* Here, teachers seek feedback and consensus on decisions and make sure students understand their decisions. This is more effective than either authoritarian rule (where decisions are absolute) or non-directed *laissez-faire* leadership.

The experts also "keep the lid on" by offering challenging and varied seatwork, providing opportunities for all students to succeed, offering plenty of direct instruction, maintaining student engagement, and avoiding "downtime." These and other effective instructional strategies are covered in Chapter 4.

In addition, teachers must know their own wants and needs, says Lee Canter, developer of the Assertive Discipline approach.

What is it you want students to do? How do you want them to behave? Answering these questions is the first step toward establishing good discipline, says Canter. He advises you to be specific. Do you want students to follow directions? Sit in their seats? Take turns? Keep their hands to themselves? Complete assignments? Not leave the room without permission? Work independently? List a maximum of five, says Canter, and these can serve as the general rules for your class.

Last but not least, teachers who are warm, patient, tolerant, interested in students, and enjoy sharing a sense of humor are most able to influence behavior and performance in positive ways. You can smile and be cheerful and still maintain a businesslike, work-oriented approach. Just show students that you care.

Le Langran, a fifth-grade teacher from Agoura Hills, California, found a way to show she cares. She began by hanging a bumper sticker in her classroom that read, "Have you hugged your teacher today?"

"Webster may define a hug as 'to clasp tightly in the arms, especially with affection; embrace'; but I know that hugging to me meant a meaningful connection between two human beings," Landgren says.

The bumper sticker hung unnoticed for weeks until Landgren couldn't resist pointing it out. The kids looked at her skeptically, so she said no more.

Weeks later, a boy came up to her after school and said, "I think I'd like to hug you today." After that, she began taking small, careful steps toward meaningful contact. She adopted three rules from Kathleen Keating's *The Hug Therapy Book*. (See box.)

"Build an atmosphere of trust and warmth by using notes, winks, praise, pats, phone calls, smiles, and jokes," Landgren suggests. "Express your emotions; be consistent; don't use hugs as rewards or punishments. Be aware of your actions, for the children you may be overlooking might be the ones who need your attention most."

Hug therapy

1. Hug therapy is always nonsexual, so be sure the hugs you dispense are compassionate, comforting, and playful, not passionate.

2. Go slow. Be certain you have permission before giving a hug.

3. If you need a hug, ask permission.

From *The Hug Therapy Book.* Kathleen Keating. Comprehensive Care Corporation, Irvine, C.A., 1987

Psychologists claim that hugging can lift depression and make us feel younger and more vibrant." And Landgren agrees.

"I began to notice a change in the atmosphere of the room. I had always maintained good control and saw myself as a warm, loving person. But as I became more sensitive to students' moods and more physically demonstrative, the students became more cooperative, responsible, and willing to work."

Landgren's way may not be yours. But as you begin to show your warmth and caring in ways that are natural to you, the students will respond and return that warmth in ways that are natural for them.

What Do You Expect?

Expectations are a powerful phenomenon. Our expectations about people influence our actions and attitudes toward those individuals, and their behaviors in response. That's why expectations tend to become self-fulfilling prophecies.

In a variety of ways, often unintentionally, we communicate the messages that some students are winners and others are losers. Whom we call on, how long we wait for responses, and how we group students all reveal our expectations. If your expectations for students are high, chances are very good they will perform well, both socially and academically. Unfortunately, the reverse is also true.

The effect of expectations

How are our expectations translated into actions—either beneficial or harmful? How do we knowingly or unknowingly treat kids unequally based on our expectations? Here's what the research shows:

• Teachers call more on those they think are most capable and give them more time to respond.
• Some teachers actually "shun" children labeled low achievers. They offer no eye contact, praise, interaction, or opportunity to answer in class.
• Children perceived as low achievers receive less praise and more criticism.
• Teachers tend to stress conduct more than learning with low achievers.
• Attempting to encourage, teachers may praise low achievers for insignificant accomplishments or simple tasks. This is often interpreted by the students as further proof the teacher thinks they're "dumb."
• Low achievers experience more rudeness, lack of interest, and inattentiveness from their teachers.
• Teachers touch fast learners more often than slow ones.
• Students perceived as low achievers are often physically separated from the rest of the class.

These teacher behaviors and others based on expectations directly affect student performance. Expectations can do much harm or much good. Your ability to recognize and control their effects will determine which.

Not surprisingly, children perceived as low achievers usually develop poor self-images. And poor self-images cause many kinds of behavioral and academic problems.

Also, if a teacher consistently avoids calling on a student he or she perceives as low-achieving, that student becomes even less able to achieve because the student is denied the chance to think and exercise intellectual skills.

The effect of your expectations is magnified by students' expectations—for themselves and their classmates. Students take their cues from teachers. If a teacher expects a child to do poorly, the child expects as much. So do his or her classmates. It is this mirroring effect that magnifies the power of expectations. Students form expectations for classmates as early as kindergarten, where children in high-ability groups can be heard making unkind remarks about the drawings and work of children in low-ability groups. In kindergarten children first perceive others' expectations for them. They use these perceptions to develop a self-image.

It's a vicious cycle as students live up or

down to our expectations, constantly reinforcing them.

How expectations develop

To break the vicious cycle of poor expectations, you must first understand how they develop.

Expectations are frequently associated with a student's cultural or racial backround, gender, or socioeconomic status, reports Jere Brophy. Teachers and parents "know," for example, that girls are more verbal than boys.

Our expectations are also influenced by the labels assigned to students, comments from previous teachers, and grades or standardized test scores.

Reading ability is another critical factor. Stanford University researcher Elizabeth Cohen claims that our entire education system is misguidedly based on the notion of reading ability as the sole indicator of intelligence. Cohen has shown through extensive research that teachers assume good readers will be competent in any content area, and that those with poor reading ability will do poorly on any task.

Classrooms create and maintain a whole status order based on reading abilities, says Cohen. This status order is reinforced by ability grouping. The order is understood and accepted by teacher and students, and their expectations and actions are influenced accordingly. Unfortunately, this order ignores the fact that there are many types of abilities, and each child "shines" in his or her own way.

Consider the different types of "intelligence" identified by Howard Gardner of Harvard University, who claims, "Human beings have evolved over a long period of time to think in at least seven ways, which I call intelligences."[1]

Mathematical and linguistic intelligence are the two types emphasized in schools. But equally important, Gardner explains, are five other types: musical, spatial, bodily-kinesthetic, interpersonal, and intrapersonal.

"We all have strengths and weaknesses among the 'seven intelligences,' " says Gardner. "Strength in one intelligence does not have predictive value for strength in another intelligence," he stresses. "Psychologists who claim that intelligence is a single entity— educators who think of students as either smart or dumb—are wrong. A person can be smart in one area and dumb in others."

That's the lesson we must teach our students. We must help them raise their expectations for themselves and each other by teaching them to recognize that everyone is "intelligent" in his or her own way.

The Multi-Ability Classroom

One of the most promising strategies for helping kids discover that they're able human beings—and raising expectations in the process—is the "multi-ability classroom." This approach, developed by Elizabeth Cohen, demonstrates that there are many important skills besides reading ability. Students' expectations change when they learn that everyone has skills to contribute. And racial and gender attitudes improve, too.

The "other abilities" Cohen has identified include (but are not limited to):
• creativity
• suggesting new ideas
• helping a group reach a decision
• visualizing problems and solutions
• physical skills, such as strength and dexterity
• reasoning (identifying relationhips and patterns, categorizing, and so on)
• problem solving
• curiosity and inventiveness
• persistence

Cohen suggests five steps for creating a multi-ability task. (Try brainstorming with a colleague to develop these activities.)

1. Choose a task that involves these features: multiple abilities, leadership roles for all students, private evaluations, feedback from peers, and little emphasis on grading or competition. Appropriate tasks could be anything from a science experiment to role-

playing to a class newspaper project.

2. Prepare the task by making sure that the multiple skills you want to emphasize really are essential to successful completion.

3. Describe the task to students and explain that what they are doing is the same thing adults do in the real world—they draw on many different skills. Identify and discuss the abilities and skills necessary for the task. What does the situation call for? What skills will help accomplish this task? (Charting and posting the abilities is helpful.) Explain that every child will be good in at least one of the abilities. Give examples involving all students, especially those who have low self-esteem or little respect from classmates. And tell students they may help each other in reading and writing.

4. Monitor the task to make sure everyone participates and no one dominates.

5. Have the class evaluate the activity. Ask students to evaluate themselves on different abilities.

What About Discipline?

Good discipline is not punishment. It is a broad concept encompassing the steps taken to ensure good behavior or to correct misbehavior. Discipline is:

• *instruction*—teaching children responsibility for their behavior, strategies for governing their own actions, and the value of following reasonable rules.

• *management*—working with students to create and enforce classroom rules and routines.

• *positive reinforcement* of good behavior as well as negative consequences for misbehavior.

Discipline is integrally entwined with classroom management and effective instructional strategies. For example, students who repeatedly fail at school tasks become frustrated. They may stop trying, or they may act out feelings of anger and hostility. Others misbehave when they are confused or bored. And there are children who don't feel they

Building Great Expectations

Individual differences in ability certainly do exist, and teachers must address these differences. But research has documented actions you can take to communicate higher expectations, encourage better performance, and increase all students' opportunities to learn. Here are some suggestions:

• Ask yourself whether you are unfairly judging a student's ability based on reports from previous years, grades or test scores, or others' opinions.

• Consciously try to call on every student.

• Give students at least five seconds to respond.

• Rephrase questions or give clues to help a child respond.

• React positively to students' answers, either affirming them or correcting them.

• When students speak, make eye contact and listen to what they say.

• Try to give all students equal attention and opportunities for success.

• Downplay ability grouping by grouping students differently for various activities. For example, use age, height, or alphabetical groupings for activities where ability differences are unimportant.

• Offer praise that is specific and sincere.

• Be aware that some students don't ask for help even when they need it.

• Model the respect and courtesy you expect students to return.

• Show an interest in the lives and experiences of all your students, and be sensitive to their emotional needs.

belong—who misbehave because they feel alienated. Teachers can prevent many of these problems by creating a strong group identity; by carefully planning and pacing lessons; by keeping kids actively involved and challenged; and by giving all students opportunities to succeed.

As former teacher Walter Doyle of North Texas State University describes, there is a beginning-of-the-year "rhythm" that characterizes all classrooms. Misbehavior gradually increases at the beginning of the year until a critical point is reached. If a teacher can successfully and firmly handle this early "testing," misbehavior decreases and stabilizes at a much lower level. But failure to handle the misbehavior at the critical point will increase its frequency and seriousness. You may even lose control of the class.

Don't panic. The strategies suggested in Chapters 1, 2, and 4 and the techniques presented in this chapter will help you prevent many problems in the first place and handle successfully those that may occur.

Let's stress the prevention part. Good discipline strategies are those that prevent problems. This means attending to the children's physical needs, so they are not uncomfortable; attending to their intellectual needs, so they are not bored, confused, or frustrated; and attending to social and emotional needs so they feel secure, valued, and part of the group.

Effective teachers help students feel good about themselves.

Behavior Problems

When does a child's behavior cause a discipline problem? When it interferes with your teaching and the children's learning. We're not talking here about the noise that characterizes happy children hard at work. Classrooms were not designed to be quiet—since the days when one teacher instructed many grades in a single room.

Behavior problems are those that interfere with classroom life; for example, an angry, hostile child who picks fights or shouts obscenities during lessons.

There are many other less extreme examples of problem behavior: children who can't seem to control annoying habits such as pencil-tapping, whistling, or talking out at inappropriate times; children who continuously whine, complain, or tattle; those who always "forget" their homework or claim their assignments are too difficult; or those who withdraw and want only to be left alone. Each of these problem behaviors interferes with your teaching and student learning.

But besides these specific problem types, there are more pervasive problems affecting a much larger portion of school-age children.

"The differences between children's behaviors and attitudes twenty years ago and today are great," writes veteran Michigan teacher Jean Medick in her publication on handling problem behaviors. With her fourth and fifth graders, for example, Medick has found that "so many children feel perfectly free to cut others down. When I ask them why they said a hurtful thing to someone for no apparent reason, they answer, 'I don't know.' It's like a sport—something to do."

Children with behavior problems share one characteristic: a very poor self-image. And a poor self-image or low self-esteem manifests itself in these pervasive problems, which Medick and other veterans find particularly disturbing:

1. Uncertainty that children feel about themselves.
2. Much physical and verbal fighting.
3. Insensitivity.
4. Lack of self-discipline.
5. Inattentiveness, poor listening skills, inability to stick to a task or concentrate.
6. Disregard for their property, that of others, or the school's.
7. Stealing, and the attitude that if they take something and can get away with it, it's okay.
8. Failure to put things away or clean up after themselves.
9. Doing only what they want to do and nothing more.
10. Constant socializing.
11. Apathy, boredom, depression, withdrawal.
12. Constant demand for their rights, with little regard for the rights of others.

Discipline techniques

Sarcasm, ridicule, and other verbal abuse are common discipline techniques that are ineffective at best and hurtful at worst. They damage students' self-esteem and only reinforce the already low opinions many kids have of themselves.

Effective teachers discipline with encouragement and kind words more often than rebukes or reprimands.

Effective teachers discipline with encouragement and kind words more often than rebukes or reprimands. They help students feel good about themselves. Their discipline techniques focus on improving a student's self-image and responsibility.

Handling behavior problems isn't easy. But when you must, try to keep this advice from veterans in mind:

• Take a deep breath and try to remain calm. It's natural to be overcome with frustration, resentment, and anger. But when you are, you become less rational and your agitation is contagious.

• Try to set a positive tone and model an appropriate response, even if it means you must take a few moments to compose yourself. Acknowledge that you need time to think, time to respond. "This is upsetting me, too, but I need a few minutes to think before we talk about it."

• Make sure students understand that it's their misbehavior you dislike, not them. "I like you, Bob, but your behavior is unacceptable."

• Give the misbehaving child a chance to respond positively by telling her not only what she's doing wrong, but what she can do to correct it.

• Never resort to blame or ridicule.

• Avoid win-lose conflicts and emphasize problem-solving instead of punishment.

• Insist that students accept responsibility for their behavior.

• Try to remain courteous in the face of hostility or conflict. Show students you care about them and their problems, earn their respect, and establish rapport.

• Follow through on commitments.

• Treat students equally and be consistent in what you let them say and do. Be careful not to favor certain students.

• Treat students respectfully and politely.

• Be an attentive listener. Encourage students to talk out feelings and concerns and help them clarify their comments by restating them.

• Use "I messages" to discuss problems. Tell students how their behavior makes you feel. For example, "Could you please move your feet? When they're in the aisle, I'm afraid I might trip over them and get hurt." This statement includes the three necessary components of effective "I-messages": describe the behavior, state the effects of the behavior, and state how it makes you feel.

• Model the behavior you expect from your students. Are you as considerate of your students' feelings as you want them to be of others'? Are you as organized and on-task as you tell them to be?

• Specifically describe misbehavior and help students understand the consequences of misbehavior.

• Be aware of cultural differences. For example, a child who stares at the floor while you speak

to him would be viewed as defiant in some cultures and respectful in others.

• Discourage cliques and other anti-social behavior. Offer cooperative activities to encourage group identity.

• Teach students personal and social skills—communicating, listening, helping, and sharing, for example.

• Teach students academic survival skills, such as paying attention, following directions, asking for help when they really need it, and volunteering to answer.

• Avoid labeling students as "good" or "bad." Instead, describe their behavior as "positive"/"acceptable" or "disruptive"/"unacceptable."

• Focus on recognizing and rewarding acceptable behavior more than punishing misbehavior.

• Ignore or minimize minor problems, instead of disrupting class proceedings. A glance, a directed question, or your proximity may be enough to stop misbehavior.

• Where reprimands are necessary, state them quickly and nondisruptively.

Specific Strategies

Reality Therapy, Assertive Discipline, Teacher Effectiveness Training, Behavior Modification and other methods offer specific techniques for handling problem behavior. Some are nationally known, while many are developed for individual schools or districts. Some are developed by researchers, others are created by practicing teachers.

Rather than rigidly following one approach or another, most teachers create their own unique styles, taking bits and pieces of several and adapting them to their situations, students, and personalities. You can too. Here are examples of the approaches some veterans take.

Token economies

Teacher Mona Wells of New Richmond, Ohio, found a combination of strategies to meet her needs. Here's how she describes the problems in her third-grade class and what she did about them:

"School had been in session for 48 days, and David had had his name on the chalkboard 48 times for disruptive behavior. Two-thirds of those times he had lost recess and had gone to the kindergarten classroom for time out. I had also called his parents, and he had gone to the principal's office. Annie was running a close second to David's record, and Tammy was coming in third. These students had become passive to any type of punishment."

What was happening?

"I realized I was reinforcing negative behavior by recognizing the students who were disrupting the class," Wells explains.

Now students who had been following rules were reinforced; disruptive students were ignored.

After scouring the research and analyzing what other teachers were trying, Wells decided she needed a "catch-the-child-being-good approach." Her plan was to reward appropriate behavior, rather than focus on misbehavior. To reinforce positive behavior, she decided to initiate a token-economy system in her classroom. This system, a form of behavior modification, allows students to earn tokens with positive behavior. These tokens can then be exchanged for rewards—privileges or material goods. Here's how the procedure works:

1. Clearly specify what behaviors will earn tokens.
2. Establish "stores" open at recess and/or after school where students can spend their tokens.
3. Decide with students on rates of payment and prices of items.
4. Design tokens that cannot be counterfeited.
5. Distribute tokens freely during the first few days, making sure that each student gets some.
6. Bestow a token immediately after "catching

a student being good" so the student will know exactly how the token was earned.
7. Once students understand the system, bestow tokens less freely and accompany each token with a smile, praise, or thanks.
8. Record students' earnings.

Following these steps, Wells was ready to roll: "I took 1 x 3-inch pieces of construction paper, wrote ONE WISH on each, then laminated them. Then I talked to students about what kind of behavior would earn tokens. We decided that a ONE WISH card was worth a sticker; two cards earned a pencil, an eraser, a sucker or a roll of Smarties; three cards earned a 10-cent box of candy or a poster; and five cards were worth a 50-cent book. I posted a WISH MENU and put items for sale in plastic tubes with the prices marked. Our store was open after the noon recess so students would have time to eat the candy they earned.

"I kept the WISH tokens with me at all times, and anytime I 'caught' a student following rules, being polite, helping a classmate, and so on, I awarded a card. Now, the students who had been following the rules were being reinforced, and disruptive students were ignored as much as possible."

"It took a couple of days for the disruptive students to begin to work harder to follow the rules, but when they did catch on, their appropriate behavior was obvious."

And it didn't stop there. Wells knew that token economies create an artificial environment and are only the first step toward long-lasting improvements. Once appropriate behaviors are learned, they should be reinforced only occasionally and randomly. This way, the behaviors become stronger and more lasting.

Thus Wells proceeded to the next stage of her new discipline program.

"I replaced the NO RECESS section of the chalkboard with a WONDERFUL section. Every time I 'caught' a child following rules, being kind, using thinking skills to answer questions, or doing his or her best on an assignment, I put the child's name in the WONDERFUL box. The selection was now limited to special performance. And I maintained a modified WISH system by putting check marks next to names in the box. Students accumulated check marks for a week, then collected their wishes at the end of the week.

"The students strived to be 'wonderful.' The atmosphere in the classroom changed. The

students watched for their peers to behave instead of misbehave. Positive reinforcement had worked to modify the students' behavior."

Like any other strategy, token economies and behavior modification work better in some situations than in others. Age, for example, is a factor. Jere Brophy and Joyce Putnam point out that behavior modification is generally more effective with younger students.

And some educators are troubled by the ethics of "buying" and "selling" good behavior, even if the scheme is only used as a first step toward learning better self-control.

But using her special knowledge of her students, Wells created a system that worked for them—and her. While it wouldn't work everywhere, her strategy met the needs of her particular situation. That's what professionals strive for.

Time out

Physically removing a disruptive child is a commonly used discipline technique referred to as time out. But while this technique stops the disturbance, it doesn't address the root of the problem. To enhance this method, Carl Calliari has developed a strategy to make "time out" a time to learn (see side box). He has found this strategy effective for many reasons.

First, kids sometimes behave disruptively without realizing it—they hum, snap their fingers, talk out loud, and so on. Or they do so many things, they aren't sure what got them into trouble. Asking them to identify the problem makes resolving it much easier.

Giving students a chance to explain their side of the story demonstrates your fairness and shows them you are interested. And asking kids what they think should happen as a result of the misbehavior helps them accept responsibility. It also gives them some control. They'll soon learn that their suggestions must be appropriate and fair to be acceptable.

Time for learning

You can make "time out" a time for learning with a strategy developed by Carl Calliari, Glassboro State College, New Jersey. Just follow these steps:

- Put a "time out" chair where you can see it, but the children can't.

- Explain the procedure to the whole class before you start using it. Tell them that the purpose of "time out" is to help them become better behaved and to learn how to make better decisions. Emphasize that when students are sent to the "time out" chair, they need to go there immediately, without argument. And explain that it's not an automatic conviction—they get a chance to tell their side.

- After you send a student to the "time out" chair, ask him or her to answer, in writing, the questions on a "Time to Think" sheet. The sheet should include these questions:
  1. Why do I think I was sent here?
  2. What is my side of the story?
  3. What do I think should happen to me?

  If your students can't read or write yet, record their answers on a tape player.

- As soon as possible, confer with the student about his or her misbehavior.

"Never assume anything, never prejudge, and be consistent," Calliari recommends. He explains that the "Time to Think" questions raise key points about misbehavior.

Behavior contracts

Another technique that can be adapted to all grade levels is contingency contracting. Here, teachers (and sometimes parents) contract with students to carry out certain responsibilities in exchange for certain rewards. Contracting helps students develop self-control and self-management by letting them experience the consequences of personal choices.

Contracts can help students improve their work habits, behavior, or both. Many teachers favor contracts over other forms of behavior modification. This technique has several major advantages, according to Jere Brophy and Joyce Putnam.

• Contracts allow students responsibility and independence in managing their school time.
• By listing specific responsibilities, contracts underscore their importance and help students remember them.
• Contracts provide necessary structure for students who are disorganized and easily distracted.
• Students have some control by being able to "negotiate" the terms of their contracts.
• Contracts emphasize student responsibility more than the rewards for terms met.
• They can be custom-tailored to each individual student.

Included on pp. 114-116 are reproducible samples of contracts you can use to negotiate with your students. also, see p. 49 in Chapter 2 for more tips on developing contracts.

"Frequently offered the responsibility for solving their school problems, children can learn through practice to be very adept problem solvers," say Michigan teacher Jean Medick. "This produces positive feelings, confidence, and a sense of being in control of one's behavior and life. It develops socially responsible youngsters."

Medick describes how her fourth and fifth graders solve the problem of fighting.

"When children fought, I used to resort to scolding, lecturing, taking away recess, isolating, or sending children to the office," Medick recalls. "These procedures did not help children learn anything about how to prevent fighting or better ways to solve disagreements.

"But children can learn a great deal about the feelings people experience in fights, causes of fights, and better ways to deal with situations that cause fights through group discussions using the problem-solving process. Even if only a handful of students seem to be doing the fighting, the whole class gets together for a discussion to help think of better alternatives. They learn much about the way their classmates think and feel during these discussions. This promotes understanding and empathy that simply was not possible when I used the old methods. I, too, learn many things about the children from listening."

Solving problems— Together!

Many of the discipline strategies advocated by teachers and child psychologists offer similar approaches to problem solving. The problem-solving process, especially effective for older children, requires that you:

1. Identify the problem.
2. Determine the circumstances and behaviors that led up to the problem.
3. Identify the feelings experienced by those involved.
4. Ask yourself, "Have I ever experienced something like this before? What did I do? Did it work?"
5. List and think through many different alternatives for handling the problem.
6. Select one alternative and develop a plan.
7. Put the plan into action.
8. Evaluate the plan. Is it working? If not, choose another alternative.
9. Involve kids in the problem-solving process, too!

Active Listening: An example

Child: Jane doesn't like me anymore. She won't play with me at recess, and she won't eat lunch with me today.

Teacher: You're upset because Jane didn't play with you at recess and won't eat lunch with you today.

Child: Yes! She's my best friend and she's being mean.

Teacher: Having Jane as a best friend is important to you and it hurts you when she is mean to you.

Child: Yes, Jane's the best friend I ever had and I don't want to lose her.

Teacher: You're worried about losing Jane as your best friend.

Child: She likes Patsy. Yesterday she said she'd play with me after school but she didn't. She played with Patsy and they're going to eat lunch together today. I don't like Patsy! It's not fair!

Teacher: Your feelings are really hurt and you feel left out. And you don't like Patsy?

Child: Yes, I'm scared I won't have anyone to play with and I don't like to eat lunch alone. Actually, I don't dislike Patsy. She's nice, but I guess I'm jealous.

Teacher: You feel scared and jealous at the same time.

Child: Yeah, but it's partly my fault. I haven't been very nice to Jane since I found out she played with Patsy.

Teacher: You think that you contributed to the problem by not being as nice as you usually are to Jane. What alternatives do you think you have?

Child: I guess I'll tell Jane I'm sorry for being mean, but I'm going to tell her she hurt my feelings, too.

Contributed by Jean Medick

Indeed, *listening* is something you need to do a lot of in problem-solving situations.

"An important discovery for me as a teacher was that my perceptions of what goes on in the classroom are not necessarily the same as those of the children," says Medick.

Only by listening can you get the whole picture. Only by listening can you discover children's motives, thoughts, and feelings while at the same time communicating the message that you have confidence in their abilities to solve the problem.

When you actively listen, you attempt to understand what is really being said. You clarify and restate what students are saying. Active listening does not mean offering advice, opinions, judgments, analyses, or solutions— only restating what you hear the person saying. Medick offers the dialogue from an experience in her classroom in the adjacent box.

"I believe that active listening, even in the simplest of exchanges, helps a child to grow," says Medick. Developing the skill takes much practice. But even beginners can become good at this important technique.

Medick also insists that her kids be honest in problem-solving situations and never resort to the "I don't know" response. This frequent response "gets a kid off the hook" by allowing him or her to avoid responsibility in unpleasant or threatening situations.

"Sometimes I think the response 'I don't know' really means, 'You figure it out, teacher—read my mind.' Early in the year, I tell all the children that responding with 'I don't know' on matters of behavior or interpersonal problems will be unacceptable because they are intelligent human beings capable of thinking. I also tell them that all other responses except put-downs are permitted in problem-solving situations—even 'I don't like you' or 'I think you are a mean or unfair teacher.' Once we know how people are honestly feeling, we can proceed to work things out."

Accepting responsibility is an important aspect of solving behavior problems. Allow children to take responsibility for their problems and responsibility for solving them. Consider this real-life example:

> John one day refused to do his schoolwork. His teacher explained to him that teaching was her responsibility, but learning was his. After signing a statement (at his teacher's suggestion) that he refused to do his work, he elected to go home. His mother picked him up (according to prearranged plans) and took him to work with her, where he spent the day alone . . . After that, he never refused to do his work again. Nor did he show resentment toward his teacher or his mother, because the choice had been his.

When you provide students with a choice, you place responsibility with them. And this is where it belongs, stress the experts. Make sure they understand the consequences of their choices; then let them decide. But also be sure to follow through. If a child elects to "suffer the consequences" rather than comply with the rules, those consequences had better be forthcoming. Make sure you involve the principal in something as unusual as the case cited above.

Resolving Conflicts

In his book *Creative Conflict Resolution* (copyright Scott, Foresman and Company), elementary teacher William Kreidler offers interesting techniques for handling conflicts between students. Among them:

• *The Fight Form*. This technique encourages students to write about a problem, defusing anger in the process. For either verbal or physical encounters, develop a form that asks students to write answers to these questions:

1. With whom did you fight?
2. What was the problem?
3. Give two reasons why you started fighting.
4. Why did the other person fight with you?

5. Did fighting solve the problem?
6. What are three things you might try instead of fighting if this happened again?
7. Is there anything you would like to say to the person you fought with?

When you review the forms with the students involved, concentrate on their suggestions for more constructive ways to face the problem.

• *Role Reversals*. Here, children first act out their conflict, then change roles to argue the opposite point of view. After the players begin to understand the other viewpoint, have them discuss possible solutions satisfactory to both views.

An interesting variation to use with large groups split into factions is the *Hassle Line*. Have the opposing groups form lines and face one another. Give the children in the first line one minute to convince the child facing them of their position. Then give the other line the same opportunity. The next step is to have the

Have children act out a conflict by using puppets.

two lines switch roles and argue the other position. Then lead a group discussion to explore solutions and find one that is acceptable to most of the kids.

• *Problem Puppets*. Puppets acting out a conflict can give young children the distance they need from a problem to freely discuss their feelings. Obtain several puppets and explain to the class that these friends will help them handle problems. Use the puppets to re-enact conflict situations, before the whole class or privately. Stop the action at the point of conflict and ask the children to suggest solutions. Have the puppets demonstrate several, even those you know won't work. This helps them think through the consequences of their actions. When you find a solution that works, ask the children in conflict if they agree to such a solution and why.

• *3-R Strategy*. For older children, try this three-step process for solving long-standing disagreements or dislikes. In the first step, *resentment*, ask both parties to state what they dislike about each other and what has happened to fuel this resentment. The *request* phase requires each child to tell the other what must be done to ease the resentment or solve the conflict. Finally, in the *recognition* phase, the children negotiate which requests they are willing to honor. End the session with both students stating qualities they like or admire in each other. (The 3-R Strategy works best in private, where you won't be interrupted— perhaps after school.)

• *Worksheet in Upgrading Behavior* (see p. 117.) This strategy applies to conflicts between a teacher and a student. It works best with a child who has a specific problem behavior, such as teasing or talking back, and is genuinely interested in changing the behavior. Ask the child to complete the worksheet. Then go over the sheet with the child, examining and discussing the behavior. Keep a record of when the child avoids conflict by enacting the new behavior. Make visible a chart showing the child's progress.

Cooling hot tempers

Hot tempers heat up many classrooms. Flare-ups usually occur unexpectedly so that you're forced to cool things down by using external control. But the only permanent solution is to teach children self-control. (See box next page.)

Helping the Underachiever

Millions of very capable children spend most of their school time trying to avoid learning, says psychologist and former teacher Sylvia Rimm, director of the Family Achievement Clinic in Wisconsin. These children are called "underachievers." They don't do as well in school as they could. And they honestly don't believe they can do any better.

"All their energy is spent manipulating their home and school environments to hide their low self-concepts," Rimm explains.

Underachievers exhibit one or more of these characteristics: inconsistent work, poor study habits, lack of concentration, hyperactivity, daydreaming, perfectionism, disorganization, and aggressive behavior.

Rimm offers strategies for helping two different types of underachievers: those who are overly dependent and those who are overly independent or dominant.

The dependent underachiever seldom completes assignments, loses homework, has a messy desk, and makes excuses for why he or she can't do assigned work. Typically, says Rimm, this type of child has had too much parental help all his or her life. The child has no self-confidence because he/she has had no experience at working out problems. This dependency becomes debilitating.

What can you do to help? Here's what Rimm suggests:

• Realize that this child will require much effort and positive support while being weaned from dependency.

• Insist on the child's independent activity on tasks you know he or she can do. The child will beg for help and you'll be tempted. But don't give in. Even a little extra help is a vote of no confidence. "Giving sympathy won't help and neither will one-to-one instruction," says Rimm. "Fostering these well-developed dependencies continues to rob children of their self-confidence."

• Request a parent conference to enlist home support. Discuss (tactfully!) the child's behavior at home and patterns you see at school. Encourage parents to set up home situations for the child that require hard work but enable him or her to succeed. Tell the parents you'll do the same thing in school. Remind them to let the child work alone.

Encourage them to express pleasure and pride at each independent accomplishment.

• Target work completion as your first goal for the child; emphasize quality later.

• Always recognize completed work with a sincere smile, stickers, privileges, or some other reward. Ask parents to set up rewards at home, based on the child's suggestions.

Dominant underachievers have always been given too much power and try to control every situation. They are independent to a fault. They can't accept *No*, put a high priority on social life, and manipulate most of the people

---

Controlling tempers

Following are strategies for helping kids learn to control their tempers. They are adapted from those suggested by school psychologist Michael Petti, Woodbridge Township, New Jersey.

• Show children that it's possible to change. Remind them of instances in which they have exercised self-control. "Sheila, I know you can control your temper. Just yesterday you remained calm after Jennifer accidentally tripped you."

• Explain in a calm situation that everyone gets angry enough to explode, but they don't do it. It doesn't solve anything, and wastes a lot of time.

• Help them understand that they can lose a dispute without losing self-respect. Most arguments are no-win situations, and it's best to just back away. No one admires a sore loser.

• Use role reversal or puppet shows to try to get students to understand others' feelings. Demonstrate that no one likes to be screamed at, picked on, or always told what to do.

• Encourage kids to talk about their concerns. A lot of little annoyances all bottled up lead to big bursts of anger. Tell them it's okay to let people know what's bothering them.

• Teach students to ask for clarifications before confronting someone angrily. Hotheads frequently misinterpret comments. Teach them to say, "I think you are saying . . ." They'll avoid a lot of battles by finding out what the other person really means.

• Discourage jealousy. Try to explain that when we act jealously, we are only putting ourselves down. Boost the jealous child's self-esteem by reviewing her past accomplishments. You could list them on a special card for her to look at when she feels jealous.

• Help children recognize their boiling points. Tenseness, throbbing temples, and bursts of energy are all physical cues they can learn to identify. Suggest a way they can relax when they feel themselves about to boil—counting to 10; assuming a "turtle" position (head on desk, eyes closed, fists clenched); thinking of a favorite TV show.

• Suggest some ways to release pent-up anger—running, bouncing a ball, discussing the matter with a friend.

• Teach kids to ask themselves, "Is this really worth getting upset about?"

• Encourage them to pat themselves on the back any time they control their tempers.

around them. ''Though dominant underachievers may appear tough, theirs is a very precarious position fraught with the fear of being exposed as vulnerable and imperfect,'' Rimm explains.

Here's how you can help:
• Let these kids know you are an ally—that you see how bright and creative they are, and you recognize their special qualities.
• Avoid useless power struggles. Don't be tempted to use grades or your power to put them down. They'll just struggle harder.
• Permit them some control within clearly defined limits. Negotiate these limits and write them down.
• Be firm, but fair. Offer your kind persuasion and support.
• Teach dominant children to examine the perspectives of others.
• Remind parents that the dominant child needs a clear *yes*, a clear *no*, and most of all, consistency.

Punishment

CAUTION: Punishment can potentially do more harm than good. It can reinforce the very behavior you are trying to correct.

If misbehaving is the only way a child has of getting attention, then punishment plays right into his or her hands and reinforces an already low self-image. Misbehavior gets the child the attention he or she wants, and the child usually continues to misbehave.

The experts—experienced teachers and researchers who study teaching—claim that punishment works best in settings where positive behavior is acknowledged and reinforced, and add that the punishment should always match the problem. Here's what they recommend:
• Never punish in the heat of the moment.
• Make sure the child knows why the punishment is necessary.
• If necessary, delay punishment until an appropriate time.
• Punish mildly, briefly, and infrequently.
• Never use schoolwork or homework as punishment.
• Don't punish the class for one child's misbehavior.

Some examples of mild punishments include:
• being last in the lunch line;
• a reassigned seat;
• staying after school just long enough to miss walking home with friends;
• removal of a privilege, such as recess or free time;
• arranging with parents for a child to lose home privileges, such as watching television.

Shoring Up Self-Esteem

It's not just another educational buzzword. Self-esteem is the driving force behind many of our actions and behaviors. Self-esteem, says psychologist Patricia Berne, is the foundation of self-confidence. Without it, kids can't succeed. And unsuccessful, unhappy students not only fail academically, they fail to behave properly in the classroom. They make life miserable—for you, the other students, and themselves.

Raising students' perceptions of themselves is treating the cause of poor behavior, rather

Building self-esteem

Eight suggestions for helping children feel good about themselves

1. Build in success.
2. State the positive.
3. Capitalize on successes.
4. Watch for growth sparks.
5. Value and acknowledge.
6. Keep expectations realistic.
7. Explore various approaches to tasks and suggestions from students.
8. Don't be boring.

than the symptoms. It's probably the most important discipline strategy you can employ.

"[Children] need to realize what others appreciate about them in order to feel self-worth," Berne explains. She offers eight suggestions for helping children feel good about themselves.

1. Build in success. Success builds self-esteem, especially when the success is continuous. Exploring a child's own interests makes success more probable for a child with low self-esteem. Berne offers the example of a nine-year-old nonreader who loved to draw pictures. In helping him learn to read, she asked him to draw pictures and tell stories about his pictures. Berne typed the stories he told her, and he later learned to read them. Because the child had produced the stories, "his potential for reading them successfully was built in," she says.

2. State the positive. Nurture success by acknowledging the positive in a nonevaluative but validating way. How? By describing a student's work rather than evaluating it. "I try to talk with them about their effort, choice of materials, subject matter, and the details in the work that particularly reflect their creativity," Berne says. "This is an affirmation of them rather than an evaluation of their product."

   For example, point out all the details in a picture instead of simply commenting, "That's a good picture." Even on test papers, you can use positive comments to draw attention to a child's strengths.

3. Capitalize on successes. If you build on a child's interests to enable him or her to succeed, go a step further and use those successes to broaden interests. One child Berne worked with loved toys, so she encouraged him to write the descriptions and prices of toys in a notebook. Later, his interests expanded to collecting and classifying plants. Berne suggests you share successes with parents by sending notes home (after you've read them to the child).

4. Watch for growth sparks. Children with low self-esteem believe they can't learn or relate successfully to others. Help ignite a spark of interest they never knew they had. When a learning-disabled child showed Berne a magic trick he learned from a cereal box, she detected his delight in the trick and noticed how his self-esteem was heightened by her enjoyment. She nurtured this newborn interest and built on it to provide success and positive experiences to share with his classmates.

5. Value and acknowledge. Visible, tangible evidence of success greatly increases a child's self-esteem. If a child is discouraged over the newest spelling list, show her the lists she's already mastered. Collect children's artwork and writings to show them the improvements they're making over time. Encourage parents to display children's work, especially work that shows

the child's accomplishment.

6. Keep expectations realistic. Don't communicate the message that "you can only learn it the way I think you should."

7. Explore various approaches to tasks and suggestions from students. "Self-esteem grows when children feel involved and in control of their lives," says Berne.

8. Don't be boring. Boredom depresses self-esteem, says Berne, while interest and excitement increase a sense of self. Teach students to look for creative alternatives to their frustrations and problems, like the child who turned her spelling words into cheers—complete with body movements.

Empathize with students by acknowledging when a task is boring or frustrating. When their feelings are recognized, children often are less resistant to the tasks, says Berne. She adds that empathizing is another way to make children feel valued.

But what about your self-esteem? Teachers must feel good about themselves before they can help kids feel good. That's the approach Cathey Graham of San Jose takes in a schoolwide effort to raise self-esteem. As a site mentor for her school, Graham uses several strategies to help her fellow teachers improve their self-images.

At faculty meetings, she shares a monthly set of mini-ideas to make teachers feel better. The ideas focus on such things as professional stimulation, meeting emotional needs, pampering oneself, taking good physical care, and so on. "Teachers end up centering their lives on everyone but themselves," she notes.

Graham also shares classroom ideas for raising self-esteem and ideas for parents (see the Tips for Parents reproducible on p. 105).

But the biggest shot in the arm for the teachers is the "Teacher of the Week" program Graham has initiated and developed. Here's how it works:

At the beginning of the year, Graham draws names and assigns each of her 28 colleagues a special week. She keeps the schedule a secret.

A teacher's special week begins Monday morning, when he or she is featured on a bulletin board in the school lobby. (Graham prepares the board the weekend before to keep it a surprise.) The board includes biographical background, information about family, favorite books, favorite places, things he or she likes to do, and goals in life.

"Many kids seem to think that teachers live in the closets at school, and they're surprised to find out we have lives of our own," says Graham. "They're also surprised to see we're still working toward goals," she continues. "They think we're just sitting tight, not having to work anymore."

The "teacher of the week" is then officially announced to the students on Monday at lunch time.

"The students' job is to tell that teacher all week how wonderful he or she is," Graham explains. "Children need to learn to say thank you," she adds. "They need to appreciate a good teacher and a good education."

The rest of the week contains more special treatment. On Tuesday, the teacher receives a balloon bouquet. On Wednesday, the school newsletter features the teacher, and on Thursday, lunch is served on a tray (after the teacher chooses from a special menu). On Friday, there's a box with a note and a special treat inside.

"This special treatment tells us we're doing a good job," says Graham. "We tend to forget that." She also reports that the program raises self-esteem all the way around. The students whose teacher is featured feel proud and excited, and the whole school gets fired up.

Motivation

Motivation is a need or desire that causes us to act. Helping kids be motivated to learn will be one of your greatest challenges—and rewards.

Highly motivated children achieve more than others. And they're also better behaved. Motivated students succeed in school and feel good about themselves and others. They are creative, curious, and confident.

Too often, though, students are externally motivated. That is, they do schoolwork to please a teacher or parent, avoid punishment, or receive a reward.

"By the sixth grade, students have apparently settled into a dull routine of doing assignments in order to get rewards, like good grades, and avoid punishments, like staying after school," says educational psychologist Jere Brophy. They are motivated to perform, but not to learn.

On the other hand, students who are internally motivated to learn approach learning tasks seriously, do them carefully, and expect to benefit from them, says Brophy. This does not mean they will always find learning tasks interesting or enjoyable, Brophy explains. Rather, they are convinced of the value of learning and believe it will directly benefit them.

Brophy points out that students can find academic activities pleasing and rewarding without being motivated to learn. For example, they can play a learning game in class and thoroughly enjoy its social or competitive aspects without thinking at all about what they are supposed to be learning.

The point is, you can design lessons and activities to capitalize on student interests, but that's not enough. The main goal of your motivational strategies must be to develop students' motivation to learn. You must convince them of the importance of learning and its benefits. Students properly motivated are students who value knowledge and skills for their own sake.

How can you help children become motivated to learn?

Let them see and hear your interest and motivation for learning. You are an important role model. And don't forget to communicate your expectations that they will enjoy learning. Also, Brophy suggests you try to ease the performance anxieties some students experience during learning activities. Stress learning as an enjoyable activity, not a

Success breeds success

Both research and common sense show that students try harder when they expect to succeed. Success is a powerful motivator for most of us, so providing opportunities for success is a great way to help keep students motivated. Remember, students need a very high success rate to keep motivated and engaged in their work—as high as 95 percent when they are working independently. Facilitate success by:

• Selecting appropriate content and tasks.

• Teaching students how to set goals, appraise their own performance, and use strategies for self-reinforcement.

• Teaching students to recognize the relationship between effort and outcome. Just spell it out. And model the effort-outcome linkage in your own actions. Don't assume students already understand the relationship. Researcher Jere Brophy suggests portraying effort as investment rather than risk. (For example, *Learning spelling words helps us read and write better*), portraying skill development as incremental (*We must learn several different skills that, together, enable us to do long division*), and focusing on mastery rather than normative comparisons (*We learn to read to enjoy a life-long pleasure, not to be better than someone else*).

competitive or high-pressure one.

Following are more strategies for motivating students to learn, based on the extensive research studies done by Brophy and his teacher and researcher colleagues.

Think positively

You can go a long way in helping kids become motivated just by presenting learning tasks in a positive way. It sounds obvious. But how many times have you heard or uttered comments such as those on the following page.

"You won't ever make it in sixth grade if you don't learn how to do this."

"Get your head in that book or I'll give you an extra writing assignment."

"I'm sorry to make you do this boring task, but you need to learn this material."

"I don't expect you to like this, but it's important."

"You've only got 20 minutes to complete this assignment, so you'd better concentrate."

No wonder kids don't value learning. We give them very little indication that they should. In his classroom studies, Brophy found that teachers made positive comments about a task only 25 percent of the time. At other times they made negative comments, neutral comments, or just launched into a task with no introduction at all.

Here are some ways to use the positive approach:
• Stress the value of the task by pointing out how knowledge and skills can bring pleasure and satisfaction.
• Personalize by expressing your beliefs, attitudes, or personal experiences that illustrate the task's importance.
• Be enthusiastic by stating your liking for this type of task.
• State positive expectations by telling students you know they will enjoy the task and do well on it.
• Explain personal relevance by tying the task to students' lives and interests.

Tempting tasks

Careful packaging of learning tasks is another good strategy. You can select or design activities to capitalize on students' existing intrinsic motivation, says Brophy. He offers these suggestions:
• Adapt tasks to students' interests. (The Student Motivation Information form on p. 110 will reveal not only student interests, but also what rewards they value and what they are curious about.)
• Include novelty or variety elements.
• Allow opportunities to make choices or decisions.
• Provide opportunities for active response.
• Include activities that provide immediate feedback to responses.
• Allow students to create finished products.
• Include elements of fantasy or simulation.
• Incorporate game-like features.
• Include higher-level objectives and divergent questions.
• Provide opportunities to interact with peers.

The specifics

Okay, by now you know some general motivational strategies. But how do you put it all together? How should you approach a particular activity to get students fired up about learning? Try these suggestions:
• Emphasize the importance of the activity.
• Project your enthusiasm.
• Induce curiosity or suspense.
• Cultivate interest or appreciation for the activity by tying it to students' lives or making abstract content more concrete and familiar.
• Shake things up a bit by introducing dissonance or cognitive conflict.
• Give students a chance to work together. Cooperative learning teams are one good example. (See p. 98.)
• Specifically state the learning objectives and provide advance organizers.
• Provide informative feedback.
• Model task-related thinking and problem solving.
• Make students aware of the various learning activities they undertake during the task—actively preparing to learn, memorizing material, encoding or elaborating on information presented, organizing and structuring content, and monitoring their own comprehension.

Rewarding behavior

When we expect external rewards for completing an activity or behaving a certain way, we are externally motivated. These extrinsic motivators—good grades, a teacher's or parent's praise, extra privileges and free time, public recognition, competition, even material goods such as stickers or candy—are expected or relied on by many students. Too often these motivators get in the way of real learning.

But while they are sometimes overused or abused, extrinsic motivators can be very effective in helping students develop intrinsic motivation to learn or behave. They can be especially effective with young and lower-ability children. Perhaps the most important role of extrinsic motivators is to make students aware of the powerful social reinforcement given to those who try hard, learn, and succeed.

Just remember that extrinsic motivation is a means to an end. More important and certainly more long-lasting, is helping kids develop internal motivation.

Suppose you decide external rewards are necessary for at least some of your students. Which ones should you use? Clearly, what is reinforcing or rewarding to one individual may not be to another. For example, a shy, withdrawn child might need your attention; a reward to a second child might be to get to read another story. See page 111 for a Motivation Menu of rewards developed by teachers. Consider these rewarding tips:

• Reinforcement is most effective at irregular intervals. For example, for a period of time offer a reward after each successful performance; later, offer the reward at random.

• Rewards related to individual students' needs are most powerful. Older students are much more likely to be reinforced by peer esteem or free time, while younger children may prefer gold stars, smiley faces, or other tangible rewards. A teacher's recognition or nod of approval for a lonely child is often more effective than candy or tokens. Observe and talk to your students to learn their personal needs.

The Pac-Man theory

Ever notice how motivated kids are to play Pac-Man or other popular video games? What's the big attraction? Writer Richard Bowman analyzed the game and interviewed many players. He found some striking parallels between Pac-Man and the ways teachers can help students become motivated. The list of motivating factors he identified reads like a quick review of the most important aspects of student motivation:

- immediate rewards and feedback;

- the game plays no favorites—everyone has an equal opportunity;

- a caring competitiveness where kids help each other;

- clarity of task;

- clear awareness of roles and responsibilities;

- choice in selecting problem-solving strategies to be used;

- a balanced system of skills and challenges, where a progressive hierarchy of challenges sustains interest;

- unambiguous feedback and ample opportunity for improvement;

- tasks with a high probability of success;

- freedom from fear of reprisal, ridicule, or rejection.

Adapted from *Educational Technology*, Sept. 1982.

• Try different types of rewards, such as the chance to be first in the lunch line, extra library privileges, or opportunities to run errands or perform other fun tasks. These reinforcements, say the experts, are more closely tied to educational goals.

• The reward should match the size of the

task. The smallest possible reward is most effective.

• Rewards must depend on actual performance, not on what is promised.

Praise: User beware

Teacher praise has been oversold as a management or motivation strategy. The fact is, verbal praise is not often effective as a reward. And it may seem more like punishment to a child who is embarrassed or threatened by special attention. Delivered insincerely or inappropriately, praise does more harm than good.

There are hidden messsages in the ways we praise people. Even if we don't intend these messages or are unaware they exist, others hear them loud and clear.

Suppose, for example, that you praise a lower-ability child who has just stumbled her way through reading a passage out loud. You are trying to encourage the child, but she feels humiliated and wonders why you have just called attention to her poor performance.

Or you praise a student for completing an easy assignment. The student reasons that, "Any dummy could do this, so Teacher must really think I'm stupid." You're only trying to be kind. But you've just shot down his self-esteem another notch.

There are often hidden messages in the ways teachers praise boys and girls.

Studies show that we tend to praise girls more for matters of form (neatness, following directions, speaking clearly) and praise boys more for substance (academic performance and intellectual responses). The messages received from these types of praise are that

Classrooms are social places and teachers play critical roles in influencing students' attitudes about themselves, classmates, and schoolwork.

boys are more capable than girls when it comes to academic tasks. Clearly, this is not the message we intend to send.

So *user beware*. Praise can undermine efforts to encourage or reinforce if it's used inappropriately.

Based on extensive analyses, Jere Brophy has developed guidelines for effective praise (see p. 106). Praise, says Brophy, is most often effective when it is:

- sincere (spontaneous);
- delivered privately;
- directed to noteworthy accomplishments;
- specific about what is being praised and why it is praiseworthy;
- focused on individual improvement and not compared to the accomplishments of others;
- phrased to emphasize the accomplishment, not the teacher's role as authority or expert.

Atmosphere Counts in Classrooms

"I consider it a moral responsibility as a teacher to help a child assume responsibility for his or her behavior, develop self-awareness, and learn to interact with others. Through attending to emotional as well as intellectual and physical development, I am a teacher in the fullest sense of the word—reaching and responding to the whole child."

—*Jean Medick*

Is your classroom a proper environment? Is the atmosphere right? The social atmosphere, that is. Are your students cooperative, responsible, caring, sharing, self-controlled, trusting, and accepting of themselves and others?

Classrooms are social places, and teachers play critical roles—consciously or unconsciously—in influencing students' attitudes about themselves, classmates, and schoolwork. Effective teachers help their students develop important social skills.

It all has to do with creating conditions conducive to teaching and learning. In the right atmosphere and environment, students (and teachers) grow and flourish; problems and misbehavior do not.

What is the "right" atmosphere? Studies consistently show that in positive classroom environments, students:

- Dare to take risks.
- Share their talents and encourage each other.
- Know they are important.
- Respect themselves and each other.
- Care for and trust each other.

It sounds like a tall order. But you can create such an environment. Many of your experienced colleagues have. In this section, teachers share their ideas and strategies for teaching the other lessons and life skills which are as important as reading, writing, and arithmetic.

Acceptance of self and others

Helping children feel good about themselves gives them the self-confidence to accept themselves—and others—for what they are. But along the way are some difficult lessons. For example, children must learn it's not only okay to be different, it's wonderful! The world is full of people with interesting differences.

To teach these lessons, elementary guidance counselor Marcia Leverte developed a unit called "Me Month." Here are some of her ideas.

Activity: Have students form a circle. Ask them to take turns looking in a hand mirror and pick out one thing they see that they like about themselves. Then ask each one to give an "I like" statement. It's best if the teacher begins with his or her own "I like" statement, such as, "I like my blue eyes." If a child cannot think of anything, help the child. Ask others to help too. Talk about how it felt to say something nice about themselves in front of others. Talk about how you felt first.

Activity: Using brown mural paper and crayons, choose one student each day to lie down and be traced by a classmate. Have others help the student color in the silhouette, adding specific body characteristics.

Then write or have the child write important personal information on the portrait—age, address, birth date, phone number, favorite subject, hobbies and interests. Display each portrait for a day.

Activity: (complements previous activity) Discuss what a positive statement is and help students come up with several. Then give children each a "smiley face" (or a shape such as a lightning bolt) cut out of construction paper (at least six inches in diameter, with room to write) and ask them to write a descriptive positive statement about the "Student of the Day"—the child whose outline was traced. Place these shapes on the silhouette. Allow each student to take home his or her portrait and the attached positive statements.

Activity: Create a learning center or bulletin board with children's photographs. Ask students to bring in pictures of themselves as babies and toddlers, along with current pictures. (Make sure to bring in your own photos.) Display the baby and toddler pictures on one side of a bulletin board and the current pictures on the other side. Have students try to match baby pictures with current ones. With younger children, discuss how everyone has grown and changed.

Activity: At the end of the "Me" unit, have students write a "Me" essay describing what they have discovered about themselves.

Self-confidence through self-awareness is also the goal of the "Me Museums" activity developed by Susie Edmond. Ask each student to bring in one empty shoe box. Then have the child print his or her name on the box and decorate it with magazine photographs or illustrations that depict the child's hobbies, interests, favorite foods or toys, television programs, and so on. (Again, make sure you participate.) Place the finished museums in a row on the window sill and ask the children to bring in one small but special item each day for the next two weeks—items such as family photographs, souvenirs, small collectibles, and greeting cards. The items are exhibited in the museums, and students view each other's exhibits during free time.

Ann McCutcheon boosts kids' confidence with this quick bulletin board idea: Make one construction-paper star 8 inches in diameter for each child. In bold letters, title the bulletin board, "I'm the star! I shine because . . ." Each student prints his or her name in the center of the star, then writes positive words describing him- or herself on each of the star's points. Let each child read his or her star aloud; then pin it on the bulletin board.

To encourage her fourth and fifth graders to tolerate and respect each other, Jean Medick uses this approach:

"A rule which I propose each year is that no name-calling, put-downs, sarcasm, or ridicule be permitted in our classroom. This rule fosters an environment where individuals are free to be themselves, where students tolerate and come to accept others, and where all are free to learn. This is perhaps the most important rule in my classroom, and I enforce it. After a while, the children help enforce it."

The "Personal Passport" and "My Bag" reproducibles on pp. 107-108 are two more vehicles for helping kids get to know themselves and each other.

Group identity

Humans are social creatures who function best as members of a group. The feeling of belonging is a basic human need. Foster group identity among your students with these activities:

• Ask each student to share with the rest of the class something he or she likes to do—play a musical instrument, play a sport, pursue a hobby, develop a skill. Children who share experiences and learn about each other develop a closeness with one another.

• Create "proud-of" bulletin boards. Kids can post individual and group work, drawings, and photographs they're proud of. (Be sure to display work of your own!)

• Encourage each child to consider the positive qualities of a friend (or friends); then send that person a note describing those qualities.
• Have the children conduct a group survey. Ask each child to complete a questionnaire that requests such information as birthplace, states visited or lived in, height and weight, number of siblings, favorite hobbies, favorite subjects, and so on. In compiling the results, students should detect an interesting phenomenon: a group is composed of individuals with many different traits and experiences. Older students can use their math skills to create a composite student by averaging the questionnaire responses. For example: The composite student is a girl weighing 65 pounds and standing 4 ft. 5 in. tall. She has one sibling, has visited three states, attended two different schools and likes math best. Point out how all of the students contribute to this composite (it would be fun to make her the class mascot and develop stories or activities around her). Think of other interesting ways to handle the questionnaire data. For example, create a verbal class portrait: "Our class consists of twelve boys and eleven girls. There are no only children. We range in height from . . ."
• Include yourself as part of the group and model your own sense of belonging. For example, describe activities as things "we" will do. Reminisce about events and activities as things "we" did together.

Cooperation

No doubt your students have been hearing about cooperation since they were old enough to watch Sesame Street. But do they really know what it means? Teach them with tried-and-true activities such as painting a classroom mural or putting on a play. And always stress these three concepts of cooperation:
• Everyone gets to participate.
• Everyone wins or loses.
• The better the students work together, the more enjoyable and successful the activity will be for all who participate.

Teachers who stress cooperation and social responsibility in their classrooms offer their students peer tutoring, small-group cooperative activities, and other chances to work together. Massachusetts teacher William Kreidler, author of *Creative Conflict Resolution*, notes that cooperative activities enhance group identity and significantly decrease classroom conflicts. Kreidler suggests these noncompetitive games and activities for setting a cooperative tone:

Activity: *Monster Making*. This is a good introduction to the process of cooperation. In small groups, students use paper, crayon, and scissors to create a monster. There are only two rules: each person in a group has a say in what the monster will look like, and each gets to help make it. Afterwards, discuss the process and ask students what problems they encountered in working together. Also ask them how they solved or could have solved the problems.

Activity: *Cooperative Musical Chairs*. This game, especially effective with young children, begins like traditional musical chairs—with one fewer chair than players. The difference is that only chairs are eliminated— players are not. When the music stops unexpectedly, the group is responsible for seeing that everyone gets a seat, even if some children have to sit on others' laps. Continue playing and stopping the music, eliminating one chair each time. All the children must help each other sit together on the remaining chairs. If anyone falls off, the group loses and the game begins again.

Activity: *Tug of Peace*. Any age group will enjoy this. Tie the ends of a large rope securely together and lay it in a circle on the floor. Ask children to sit outside the circle and grab hold of the rope. The object is for the students to raise themselves to a standing position by pulling hard on the rope. Obviously, they must all pull together. When they succeed, the group wins.

Activity: *Peace Teams*. Upper-grade children test their problem-solving skills in this activity.

Divided into small "peace teams," groups of children try to solve a written problem (home or school situations) you have given them. (Each team works on the same problem at the same time.) At your signal, each team must develop and write a solution within a specified number of minutes. When time is up, read aloud and discuss the various solutions. The activity continues with teams having less and less time to develop solutions as they work more and more cooperatively. Discuss how groups reach solutions and what helps the process occur more rapidly.

Responsibility

Individual and social responsibility are important goals in classrooms. Effective teachers believe that students must be responsible for their own learning and behavior, and responsible for acting in the best interests of the group. Jean Medick reports:

"A theme we discuss and explore all year is that freedom and responsibility go together. The children are free to sit where and with whom they wish, as long as they behave responsibly and do their work. Seating arrangements change frequently. The freedom to move desks fosters social growth, and provides me with important information about the social dynamics within the room. It also involves the children in relevant, and sometimes difficult, decision-making.

A large number of classroom management responsibilities are handled by the children, including room cleanup. I do nothing for the children that they can do for themselves."

Indeed, assigning students to routine classroom tasks is a proven method of helping them become more responsible. And with increased responsibility comes increased self-esteem and self-confidence, and a decrease in problems.

Activity: *Employing Students in the Classroom.* New York teacher James Ellis has developed a "job responsibility" program that helps his students learn the self-discipline to complete tasks they attempt. At the same time, they become productive, cooperative members of the group.

Messenger, chalkboard caretaker, classroom librarian, file clerk, and AV equipment operator are jobs students can easily and willingly handle. Ellis suggests grouping the jobs into four categories and asking students to sign up for three-week shifts. The jobs and the responsibilities of each are listed below.

• Librarian: straighten bookshelves; keep encyclopedias and dictionaries in proper place and sequence; straighten materials in closets, tables, and shelves; keep track of materials signed out.

The Responsible Classroom

Marcia Leverte, Arden Smith, and JoAnn Cooper offer the following description of a responsible classroom.

Inside a responsible classroom there is:

• Mutual respect, not fear of ridicule;

• Encouragement, not criticism or unconcern;

• Shared responsibility, not sole responsibility or undependability;

• Consequences for behavior, not punishment or inconsistency;

• Shared decision-making, not judgment or indecision;

• Influence, not power or weakness;

• Cooperation, not competition or control;

• Teacher facilitation and leadership, not command or desertion;

• Desire to learn from within, not imposed learning or indifference to learning;

• Freedom and order, not dictatorship or chaos.

• Audio-visual Equipment Operator: obtain, set up, operate, and return necessary equipment.

• Messenger: run errands; deliver messages whenever and wherever necessary; take the lunch count and absentee attendance cards to the office in the morning.

• Secretary: file and correct student work when necessary; staple; hole-punch papers for notebooks; distribute and collect student work; take attendance and keep an accurate record of absences; appoint helpers on jobs that require more time or effort than usual.

Ellis suggests posting the jobs, listing the requirements under each a job description (for example, patience, neat handwriting, or mechanical inclination), and a sign-up sheet (dated and broken down into three-week intervals). Also, he asks students to sign a contract and compensates them for their work by allowing them to earn credits toward a reward. He words the contract as follows:

> It is hereby agreed that I will fulfill the job for which I signed up for a three-week period of time. I will receive _____ task credits per week toward a reward, providing my job has been done satisfactorily. I will sign up only once in each of the four categories unless there are vacancies after everyone has had a chance to sign up.
>
> Pupil's signature
> Teacher's signature
> Date signed

If a student does not fulfill the contract's terms, he or she does not receive the credits. Once an "employee" earns a designated number of credits, he or she is eligible for a reward— free reading, listening to music with headphones, time for quiet table games or a favorite craft, or something more tangible.

Of course, it's up to you to adapt this program to your particular students and classroom.

One variation is to have children actually apply for a job. They complete an application form, list their qualifications and state why they want the job and think they can do good work. (It might boost their self-esteem to see how qualified they are!)

Strategy: Let kids make decisions. Responsibility and decision-making go hand in hand. If we believe we are in control of our lives, we are much more likely to accept responsibility for our behaviors and actions. Give students the training and opportunities necessary to make responsible decisions, and help them realize how many decisions they make each day.

Marcia Leverte, Arden Smith, and JoAnn Cooper, former teachers and authors of *Giving Kids a Piece of the Action*, offer these suggestions:

• Before beginning a new curriculum unit, discuss the topics you're planning to cover and ask students for ideas on how they could learn about these topics. Their ideas will help you plan a more meaningful unit. And they will feel more responsible for the unit because it's "theirs."

• Allow children to choose between different activities—two learning center activities, two ways to approach a research project, two different reading assignments, etc.

• Ask children to apply for classroom jobs, rather than simply assigning them.

• Have students practice decision-making skills by pretending they have just moved into a new house and have a certain amount of money to furnish it. Pass out catalogues and ask them to list the items they would purchase and the price of each. Make sure they don't exceed their budget. Afterwards, discuss their decisions and the reasons behind them.

• Periodically set aside time at the end of the day to review decisions students have made. Ask them to list ten decisions they made for themselves that day and ten that others made for them. Have the children rank-order their decisions and discuss the reasons behind them.

• Always seize opportunities to point out decisions kids have made and the responsibilities and consequences (good or bad) that accompany those decisions.

See p. 113 for a self-evaluation test you can ask students to take. The test, developed by Leverte, Cooper, and Smith, should help them understand their actions and the choices they make every day.

Communication

A positive classroom environment and healthy atmosphere require that children learn to communicate effectively and honestly—and perceive that you are doing the same. Effective communication leads to mutual trust and respect.

Activity: *Focus on Finger-Snapping.* Actor and educator Mark Lynch of Arts E.T.C. (Educational Training Center) in Cleveland uses a finger-snapping exercise to develop focus. Students toss imaginary snaps to one another, slowly and carefully. As a snap leaves one child's hand, the next one gets ready to catch it on his fingertips. Without speaking or pointing, each child must focus intently on the tosser to determine where the toss will come and how fast.

Activity: *Dramatic Interactions.* Lynch also uses drama to teach kids how to interact, "connect," and really listen. He has them practice eye contact and short dialogue as they share an object. *This is a ball; Thank you.* Then he has the children share an emotion while exchanging the object. For example, they may express happiness, sadness, or fear.

In addition, drama enables a child to approach a problem, dilemma, or conflict while the other children analyze the situation themselves.

Strategy: The Sounding Board. Problems and pressures affect Janice Kahn's third graders just like every other class. To help them cope, she nailed up a mailbox in a corner of the room and invited them to express their thoughts, feelings, and wishes in notes (anonymous or signed). Children used the mailbox to vent their emotions, once they realized there was no fear of retaliation.

"These expressions of growing pains allowed me an opportunity to respond with caring and compassion," Kahn reports. "Our mailbox became a collection of emotions: the anger, fear, love, jealousy that dwell inside us all."

"It is by reaching the heart of a child that we gain trust. And this trust spills over into a willingness to learn," Kahn continues. "Through heightened communication in our classroom, we all learned that happiness shared is doubled. And we have come to think that a trouble shared is halved."

Activity: *The Daily Diary.* Another way to encourage students to air their feelings and frustrations is to have them keep daily diaries. Diaries serve the dual purpose of allowing children to practice writing skills while expressing their feelings about each day's events. Shared with teachers or other children, these diaries can enhance communication and interaction. Diaries can be an effective strategy for reaching children with serious behavior problems. But make sure they understand that the diaries will be shared.

Sweet harmony
(The Nonsexist, Nonracist Classroom)

Discrimination based on sex or race is a fact in elementary classrooms. Teachers discriminate and so do children. Much of the time our discriminatory actions are unintentional—we act on ingrained attitudes and behaviors and don't realize the implications or consequences of our actions.

We don't mean to discriminate. But we do—in the questions we ask, the praise we offer, the tasks we assign, the attention we give. With actions that speak louder than words we are telling some children that they are not as capable as others simply because of who they are. Low expectations, poor self-concepts, low self-confidence, low achievement, fewer opportunities and options, conflict, behavior problems—these are the consequences of discrimination in the classroom.

Sometimes all we need is to be made aware

of our discriminatory actions. And here's where research can help. (See box.)

Are your classroom actions and attitudes based on underlying stereotypes? Find out with the consciousness-raising scale on p. 118. And give students a chance to say whether or

Documented Results

The following systematically documented behaviors show ways that teachers treat boys and girls differently. Are these behaviors discriminatory? Do they result in unequal opportunities to learn? You decide. Research demonstrates that teachers:

- give boys more direct instruction, approval, disapproval, and attention (listening);
- ask boys more factual, abstract, and open-ended questions;
- give more teaching attention to boys during mathematics instruction and to girls during reading instruction;
- expect boys to be more assertive and active and girls to be more quiet and passive;
- ask boys to assume leadership roles, repair equipment, run movie projectors, move furniture, and carry books;
- ask girls to assume supportive roles, write class invitations and thank-you notes, water plants, and do classroom housekeeping chores;
- reprimand boys more frequently and more harshly and punish them more severely, even when girls and boys are misbehaving equally;
- praise boys more for the intellectual quality of their work and girls more for neatness, following directions, and other matters of form;
- criticize girls more for skill deficiencies and boys more for behavior.

Helpful suggestions

First, resolve to avoid the discriminatory practices identified above. Here are some suggestions for nonbiased teaching:

- Direct lower-order and higher-order questions to both boys and girls.
- Assign leadership and support roles equitably.
- Eliminate segregated play areas, and discourage students from segregating themselves.
- Avoid grouping on the basis of gender or race.
- Encourage boys and girls to participate in nontraditional activities.
- Avoid stereotyping girls as compliant and obedient and boys as disruptive and aggressive.
- Reinforce boys and girls or students of different races who are working and playing together.
- Avoid thinking only of girls as being "neat" and only of boys as "intellectually competent."

not they think teachers treat boys and girls fairly by asking them to complete the questionnaire on p. 127. Their evaluations could initiate an enlightening class discussion.

There are many ways to make the classroom a more equitable place for boys and girls of all races and ethnic origins. (See box, this page.)

Another option is to examine classroom textbooks and reading materials for racist or sexist content. The Council on Interracial Books for Children offers ten guidelines for detecting sexism or racism (see p. 120).

Teachers can also present activities that teach valuable lessons about prejudice and stereotyping. On pp. 124-126 are two of many lessons developed by teachers at Waiahole

Elementary School in Hawaii. (For many more activities, see *Oceans of Options*, listed in the bibliography.) You can also design a classroom discussion around a homework assignment to watch cartoons (see p. 119).

Cooperative Learning

How can teachers get kids to like and respect their peers of different races and opposite gender? By assigning them cooperative tasks and responsibility for each other's learning. Discussion and awareness activities expose social prejudice. But cooperative activities help defeat it.

The research evidence is consistent: racial and gender relations improve markedly in classrooms where students interact cooperatively to meet learning goals. Just plain common sense tells you that getting to know people as individuals helps dispel generalized social stereotypes.

Perhaps the most promising strategy for creating classroom harmony is the Student Team Learning approach developed by Robert Slavin and colleagues at the Center for Research on Elementary and Middle Schools, Johns Hopkins University. This approach dramatically improves racial and gender attitudes and along the way promotes fairness, cooperation, respect, and responsibility; increases motivation and achievement; decreases behavior problems; and even facilitates mainstreaming—the placement of academically-challenged students in regular classrooms.

It sounds too good to be true. But for more than ten years, teachers have been

implementing Student Team Learning with great results. Teachers report that the kids love it. And if teacher testimonials don't convince you, the research will. Research experiments and extensive studies have repeatedly documented not only improved attitudes, but improved achievement and behavior for all students participating on student learning teams.

Here's how it works:

Teachers assign students to four- or five-member groups mixed in ability, sex, and ethnicity. (Typically, there is one high achiever, one low achiever, and two average achievers per group.) They present a whole-class lesson, then ask students to work as teams to learn and master the academic material.

In math, for example, team members can work on problems, then compare answers and resolve discrepancies. In spelling, they can drill each other on new words. They can look for key information in a social studies text, or complete a science experiment together.

After studying the material, students are quizzed individually. Their quiz scores are combined to derive a team score. One version of the technique allows students to play academic games to demonstrate their learning.

Each team member's efforts contribute to the group because individuals compete against their previous achievement records to earn points. "This makes every member important to his or her groupmates and increases positive feelings and respect among teammates," Slavin explains.

"Making a child who's failing a subject part of a team that's working toward a goal is a very effective way to motivate that child to try harder," Slavin continues. "And the team goal motivates kids to care how well others on the team are learning."

There are three essential elements of the Student Team Learning approach:

1. Team rewards, such as certificates or special mention in the class newsletter, when teams meet goals.

Implementing STAD

This version of Student Team Learning can be adapted to many subjects and grades. Follow these steps to implement Student Teams Achievement Divisions:

- Choose a lesson and assign students to four-member heterogeneous teams.
- Set individual achievement goals for students based on previous performance.
- Present the lesson to the whole class.
- After the lesson, have students work in pairs within their teams, helping each other with problems, comparing answers, discussing solutions, or testing each other to prepare for the quiz. Make sure they realize that the team can only succeed if all team members understand the lesson.
- Quiz the students individually.
- Award quiz points based on improvements from each child's earlier performance and combine the individual scores to arrive at team scores. (Perfect papers always produce a maximum score, regardless of previous progress.)
- Reward the teams that meet their goals with a certificate or some other form of recognition.

2. Individual accountability, where team success depends on the individual learning of each member. Here, team activity focuses on members tutoring one another and making sure everyone understands the material on the quiz.
3. Equal opportunities for success, where students try to outscore their own past performance and each can make a valued contribution.

One version of Student Team Learning that can be adapted to most subjects and grade levels is Student Teams Achievement

Division. It is especially appropriate for math computation and applications, language use and mechanics, map skills, science concepts, and other areas characterized by well-defined objectives with single correct answers.

Team-Assisted Individualization is another form of Student Team Learning. This version features individualized rather than whole-group instruction. It's specifically designed for math computation in grades three through six.

After a placement test, each student enters an individualized sequence. Team members, all working on different units, check each other's work against answer sheets, discuss possible answers, and help solve problems. Students take individual unit tests and again, their scores contribute to the team score.

Slavin suggests reorganizing teams every six weeks to keep learning and cooperation at optimum levels.

For more information, see the references on cooperative learning listed in this chapter's bibliography.

Chapter 3—Read more about it

1. *The Hug Therapy Book.* Kathleen Keating. Irvine, CA: Comprehensive Care Corporation, 1987.

2. *Building Self-Esteem in Children.* Patricia H. Berne and Louis M. Savary. New York: Continuum Publishers, 1981.

3. *100 Ways to Enhance Self-Concept in the Classroom.* Jack Canfield and Harold C. Wells. Englewood Cliffs, NJ: Prentice Hall, 1976.

4. *Classroom Organization and Management* (Occasional Paper No. 54). Jere E. Brophy. East Lansing, MI: Institute for Research on Teaching, 1982. Also in *Elementary School Journal,* 1983, 83, 265-85.

5. Research on the Self-Fulfilling Prophecy and Teacher Expectations (Research Series No. 119). Jere E. Brophy. East Lansing, MI: Institute for Research on Teaching, 1982. Also in *Journal of Educational Psychology,* 1982, 75, 631-661. (Also available as Research Series No. 119 from the Institute for Research on Teaching, East Lansing, MI 48824.)

6. "On Praising Effectively." Jere E. Brophy. *Elementary School Journal,* 1981, 81, 269-278.

7. "Teaching Self-Discipline." *Theory Into Practice* (special issue), 1985, No. 24.

8. "Responsibility in the Classroom: A Synthesis of Research on Teaching Self-Control." Richard Prawat and Linda Anderson. *Educational Leadership,* 40, 62-66.

9. "The Relationship Between Teacher Thought and Action and Student Affective Outcomes." R. S. Prawat and J. N. Nickerson. *Elementary School Journal,* 1985, 85, 529-540.

10. *A Bibliography for Teachers of the Behaviorally Disordered.* (Occasional Paper No. 55). E. Pernell. East Lansing, MI: Institute for Research on Teaching, 1982.

11. *Effective Strategies for Three Problem Behaviors: Hostile-Aggressive, Passive-Aggressive, and Withdrawn/Failure Image.* (Occasional Paper No. 30). Jean M. Medick. East Lansing, MI: Institute for Research on Teaching, 1979.

12. *Classroom Misbehavior: Turning It Around.* Jean M. Medick. East Lansing, MI: Fanning Press, 1981. (Write to 524 Woodland Drive, East Lansing, MI 48823.)

13. *21st Century Discipline.* Jane Bluestein. Cleveland, OH: Instructor Books, 1988.

14. *Assertive Discipline.* Lee Canter. Seal Beach, CA: Canter and Associates, Inc., 1976.

15. *Schools Without Failure.* William Glasser. New York: Harper and Row, Colophon Books, 1975.

16. *Reality Therapy.* William Glasser. New York: Harper and Row, Colophon Books, 1975.

17. *TET: Teacher Effectiveness Training.* T. Gordon. New York: Peter H. Wyden, Inc., 1974.

18. *Learning and Motivation in the Classroom.* S. Paris, G. Olson, H. Stevenson (eds.). Hillsdale, NJ: Erlbaum, 1983.

19. *Socializing Student Motivation to Learn* (Research Series No. 169). Jere Brophy. East Lansing, MI: Institute for Research on Teaching, 1986.

20. *Looking in Classrooms* (third ed.). T. Good and J. Brophy. New York: Harper and Row, 1984.

21. *Designing Groupwork: Strategies for the Heterogeneous Classroom.* Elizabeth G. Cohen. New York: Teachers College Press, 1986.

22. *Oceans of Options: Sex Equity Lessons for the Classroom.* Lisa Hunter with Donna Bellorado (compilers). San Francisco: Far West Laboratory for Educational Research and Development, 1983.

23. *Gender Influence in Classroom Interactions.* L. Wilkenson and C. Merrett (eds.). Orlando, FL: Academic Press, 1985.

24. *Cooperative Learning.* Robert E. Slavin. New York: Longman, 1983.

25. "Cooperative Learning and the Cooperative School." Robert E. Slavin. *Educational Leadership,* Nov. 1987, 7-13.

26. "Cooperative Learning: Where Behavioral and Humanistic Approaches to Classroom Motivation Meet." Robert E. Slavin. *Elementary School Journal,* 1988, 88, 29-38.

27. *Creative Conflict Resolution.* William Kreidler. Glenview, IL: Scott, Foresman and Co., 1984.

28. *Discipline and Group Management in Classrooms.* Jacob Kounin. New York: Holt, Rinehart and Winston, 1970.

NOTES

N O T E S

Self-Esteem
15 Ways to Help Children Like Themselves

1. Reward children. Give praise, recognition, a special privilege, or increased responsibility for a job well done. Emphasize the positive things they do, not the negative.

2. Take their ideas, emotions, and feelings seriously. Don't belittle them by saying, "You'll grow out of it" or "It's not as bad as you think."

3. Define limits and rules clearly and enforce them. But allow latitude for your children within these limits.

4. Be a good role model. Let your children know that you feel good about yourself. Also let them see that you too can make mistakes and can learn from them.

5. Teach your children how to deal with time and money. Help them spend time wisely and budget their money carefully.

6. Have reasonable expectations for your children. Help them to set reachable goals so they can achieve success.

7. Help your children develop tolerance toward those with different values, backgrounds, and norms. Point out other people's strengths.

8. Give your children responsibility. They will feel useful and valued.

9. Be available. Give support when children need it.

10. Show them that what they do is important to you. Talk with them about their activities and interests. Go to their games, parents' day at school, drama presentations, award ceremonies, and so on.

11. Express your values, but go beyond "Because I said so" or "I want you to do that." Describe the experiences that determined your values, the decisions you made to accept certain beliefs, the reasons behind your feelings.

12. Spend time together. Share favorite activities.

13. Discuss problems without placing blame or commenting on a child's character. If children know that there is a problem but don't feel attacked, they are more likely to help look for a solution.

14. Use phrases that build self-esteem, such as "Thank you for helping" or "That was an excellent idea!" Avoid phrases that hurt self-esteem: "Why are you so stupid?"; "How many times have I told you?"

15. Show how much you care about them. Hug them. Tell them they are terrific and that you love them.

Me . . .
in a nutshell

Words and phrases can tell a lot about a person. I think these five words describe me best.

_____

_____

_____

_____

_____

My best characteristic is . . .

_____

These three words are the ones I'd like people to think of when they think of me.

_____

_____

_____

If I could change myself, I would try to be . . .

_____

_____

_____

_____

_____

_____

GUIDELINES FOR
EFFECTIVE PRAISE

EFFECTIVE PRAISE	**INEFFECTIVE PRAISE**
1. is delivered contingently	1. is delivered randomly or unsystematically
2. names the specific accomplishment	2. is restricted to global positive reactions
3. shows spontaneity, variety, and other signs of credibility; suggests clear attention to the students' accomplishment	3. shows a bland uniformity that suggests a conditioned response made with minimal attention
4. rewards attainment of specified performance criteria (this can include effort criteria, however)	4. rewards mere participation, without consideration of performance processes or outcomes
5. provides information to students about their competence or the value of their accomplishments	5. provides no information at all or gives students information solely about their status
6. orients students toward better appreciation of their own task-related behavior and thinking about problem solving	6. orients students toward comparing themselves with others and competing
7. uses students' own prior accomplishments as the context for describing present accomplishments	7. uses the accomplishments of peers as the context for describing students' present accomplishments
8. recognizes noteworthy effort or success at difficult tasks for *this* student	8. is given without regard to the effort expended or the meaning of the accomplishment for *this* student
9. attributes success to effort and ability, implying that similar successes can be expected in the future	9. attributes success to ability alone or to external factors such as luck or low task difficulty
10. encourages students to expend effort on the task because they enjoy the task and/or want to develop task-relevant skills	10. encourages students to expend effort on the task for external reasons—to please the teacher, win a competition or reward, and so on
11. focuses students' attention on their own task-relevant behavior	11. focuses students' attention on the teacher as an external authority figure
12. fosters appreciation of task-relevant behavior through logical attribution after the process is completed	12. intrudes into the ongoing process, distracting attention from task-relevant behavior

Developed by Jere Brophy, the Institute for Research on Teaching, College of Education, Michigan State University. Published as "Teacher Praise: A Functional Analysis," *Review of Educational Research*, Vol. 51, 1981, pp. 5-32, Table p. 24. Copyright 1981, American Educational Research Association, Washington, D.C.

My Bag

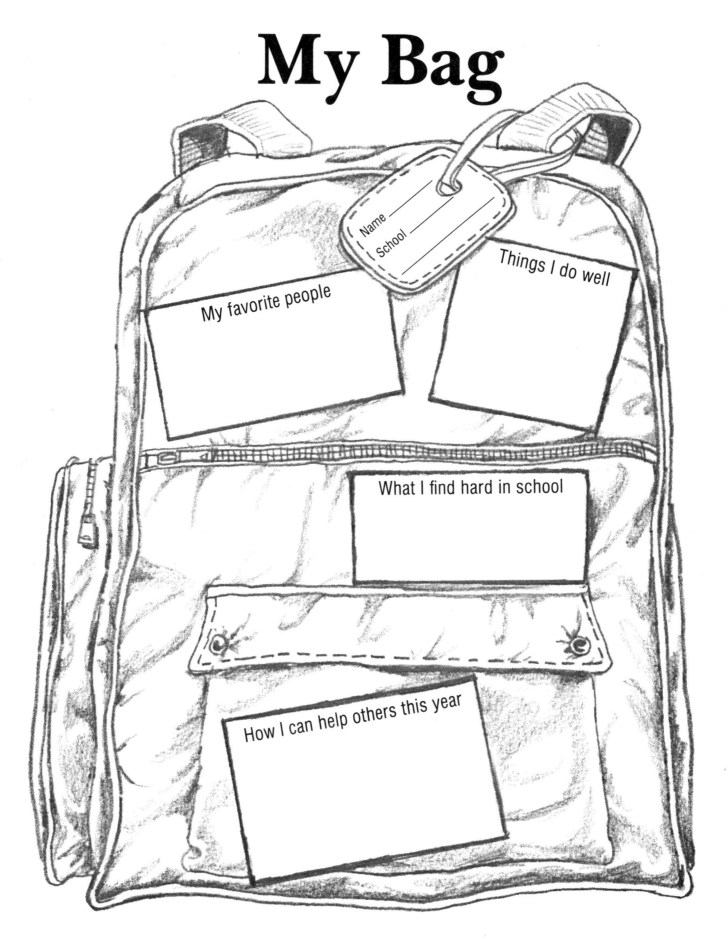

Name _____

School _____

My favorite people

Things I do well

What I find hard in school

How I can help others this year

Cut out your bag. Stick it on your locker, notebook, knapsack, or lunch box.

PERSONAL PASSPORT

This passport belongs to

_____
name

who was born on _____
date of birth

in _____
city

_____
state

_____
country

and is a student at

_____
name of school

_____
address of school

photograph or drawing of
the bearer of this passport

_____
home address

_____
telephone number

Student Motivation
Information Form

Name _____

Date _____

1. The best movie I've seen recently is _____

2. I'm very proud that I _____

3. A reward I like to get is _____

4. A beautiful thing I once saw was _____

5. My favorite school subject is _____

6. One thing I do very well is _____

7. My two favorite TV programs are _____

8. What seems mysterious to me is _____

9. When I read for fun I like to read stories about _____

10. One of my better accomplishments has been _____

11. If I had ten dollars I'd spend it on _____

12. I wonder about _____

13. When I have free time I like to _____

14. I know that I can _____

15. I enjoy _____

16. Something I want to do more often is _____

17. If I could go anywhere, I would go to _____

18. One of the things I like best about myself is _____

19. A good thing my teacher could do for me is _____

20. The question I want answered is _____

21. My favorite game is _____

22. In schoolwork my best talent is _____

23. Something I really want is _____

24. What really makes me think is _____

25. An important goal for me is to _____

26. I know a lot about _____

27. If I did better in school, I wish my teacher would _____

28. If I could get the chance, I would try _____

29. Sometimes I worry about _____

30. I feel satisfied when I _____

31. I spend most of my money on _____

32. When I get older I want to _____

33. Something I want to know more about is _____

34. The thing I like to do with my friends is _____

35. I like it when my parents give me _____

Motivation Menu

When the Mid-continent Regional Educational Laboratory held "school improvement" workshops in several states, participating teachers contributed ideas that they've used successfully to motivate students. The following list is adapted from their "menu."

Recognition/Reward

Teaching Others
Attention
Happy-Grams
Stickers
Peer-Tutoring
Pat on the Back
Special Jobs
Complimentary Comments
Happy Notes to Parents
Daily Helpers
Tangible Rewards
Specific Praise
One-to-One Counseling
Smiles
Laughter
Special Table in Lunchroom
Pictures Displayed with Biographies
Artwork Displayed in Local Businesses
Good Behavior Coupons-Raffle
Certificates
Phone Call Home
Display of Class Work
Taking Work to Show Principal
Talent Show (Parents, Teachers, Students)
Art Show
Hobby Display
First in Line
"I Got Caught Being Good" T-Shirt Awards

Special Projects

Making Books
School Newspaper
Special Lunch or Dinner with Decorations
School T-Shirts
"Helping Projects"
Canned Food Drive
Mentors from the Community
Adopt-a-Grandparent

Days & Special Events

Friendship Day
Crazy Hat or Special Hat Day
T-Shirt Day
School Colors Day
Everybody-Wear-Red-Day
Everyone-Compliment-Someone Day (e.g., give 3 compliments; learn to accept compliments)
Everyone-Do-Something-Nice Day
Halloween (teachers in costume, too) & Costume Parade
Clash Day or Mismatch Day
Storybook Character Day

Contests/Competitions/Goals

Drawing
Math Contests
Spelling Bee
Games
Earn Free Time
Tournament
Faculty Sports Contest
Interschool Competition
Points
Spelling Week
Bingo
Design School Flag, Insignia, Newsletter, Mascot
PTA Membership Competition
Jeopardy
Spelling Monopoly
Student of the Month
Individual Competition
Time-test Winner for Breaking Own Record
Challenge
Candy Bar Question
Intramurals
"Whiz-a-matic Machine" Quiz Show (teams of students develop test items from their own current-events reading)

Everybody Can Participate

Songfests
Art Fests
Field Days
Non-Competitive Games, Skiing, Skating
Grade-Level Lunches with Principal
"Birthdays" Party Honoring Birthdays (Parents Invited)
Board Work
Schoolwide Breakfast
Free After-School Movies
Popcorn Party
Review Teams for Tests
Mini-Courses

Book club
Birthday Club
Read-a-thon

Suspend the Rules

Free Time
Special Privileges
Write on Hands—to Show Last Year's Teacher
Mascot Travels from Room to Room
Sit-Where-You-Want in Lunchroom Day
Outside Play Time
Lunch Out
Take Work to Principal
Shirttail Day
Gum in Class
Crib Notes for Tests

Parents

Parent Volunteer Program
Parent Luncheon
Phone Call Home
Happy Note to Parents
Parent-Teacher Cookout
"Birthdays" Party
Grade-Level Family Night Dinner and Program
Parent-Teacher-Student conferences
Ask Mom/Dad for Information

"Extra" and Fun

A Surprise
Films
School Assemblies
Concert
Reading Corners
Change Classrooms (e.g., on April 1)
School Sing-Along
Outside Play Time
Plays
Field Trips
Special Guest Day
Parent Day Luncheon
Staff Recognition Day
Lunch with Teacher
Skating Parties
Spring Carnival
Computer Time for Time on Task
Lunchtime Dances

With permission of the Mid-continent Regional Educational Laboratory, 12500 E. Iliff Ave., Suite 201, Aurora, Colorado 80014.

Checklist on
Human Relations

In the Classroom ✓

_____ Do I accept each child as he/she is?
_____ Do I help all children feel they belong?
_____ Do I show confidence in my students?
_____ Do I let them know I like them?
_____ Do I make each child feel he/she has something to contribute?
_____ Do my pupils bring their problems to me?
_____ Do I help them accept one another?
_____ Do I let everyone express his/her feelings?
_____ Do I live up to agreements with students?
_____ Do I succeed in getting everyone to assume some responsibility?
_____ Do I help the group form a behavior code?

Outside of Class ✓

_____ Do I try to develop faculty cooperation?
_____ Do I do my share in determining and carrying out school policies?
_____ Do I aid associates with constructive ideas?
_____ Do I refrain from interfering with the classroom affairs of associates?
_____ Do I refrain from shifting my responsibility to other teachers?
_____ Do I hold inviolate confidential information about my associates?
_____ Do I transact school business through the proper channels?
_____ Do I avoid petty conversation about my associates?

With Parents and Community ✓

_____ Do I maintain friendly, cooperative relationships with parents?
_____ Do I hold all information confidential?
_____ Do parents feel sure that I deal justly and impartially with every child?
_____ Do I give all parents their fair share of time?
_____ Do I present a complete, fair, and meaningful evaluation to parents?
_____ Do I listen to and give fair thought to parents' opinions?
_____ Do I take an active part in community life?

Maturity ✓

_____ Do I seek to develop sufficient social skills?
_____ Am I increasingly willing to accept myself as having worth?
_____ Do I seek to become more self-directing?
_____ Do I continually seek to improve my problem-solving techniques?
_____ Do I attempt to face my frustrations?
_____ Do I recognize my own needs? My own shortcomings?
_____ Do I volunteer my special skills?
_____ Do I try to take disappointments without becoming discouraged?
_____ Do I seek to control myself and adjust my behavior to the situation?

Ethical Standards ✓

_____ Do I treat each child without prejudice or partiality?
_____ Do I respect the confidence of a student? Of a group of students?
_____ Do I refuse to use my position to promote partisan policies and sectarian views?
_____ Do I listen to and weigh parents' viewpoints carefully?
_____ Do I avoid making remarks that might discredit parents?
_____ Do I evaluate the attitudes and activities of the community with an open mind?
_____ Am I civic-minded?
_____ Do I do my share in keeping the public informed about school achievements?
_____ Do I exercise my right to participate in the processes which determine school policy?
_____ Do I support school policy once it has been determined?
_____ Do I keep a legal contract unless canceled by mutual consent?
_____ Am I kind, tolerant, and loyal in my dealings with professional associates?
_____ Do I take pride in the achievements of my associates?
_____ Do I avoid pettiness, jealousy, rancor?
_____ Do I criticize with discretion?
_____ Am I proud of my profession?

This list appeared in INSTRUCTOR, August 1978.

How **Responsible** are you?

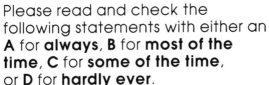

Please read and check the following statements with either an **A** for **always**, **B** for **most of the time**, **C** for **some of the time**, or **D** for **hardly ever**.

_____ I get myself up in the morning.

_____ I eat breakfast when it is ready.

_____ I get myself dressed for school in plenty of time.

_____ I brush my teeth and comb my hair before I leave.

_____ I remember my books, lunch, and materials needed for the day.

_____ I get to the bus stop before the bus arrives.

_____ I get to my classroom on time.

_____ I keep my desk and the area around it clean.

_____ I remember my homework assignments and turn them in on time.

_____ I complete my work assignments during the day.

_____ I am careful not to disturb my friends when they are studying.

_____ I remember other students are working when I walk down the hall; so I walk softly.

_____ I bring my lunch money or remember my lunch every day.

_____ I write down homework assignments and prepare my books to take home with me.

_____ I get in the bus line in time to walk to the bus.

_____ I hang up my coat and put my books away when I arrive home.

_____ I remember to do my jobs or chores at home.

_____ I get myself to bed at my bedtime without being reminded.

Developed by Marcia Leverte, Arden Smith, and JoAnn Cooper. Original appeared in INSTRUCTOR, October 1978.

I think I can

The subjects that are hardest for me to hand in on time are _____

_____

_____

_____

The reasons why my work is late are_____

_____

_____

_____

This is my plan of action to improve_____

_____

_____

_____

We'll meet again to talk about it on _____

_____

Student

_____

Teacher

I need to give myself a boost!

This part of school bothers me: _____

_____

I would do this to make it better: _____

_____

_____

_____

I'll try to do this to make it better for me: _____

_____

_____

_____

_____

I'll give it a try for this length of time: _____

_____

_____

We'll meet again to talk over how I feel on _____

_____

_____
Student

_____
Teacher

Oops!

I don't mean to do this in class but it just happens: _____

_____

_____

_____

I want to concentrate on this problem by _____

_____

_____

_____

I'll really try for this length of time: _____

My reward for solving the problem will be _____

_____

_____

_____

_____
Student

_____
Teacher

Worksheet in
Upgrading Behavior

We have a problem. It's a problem we can solve if we give it some thought and a good try. The following questions will help us examine the problem. Please fill in answers to the questions. Take your time and really think about what you say.

1. What is the behavior that needs to be changed?

2. Exactly when do you use this type of behavior?

3. Because of this behavior, I can _____

   and I don't have to _____ .

   My behavior _____ .

4. However, because of this behavior,

   I don't get to _____ .

   This behavior costs me _____ .

5. It seems to me my behavior (gets me more than it costs me/costs me more than it gets me);

   therefore, I (do/do not) want to change it.

6. Instead of _____ , I think that _____ would be more satisfying.

   Something I could try next time would be to _____ .

Adapted from an article by William Kreidler which appeared in INSTRUCTOR.

HOW RAISED IS YOUR
CONSCIOUSNESS?

Teachers, it's your turn to take the test today. Let's see how you rate yourself on the following consciousness-raising scale.

YES NO

1 When assigning reading material to my class, I carefully check to see whether the characters have been cast in stereotypic roles. ____ ____

2 When disciplining the children in my class I tend to be easier on the girls than on the boys because girls are more emotional. ____ ____

3 We are having a class party and the organization has been left up to me. I tend to ask the girls to bring baked goods and the boys to bring games and records. ____ ____

4 I would be more inclined to leave a group of girls unsupervised than a group of boys because girls are generally better behaved and less rowdy. ____ ____

5 When I need audio-visual equipment brought into the class I always ask the boys to bring it in or set it up. ____ ____

6 In my experience, girls appear to have a better understanding of the feelings of others than boys do. ____ ____

7 When discussing career education with my class, I usually include examples of male secretaries, nurses, and teachers as well as female lawyers, truckers, and those in other nontraditional roles. ____ ____

8 A student tutor is needed for the kindergarten class. I would probably send a girl because girls relate better to smaller children than boys do. ____ ____

YES NO

9 I am preparing a social studies lesson and must complete a large wall map by shading it with color. I will probably ask some boys in my class to work with me. ____ ____

10 I have been asked to organize the school sports day. I will probably separate the girls from the boys in most of the events. ____ ____

11 I would much rather work for a male principal than a female one. ____ ____

12 The principal has asked me to address the school newsletter to the parents in our community. I will probably ask a group of girls to help address the envelopes because they have neater handwriting than boys. ____ ____

13 When the principal comes to my door asking for two students to help in the gymnasium, I send boys because they are stronger. ____ ____

14 The boys in my classes need to be challenged through competition in order for them to achieve the motivation that the girls already have. ____ ____

15 I think the girls in my classes are more easily persuaded than the boys. ____ ____

16 The school is having a concert next week and a student host is required to help greet the parents. I would probably choose a girl because girls are generally more polite and better mannered. ____ ____

ANSWERS

Give yourself one point for each answer indicated here. The closer your score is to 16 points, the less you stereotype. 1) yes; 2) no; 3) no; 4) no; 5) no; 6) no; 7) yes; 8) no; 9) yes; 10) no; 11) no; 12) no; 13) no; 14) no; 15) no; 16) no

How did you do? For those people who scored above 10—*bravo*, and please continue generating a liberating education for boys and girls. You are on your way toward developing a host of nontraditional roles and attitudes that are free of debilitating stereotypes. Those who scored below 10 need to become more aware that the school is a major factor in the reinforcement of sex roles.

Developed by Dr. Barbara Samuels. Original appeared in INSTRUCTOR, February 1980

Assignment:
Watch Cartoons!

Cartoons are more than just fun entertainment. They influence how we think and behave. For example, they tell us how good people and bad people act. But these messages are often stereotypes. They may limit what we think we can and cannot do. Watch cartoons, and the commercials in between, on Saturday morning and write what you see the characters doing. Discuss your observations with your family.

Name of cartoons:

Name of characters: (male or female?)

What do characters do in the cartoon?

Select one commercial.
Name the product advertised:

What are boys doing in this commercial?

What are girls doing in this commercial?

How are the actions of boys and girls different?

With what types of toys do girls play in this commercial?

With what types of toys do boys play in this commercial?

With permission of the Mid-continent Regional Educational Laboratory, 12500 E. Iliff Ave., Suite 201, Aurora, Colorado 80014.

 # Ten *Quick* Ways

*Both in school and out, young children are exposed to racist and sexist attitudes.
These attitudes—expressed over and over in books and in other media—gradually distort
their perceptions until stereotypes and myths about minorities and women
are accepted as reality. It is difficult for a librarian or teacher to prompt children
to question society's attitudes. But if a child can be shown how to detect racism
and sexism in a book, the child can proceed to transfer the perception
to wider areas. The following ten guidelines are offered as a starting point
in evaluating children's books from this perspective.*

1. Check the Illustrations

Look for Stereotypes. A stereotype is an over-simplified generalization about a particular group, race, or sex which usually carries derogatory implications. The following are some infamous overt stereotypes: Blacks—Happy-go-lucky, watermelon-eating Sambo, and the fat, eye-rolling "mammy"; Chicanos—sombrero-wearing or fiesta-loving, and the macho bandito; Asian Americans—the inscrutable, slant-eyed "Oriental"; Native Americans—the naked savage or "primitive brave" and his "squaw"; Puerto Ricans—the switchblade-toting teen-age gang member; women—the completely domestic mother, the demure, doll-loving little girl and the wicked stepmother. While you may not always find stereotypes in the blatant forms described, look for variations which in any way demean or ridicule characters because of their race or sex.

Look for Tokenism. If there are racial minority characters in the illustrations, do they look just like whites except for being tinted or colored in? Do all minority faces look stereotypically alike, or are they depicted as genuine individuals with distinctive features?

Who's doing what? Do the illustrations depict minorities in subservient and passive roles, or in leadership and action roles? Are males the active "doers" and females the inactive observers?

2. Check the Story Line

Liberation movements have led publishers to weed out many insulting passages, particularly from stories with Black themes and from books depicting female characters; however, racist and sexist attitudes still find expression in less obvious ways. The following checklist suggests some of the subtle (covert) forms of bias to watch for.

Standard for Success. Does it take "white" behavior standards for minority persons to "get ahead"? Is "making it" in the dominant white society projected as the only ideal? To gain acceptance and approval, do persons of color have to exhibit extraordinary qualities—excel in sports, get A's, etc.? In friendships between white and nonwhite children, is it the child of color who does most of the understanding and forgiving?

Resolution of Problems. How are problems presented, conceived and resolved in the story? Are minority people considered to be "the problem"? Are the oppressions faced by minorities and women represented as related to social injustice? Are the reasons accepted as inevitable? Does the story line encourage passive acceptance or active resistance? Is a particular problem that is faced by a racial minority person or a female resolved through the benevolent intervention of a white person or a male?

Role of Women. Are the achievements of girls and women based on their own initiative and intelligence, or are they due to their good looks or to their relationship with boys? Are sex roles incidental or critical to characterization and plot? Could the same story be told if the sex roles were reversed?

3. Look at the Lifestyles

Are minority persons and their setting depicted in such a way that they contrast unfavorably with the unstated norm of white, middle-class suburbia? If the minority group in question is depicted as "different," are negative value judgments implied? Are minorities depicted exclusively in ghettos, barrios or migrant camps? If the illustrations and text attempt to depict another culture, do they go beyond ovesimplifications and offer genuine insights into another lifestyle? Look for inaccuracy and inappropriateness in the depiction of other cultures. Watch for instances of the "quaint-natives-in-costume" syndrome (most noticeable in areas like clothing and custom, but extending to behavior and personality traits as well).

4. Weigh the Relationships Between People

Do the whites in the story possess the power, take the leadership, and make the important decisions? Do racial minorities and females of all races function in essentially supporting roles?

How are family relationships depicted? In Black families, is the mother always dominant? In Hispanic families, are there always lots of children? If the family

is separated, are societal conditions—unemployment, poverty, for example—cited among the reasons for the separation?

5. Note the Heroes

For many years, books showed only "safe" minority heroes—those who avoided serious conflict with the white establishment of their time. Minority groups today are insisting on the right to define their own heroes (of both sexes) based on their own concepts and struggles for justice.

When minority heroes do appear, are they admired for the same qualities that have made white heroes famous or because what they have done has benefited white people? Ask this question: "Whose interest is a particular hero really serving?"

6. Consider the Effects on a Child's Self-Image

Are norms established which limit any child's aspirations and self-concept? What effect can it have on Black children to be continuously bombarded with images of the color white as the ultimate in beauty, cleanliness, virtue, etc., and the color black as evil, dirty, menacing, etc.? Does the book counteract or reinforce this positive association with the color white and negative association with black?

What happens to a girl's self-image when she reads that boys perform all of the brave and important deeds? What about a girl's self-esteem if she is not "fair" of skin and slim of body?

In a particular story, are there one or more persons with whom a minority child can readily identify to a positive and constructive end?

7. Consider the Author's or Illustrator's Background

Analyze the biographical material on the jacket flap or the back of the book. If a story deals with a minority theme, what qualifies the author or illustrator to deal with the subject? If the author and illustrator are not members of the minority being written about, is there anything in their backgrounds that would specifically recommend them as the creators of this book?

8. Check Out the Author's Perspective

No author can be wholly objective. All authors write out of a cultural as well as a personal context. Children's books in the past have traditionally come from authors who were white and who were members of the middle class, with one result being that a single ethnocentric perspective has dominated children's literature in the United States. With any book in question, read carefully to determine whether the direction of the author's perspective substantially weakens or strengthens the value of his/her written work. Is the perspective patriarchal or feminist? Is it solely Eurocentric, or do minority cultural perspectives also receive respect?

9. Watch for Loaded Words

A word is loaded when it has insulting overtones. Examples of loaded adjectives (usually racist) are *savage, primitive, conniving, lazy, superstitious, treacherous, wily, crafty, inscrutable, docile,* and *backward.*

Look for sexist language and adjectives that exclude or ridicule women. Look for use of the male pronoun to refer to both males and females. The following examples show how sexist language can be avoided: ancestors instead of forefathers; community instead of brotherhood; firefighters instead of firemen; the human family instead of the family of man.

10. Look at the Copyright Date

Books on minority themes—usually hastily conceived—suddenly began appearing in the mid-1960s. There followed a growing number of "minority experience" books to meet the new market demand, but most of these were still written by white authors, edited by white editors and published by white publishers. They therefore reflected a white point of view. Not until the early 1970s did the children's book world begin to even remotely reflect the realities of a multiracial society. The new direction resulted from the emergence of minority authors writing about their own experiences. Nonsexist books, with rare exceptions, were not published before 1973.

The copyright date, therefore, can be a clue as to how likely the book is to be overtly racist or sexist, although a recent copyright date, of course, is no guarantee of a book's relevance or sensitivity. The copyright date only indicates the year the book was published. It usually takes about two years from the time a manuscript is submitted to the publisher to the time it is actually printed and put on the market. This time lag meant very little in the past, but in a time of rapid change and changing consciousness, when children's book publishing is attempting to be "relevant," it is becoming increasingly significant.

From: *Ten Quick Ways to Analyze Children's Books for Racism and Sexism.* Reprinted by permission of the Council on Interracial Books for Children, Inc., New York.

PHYSICAL ABILITIES CHECKLIST

Draw a happy face

😊 **if you can.**

Draw a square ☐

if you want to learn.

	I can 😊	I want to learn ☐
1. hop		
2. skip		
3. jump		
4. run		
5. turn somersaults		
6. do cartwheels		
7. yawn		
8. wink		
9. walk a balance beam		

	I can 😊	I want to learn ☐
10. blow my nose		
11. swim		
12. ride a bicycle		
13. tie my shoelaces		
14. hammer a nail		
15. turn on a faucet		
16. eat with a fork		
17. throw a ball		
18. catch a butterfly		
19. button my shirt		
20. snap my fingers		
21. sing a song		
22. laugh		
23. blush		
24. walk to school		
25. clap my hands		

Adapted from: *Foundation Program: Career Education and Guidance for Grades K - 3.* ESEA Title IV, Part B consortium: Department of Education, State of Hawaii. From: *Oceans of Options: Sex Equity Lessons for the Classroom.* Published by Far West Laboratory for Educational Research and Development, 1855 Folsom Street, San Francisco, California 94103.

Values Voting

YES   NO

____ ____ 1. It's all right for boys to cry.

____ ____ 2. It's all right for girls to cry.

____ ____ 3. Being a nurse is a good job for a woman.

____ ____ 4. Being a nurse is a good job for a man.

____ ____ 5. Boys can be babysitters.

____ ____ 6. Girls can be babysitters.

____ ____ 7. Women can be firefighters.

____ ____ 8. It's all right for boys to play with dolls.

____ ____ 9. It's all right for girls to play with dolls.

____ ____ 10. Girls are smarter than boys.

____ ____ 11. Boys are afraid of spiders.

____ ____ 12. Girls are afraid of spiders.

____ ____ 13. I like to help out cooking in the kitchen.

____ ____ 14. I like to help out fixing things around the house.

____ ____ 15. Boys are better in math than girls.

____ ____ 16. Girls behave better than boys.

____ ____ 17. Boys can be secretaries.

____ ____ 18. Girls have more patience than boys.

____ ____ 19. Boys are stronger than girls.

____ ____ 20. Girls are better cooks than boys.

____ ____ 21. A woman can be President.

____ ____ 22. Men are better drivers then women.

Developed by Gordon Tokushige, Waiahole Elementary School, Oahu, Hawaii. From: *Oceans of Options: Sex Equity Lessons for the Classroom.*
Published by Far West Laboratory for Educational Research and Development, 1855 Folsom St., San Francisco, California 94103.

Awareness of
Sex Bias & Equity

GRADES
Three through six

SUBJECT
Language Arts, Social Studies

EQUITY OBJECTIVES
(1) The teacher will find out the extent to which students have stereotyped expectations about who should hold various jobs, and (2) the students will show that they understand the word *stereotype* by correctly identifying certain expectations about jobs as stereotypical.

SKILL OBJECTIVES
The students will practice comprehension and analytical skills by: (1) following directions, and (2) explaining why they think as they do.

TIME
30 minutes for filling out questionnaire; 30 minutes for discussion.

ACTIVITY DESCRIPTION
Have students fill in the "Who Should" questionnaire on page 125. Students indicate whether they think various activities are appropriate for girls, boys, or both. After handing in their questionnaires, discuss reasons the students responded as they did.

ACTIVITY PROCEDURE
1. Discuss the vocabulary important to this lesson: *stereotype, bias, opinion.*
2. Discuss the questionnaire. Make sure that students understand that you want honest opinions. Stress that there are no right or wrong answers and that you are not testing them on facts. Make it clear that they should write their opinions, not what they think the teacher wants to hear, and that they don't need to put their names on the questionnaires.
3. Hand out the questionnaire. Allow students about 30 minutes for filling them out.
4. Collect the questionnaires before you hold a discussion (so students won't change the answers). Compile data later.
5. Tally the results, so that you can see what the students' expectations are.
6. Lead a group discussion. You might ask:
   • What are the occupations that only men go into? Why do you think so?
   • What are the occupations that only women go into? Why do you think so?
   • Could both men and women hold those jobs? Why do you think so?
   • Do you think they should both have the opportunity to hold those jobs?
   • What job would you like to have?
7. Be ready to counter stereotypical ideas with information about women astronauts, women scientists, male librarians, male secretaries, and male nurses. Ask children for examples from their own experience, or from TV or magazines, and so on.

Developed by Carol Hankinson, Waiahole Elementary, Oahu, Hawaii; and Amy Okumura, Beverly J. Pu, and Yuriko Wellington, Hana High and Elementary, Maui, Hawaii. From:*Oceans of Options: Sex Equity Lessons for the Classroom.* Published by Far West Laboratory for Educational Research and Development, 1855 Folsom St., San Francisco, California 94103.

Who should?

Grades 3-6

What is your school? _____ What is your grade? (Circle your grade.) 3 4 5 6

What is your teacher's name? _____ Are you a boy or a girl? (Circle the right word.) BOY GIRL

Part I For each of these jobs, circle the 1 under MAN if you think only a man should do the job; circle the 2 under WOMAN if you think only a woman should do the job; or circle the 3 under BOTH if you think both a man and a woman should do the job. Be sure to *circle only one answer* for each job.

	MAN	WOMAN	BOTH
1. airplane pilot	1	2	3
2. artist	1	2	3
3. astronaut	1	2	3
4. carpenter	1	2	3
5. cook	1	2	3
6. doctor	1	2	3
7. forest ranger	1	2	3
8. lawyer	1	2	3
9. librarian	1	2	3
10. lifeguard	1	2	3
11. nurse	1	2	3
12. President of the United States	1	2	3
13. race car driver	1	2	3
14. secretary	1	2	3
15. store clerk	1	2	3
16. sixth grade teacher	1	2	3
17. telephone operator	1	2	3
18. truck driver	1	2	3
19. nursery school teacher	1	2	3

Part II When there are class jobs to be done, who do you think should do them? Circle the 1 under BOY if you think only a boy should do them; circle the 2 under GIRL if you think only a girl should do them; or circle the 3 under BOTH if you think both a boy and a girl should do them.

	BOY	GIRL	BOTH
20. messenger	1	2	3
21. class president	1	2	3
22. eraser cleaner	1	2	3
23. librarian	1	2	3
24. class secretary	1	2	3
25. class treasurer	1	2	3

Part III Now what about things at home? For each of these things, circle who *should* do it: a man, a woman, or both.

	MAN	WOMAN	BOTH
26. When children misbehave at home, who should correct them?	1	2	3
27. Who should teach good manners?	1	2	3
28. Who should take care of a sick child?	1	2	3
29. Who should teach children right from wrong?	1	2	3

Part IV Here is a list of jobs that people do at home. Circle who *should* do the job: a man, a woman, or both.

	MAN	WOMAN	BOTH
30. washing dishes	1	2	3
31. taking out the trash	1	2	3
32. grocery shopping	1	2	3
33. paying bills	1	2	3
34. cooking	1	2	3
35. fixing things around the house	1	2	3
36. dusting furniture	1	2	3
37. scrubbing floors	1	2	3
38. sewing	1	2	3
39. working in the yard	1	2	3
40. moving furniture around	1	2	3
41. doing laundry	1	2	3

Part V Here is a list of spare-time activities. Circle who *should* do them: a man, a woman, or both.

	MAN	WOMAN	BOTH
42. playing football	1	2	3
43. swimming	1	2	3
44. playing the violin	1	2	3
45. going to sports games (like baseball)	1	2	3
46. gymnastics	1	2	3
47. helping in a hospital every week	1	2	3

Developed by the Highline School District, Project Equality, Seattle, Washington 98166.

Bias-free
Interactions

GRADES
Three through six

SUBJECT
Reading

EQUITY OBJECTIVES
(1) The teacher will find out if he or she is treating students of both sexes fairly, and
(2) The students will show they understand the concept of equal treatment by backing up the opinions they express with reasons or examples.

SKILL OBJECTIVES
Students will improve their skills in: reading, following oral instructions, and expressing themselves verbally.

TIME
45 minutes

ACTIVITY DESCRIPTION
Students will fill out a teacher-made questionnaire that assesses whether they think the teacher treats both sexes fairly. Then they'll discuss their responses.

ACTIVITY PROCEDURE
1. Hand out the questionnaires and have the students read the instructions along with you.
2. Make sure the students understand that they should *not* put their names on the questionnaire, so they can be perfectly honest in their answers.
3. Allow the class ten minutes to complete the questionnaires; collect them.
4. Use the balance of the time to discuss the questions in a magic circle (i.e., each person who wants to speak gets a turn; nobody gets put down for his or her opinion). When you present a question, ask each student who wants to respond to tell what he or she thinks about the issue *and* to give one reason why (or one example of a specific incident).
5. See whether there seems to be a pattern to the responses (e.g., do the girls all say that the teacher is fair and the boys think the teacher scolds the boys too much?) If there is a pattern, point it out and search for an explanation with the help of the class. If there doesn't seem to be a pattern during the discussion, tally the written responses and discuss them with the class.
6. To make this a shorter lesson, consider only those questions that relate to the classroom jobs children are given and to praising and scolding. These are the questions that precipitate the most lively discussions.

Developed by Carol Hankinson and Arleen Ogasawara, Waiahole Elementary School, Oahu, Hawaii. From: *Oceans of Options: Sex Equity Lessons for the Classroom*. Published by Far West Laboratory for Educational Research and Development, 1855 Folsom Street, San Francisco, California 94103.

Are teachers fair?

This is a questionnaire to see if you think that *teachers are fair* to their students and if they treat boys and girls the same in the classroom. You do *not* need to put your name on the paper, so give honest answers!!

	Boys	Girls	Both
1. When heavy things have to be carried to and from the office, library or car, who gets the job?			
2. When the boards need to be erased, who gets the job?			
3. When errands need to be run, who gets the job?			
4. Who gets praised the most in the class?			
5. Who gets scolded the most?			
6. When papers need to be passed out, who gets the job?			
7. When it is time to line up for lunch, recess, gym or to go home, who lines up first?			
8. Who gets the most help from the teacher during class time?			
9. Who gets reminded to be quiet the most?			
10. Who gets to write on the board the most?			
11. Who gets the special favors and fun things to do?			
12. Who does your cleaning-up jobs?			
13. Who gets picked the most to answer questions?			
14. Who gets the hardest questions to answer?			
15. Which does your teacher think are better readers?			
16. Which does your teacher think are better in math?			
17. Which do you think that your teacher likes the best?			
18. Who gets punished the most in your class?			
19. Who seems to get in trouble the most?			
20. Who gets to talk to the teacher the most?			
21. Who gets to be chosen for leader or Captain the most?			
Total Score			

Developed by Carol Hankinson, Waiahole Elementary School, Hawaii. From *Oceans of Options: Sex Equity Lessons for the Classroom.* Published by Far West Laboratory for Educational Research and Development, 1855 Folsom Street, San Francisco, California 94103.

Instructional strategies that work

> *" As a profession, we know a great deal about what makes for effective teaching, and it is time we share this knowledge clearly and directly with those who are joining our ranks. "*
>
> *—Susan Loucks-Horsley et al.*
> *Continuing to Learn: A Guidebook for Teacher Development*

The school year is well under way. You and your students have the classroom routines down pat, and most days things run pretty smoothly. The nightmares, crying spells, and attacks of the cold sweats have subsided.

Go ahead. Give yourself a big pat on the back. You deserve it. You know how to survive in the classroom.

But that's not enough. The next big step is learning to actually teach.

With survival skills mastered and classroom management under control, the stage is set. The students are ready to learn, and you are ready to concentrate on teaching them. Now's the time to focus on instructional strategies and how and when to use them.

This chapter presents instructional strategies that work—those expert teachers swear by and researchers have demonstrated to be effective. How do we know they work? Because the students whose teachers use these strategies learn and achieve more than other students.

We're talking here about an emerging "science of teaching." Scholars refer to it as the professional knowledge base—knowledge unique and essential to good teaching. These are teaching behaviors that make a predictable difference.

To identify effective instructional strategies, researchers observe, interview, and study effective teachers. They look for key behaviors and what it is these teachers do differently from others. Strategies identified can then be tested in experimental studies. That is, other teachers learn to use the strategies in their classrooms, and researchers document the effects.

But as researcher Jere Brophy and others caution, research offers guidelines for understanding particular situations involving particular students—guidelines for determining the likely consequences of certain strategies in certain contexts. Researchers and authors Christopher Clark and Robert Yinger contend that:

"Teachers should be helped to think from theory and research, but not be controlled by them."

You, as a professional, must ultimately decide what, where, when, and how to teach, keeping in mind the particular needs of your students. Research provides information to help you make those decisions. It increases your repertoire of options.

It would be easier if someone could just tell you exactly what you need to do. Teachers sometimes criticize educational research for not being more specific—for failing to offer "recipes" for practice.

But teaching isn't cooking. You can't mix together a specific list of ingredients and produce a product that looks the same every time. Teaching is a complex human endeavor that can be guided, but not prescribed, by research. The key word here is "human"—human variation among teachers and students. No two teachers, students, or situations are the same. That's why your judgment calls are so important.

Judgment calls and decision-making, constant challenges, variety, and change—these are the factors drawing many talented and multi-faceted people into teaching. These are the reasons why good teaching invigorates and extends us.

What Do They Know?

Each year, you and your students will take a long trip together. Destination: increased learning and achievement. Where you start, the route you take, and where you end up will vary from class to class and student to student. But the map that guides you along your way—evaluation—remains the same.

Effective evaluation or assessment (the terms will be used interchangeably) involves much more than giving paper-and-pencil tests and assigning letter grades. The process occurs before, during, and after lessons, units or marking periods. It is a way of charting students' progress—a means to ensure they (or you) don't get off track.

Assessment is the vehicle for instructional planning. You can't plan for effective instruction until you know where students are, where you want them to go, and how you want them to get there.

Where are we going?

Common sense tells you that you won't know when you've arrived somewhere if you don't know where you're going. You must determine a destination. For teaching, that means setting goals and long-term planning. You can get started before school begins. In listing your goals, don't forget to include:

• Mandated objectives. Does your school, district, or state specify certain goals? Completing a certain text or reader? Learning specific math facts or spelling words?

• Your own curriculum priorities. What subjects or topics will you emphasize? Where do you want to concentrate your time and energy? How will you allocate teaching time to various subjects?

• Goals for the class. How should students be different after spending a year with you? What will they know then (academically and socially) that they don't know now?

• Goals for individual students. What are your special goals for mainstreamed or gifted children? How will you help your slow readers this year? Are there ways you can teach the shy student, the underachiever, the kid who pretends to hate school?

• Goals for yourself. What are your personal

Where are we going?

To know where you're going in teaching, you must first determine a destination. That means setting goals and long-term planning. Get started before school begins. List your goals; be sure to include:

- Mandated objectives.
- Your curriculum priorities.
- Goals for the class.
- Goals for individual students.
- Goals for yourself.
- Student interests and characteristics.
- Your interests.

(Some of these ideas are adapted from suggestions by Kenneth Bierly.)

LEARNING TO TEACH

and professional goals? Would you like to experiment with peer coaching this year (see p. 272) or try some joint lessons with a colleague's class?

• Student interests and characteristics. What are the special interests or needs of this year's class? (See student interest survey on p. 110). How can you develop curriculum around those interests? (Students also have different learning styles, for which you must plan. See pp. 157-158 for descriptions of visual and auditory learners.)

• Your interests. How can your personal passion for birdwatching, for example, translate to exciting lessons and activities?

Keep this list of goals handy so you can refer to it throughout the year, revising when necessary. Even when the going is smooth, it can't hurt to check your map once in a while.

(These ideas are adapted from suggestions by Kenneth Bierly.)

Where are you now?

Your destination is set. But you can't plot your course until you know your starting point. And you can't tell how far you've come unless you know where you began.

What skills and abilities do students bring to your class? What are their weaknesses, and where do they need to improve? To find out, you need to do some investigative work to gather baseline data. Here's how:

• Develop a few short tests to give students at the beginning of the year. For example, if the district mandates completion of a certain task, pull sample problems from the test and use it as a pretest. Be sure to include skills and concepts students should have already mastered. Identify weaknesses and problem areas. You can use the same test to check on progress during the year or to assess overall achievement at year's end.

• Continue to use pretests throughout the year. Before a major curriculum unit, find out what each student already knows about the particular topic and related skills or concepts. Then fine-tune your lessons accordingly.

• Make an evaluation folder for each student. Place the pretest results inside, along with other diagnostic information you collect throughout the year.

• By consulting with parents or school records, determine children's special physical needs. For example, students with visual or auditory impairments may need seats up front.

• Examine grades, comments, and standardized test scores in students' cumulative folders. There is a lot of potentially useful information in a cumulative folder, but approach this information cautiously. It could bias your judgments and color your expectations. Most veterans and other experts suggest getting to know your students before reading their cumulative folders. Also, proceed cautiously with standardized test results. Used properly, these tests can be valuable tools for guiding classroom instruction. But they can also be misused to support unfair tracking programs and other discriminatory practices. (See this chapter's section on standardized tests, p. 133.)

• Observe individual behaviors, looking for strengths, interests, special needs, and problems. Note all these in the student folders. But remember, you'll need a safe place to keep these folders. Information you include is for your eyes only!

Chart the direction

The next step is deciding how to try to reach your destination. Which route should you take? In which direction should you go? In terms of teaching, this means deciding what curriculum you will use and how you will teach it.

• Review your goals and priorities and begin to schedule instructional units and activities, allocating the most time to subjects you think are the most important or the skill areas where students need the most help. (Sometimes, time allocations are decided by the district.)

• Identify "chunks" or conceptual segments that can be learned separately before they are integrated or reorganized into larger chunks.

• Plan activities around students' special interests and needs. Do they love sports? Then tailor a health unit to sports and sports figures.
• Decide how you'll teach—which instructional strategies and grouping (whole-class, small-group, etc.) will best serve students' needs.

As you teach your students, guiding them toward increased learning and achievement, you will periodically need to check their progress. How far have they come? Are they progressing adequately? Have they reached the destination, or are they lost and in need of a better route?

Are we there yet?

Keep these ideas in mind when assessing student learning:
• Use daily reviews to judge how students are progressing—homework checks, learning games, group discussions, random questioning, and so on. Experts include review as part of every lesson.
• Continue using pretests and gathering diagnostic information to decide which skills or knowledge students need to acquire next.
• Assess learning in many different ways, including paper-and-pencil tests, academic games where mastery is demonstrated, participation in group discussions or projects, asking students to apply knowledge to new situations, and so on.
• Make sure students can apply or transfer new knowledge to other situations. Learning hasn't occurred until they can, according to mastery learning experts.
• Students must master material to the point of overlearning to be able to apply it to new situations.
• Take advantage of the help and advice available from testing experts and evaluation specialists in your district. They can help you construct good tests, offer insights on commercially available tests, and teach you how to interpret standardized test results, among other things.
• Tests and quizzes are learning tools as well as measuring tools. Encourage students to learn from their mistakes and improve their test scores by mastering the materials they were unable to master the first time. Emphasize learning over competition. Say, "The test will show us how well we've learned this and whether we still need more work," rather than, "Let's see who knows this and who doesn't."

Are we there yet?

Keep these ideas in mind when assessing student learning:

- • Use daily reviews to judge how students are progressing.
- • Continue using pretests and gathering diagnostic information.
- • Assess learning in many different ways.
- • Make sure students can apply/transfer new knowledge to other situations.
- • Students must master material to the point of overlearning.
- • Tests and quizzes are learning tools as well as measuring tools.

- • Take advantage of the help and advice available from testing experts and evaluation specialists in your district.
- • If students have not learned and retained what you've taught them, you must reteach the lesson using new strategies.
- • Record what students think they know about a topic before they study it, then review their statements after the unit.
- • Recognize each student's success and let parents know when a child has reached a milestone.

• If students have not learned and retained what you've taught them, you must reteach the lesson using new strategies or approaches. (The old ones didn't work!)

• Compare the assessment information collected early in the year with later evaluations so you can target areas for improvement.

• Record what students think they know about a topic before they study it, then review their statements after the unit. They'll be tickled to hear their misconceptions and pleased at the progress they've made. Try making a chart with the students where you list "What We Know" on one side and "What We Want to Learn" on the other. By involving them this way, you'll get some good ideas about what interests them and give them some control over what they learn. They'll have a vested interest in learning.

• Recognize each student's successes (even small ones) and let parents know when a child has reached a goal or milestone.

Using standardized tests

Just mention the phrase "standardized test" and watch those around you squirm. The very words cause eyebrows to raise. Standardized tests make people uncomfortable. Their use is associated with unfair tracking policies, discrimination, denied opportunities, negative labeling of students, teacher evaluation, and other such practices.

Before you write them off, take a closer look. You'll discover that the controversy stems from abuse—not proper use—of the tests.

Standardized achievement tests are potentially powerful tools for instruction. They are the most objective and scientific measures available. They identify students' strengths and weaknesses and allow teachers to tailor instruction accordingly.

How? One way is to study the breakdown of skill area objectives on the test and examine how many questions students answer correctly for each objective. You can pinpoint where students need help.

Teachers talk about testing

In her study of "A + Teachers," teacher Ruth Tschudin found that effective teachers use written tests sparingly, more often relying on other evaluation techniques. Here are some of their suggestions:

• **Observation is a good way to evaluate learning.** Observe students in practical problem-solving situations—collecting milk money, writing letters, finding information in an encyclopedia, and so on.

• **Use oral and open-book quizzes.** For example, have students consult reference materials while taking an open-book test, then demonstrate their knowledge through an oral quiz. Many teachers believe individual oral tests are more accurate and less threatening than paper-and-pencil tests.

• **Have students test each other** in areas such as math facts and spelling skills. The payoffs? Students who are more relaxed and fewer papers to correct, say teachers.

• **Ask students to help you write test questions.** This is especially effective in social studies. It's a great review technique that involves kids more with the material.

• **Use frequent small tests instead of fewer large ones.** This minimizes test anxiety, encourages small successes, and reveals problems sooner.

Suppose you discover that four children had serious trouble with one reading skill—extracting the main idea from a passage. They've answered correctly only one or two of the eight questions testing this skill.

Differences in standardized test scores often reveal differences in opportunities to learn.

Now what? The next time you work with these children you emphasize main ideas. You call on them in reading groups to identify main ideas. You provide them with other opportunities to practice this skill, and you ask their parents to do the same. You might decide to actually reteach this skill to these students.

A test's usefulness depends on how much you know about it. What do you actually know about standardized achievement tests? Give yourself the quiz on p. 156 to find out. What you don't know may surprise you.

Following are some more facts about standardized tests:

• Test results should never replace teacher judgment; they should supplement and support it.

• Test results are potentially most useful where they disagree with teacher judgments. Like a red flag, they warn us to proceed cautiously. Are there learning problems you haven't perceived? Is a child achieving more than you thought? Was a student sick or distracted during the test?

• Results are reported in various ways, including composite scores (stanines, grade equivalents, percentile ranking), scores in major skill areas, individual item analysis (students' responses on each test question), and so on. Each type of score serves a specific purpose and is more appropriate or helpful in some situations than in others.

• Test manuals are full of useful information about interpreting and using test results. Too often, though, districts deny teachers access to the manuals.

• Differences in average test scores among certain groups often reveal differences in opportunities to learn.

• Not all standardized tests are created equally.

• Comparing one child's test performance to a national norm allows us to see how that child learns in given subject areas in relation to other children.

• Students, especially younger ones, need to learn how to take standardized tests. They need practice in marking answer sheets, pacing themselves, and making reasonable guesses on questions they don't know. They need to understand the purpose of standardized testing, and practice with special strategies—for example, eliminating incorrect answers for multiple-choice questions.

A good reference on teaching kids how to take tests is *Test Scores Count! A Handbook for Teaching Test-Taking Skills*, by Sharon Koenigs (see this chapter's bibliography). Briefly, Koenigs identifies these four major skill areas:

1. Understanding instructions and following directions. (Following oral and written instructions, understanding the vocabulary of test directions, using answer sheets, interpreting different formats.)

2. Using time efficiently. (Budgeting time, saving unknown questions for last, using extra time to check answers.)

3. Guessing wisely. (For example, eliminating answers in multiple-choice questions.)

4. Applying special strategies to specific types of test questions (such as eliminating incorrect responses in multiple-choice items or avoiding, in most cases, answers that include 'all' or 'none' in true/false items).

Instruction in test-taking at any grade level, says Koenigs, should:

• Help students develop an understanding of the purpose of testing and how results are used.

• Provide practice in taking tests, especially timed tests, and provide practice with different item formats.

• Make students familiar with the vocabulary of test instructions.

• Offer opportunities to use separate answer sheets and/or instructions for marking.

• Present special test-taking strategies and offer practice.

Teaching The Lesson

What is it that effective teachers actually do when teaching a lesson? What instructional strategies lead to increased learning?

The same answers keep emerging. Researchers working with teachers in varied settings are drawing basic conclusions about what works and what doesn't. Regardless of personal teaching style, experience, or preferences, these instructional principles help students succeed academically.

Effective instructional strategies can be organized around five basic steps of teaching a lesson: task focus, lesson presentation, guided practice, independent practice, and review.

Five basic steps: task focus, lesson presentation, guided practice, independent practice, review.

The strategies described below cut across subject areas. They are the common denominators in many different models of teaching—the strategies verified by research. And most of these strategies depend on good classroom management practices, just as the reverse is true. Effective instructors tend to be effective classroom managers and vice versa.

Get ready, get set . . .

With each new lesson, teachers must focus student attention and interest on the task at hand. Here's how to get students set to work:
• Introduce the lesson in an interesting way. Pique curiosity with a "teaser" or a provocative question, for example.
• State academic goals clearly. Maintain an academic focus.
• Assess how much students already know about the topic. You could do this with a simple pretest. If you've opened a science lesson by asking why okra could legitimately be served in a fruit salad, use student responses to gauge previous knowledge.
• Exhibit examples of acceptable and unacceptable work, where appropriate. (Make sure you use your own work samples or those of previous students; avoid comparisons among the current class members.)
• Make sure the students know what they must learn. Head nods or hand signals such as "thumbs up" can indicate that students understand. (These "every-pupil response techniques" are also helpful during reviews.)
• Review prerequisite skills or concepts (checking homework is one way).

Become better thinkers

Francis Hunkins offers three questioning techniques for helping students become better thinkers:

1. Probe for answers, leading students to appropriate responses. For example, lead students to explain why leaves change color with questions like: *What do you know about autumn? Are days longer or shorter in the fall? What does sunlight have to do with the color of leaves?*

2. Ask children to clarify or elaborate on their answers. *Why do you say that? Can you explain your answer?*

3. Use questions that elicit different opinions or more than one correct response. *What risks did the colonists face in declaring independence?* Do you think *The Wizard of Oz is a good movie?* This strategy is called **distribution.**

Presenting the lesson

The next step is to present the new material and information. When effective teachers present new lessons, they use the following techniques:
• Communicate distinct openings and closings for each new lesson.
• Proceed in small steps at a brisk pace. Appropriate pacing maximizes student involvement and minimizes behavior problems. Pacing should vary according to students' capabilities.
• Focus on one thought at a time, avoid digressions, and organize the lesson so that one point is mastered before you move on.
• Check for understanding at each step. Always make sure the kids are with you before you proceed. Asking students to nod their heads, make a hand signal or respond in unison to a question are some of the ways you can do this.

Teachers can also check for understanding by sampling individual responses: Pose a question, wait a few seconds, then call on representative students. If the quick learners are confused you can be sure the rest of the class is. Conversely, if slower students know the answer, you're undoubtedly ready to move on.

• Interact constantly with students using questions, direct eye contact, and so on.

• Give explicit instructions and detailed explanations. Students need to know what to do and how to do it.

• Model skills and strategies necessary for completing the tasks. Show them how you'd memorize factual material or search for information in a printed passage, for example.

• Provide many and varied similar and dissimilar examples.

• Teach facts *and* concepts. Students need both. Facts are building blocks, concepts are bridges. Concepts enable students to apply knowledge to other situations—to transfer learning. Experts say that learning hasn't occurred until it transfers to new situations.

Experts say that learning has not occurred until it transfers to new situations.

• Relate new material to students' personal lives and existing frames of reference. This, too, facilitates transfer of learning.

• Make smooth, rapid transitions between lessons.

• Ask a lot of the right questions. Students need both lower-level-thinking questions (How many states are there in the United States?) and higher-level-thinking questions—those that require processing of information, not just simple recall (How did the Louisiana Purchase change the face of a young nation? What was the turning point in the transition from colonies to states?)

Test your questioning skills with the quiz on p. 154. Learn some new strategies for asking better questions from those described on p. 153.

Guide them along

After presenting new material, teachers must skillfully guide students in practicing new skills and concepts. Guided practice means working together as a group. During a math lesson, for example, students might go to the board several at a time to work sample problems.

Guided practice reveals whether or not students understand the material and whether any reteaching is necessary before students practice on their own. Guided practice must always precede independent practice, or students risk practicing their mistakes.

Guided practice must precede independent practice. Immediate feedback and corrections are critical at this point.

At this point, immediate feedback and corrections are critical. Mistakes or misconceptions occurring early in the learning process enlarge over time, affecting subsequent learning. The longer errors persist, the more difficult they are to correct.

Effective elementary teachers spend more time than others in guided practice, asking questions, correcting errors, and repeating new material. One study showed that the most effective teachers ask approximately 24 questions per 50-minute math period, compared to an average of nine asked by others.

Elementary students need guided practice. Of course, the amount varies with the difficulty of the material and the age of the students. Young students need more guided practice than older ones, particularly in mathematics and reading.

When guiding students through new material or skills:

• Present only a small amount of practice material at one time.

• Allow sufficient time for practice.

• Continue to gauge understanding, reteaching certain steps if necessary.

• Give every child a chance to respond and receive feedback. Involve them all in classroom recitations or discussions. Researcher Linda Anderson and her colleagues found that during small-group instruction, effective teachers move around the group in a fixed order rather than calling on students randomly. This accomplishes several things. It gives everyone an equal opportunity to participate; it eliminates the distractions of hand waving and other attention-getting behaviors; and it takes less time.

• Give students adequate time to respond to your questions. Based on her extensive research, Mary Budd Rowe of the University of Florida recommends a "wait time" of 3-5 seconds. Any less is unfair to slower responders, and any more causes behavior problems as other students become restless.

• Continue to practice until students achieve about an 80 percent success rate (compared to a 95 percent success rate when they work alone).

• Offer speedy and specific feedback. Research suggests that academic feedback is more conducive to achievement than any other teaching behavior. When children anwer your questions, let them know how they're doing.

• Explain or follow up on student answers that are correct but hesitant. "Yes, that's right, because . . ."

• Lead students to correct their own errors by simplifying the questions, giving clues, explaining or reviewing steps, or even reteaching, if necessary.

• Wrong answers due to carelessness (as opposed to lack of understanding) need to be corrected, not explained.

Independent practice

Now you are confident that students can go it alone. You've presented the new material, guided them in practicing it, and are reasonably sure they won't make any serious mistakes. Let them get to it!

• Homework, seatwork, learning games, and cooperative activities are all ways to give

Overlearning

Over and over, research demonstrates the importance of **overlearning**—particularly for hierarchically organized material. Overlearning helps students become confident with the material, retain it longer, and be able to apply it to new situations.

Give kids independent work they can handle successfully to keep motivation and involvement high. But don't forget they need challenge. Teaching skill comes in finding the fine line between challenging students and allowing them to overlearn.

students the independent practice they need.

• Always make sure independent practice directly follows guided practice so new material is fresh in students' minds. Also, with guided practice preceding independent practice, students are less likely to practice their mistakes.

• During independent practice, make sure students master content to the point of "overlearning." Their responses to questions and problems should become rapid and automatic. Researchers recommend a 95 percent success rate!

• Always monitor independent practice. Circulate around the classroom, actively explaining, observing, asking questions, and giving feedback. But try not to spend more than 20 seconds with any one student, lest the others become restless.

• Researcher Thomas Good suggests that math seatwork and homework assignments should take no longer than 15 minutes.

• Demonstrate the importance of independent practice by collecting all assignments. Review the material by having students grade their own or each other's papers.

• Always explain the purpose and nature of independent practice.

• Divide difficult material into several segments of instruction and seatwork during a single period.

See Chapter 2 for more tips on managing seatwork, the most common form of independent practice.

Regular reviews

Daily, weekly, and monthly reviews help students remember what they've learned. And retention says a lot for your effectiveness as a teacher.

Periodic reviews reveal where students need more work—more help from you. Frequent review also gives students a greater chance to succeed. Effective teachers provide many opportunities for review.

• Homework and seatwork assignments should regularly concentrate on reviewing previous work. In math, for example, assign homework on Thursday or Friday that reviews the week's work.

• Games, class discussions, and quizzes that "don't count" are good ways to review a week or a month after material is taught.

• "Sponges" help kids review. These 3- to 10-minute activities soak up transition times between lessons. They focus students on the upcoming lesson by having them review recent material. A sponge can be a question or activity written on the board. ("Write down 10 words that have the 'th' blend.") Prepare a handout using activities such as those on p. 159.

• When students do poorly on reviews, think about adjusting your lesson pace or offering more guided practice.

Plan Your Strategy

You see, there really is a science of teaching. All of these strategies are effective and well-documented—when used appropriately, of course.

But how will you ever remember all this when you are standing in front of 30 expectant faces?

You don't have to. Plan for instructional effectiveness as a routine part of lesson planning. Plan the questions you'll ask and the examples you'll provide. Think ahead of time how to make the new knowledge relevant to students' lives and how to model the skills they must learn. Plan how to guide students in practicing the new material, and decide how you'll offer opportunities for independent practice.

Remember, behind every good lesson is a good lesson plan.

Keep Them Actively Engaged

Active teaching helps students learn because it keeps them motivated and attentive by allowing them to succeed at academic tasks.

It's as simple as that. No matter what your instructional style or how much teaching experience you have, you must actively engage students and offer them plenty of chances to succeed.

Active teaching

Call it direct instruction, explicit instruction, active teaching, structured learning, or any other phrase. But when it means teachers organizing and clearly leading learning activities, it works.

Direct instruction means that teachers carefully structure academic tasks. They tell students how to accomplish these tasks, and they guide them through exercises leading to mastery. They give students frequent

---

Teaching tip

What does active teaching look like in the classroom? To actively teach a lesson, focus student attention on the new material, present the new material, guide students in practicing it, give them a chance to practice independently, and conduct frequent reviews—in that order.

opportunities for practice, and they assess whether or not reteaching or more practice is needed.

First-grade teachers directly instructing reading groups, for example, introduce new words to the students and point out important phonetic features. They talk about what a word means and give examples of how it is used. They let students practice words in oral reading and ask questions to make sure students understand what they read and can analyze the words.

Active teaching works best when cognitive achievement is the goal. Other approaches may be more appropriate for developing attitudes, emotions, interests, and social skills.

To actively teach fractions, a teacher introduces the topic, explains what fractions are, gives concrete examples, works problems on the board, guides the class in working problems together, makes sure kids understand the lesson, then gives them opportunities to practice independently with problems they can handle.

Active teaching really works. On this point the research is loud and clear: active teaching, more often than not, is superior to individualized or student-guided "discovery" approaches to learning. In small groups or large ones, children pay more attention and learn more when the teacher leads the lesson.

Jere Brophy makes no bones about it: "The emphasis of the 1960s and early 1970s was on teacher-proof curricula and individualized learning packages that changed the teacher's role from instructor to instructional manager," Brophy writes. "This, coupled with the notion that there is too much 'teacher talk' and not enough 'student talk,' has displaced many teachers from their traditional role as instructional leader in the classroom. The research . . . suggests that this has been a mistake."

"To learn independently, students must be able to read, understand and follow directions, identify key concepts, and correct their own errors," Brophy explains. "Furthermore, they must be willing and able to sustain sufficient levels of concentration and effort. This combination of skills and self-sustaining motivation does not exist at all among students in the early grades, and probably exists in only a minority of older students."

Higher achievement gains are associated with persistent attention to academic tasks, teachers' active involvement with students,

Active teaching

Here's the evidence cited by Jere Brophy, Carolyn Evertson, Barak Rosenshine, Linda Anderson, Thomas Good, Donald Cruickshank, and many other researchers of teaching:

- Active teaching is associated with higher achievement across subjects and grade levels.

- Teacher explanations and demonstrations, lectures, recitation, drill and practice—all features of direct instruction—clearly contribute to increased learning.

- Structured programs produce greater achievement than open programs.

- Students even need explicit instruction in becoming independent learners (how to work alone, how and when to seek help, seeking solutions to problems that might arise, knowing what resources are needed, and so on).

- Most forms of "open education" and "individualized instruction" involve unrealistic expectations about how well young students can manage their own learning. Young children frequently don't understand what they are supposed to do or learn.

students' active engagement in learning tasks, well-organized learning environments, and orderly classrooms.

Lower achievement gains are related to students choosing their own activities and seating, teachers working with individuals for extended periods, teachers doing clerical tasks while students work, and students socializing and misbehaving.

Active teaching clearly works. But like other strategies, it works best when adapted to particular students and situations.

Younger children, for example, require more practice than older students. In upper grades, you'll be able to spend more time presenting and less time directing practice.

Active teaching also works best when cognitive achievement is the goal. But other approaches may be more appropriate for growth in noncognitive areas, such as attitudes, emotions, interests, and social development.

Further, younger and lower-ability students, as well as those who are anxious or dependent, need the structure that active teaching provides. But older, more independent students may do quite well in some situations that are less teacher-directed or structured.

It's your judgment call. Use your professional knowledge of students and situations to decide when and where you'll actively teach.

Time to learn

Time is opportunity to learn. And some students have more opportunity than others. On a typical school day, a child in one classroom might spend 84 minutes on reading instruction, while a child in another spends only 24 minutes. (These figures come from a study at the Institute for Research on Teaching.) Add to this the variations in time students spend concentrating on the instruction (and not daydreaming or using the restroom) and you have some idea of the tremendous differences in opportunities to learn.

Effective teaching strategies won't help if you don't have time to teach and students don't have time to learn. Studies nationwide have documented huge differences in teaching and learning time among classrooms. Here's a sample of the findings:

• In the same school district and same grade level, one teacher regularly spends 137 minutes a day on reading and language arts, while another spends just 45 minutes per day.

• One teacher spends 16 minutes each day on mathematics, compared to the 71 minutes allocated daily in another classroom.

• Some teachers, perhaps without realizing it, allocate insufficient time to subjects they do not enjoy—particularly, mathematics and science.

• Teachers differ in the amounts of time they devote to certain subjects. Those who emphasize mathematics tend to spend much less time on social studies than other teachers, and vice versa.

• Reading comprehension skills accounted for 50 hours of instructional time in one classroom for the whole year and only 5 hours in another.

• The time children spent doing seatwork ranged from 52 minutes per day in one classroom to 145 minutes in another.

• Within a class, some children receive more seatwork and less direct instruction than others.

• Children of the lowest socioeconomic status consistently spend less time and receive less instruction in math and reading than their classmates.

• The time students actually spend working or paying attention to instruction ranges from about 35 percent to 90 percent.

• Students are successfully engaged—actually succeeding at their work—from four to 52 minutes per day.

Get the picture? Even small differences in teaching and learning time add up to big ones. Just 25 minutes more (or less) instruction a day amounts to two hours a week or 80 hours a year!

Fortunately, there are ways to increase children's opportunities to learn. Consider three distinct aspects of classroom time:
• *Allocated time*—the amount of time allotted to various subject matters and topics within a subject. Teachers also allocate different types of time: whole-group teaching, seatwork, and tutorial or cooperative activities.
• *Instructional time*—the time you actually have to teach. This is the time allocated to a lesson minus disruptions (inside or outside the classroom), transitions from one activity to another, and other time-wasters.
• *Engaged time*—the time students are paying attention or busily involved during instruction. This is often referred to as *time on task.* Instruction does not automatically translate to learning. Students only learn when they're engaged— successfully.

Give yourself more time to teach by establishing good classroom management. For example, reduce transition times with efficient routines. Save time with careful planning and preparation. (See Chapter 2 for more ideas.)

Another good time-saver is integrating different subject matters into one lesson— teaching multi-purpose lessons to cover more ground in less time. Have students read about current events or write a science report, for example. (See the section on subject matter integration in Chapter 5.) The language arts are particularly suited to subject matter integration. We have to write, read, speak, and listen to something, and that something can be a specific subject or topic.

Is your teaching engaging?
Engaged time is the major concern in this chapter. Whereas effective management can increase teaching time, effective instructional strategies increase the time children spend attending to lessons. And no matter how much time you spend teaching, students won't learn unless they're paying attention. Here's how to ensure they do:
• Offer plenty of direct or active teaching. When you direct the action, kids are more

likely to sit up and take notice. Direct instruction means building in lots of teacher-student interaction.
• Strive for eye contact from all students while you give directions or offer an explanation. Students are more likely to attend to what you're saying when they are looking at you instead of the wall, the ceiling, or another student.

Researchers recommend a success rate of 80 percent during initial learning, 95 to 100 percent during independent practice.

• Make sure they succeed. Success is as sweet as candy, and kids keep coming back for more. Success raises self-esteem, which feels good, and motivates children (or anyone) to engage in the same activities. Learning occurs during that portion of engaged time when students are actually succeeding at a task. Researchers call this *academic learning time.*

When are kids successful? When they know the material so well they make only occasional mistakes. Researchers consistently recommend a success rate of 80 percent during initial learning and 95 percent or higher during

---

Ask yourself

There are only so many hours in a day and so many school days in a year. So use carefully the limited time available. Former teacher Ursula Casanova of Stanford University suggests monitoring your classroom activities for a few days and recording in a journal how you spend class time. Ask these questions:

1. How closely do I keep to my schedule?

2. Am I giving enough attention to those areas students must master by the end of the year?

3. How much time is used for transitions?

independent practice.

This doesn't mean offering students only easy material. It means offering challenging material in the proper way—in small steps, with plenty of guided practice and review.

• Pace lessons as briskly as possible. Many teachers underestimate the rate at which their students can move through the curriculum.

"The scope and sequence of the typical American school curriculum allows for a relatively leisurely pace, so it is reasonable for teachers to try to move through the material efficiently," claims researcher Jere Brophy. This means briskly pacing material that is appropriately difficult, not trying to teach material that is too difficult in the first place, he stresses.

There's a happy medium between lessons so slow and easy they bore students and those so fast and difficult they cause frustration. At either extreme, students become restless and give up. And that means trouble. That's when learning stops and behavior problems begin.

Appropriate pacing can also increase learning efficiency by covering more material during a given period. Adjust your pace by monitoring and assessing student progress.

• Motivate your students to want to learn. When we genuinely enjoy something, are convinced of its worth, or feel good for doing it, we naturally want more. Motivation for learning is such a vital part of good teaching that Chapter 3 features a whole section on it (see p. 86).

You can also keep kids engaged with the way you manage the classroom. Do you

monitor seatwork and other independent practice? Have you established routines to reduce the time students spend waiting—for you, for supplies, for each other? Do your management practices prevent time-consuming behavior problems? Not surprisingly, there's a strong correlation between good management and good instruction. Both require efficient organization and careful planning.

How attentive are your students? Find out by monitoring the time they spend "on task." To do this, Ursula Casanova suggests working together with a colleague. She explains how:

Visit each other's rooms for 20 minutes, four or five different times. The visiting colleague should focus on six or eight students to check whether or not they are paying attention to a task at a given moment. Make decisions quickly, using judgment of what constitutes time on task. You can check on all eight students in under three minutes. Then repeat the cycle for a total of 20 minutes.

Determine a student's attending rate by dividing the number of times the child was on task by the total number of times you checked. In other words, if a child was paying attention three of the six times you checked him, his attending rate would be $3/6$, or 50 percent.

Average the individual percentages to obtain a group rate. Group rates averaged over four or five sessions—preferably at different times of the day—will yield a rough estimate of the percent of time students are paying attention.

Also monitor students' success rates, Casanova advises. Examine workbooks, tests, and written work, asking these questions:
1. Are students consistently getting less than 75 percent correct?
2. Do you find yourself having to reteach often?
3. Do kids complain that "it's too hard"?

Ability Grouping

Teachers group students in many different ways. Learning centers, ability groups for different subjects, cross-age and peer tutoring, gifted and special education pull-out programs, and cooperative learning teams are all examples.

Grouping serves many purposes. Heterogeneous student teams can improve student relations and increase achievement while multi-ability groupings increase self-esteem (see Chapter 3). Learning centers give students choices and exciting alternatives to traditional seatwork (see Chapter 2). Tutoring programs help both tutor and tutee learn more without demanding more of a teacher's time (see Chapter 2).

But most directly related to instructional effectiveness is grouping by ability. Ability grouping allows teachers to tailor instruction and curriculum to the needs and readiness levels of individual students.

Among the several types of ability grouping practiced at the elementary level, within-class grouping is the most common. Here, students spend most of the day in a heterogeneous classroom, moving into ability groups only for certain subjects such as reading or mathematics.

Most teachers swear by ability grouping. And theoretically, it's a great idea. Teachers can meet children's needs in much less time than it would take to individualize instruction

Low achievers

These students suffer both academically and psychologically when other low achievers are their only role models. Some researchers report, for example, that kids in the lowest reading groups are actually depressed. And no wonder. They're ridiculed by their peers. Their teachers hold low expectations for them and offer them less and lower-quality instruction than other students. They perceive themselves as losers. In one classroom, the lowest group was actually called the "Class Clowns."

for every student. They can increase the pace and level of instruction for high achievers and give low achievers more guided practice and review.

And everybody wins, right?

Not according to the research. Studies document the often-times deleterious effects of grouping students by ability. Among other things, ability grouping:

• decreases achievement in low or average-ability groups;
• reinforces negative self-images and low expectations held for lower-achieving students;
• deprives lower achievers of the stimulation of working with high achievers;
• carries a stigma more debilitating than one of being a poor achiever in a heterogeneous group.

Further, teachers often discriminate among the groups. For lower-ability groups they:

• give students fewer and poorer opportunities to learn;
• spend more time on management and discipline than teaching;
• spend less time on preparation;
• present less interesting material.

Yet for all its faults, ability grouping remains a viable option for teaching complex, hierarchical subjects to large and diverse groups of students. If you do it right, it can work.

There's probably no one more familiar with the pros and cons of ability grouping than Robert Slavin of the Center for Research on Elementary and Middle Schools. In an exhausting review of research, Slavin found that ability grouping can be handled effectively. Here's what he suggests:

Don't overdo it

Keep students in heterogeneous classes or groups most of the time and regroup by ability only in subjects where it really makes a difference, says Slavin. Here, he refers to the effectiveness of within-class ability grouping for mathematics in the upper elementary grades and across-grade ability grouping for reading.

"There is good reason to avoid ability-grouped class assignment, which seems to have the greatest potential for negative social effects since it entirely separates students into different streams," Slavin continues. He cites lower expectations, lower self-esteem, lower quality of instruction (most teachers dislike teaching low achievers), and lack of high-achieving role models as serious problems in ability-grouped classes of lower achievers.

But the most compelling argument against ability grouping, says Slavin, is that it "goes against our democratic ideals by creating academic elites. Because ability groupings often parallel social class and ethnic groupings . . . [they] may serve to increase divisions along class, race, and ethnic lines."

The evidence shows that all students benefit from interacting with a wide variety of peers in a variety of settings.

Remember why you're grouping

The instructional purpose of ability grouping is to accommodate different needs and capabilities, tailoring instruction as closely to individual students as possible.

To effectively use ability grouping, you must first establish groups that actually reflect different abilities. Grouping plans must measurably reduce student ability differences in the specific skill being taught, Slavin stresses.

Make assignments based on several factors:

• your personal knowledge and judgment of the child;
• achievement as indicated on standardized achievement tests or some other objective measure;
• class performance;
• past performance and the recommendations of previous teachers.

Further, you must adapt your instruction to the group. "Teachers must actually vary their level and pace of instruction to correspond to students' levels of readiness and learning rates," Slavin explains. But this doesn't mean you can't give high-quality instruction to all groups.

Teachers grouping kids by ability should keep the number of groups small enough to allow for adequate direct instruction for each group. Slavin suggests a maximum of three groups. Beyond that number you can expect serious management problems.

With reading instruction divided among three groups, for example, students must spend at least two-thirds of their reading time working without direct instruction or supervision. And assigning large amounts of unsupervised seatwork results in less achievement and more behavior problems as students become bored or restless.

Also, the transition time between ability groups reduces precious instructional time. The more subjects you group for, and the more groups per subject, the greater the loss.

Keep it flexible

Finally, teachers must keep group composition fluid. That is, watch for misassignments and changes in student performance that warrant regrouping.

"Grouping plans must frequently reassess student placements and must be flexible enough to allow for easy reassignments after initial placement," Slavin concludes.

Monitor changes with the same criteria you used to assign the groups in the first place—personal judgment, test scores, and class performance.

Chapter 4—Read more about it

1. Continuing to Learn: A Guidebook for Teacher Development. Susan Loucks-Horsley, et al. The Regional Laboratory for Educational Improvement of the Northeast & Islands, 1987.

2. "Synthesis of Research on Explicit Teaching." Barak Rosenshine. *Educational Leadership*, 43 (April 1986), 60-69.

3. *What's Noteworthy on Teaching*. Aurora, CO: Mid-continent Regional Educational Laboratory, 1987. (Includes summaries of The Hunter Model (Madeline Hunter), Active Mathematics Teaching (Good, Grouws, and Ebmeier) and Explicit Teaching (Rosenshine).

4. *Teaching is Tough*. Donald R. Cruickshank and Associates. Englewood Cliffs, NJ: Prentice-Hall, 1980.

5. *Models of Teaching* (third ed.) B. Joyce and M. Weil. Englewood Cliffs, NJ: Prentice Hall, 1986.

6. Research Perspectives: Direct Instruction. G. Duffy. *Michigan Reading Journal*, 13 (1980), 23-25.

7. *Test Scores Count: A Handbook for Teaching Test-Taking Skills*. Sharon Koenigs. Aurora, CO: Mid-continent Regional Educational Laboratory, 1987.

8. "The Role of Testing in Effective Schools." A. C. Porter. *American Education*, (1983), 1, 25-28.

9. *Mastery Teaching*. Madeline Hunter. El Segundo, CA: PIP Publications, 1982.

10. *Teacher Behavior and Student Achievement* (Occasional Paper No. 73). J. Brophy and T. Good. East Lansing, MI: Institute for Research on Teaching, 1984. Also in M. C. Wittrock (ed.) *Handbook of Research on Teaching* (third ed.). New York: Macmillan, 1986.

11. "Relationships Between Teachers' Presentations of Classroom Tasks and Students' Engagements in Those Tasks." J. Brophy, et al. *Journal of Educational Psychology*, 75 (1983), 544-552.

12. *Looking in Classrooms* (third ed.). T. Good and J. Brophy. New York: Harper & Row, 1984.

13. *Learning and Motivation in the Classroom*. S. Paris, G. Olson, and H. Stevenson (eds.) Hillsdale, NJ: Erlbaum, 1983.

14. *"Using Textbooks and Teachers' Guides: What Beginning Teachers Learn and What They Need to Know"* (R. S. No. 174). D. L. Ball and S. Feiman-Nemser. East Lansing, MI: Institute for Research on Teaching, 1986.

15. *"Ability Grouping and Student Achievement in Elementary Schools: A Best Evidence Synthesis"* (Rep. No. 1). Robert Slavin. Baltimore, MD: Center for Research on Elementary and Middle Schools, 1986.

Special Instructional Concerns:

1. *Advances in Bilingual Education Research*. E. E. Garcia and R. V. Padilla (eds.). Tucson, AZ: University of Arizona Press, 1985.

2. *Culture and the Bilingual Classroom: Studies in Classroom Ethnography*. H. T. Trueba, G. P. Guthrie, and K. H. Au (eds.). Rowley, MA: Newbury House, 1982.

3. "How Do We Help the Learning Disabled Child?" *Instructor*, February 1984, 30-36.

4. *What are Learning Disabilities?* (Item 438). Mary M. Banbury. Washington, DC: American Federation of Teachers.

NOTES

N O T E S

HOW DO YOU RANK AS A
TEACHER-MANAGER?

Take this quiz and find out! It's just for you—to help you learn more about yourself and your job. The sole purpose of this test is to help you reflect on your effectiveness as a leader and adviser, as a pacesetter and goalmaker, as a creator of a successful learning environment, and most important of all, as a teacher of your students.

Read each statement; then place a number from 1 to 5 in the **first** column, 5 being the highest, and 1 the lowest. Next year, come back and take the quiz again. Your improvement should be obvious.

Each item has two columns: **Now** and **1 Year Later**.

1. Self-management
a. You are confident of your professional abilities.
b. You look forward to going to work.
c. You are organized.
d. Your appearance satisfies you and pleases others.
e. At the end of the day you feel happily exhausted.
Total

2. Preparation and planning
a. You establish goals, then select strategies to achieve them.
b. You evaluate a total unit, rather than each individual task.
c. Preparation time equals a fourth or more of teaching time.
d. You plan for the class as a whole.
e. You review used plans and file better ones for future use.
Total

3. Utilizing learning tools
a. Your teaching strategies include having students compare and confirm evidence.
b. You steer a student toward the learning tool or method that works most effectively for him or her.
c. You want children to recognize there is often more than one right answer to a question.
d. You utilize both human and media resources liberally in your teaching.
Total

4. Organization of learning resources available
a. You recognize that one objective such as "learning to read" should not be a teacher's only goal.
b. You initiate new learning from many different sources.
c. You consciously plan for students to write on a daily basis.
d. You work deliberately to help children use their acquired skills in creative or problem-solving activities.
Total

5. Quality of teaching
a. Your students know the goal behind a task and participate in immediate evaluation of their efforts.
b. Whenever you can, you put humor and fun into your teaching.
c. Daily learning tasks differ for different students.
d. Students are encouraged to select learning strategies that work well for them.
e. You work with small groups as well as the whole class.
Total

6. Classroom control
a. You recognize your power and use it effectively.
b. Discipline does not mean punishment in your class.
c. You and your students can settle personal problems easily.
d. Your students are active partners in classroom control.
Total

7. Record-keeping
a. Your record-keeping system provides good support for your management efforts.
b. You record promptly and easily.
c. Only objective evidence is reported in report card marks.
d. You share student records with parents comfortably.
e. You involve students in the record-keeping system.
Total

8. Evaluating performance
a. The purpose of evaluation is to determine future action in terms of goals and strategies.
b. Testing for marking purposes is only one aspect of your evaluations.
c. You try to evaluate promptly after task completion.
d. You sometimes have children mark their own or other students' papers.
e. Your student profiles are nearby for easy referral.
Total

9. Diagnosing
a. You consider yourself an expert in diagnosing student learning capabilities and problems.
b. You consider diagnosis high among the top five teaching tasks.
c. You regard both subjective and objective evidence as important.
d. When a student's performance differs from your diagnosis, you seek the experts' advice.
e. Individual diagnoses of students guide your selection of classroom goals and strategies.
Total

10. Teacher-student relations
a. Your ego satisfaction as a teacher comes mostly from seeing your students involved and fulfilled.
b. You feel that admitting an error of judgment or conduct on your part does not imperil your control as a teacher.
c. You make deliberate individual appraisals of your students at least once every two weeks.
d. You have a working one-to-one relationship with each student.
Total

11. Member of the teaching team
a. You share successful strategies with other teachers.
b. You could swap a "no-chemistry" student with another teacher without feeling failure or loss of face.
c. You don't feel you must live up to what other teachers are doing.
d. You are part of a subgroup of teachers in your school who professionally aid each other.
e. Teacher get-togethers in your school are sometimes social and sometimes professional in nature.
Total

Developed by Instructor January 1982.

A+Teacher
How's Your Teaching?

How's your teaching? Find out with this self-evaluated questionnaire. It's for your eyes only, so be honest! The results might suggest where you could improve.

A. WHAT GOALS DO YOU STRESS FOR YOUR STUDENTS?

	Never	Seldom	Sometimes	Often	Always
1. Learning, achieving academically	☐	☐	☐	☐	☐
2. Gaining practical skills	☐	☐	☐	☐	☐
3. Being neat, accurate, organized	☐	☐	☐	☐	☐
4. Questioning and seeking own answers	☐	☐	☐	☐	☐
5. Developing talents and interests	☐	☐	☐	☐	☐
6. Becoming involved in current issues	☐	☐	☐	☐	☐
7. Developing a positive self-image	☐	☐	☐	☐	☐
8. Being creative	☐	☐	☐	☐	☐
9. Behaving in an acceptable manner	☐	☐	☐	☐	☐
10. Cooperation	☐	☐	☐	☐	☐

B. WHERE DO YOU GET YOUR IDEAS AND INSPIRATIONS FOR SUBJECT MATTER, METHODS, AND ACTIVITIES?

	Never	Seldom	Sometimes	Often	Always
1. Commercial texts, workbooks, programs, etc.	☐	☐	☐	☐	☐
2. Curriculum guide	☐	☐	☐	☐	☐
3. Educational television	☐	☐	☐	☐	☐
4. Workshops, courses, seminars	☐	☐	☐	☐	☐
5. Educational books, magazines, etc.	☐	☐	☐	☐	☐
6. Holidays, events, special occasions	☐	☐	☐	☐	☐
7. Your students	☐	☐	☐	☐	☐
8. Other teachers	☐	☐	☐	☐	☐
9. Your own creative ideas	☐	☐	☐	☐	☐

10. Which book has most influenced your teaching?

C. WHICH EDUCATIONAL MAGAZINES DO YOU READ?

	Never	Seldom	Sometimes	Often	Always
1. American Teacher	☐	☐	☐	☐	☐
2. Changing Education	☐	☐	☐	☐	☐
3. Instructor	☐	☐	☐	☐	☐
4. Learning	☐	☐	☐	☐	☐
5. Scholastic Teacher	☐	☐	☐	☐	☐
6. Today's Education (NEA)	☐	☐	☐	☐	☐

D. HOW DO YOU PLAN AND PREPARE YOURSELF?

	Never	Seldom	Sometimes	Often	Always
1. Use commerical plan book	☐	☐	☐	☐	☐
2. Follow teacher manuals	☐	☐	☐	☐	☐
3. Establish objectives for the year	☐	☐	☐	☐	☐
4. Make long-range plans (month or more)	☐	☐	☐	☐	☐
5. Plan weekly	☐	☐	☐	☐	☐
6. Plan daily	☐	☐	☐	☐	☐
7. Use spur-of-moment teaching opportunities	☐	☐	☐	☐	☐
8. Plans checked by principal	☐	☐	☐	☐	☐
9. Plan with students	☐	☐	☐	☐	☐
10. Plan with other teachers	☐	☐	☐	☐	☐

11. How much of your own time do you spend on school-related work each week?
☐ 0 ☐ Less than 5 hours ☐ 5-10 hours ☐ 10-20 hours ☐ More than 20 hours

E. HOW IS YOUR CLASSROOM SET UP?

	Never	Seldom	Sometimes	Often	Always
1. Desks in rows	☐	☐	☐	☐	☐
2. Desks in groups	☐	☐	☐	☐	☐
3. Tables instead of desks	☐	☐	☐	☐	☐
4. Displays of student work and projects	☐	☐	☐	☐	☐
5. Learning centers and exhibits	☐	☐	☐	☐	☐
6. Specialized work areas (science, math)	☐	☐	☐	☐	☐
7. Live animals	☐	☐	☐	☐	☐
8. Plants	☐	☐	☐	☐	☐
9. Chalkboards that are utilized	☐	☐	☐	☐	☐
10. Bulletin boards that are utilized	☐	☐	☐	☐	☐

F. WHAT MATERIALS AND EQUIPMENT DO YOU USE?

	Never	Seldom	Sometimes	Often	Always
1. Camera	☐	☐	☐	☐	☐
2. VCR	☐	☐	☐	☐	☐
3. Computer	☐	☐	☐	☐	☐
4. Tape recorder	☐	☐	☐	☐	☐
5. Phonograph	☐	☐	☐	☐	☐
6. Motion pictures, slides, filmstrips	☐	☐	☐	☐	☐
7. Opaque or overhead projector	☐	☐	☐	☐	☐
8. Duplicating masters and machine	☐	☐	☐	☐	☐
9. Commercially produced games, kits	☐	☐	☐	☐	☐
10. Newspapers, catalogs, magazines, etc.	☐	☐	☐	☐	☐
11. Scraps, leftovers, etc.	☐	☐	☐	☐	☐
12. Teacher-made materials	☐	☐	☐	☐	☐
13. Student-made materials	☐	☐	☐	☐	☐

14. How much of your own money do you generally spend for school materials per school year?
☐ Less than $10 ☐ $10-25 ☐ $25-50 ☐ $50-$100 ☐ More than $100

G. HOW DO YOU HANDLE DISCIPLINE PROBLEMS?

	Never	Seldom	Sometimes	Often	Always
1. Small reminders (look, snap of finger)	☐	☐	☐	☐	☐
2. Verbal reprimand	☐	☐	☐	☐	☐
3. Physical reprimand	☐	☐	☐	☐	☐
4. Punishment (written work, separation, detention, withholding privileges)	☐	☐	☐	☐	☐
5. Involve principal	☐	☐	☐	☐	☐
6. Involve parents	☐	☐	☐	☐	☐
7. Ignore bad behavior, praise good	☐	☐	☐	☐	☐
8. Private conference with offender	☐	☐	☐	☐	☐
9. Involve class in solving problem	☐	☐	☐	☐	☐
10. Have student work out problem independently	☐	☐	☐	☐	☐

H. HOW DO YOU ALLOW FOR INDIVIDUAL DIFFERENCES IN YOUR STUDENTS?

	Never	Seldom	Sometimes	Often	Always
1. Vertical grouping	☐	☐	☐	☐	☐
2. Using multilevel materials	☐	☐	☐	☐	☐
3. Stressing individual growth and achievement	☐	☐	☐	☐	☐
4. Homogeneous groupings in class	☐	☐	☐	☐	☐
5. Enrichment work for the gifted	☐	☐	☐	☐	☐
6. Extra help for slow learners	☐	☐	☐	☐	☐
7. Activities for individual interests	☐	☐	☐	☐	☐

Rating scale for sections I–M and N–R: **Never · Seldom · Sometimes · Often · Always** (five checkboxes each)

I. WHAT TEACHING METHODS DO YOU USE?
1. Formal class lessons .... ☐☐☐☐☐
2. Class discussions .... ☐☐☐☐☐
3. Team teaching .... ☐☐☐☐☐
4. Small-group instruction .... ☐☐☐☐☐
5. Individualized approach .... ☐☐☐☐☐
6. Following texts and other sequential materials .... ☐☐☐☐☐
7. Relating all work to overall themes .... ☐☐☐☐☐
8. Contracting with students .... ☐☐☐☐☐
9. Using commercially prepared programs ☐☐☐☐☐
10. Drill work and memorization .... ☐☐☐☐☐
11. Innovative or original methods .... ☐☐☐☐☐

J. WHAT ACTIVITIES OR LEARNING EXPERIENCES DO YOU OFFER YOUR STUDENTS?
1. Creative writing .... ☐☐☐☐☐
2. Role playing, drama .... ☐☐☐☐☐
3. Setting up bank, store, etc., in class ... ☐☐☐☐☐
4. Contests, games, competitions ...... ☐☐☐☐☐
5. Small-group or committee work ...... ☐☐☐☐☐
6. Field trips and guest speakers .... ☐☐☐☐☐
7. Practical, hands-on activities .... ☐☐☐☐☐

K. HOW ARE YOUR STUDENTS ACTIVELY INVOLVED IN THEIR LEARNING?
1. Class meetings .... ☐☐☐☐☐
2. Participating in planning and directing . ☐☐☐☐☐
3. Freedom of movement and expression ☐☐☐☐☐
4. Choosing individual endeavors .... ☐☐☐☐☐
5. Correcting papers .... ☐☐☐☐☐
6. Keeping personal progress records ... ☐☐☐☐☐
7. Peer editing contracts .... ☐☐☐☐☐
8. Periodic conferences with you .... ☐☐☐☐☐
9. Striving for rewards and awards ...... ☐☐☐☐☐
10. Using equipment and audiovisual aids . ☐☐☐☐☐
11. Classroom jobs and responsibilities ... ☐☐☐☐☐
12. Creating bulletin boards, exhibits, etc. . ☐☐☐☐☐
13. Celebrating birthdays, special occasions ☐☐☐☐☐

L. WHO ELSE IS ACTIVELY INVOLVED IN TEACHING YOUR STUDENTS?
1. Other teachers and specialists .... ☐☐☐☐☐
2. Principal .... ☐☐☐☐☐
3. Students (peer teaching) .... ☐☐☐☐☐
4. Classroom aide .... ☐☐☐☐☐
5. Student teacher, college helper ...... ☐☐☐☐☐
6. Parents .... ☐☐☐☐☐
7. Volunteers .... ☐☐☐☐☐

M. HOW DOES HOMEWORK ENTER YOUR EDUCATIONAL PICTURE?
1. Written assignments .... ☐☐☐☐☐
2. Study or preparation assignments .... ☐☐☐☐☐
3. Same assignment for all .... ☐☐☐☐☐
4. Individualized assignments .... ☐☐☐☐☐
5. Free-choice assignments .... ☐☐☐☐☐
6. Assignments for those who want them ☐☐☐☐☐
7. Assignments for those who need them ☐☐☐☐☐
8. Text or workbook assignments ...... ☐☐☐☐☐
9. Skill or drill assignments .... ☐☐☐☐☐
10. Creative assignments .... ☐☐☐☐☐
11. Long-range assignments (week or more) .... ☐☐☐☐☐
12. How much time per week does a student in your class spend on your assigned homework?
☐ 0　☐ Less than 1 hour　☐ 1-5 hours　☐ 5-10 hours ☐ More than 10 hours

N. HOW DO YOU USE TESTS?
1. To determine student progress ...... ☐☐☐☐☐
2. To motivate effort and achievement ... ☐☐☐☐☐
3. To encourage memorization of facts .. ☐☐☐☐☐
4. To test understanding of concepts, processes .... ☐☐☐☐☐
5. To see what student knows (e.g., pretest) .... ☐☐☐☐☐
6. To set up instructional groups .... ☐☐☐☐☐
7. To reinforce students' test-taking skills ☐☐☐☐☐
8. To evaluate your own teaching ...... ☐☐☐☐☐
9. How many tests does a student in your class take per week? ☐ 0 ☐ 1 or 2 ☐ 3-5 ☐ 5-10 ☐ More than 10

O. HOW DO YOU KEEP STUDENT PROGRESS RECORDS?
1. Rely on memory .... ☐☐☐☐☐
2. Commercial marking book .... ☐☐☐☐☐
3. Teacher checklists of completed tasks, mastered skills, etc. .... ☐☐☐☐☐
4. Individual student folders or files ..... ☐☐☐☐☐
5. Classroom displays of progress charts ☐☐☐☐☐
6. Anecdotal records .... ☐☐☐☐☐
7. Own original system .... ☐☐☐☐☐

P. IN WHICH ORGANIZATIONS DO YOU PARTICIPATE?
1. Parent-teacher group (PTA, PTO) ..... ☐☐☐☐☐
2. NEA, AFT, other education associations ☐☐☐☐☐
3. Educational committees .... ☐☐☐☐☐
4. School voluntary activities .... ☐☐☐☐☐
5. Tutoring programs .... ☐☐☐☐☐
6. Civic affairs .... ☐☐☐☐☐
7. Service organizations .... ☐☐☐☐☐
8. Little League, Scouts, etc. .... ☐☐☐☐☐
9. Religious school staff .... ☐☐☐☐☐

Q. WHICH CHARACTERISTICS DESCRIBE YOU IN THE CLASSROOM?
1. Well organized .... ☐☐☐☐☐
2. Strict .... ☐☐☐☐☐
3. Consistent .... ☐☐☐☐☐
4. Soft-spoken .... ☐☐☐☐☐
5. Creative .... ☐☐☐☐☐
6. Enthusiastic .... ☐☐☐☐☐
7. Humorous .... ☐☐☐☐☐
8. Patient, understanding .... ☐☐☐☐☐

R. DO THE FOLLOWING FACTORS CONTRIBUTE TO YOUR TEACHING SUCCESS?
1. College training .... ☐☐☐☐☐
2. Student teaching experience .... ☐☐☐☐☐
3. Past experience as a teacher .... ☐☐☐☐☐
4. Rapport with class .... ☐☐☐☐☐
5. The teaching methods you use ...... ☐☐☐☐☐
6. Effort and hard work .... ☐☐☐☐☐
7. Working well with others (parents, staff, etc.) .... ☐☐☐☐☐
8. The number of students in class ..... ☐☐☐☐☐
9. The type of students you teach ..... ☐☐☐☐☐
10. Your personal appearance .... ☐☐☐☐☐
11. Enjoyment of job .... ☐☐☐☐☐
12. Professional experiences outside of the classroom; including in-services ...... ☐☐☐☐☐
13. Interaction with colleagues .... ☐☐☐☐☐

This questionnaire was adapted from the original questionnaire by Ruth Ann Tschudin which was completed by 420 teachers. The resulting data were the basis for Miss Tschudin's study and her article, *The Secrets of A+ Teaching*, INSTRUCTOR, September 1978.

High Ideals

Which of the following "ideals" describes your performance?
Check those that apply and try working on the rest.

_____ I base my planning on learning goals and strategies rather than pages in the textbook.

_____ In basic skill areas, I use my time and work differentials to try to keep all children at least at grade level.

_____ I involve students in task identification, learning styles, use of skills, and test analyses.

_____ My classroom reflects the learning that is going on in it; it is attractive and expressive, an agreeable place to be.

_____ I diagnose individual learning problems and plan on the basis of my diagnoses.

_____ I balance the economy of group teaching with individual prescriptions for each child.

_____ I balance my time, allowing for planning, managing, teaching, and paperwork, spending at least 20 percent of my time in planning and development.

_____ Students write every day; they know the standards they should achieve.

_____ At least 40 percent of the school day involves writing, organizing, making, expressing, researching, summarizing, comparing, hypothesizing, and applying.

_____ I consult frequently with my principal about problem situations and students in my classroom.

_____ I seek to develop interest and involvement in neighborhood, community, national, and world events.

_____ I regularly plan learning tasks that cause children to reach and stretch.

_____ I strive to have a good relationship with each child; we are courteous with and supportive of each other.

_____ I provide opportunities for students to use good material, print and nonprint.

_____ I give precise directions and assignments, and when I give homework it is usually completed.

_____ I pretest or survey before introducing new material so as to use the students' time wisely.

_____ I have minimums every child must achieve, and maximums that children are encouraged to reach for.

_____ I read regularly to my students; they read at least 20 books a year for pleasure.

_____ I teach my children how to take tests and I maintain an optimum testing environment.

_____ When test scores are low, I re-evaluate and redevelop the strategies that I used.

_____ At least every three weeks, I review individual progress in major learning areas, then revise my goals and procedures as needed.

_____ If my plan book was missing, students could tell the substitute enough for them and him/her to have a worthwhile day.

_____ Other teachers and I often exchange ideas. I consider myself to be at least moderately innovative.

_____ In skill and drill areas, I have time and accuracy goals; each student knows what he or she must do to reach them.

_____ I perform special duties (hall, lunchroom) effectively and in good grace.

_____ Parents respect my authority; they think of me as a firm, fair person with whom they can comminucate.

_____ I welcome the use of new textbooks, audiovisuals, and other learning materials, including computers.

_____ My classroom is a community of children. We have defined tasks and responsibilities, and enough rules to make classroom living efficient but not confining.

_____ In standardized tests, my children rank just about where I expect them to and I am usually satisfied with what I have achieved.

Asking Good Questions

Ask better questions and help your students become better thinkers with these eight strategies converting simple questions into more challenging ones.

Yes, but why?

Ask students why an answer is correct. For example, *Why is 6 × (9 − 4) equal to 30 and not 50?* or *why does Columbus get credit for discovering America?* In each of these converted questions, it's easy to tell if students know the basic information. And the bonus is that these questions also require the processing of that information.

What's the use?

Ask questions that focus on the use of information. So, to the question *Why do you need to know the effect of light on plant growth?* students might answer, *To do landscaping, know where to plant a garden, or decide which houseplants to buy for the light exposure available.* Such questions increase the likelihood that students will remember facts, because they apply them.

A natural outgrowth of using "why" questions is that students soon begin to ask them as well as answer them.

What's different now?

Asking about the implication of a change is also worthwhile. To use this conversion strategy, first change something about the information you want the students to know. Alex Osborn in *Applied Imagination* (Scribner, 1963) suggests eight tactics for change:

1) Adapt—borrow an idea from somewhere else. *How would our lives be different if we hibernated all winter long as animals do?*
2) Modify—make a small change for the better. *If Hansel and Gretel had brought a map with them into the forest, what might have happened?*
3) Substitute—use something for something else. *How would a blueberry sandwich taste?*
4) Magnify—add, multiply, or extend. *What would Newton's Fourth Law be?*
5) Minify—make it smaller, omit something, divide it. *Can you imagine a world without gravity?*
6) Rearrange—revise the order of things. *What would be the consequences if A was the last letter in the alphabet, and Z the first?*
7) Reverse—turn things completely around. *How would you like to go to bed in the morning and get up at night?*
8) Combine—add two or more things together. *How would the world be if each continent was only one country?*

Can you prove it?

Asking for the proof of an answer requires that the student both formulate the answer and offer support for it. The question *How do we find the area of a triangle?* becomes *Does the formula you are using to find the area of a triangle always work? Why?* This strategy works especially well for literature assignments. Questions about character actions, plot events, and author style may be answered only with support from the text.

Right, wrong, or neither?

Too often, higher-level questions become lower-level ones because the questioner has a predetermined answer. One way to avoid this is to consciously suspend judgment on an issue and another is to ask a question that has no right or wrong answer.

Finding this kind of open-ended question requires the questioner to do some real exploration on the subject. For instance, a factual question about the names of the 13 colonies might become—after some thought—one of the following higher-level questions: *Why do people name places instead of using another identification system such as numbers? How important was communication among the colonies in moving toward independence?* The higher-level-thinking question you choose will depend on the direction you have chosen for your unit and your students' interests.

All of the above?

Asking questions that have more than one answer calls for careful analysis and multiple answers from the students. This strategy has wide application for teaching basic skills. Instead of asking for the definition of a noun, for example, ask: "How many words can you think of that fit this sentence: *The exhausted _____ raced around the corner.* Obviously, only nouns may be used to complete the sentence. In addition, the question has changed from asking for the recall of a memorized definition to an active search for words that meet a certain set of conditions.

Alike or different?

The questions *How are Jefferson and Lincoln alike? How are they different?* and *What do the formulas for finding the areas of the following figures have in common?* use comparison and contrast— another effective strategy. A good way to introduce students to this concept is to compare and contrast concrete objects. Give small groups of students two similar objects to compare—forks of different patterns, coins, or hats. Ask them to list similarities and differences. When all the groups' lists have been combined on the chalkboard, ask students to identify the categories they used as the basis for their comparisons, such as texture, color, size, and so on.

With a little practice, students quickly get in the habit of searching for categories and characteristics. The next step is to compare and contrast on a more abstract level: a story and poem about the same event, multiplication and division, or mammals and birds.

Square peg and round hole?

Formulating questions using unusual relationships requires creativity on the part of the teacher as well as the student. When studying verbs, for example, relate them to the actions and habits of people: *What would a helping verb say to an action verb if they happened to meet?* or *If we think of the parts of speech as a family, who would the family members be and how do you see their family roles?*

You could also proceed by placing any event or topic in an entirely remote context. The more remote the association, the more effectively it will stretch your students' thinking. The ability to break out of familiar ways of thinking is an important element in creativity.

By Hilarie Bryce Davis. Original questionnaire appeared in INSTRUCTOR, November 1980.

What's your questioning IQ?

Spend too much time asking kids lower-level-thinking questions? Take this quiz by Robet Schirrmacher and Michael Kahn of Rollins College, Winter Park, Florida, and find out. Below are questions you might ask children after reading *Goldilocks and the Three Bears.* Write L after the questions that call on only lower-level-thinking skills. Write H after those questions that involve higher-level-thinking skills.

Scoring: Now check your answers: (1) L; (2) L; (3) H; (4) H; (5) L; (6) L; (7) L; (8) H; (9) H; (10) H. If you have 8-10 correct, you know the difference between higher-level and lower-level thinking skills and are probably a questioner extraordinaire; 5-7, you've got the idea; 3-4, you need to brush up on your questioning skills; fewer than 3, cram course needed!

_____ (1) How many bears are there in the story?

_____ (2) What is porridge?

_____ (3) How would you have felt if you were Baby Bear?

_____ (4) Should Goldilocks be punished for breaking the chair?

_____ (5) Who went into the house where the three bears lived?

_____ (6) What happened first in the story?

_____ (7) What happened after Baby Bear's chair broke?

_____ (8) Do you think the three bears will lock their door the next time they leave their house?

_____ (9) Is this story like another bear story we've read? How?

_____(10) Are all little girls like Goldilocks?

Developed by Robert Schirrmacher and Michael Kahn. Original questionnaire appeared in INSTRUCTOR, November 1980.

No-Cost Strategies for LEP Students
(Limited English Proficiency)

Useful strategies for serving limited-English-proficient students (LEP) in the classroom are these:

1. Seat the student close to the front of the room where directions and instructions may be given with fewer distractions.

2. Speak naturally, but slowly, to allow for comprehension to develop.

3. Use clear, simple language, (i.e. shorter sentences, simpler concepts, and fewer multisyllabic words).

4. Repeat the explanations, directions, or instructions as needed.

5. Support content-area instruction with visual material—pictures, diagrams, stickmen, and drawings.

6. Provide manipulative materials whenever possible to make mathematics and science lessons meaningful.

7. Offer film and filmstrips with the sound track turned off and tell the story or explain the lesson in simpler language and less complex terms.

8. Do not call on the LEP student for a lengthy response. Elicit one-word or gestural answers when appropriate.

9. Avoid correcting errors of pronunciation, structure, or vocabulary. Accept the student's effort, or if necessary, state the response correctly without comment.

10. Do not expect mastery of the language or the accuracy of a native-English speaker. Enjoy the flavor of the non-native speech, especially when such usage does not interfere with comprehension.

11. Assign a dependable classmate to assist whenever additional directions are needed to follow through on assignments or seatwork.

12. Allow periods of silence for taking in the new melody, rhythm, and rhyme of English.

13. Provide a climate of warmth and caring which nurtures a sense of comfort and ease for students who are coping with the demands of a new language.

Above all, enjoy the wonder and delight of language — *everyone's!*

Developed by Dr. Eleanor W. Thonis, Wheatland, California.

It's *your* turn
to be tested

Test what you know about testing
with this little quiz developed by Riverside Publishing Company.
Some of the questions have more than one correct answer.

1. An achievement test:
   a. measures intelligence
   b. is designed to measure small increments of learning
   c. determines a child's development level and indicates strengths and weaknesses
   d. aids a teacher's diagnostic judgment, but can never replace it

2. General intelligence:
   a. is precisely measurable
   b. is not limited to cognitive abilities, but also includes social perceptiveness, creativity, and musical and mechanical ability, among other factors
   c. as measured on cognitive ability or academic aptitude tests, involves using previously learned skills to solve new problems or situations
   d. all of the above

3. T or F: Measures of academic aptitude predict how well a child is prepared for schoolwork.

4. A test is _____ when it actually measures what the user wants to measure, and _____ when students score the same on different versions of the same test.

5. T or F: A criterion-referenced test compares a student's performance on certain skill objectives with some performance standard.

6. T or F: A norm-referenced test compares a student's performance on certain skill objectives with that of other children at his or her grade level.

7. T or F: Criterion-referenced reports are available for norm-referenced tests.

8. National norms:
   a. are based on national samples of several thousand students
   b. represent a cross-section of various ethnic and racial groups in the proportion they occur nationwide
   c. are developed to make some children look good and others look bad
   d. all of the above

9. Individual item analysis:
   a. includes a breakdown of skill-area objectives and the actual test questions sampling those objectives
   b. shows the number of questions in each skill area answered correctly by each child
   c. is the most helpful aspect of test results for individualizing instruction.
   d. all of the above

10. Test bias:
    a. is revealed when one subgroup of the population correctly answers a test question more often than other subgroups
    b. occurs for all students—minority and majority, boys and girls.
    c. is ignored by test developers
    d. can be reliably predicted by teachers who examine a test

_____ *Answers:* _____

1. c & d;   2. b & c;   3. T;   4. valid, reliable;   5. T;   6. T;   7. T;   8. a & b;   9. d;   10. b.

From: *Riverside Review.* Published by The Riverside Publishing Company, 8420 Bryn Mawr Ave., Chicago, Illinois 60631-3476.

Characteristics of the
Visual Learner

He/She:

—may seem to ignore verbal directions.

—asks for questions or instructions to be repeated, frequently in different words.

—may frequently have a "blank" expression on his/her face, or may seem to daydream during classes which are primarily verbal.

—may substitute gestures for words, or may seem, by his/her gestures, to be literally groping for a word.

—may have poor speech, in terms of either low vocabulary, poor flexibility of vocal patterns, or articulation.

—often looks to see what everyone else is doing before following instructions.

—may say "What?" or "Huh?" often.

—seems to misunderstand often.

—often speaks too loudly, though he/she may dislike speaking before the group or listening to others.

—may do poorly in phonics-based activities.

—often can't remember information given verbally.

—may have trouble associating sounds and objects.

—seems to know few words' synonyms commonly known to children at his/her age or ability level.

—may do better work when assignment is demonstrated, rather than explained verbally.

—may be unable to explain in words many complex tasks he/she is able to do, such as repairing a bicycle, taking apart a clock, etc.

—often answers with a simple yes or no, rarely using complex sentences.

Characteristics of the
Auditory Learner

He/She:

—has limited attention to visual tasks.

—may have poor handwriting.

—has problems copying from the board.

—may have reversals or inversions in writing, or may leave out whole words or parts of words.

—may rub his/her eyes or show other signs of eye problems, or complain that his/her eyes hurt.

—may do poorly on written spelling work, but may perform better in spelling bees.

—may not remember much of what he/she has read and does better on material discussed in class.

—may read below grade level, or below the level expected for his/her general ability.

—may show consistent patterns: in math errors, when carefully analyzed, in attention to signs, confusion of similar numerals, and so forth.

—may not seem to observe things other children comment on: new bulletin board displays, a broken window, or Teacher's new sweater.

—may do poorly on map activities.

—may be poor at visual word attack so that he/she confuses words that look similar, such as <u>bill</u>, <u>bell</u>, <u>ball</u>, and <u>bull</u>.

—may do poorly on matching activities, especially where a series of lines must be drawn from one column to another.

—probably dislikes "ditto" activities, but given the chance, will sort through a stack of dittos for the clearest copy.

—often skips words or even whole lines in reading, and uses a finger as a guide whenever possible.

—may enjoy memory work.

—may be a "mumbler," muttering or whispering during silent reading or other quiet seatwork; may also whistle or hum without being aware of it, rather than doodling on scratch paper.

—may have trouble identifying "how many?" without counting.

—organizes papers poorly: often writes the answer in the wrong blank on workbook pages, or can't find where the answers go.

—may seem lost on material requiring a separate answer sheet.

—spells a word the way it sounds: <u>meen</u> for <u>mean</u>, and so forth.

Distributed by the San Jose Unified School District, San Jose, California.

Sponge Activities

1. Word Search   Prepare a grid with lines at the top (see sample below). Copy and hand out to students. Each child writes vocabulary words on the lines at the top of the grid, then writes as many words as he or she can on the grid, in any direction—up, down, across, diagonally, or backwards. (Any leftover words are crossed off the list.) The blank spaces are filled with random letters. The student gives the grid to a classmate who tries to find and circle words in the grid that match those on the lines at the top.

<u>   vertical   </u>

2. Puzzles   Develop crossword puzzles using vocabulary words and definitions.

3. Simple Math Activity   This activity is intended to help students practice addition or multiplication. Prepare a grid (see sample at right). Mark a plus or multiplication sign in the lefthand corner. The student circles the operations sign, then writes in each blank space the sum or product of the numbers on the top line, plus or times the number in the lefthand corner.

4. Find the Facts   The purpose of this activity is to practice addition, subtraction, multiplication, and division. Prepare a grid using the numbers in the sample at right. Copy and hand out to students. They find basic math facts hidden in the grid and circle, then insert the sign of operation and equal signs where appropriate (see sample at right). Operations appear horizontally, vertically, and diagonally.

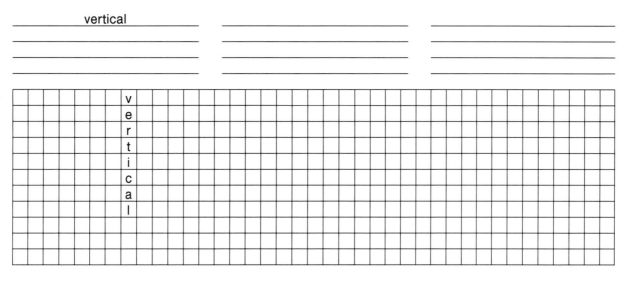

CHAPTER 5

Teaching certain subjects

Just as you adapt instructional strategies to specific students and situations, it's important to adapt them to specific subject matters.

This chapter focuses on instructional strategies unique to certain subjects—specifically, reading, writing, math, and science. It examines research findings, discusses the implications of that research, and offers classroom-tested ideas and activities for these subjects.

The exclusive emphasis here on *the basics* does not mean that other subjects aren't important. Rather, these are the subjects most thoroughly researched. These areas can definitely claim unique strategies leading to improved teaching and learning.

What's presented by no means exhausts the instructional possibilities. In fact, it barely scratches the surface. Each section includes suggestions for further reading. Also, look to the research centers and educational laboratories mentioned in Chapter 8 for information on content-specific instructional strategies.

But maybe you're worried about too much information—too many instructional strategies and ideas to implement. After all, there's a lot we now know about effective teaching in various subject matters. It's too much for a beginner—or any teacher—to absorb all at once. So don't even try. Take veteran Barb Diamond's advice and focus on one area at a time. "Establish goals and work to accomplish these goals systematically and not all at once. For example, if you're working to improve your math instruction, let other areas 'suffice' until you accomplish your aims."

Integrating Subject Matters

One second-grade teacher puts away the basal readers and devises a reading unit on folk tales. Why not give students a taste of American folklore as they practice their reading skills, she reasons.

Fifth graders listen to classical music while copying sentences. They are learning to appreciate music and practicing their penmanship at the same time.

Middle school students investigate the mathematical relationship of musical notes in a science unit on sound. Later they'll build their own simple instruments to study sound and vibrations.

Combining different subjects into multi-purpose lessons is not a new idea. But there is renewed interest in this instructional strategy as research demonstrates its tremendous benefits.

Integration pays off

There are many good reasons to integrate subject matters into multi-purpose lessons:
• Through integrated lessons, students learn the interrelatedness and interdependence of knowledge. Math skills help them solve science problems. Reading and listening skills keep them informed of current events.
• Subject matter integration saves time. Multi-purpose lessons allow teachers to cover two or more subjects in less time than it would take to teach them separately. That means kids will learn more topics their teachers might otherwise not have had time to teach.

The time factor is important for two reasons. By saving time, teachers and students can cover more subjects and topics. Integration allows students more time to practice skills. (They can focus on skills in reading, interpreting, and writing, using a historical account, for example.)

Multi-purpose lessons make instruction more meaningful. For example, students learn that writing serves a real purpose and can produce real results when, during their science class, they write letters expressing their views on a local environmental issue. And who wouldn't rather read an exciting, true-life account of American pioneers than a *Dick and Jane* story in a basal reader?

• Subject integration increases learning and achievement. More time spent on more subjects, more meaningful instruction, more awareness of how different types of knowledge and skills are related—it all adds up to more learning for students. That's a documented fact.

What to integrate

While virtually any combination of subjects is possible, most integrated lessons—including the examples in this chapter—involve the language arts.

"The language arts are tools, explains researcher Laura Roehler. "Tools are always applied to something. Teachers must choose which subjects or topics students will write, read, listen, or speak about."

Roehler and her colleagues studied language arts instruction in elementary classrooms. They found wide variations across classrooms in the time kids spend not only learning language arts skills, but also putting them to use.

You guessed it. The teachers who integrated language arts with other subjects were the ones who gave students more language arts instruction and practice opportunities.

In reading instruction, you can get more mileage if you use basal selections that expose students to different types of content. Stories based on historical events or articles about science are just two examples of specific basal content.

Reading texts vary widely on the amount of content covered. Analysis of basals at the Institute for Research on Teaching revealed that up to 50 percent of the selections are "content-neutral" in some readers. This means the selection either does not present new information, or does not develop new information fully enough to be meaningful.

That's a lot of wasted opportunity to learn!

You probably won't get to choose the basal readers your students must use. But you can choose when and how to use the reader. Where a text is content-deficient, substitute other reading materials such as newspapers, magazines, posters, or cookbooks. Team up with a colleague to identify your basal's strengths and weaknesses and think of alternatives.

Also, recognize that basals vary not only in the *amount* of content but also in *type* of content. The IRT researchers found three types:
1. specific subject matter
2. "how-to" selections that teach skills such as problem solving, reasoning, and persistence
3. selections that feature characters modeling virtues such as humility, patience, courage, kindness, honesty, or hope.

All three types are useful for creating multi-purpose lessons.

Social studies is another subject ripe with possibilities—especially in the area of multicultural studies. Cultural content can be the organizing theme for many different academic activities. (See the example of a Chinese unit on p. 164.) Multicultural units form multipurpose lessons in many ways. Aside from subject matter integration, multicultural units teach children to accept and value differences among people.

Science, too, lends itself well to multi-purpose lessons. Science and social studies, for example, are a natural combination. These subjects overlap in many topics, including energy, food production, population and other environmental problems, weather and climate, natural resources, and national defense.

Science and math team up nicely, too. To a large extent, mathematics is the language of science. As Thomas Koballa and Lowell Bethel explain in *Research Within Reach: Science Education*, "Mathematics is a discipline based on abstractions. Integrating science and mathematics experience is commonly recognized as a means of helping students learn abstractions by relating abstractions to meaningful experiences."

What about subject combinations that aren't obvious? Like science and music, for example? Sure, say Koballa and Bethel, or science and art. The authors describe programs in which students study vibrating systems to learn the tionship between science and music. They observe the physical and musical vibrating

systems of simple instruments they make from straws, rubber bands, string, or soda bottles.

In integrated science and art lessons, kids might focus on techniques common to both areas—concentration and careful observation. They learn to appreciate the beauty in science and the natural world, and are exposed to the art of biological illustration.

This chapter's section on science instruction includes more examples of integrated science lessons.

Planning integrated lessons

An integrated unit is easier to plan and visualize with a useful technique called webbing. Webbing is a graphic illustration of how a single topic (whales, for example) becomes the focus for spinoff lessons in various subjects. Here's what it might look like in a plan book. (See illustration below.)

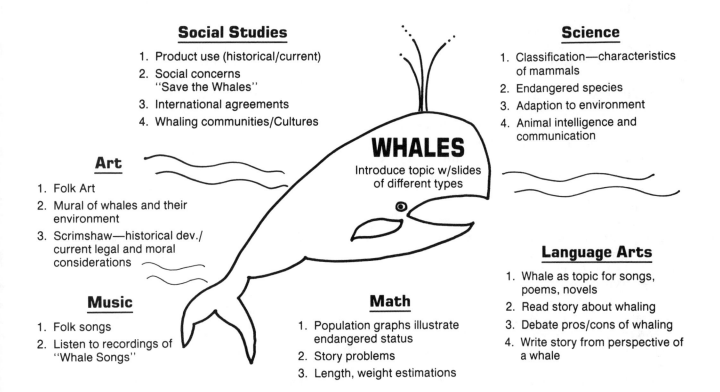

Social Studies
1. Product use (historical/current)
2. Social concerns "Save the Whales"
3. International agreements
4. Whaling communities/Cultures

Science
1. Classification—characteristics of mammals
2. Endangered species
3. Adaption to environment
4. Animal intelligence and communication

Art
1. Folk Art
2. Mural of whales and their environment
3. Scrimshaw—historical dev./ current legal and moral considerations

Music
1. Folk songs
2. Listen to recordings of "Whale Songs"

WHALES
Introduce topic w/slides of different types

Math
1. Population graphs illustrate endangered status
2. Story problems
3. Length, weight estimations

Language Arts
1. Whale as topic for songs, poems, novels
2. Read story about whaling
3. Debate pros/cons of whaling
4. Write story from perspective of a whale

Cultural unit

Here is a cultural unit on China for fifth or sixth grade (adapted from *Children's World View: The Basis for Learning Activities*, F. N. Lewis and Jane Margold, Far West Laboratory, 1981, as described in Far West's *Resources and Practice*, vol. 5, no. 1, Feb. 1987).

- geometry/history/social studies: Help students design and build models of Chinese-style homes. Then teach about the traditions concerning home and family life and the importance of aligning homes on the family property.
- health/phys. ed./philosophy/music/dance: Teach children some Tai Chi exercises and discuss their philosophical and physical purpose.
- chemistry/physiology: Study Chinese herbal remedies and acupuncture.
- reading/history/art/language arts: Have students read Chinese literature, history, and/or poetry; then design facial masks, scrolls, and costumes for a Chinese play.

Try making separate webs for resources, activities, and skills covered. Create webs or brainstorm with a colleague. You might even try making it a classroom activity; let students participate in the planning process and give them a choice about what they'll study next.

More examples

Following are examples of how to integrate subject matters into academic activities. Implement these ideas directly, or use them as guidelines for developing your own integrated lessons. Work with a colleague to plan multipurpose lessons. Besides the cultural unit described above, here are ideas to extend integrated lessons. Be creative!

1. For a thoroughly integrated middle-grade social studies unit on the pioneer movement westward, see the reproducibles on pp. 209-213.

2. Have students combine listening skills with reading comprehension in this simple activity offered by Nicholas Criscuolo: After your class has read a story, summarize it for them orally—but occasionally throw in some inaccurate statements. Ask the students to listen carefully and clap their hands every time they hear an incorrect statement. Then ask them to correct the false statements.

3. Combine history and language arts by using historical details to teach children how to expand their written sentences. On a sheet of paper, list simple sentences about historical figures in one column and descriptive phrases about places or events in another. As they match a sentence in the first column with a phrase from the second, they must combine the two. For example, the sentence, "Abraham Lincoln issued the Emancipation Proclamation" could be matched with "Freed the Slaves" and combined as, "Abraham Lincoln issued the Emancipation Proclamation, which freed the slaves."

4. Combine health and writing by having students write a descriptive paragraph about a food item from one of the four major food groups. Gather pictures of foods from old magazines, and give one to each student (do not let the students see one another's pictures). Then ask the kids to write a description of their food without actually naming it. They should discuss its nutritional value and identify which food group it belongs to, as well as physically describing it. When everyone is finished, have each child read his or her paragraph aloud while the others try to guess the name of the food.

You will undoubtedly integrate subject matters even without intending to do so. But make the most of integrated instruction by consciously planning multipurpose lessons and establishing goals and objectives for each subject covered. Help students see how these subjects intertwine.

Reading Instruction

When we read, we try to understand the relationships of words and ideas within a passage and how the meaning of the passage relates to the world around us. Many educators feel that reading is the single most important educational activity in a child's life.

Reading enables us to think, interpret others' thoughts, and ultimately, express our own.

Your job is to help students develop these skills. This section will suggest how.

Be explicit

Actively teach the skills and strategies students need to be able to read. Direct instruction in reading is critical, say Gerald Duffy and Lonnie McIntyre of the Institute for Research on Teaching.

There is overwhelming evidence demonstrating the effectiveness of direct instruction—where teachers present and explain new material, guide students in practicing it, allow them to practice independently, and frequently review. (See Chapter 4 for a more detailed definition.) Yet

in a study of highly rated first- and second-grade teachers, Duffy and McIntyre found almost no direct instruction in their reading classes. Instead, recitation from basal readers was the predominant instructional activity. "Teachers asked students to recite answers to questions in their workbooks and to questions about the basal text stories as if students ought to already know how to read."

Duffy and McIntyre found that teachers assisted students only after students made a recitation error. Even then, the assistance was a prompt or a clue, with no explanation of the error. Much more effective, the educators say, is to directly assist students to minimize error and confusion in the first place.

How?

By being more explicit in your instruction and thoroughly explaining the skills and strategies students need to become good readers. You can't just tell students what to do; you must explain how to do it.

Based on their own research and classroom teaching, Duffy and colleague Laura Roehler suggest six ways to make reading instruction more explicit:

1. Focus on strategic mental processing needed to do a task (as opposed to procedures). Include explicit information about what is being taught and why it is important. For example:

    Teacher: "Today we are again studying comprehension. We're going to focus on learning to read clues in a paragraph and make a reasonable guess of what is going to happen next—what the author has in mind. This is called making inferences— trying to figure out what happens based on the information you have."

    This type of introduction is far more effective than simply announcing, "Today we're going to study syllables."

2. Make visible the invisible mental processes involved. For example, here's how you might explain the process of searching a passage for information and combining

Reading skills and conditions

These are the skills and conditions necessary for reading, according to reading specialists:

- an adequate sight vocabulary (the ability to recognize words immediately)

- good decoding skills (the ability to figure out words one does not recognize immediately)

- fluent text segmentation (the ability to simultaneously integrate written words, syntax, and semantics into meaningful phrases)

- retentive comprehension (the ability to remember what one reads and draw inferences from it)

various pieces of information to answer a question:

"The first question in the book is: 'What are some of the supplies the early pioneers brought with them?' Look in your book on pages 47, 48, and 49. Do you see on each page there is a description of some type of provisions? By putting all of this information together, we can answer the question. The answer is (give the complete answer). We had to search the text, locate information in different spots, and put it all together to answer the question."

Direct explanation, modeling, and guided practice help you teach reading skills and comprehension.

3. Focus more on the thinking required to get a correct answer than on the answer itself. You might respond to a student's correct answer, for example, by asking how he or she got the answer.

4. Be flexible and responsive to students' needs. If they seem confused, offer another explanation or example. Here's an explicit, true-life example Duffy recorded during research:

Teacher: Connector words are what, David?
Student: Two words put together.
Teacher: What are connector words, Josh?
Student: Two words hooked together.
Teacher: They are not two words. Maybe I explained that incorrectly. A connector word is a word that connects one or more ideas. Okay, in this sentence, "They always walk to school together and always walk home together." Now in this sentence there are two ideas: they always walk to school; and they always come home. Of the four connector words I put on the board, which word is connecting the two ideas, David?
Student: And.
Teacher: And. Do you see that? And. I have it underlined here. See how it is connecting the ideas of walking to school together and coming home together? It is sort of like a

bridge that connects these two. Bridges connect different places, words connect ideas. Connector words connect ideas.

5. Make instruction cohesive and continuous across lessons. Plan lessons that follow each other in logical sequence and build upon the theme of how students make sense of what they read.

6. Specifically explain how, why, and when students should use the strategies taught. Duffy offers this example of how one teacher taught students to use the 'ou' vowel combination to sound out unknown words:

Teacher: "Okay, let me tell you how I would do this if I were reading alone. Let's suppose I was reading along and I came to the word "out" and I have never seen the word before, which is really possible. I see an "ou" and I know "ou" has the sound of "ow," like Gracie said. It sounds like a "w" is in there—*ow*—and I know it has a "t" at the end and the "t" sounds like t-t-t. So, I have "ow-t"—out."

Teachers who explain more, talk more, says Duffy. And that scares people. He points out we've been led to believe that teacher talk is a sign of poor teaching. So teachers shy away from explaining things and focus instead on asking questions, which students answer in ordered turns. Students are left to figure out the reading process on their own from the questions and answers they hear.

Teachers who want all their students to read must directly explain the reading process.

But many can't do that. Teachers who want all their students to read must directly explain the reading process, Duffy insists.

"[Explanation] is essential if all pupils are to view reading as a sense-making rather than mechanical process," he concludes.

What's the evidence that explicit teaching

helps kids become better readers?

Duffy and Roehler found that the students whose teachers used explicit instruction were more involved in their reading lessons, more conscious of specific reading skills and strategies, and could make better sense of what they'd read. They were well on their way to becoming proficient readers.

Vocabulary instruction

Children can't understand what they read if they don't know what the words mean. And that, says Wisconsin researcher Dale Johnson, is why vocabulary instruction is so important.

Yet during a survey of primary grade teachers, Johnson found that only 14 percent spend more than 45 minutes per week teaching vocabulary, and more than half teach vocabulary only during reading class, never as a separate subject.

Johnson also found that most teachers rely on workbook exercises and word attack skills to teach new words.

But there's a better way, he concludes, offering these recommendations:
• Increase vocabulary instruction by spending up to 20 minutes daily on direct instruction outside reading class.
• Relate new words to children's prior knowledge and experience—help them connect new words with something they already know.

Children who can't recognize words quickly have trouble understanding what they read, says Johnson. He explains that our brains can only process a certain amount of information at a time. If we're too busy identifying words, there's less opportunity for understanding the ideas expressed by the words.

It may be better to teach 100 new words well than to present 400 superficially, says Isabel Beck of the Learning Research and Development Center in Pittsburgh. She explains that children need repeated exposure to a word before they "own" it, or know how to use it properly. The words that are likely to cause comprehension problems for children

Reading Comprehension

Jean Sealey, in an Appalachia Educational Laboratory bulletin *Reading* (Motivation—Teaching Comprehension), recommends these strategies to balance decoding and comprehension instruction in the early grades:

• Make decoding instruction meaningful by using real words. Intersperse practice on real words with practice on decoding syllables.

• Have students demonstrate their understanding of the materials they decode. Ask them questions about what they read. Give them written directions to follow. Let them act out stories.

• Give students ample opportunity to apply their decoding skills to meaningful and enjoyable materials—books, magazines, comic books.

• Make sure students learn to identify and use new words in context.

• Explain that the primary purpose of reading is to understand what you've read. Explain and demonstrate that decoding and learning to recognize words rapidly will help them comprehend—and enjoy—what they read.

are those not frequently heard in everyday conversation. Make sure the words your students must learn are reinforced and used repeatedly throughout the day. (For example, have students raise their hands every time they hear a new vocabulary word.)

Teaching comprehension

Reading comprehension—understanding the ideas and information contained in printed passages—is a major goal of reading instruction. Reading theorists identify three levels of comprehension:

• literal (factual recall),
• interpretive (drawing conclusions, inferring emotions or motives, etc.)
• evaluative (recognizing author's viewpoint, style, purpose, tone, main idea, themes, plot, and so on).

The first step toward reading comprehension is developing accurate and automatic decoding skills. Students must know what a word is before they can read it to understand a sentence or passage. But while decoding is a primary objective of early reading instruction, it should not overshadow comprehension.

During reading instruction, focus students' attention on comprehension by asking them to predict ahead of time what a story or selection is about. Prompt them to use clues such as titles or subtitles, pictures, or what they may already know about a topic, but demonstrate how unreliable these predictions can sometimes be with the reproducible *ReQuest Procedure,* on p. 190.

Researcher Isabel Beck has identified five factors affecting children's reading comprehension:
• decoding accuracy and fluency
• increased word knowledge
• experience with various linguistic structures
• knowledge of the world
• experience in thinking about texts.

Think about the "knowledge of the world" factor for a moment. Beck gives the example of a story about going on vacation, which includes information about folding clothes or carrying bags. If a reader is unfamiliar with vacations or doesn't already know that packing suitcases is a part of preparing for a vacation, he or she may misunderstand or misinterpret the story's reference to clothes and bags.

Beck urges teachers to account for these factors affecting comprehension.

Reading specialist Nicholas Criscuolo says that when children can "really read" a story—when they can detect the author's purpose, recognize bias and propaganda, sense a character's emotional reactions, draw inferences, and form generalizations—they become discriminating readers. And "only discriminating readers enjoy all that a passage was intended for."

Criscuolo offers 45 classroom-tested activities on pp. 192-195 for improving kids' reading comprehension—activities to "help them get the message."

Writing Instruction

"Writing in everyday school life may be invisible in the sense that talk is invisible in everyday life—it is such a part of day-to-day transaction that it is taken for granted." So conclude researchers Christopher Clark and Susan Florio-Ruane of the Institute for Research on Teaching after their extensive studies of writing in the classroom.

An Activity

Teacher June Page encourages her students to make predictions.

Have each student pick one book from the school library (make sure their selections are the appropriate grade and reading level). Back in the classroom, ask them to leaf through their books without actually reading them, paying special attention to the cover and any illustrations. Then ask them to write brief paragraphs describing what they think their books are about. Collect the paragraphs and save them. Give the kids a week or two to read their books, and when they're finished, ask them to write a paragraph describing what the book was actually about. Let them compare their before-and-after descriptions. They'll probably find that their first impressions weren't very accurate. And it's also a good way to make the point that you can't judge a book by its cover.

Tests, worksheets, essays, notes, letters—they're just a few examples of the many occasions for writing in school. But these occasions are often not even counted as writing or writing instruction by teachers, children, or parents, the researchers report.

"Yet it is precisely this everyday use of language that is at the heart of the process of becoming a competent communicator."

To take advantage of these everyday occasions, Clark and Florio-Ruane suggest you draw students' attention to the purpose and other important aspects of the writing they do in completing other academic tasks.

We write to communicate our thoughts and ideas. As teachers, we can't assume children understand that—because often, they don't.

Educators and researchers agree that writing instruction should give students many opportunities to communicate their own ideas. Teach writing as a student-centered, skill-based, active process, the experts recommend.

The research says . . .

Here's what research shows about teaching writing skills and encouraging communicative ability.

• Writers need an audience. Primary-grade writers especially seem to profit from live, visible audiences, and it's important that students understand exactly who that audience is.

• Young writers need models—models of both process and product. When students see you

writing, you've conveyed the message that writing is a valuable, worthwhile activity. And you can help students visualize a finished product by showing them samples of your own work or work of students from previous years.

• Writers need a purpose. A writing activity must achieve some purpose beyond that of fulfilling an assignment or pleasing the teacher. Letters to invite or thank classroom speakers, safety posters developed for younger children, stories to entertain peers—these are examples of writing with a purpose.

At a more basic level, you need to make students understand that we write to express our thoughts, emotions, and ideas. Students certainly need the mechanics of writing— grammar, punctuation, sentence structure, spelling—but focus their attention on the communicative purpose of writing, advises educator Ursula Casanova. "By switching the focus," says Casanova, "writing can change from a tiresome, mechanical activity to a thinking, problem-solving process that requires kids to shift attention outward to the reader and inward to their own responsibility."

• *Writing assignments should address students' needs and concerns.* "Real" assignments demonstrate that writing is a useful tool, says Casanova. For example, "Sixth graders usually have complaints to write about—a TV toy that didn't live up to expectations or the lack of a neighborhood baseball field. They may want to persuade the principal to permit a school wide rock concert, or convince parents they need bigger allowances."

• *Teachers must actively teach writing skills.* "[There is] a popular educational belief, sometimes correct, that kids who read good literature will learn good writing," says researcher David Berliner. "This 'pick-up' or 'osmosis' theory of learning works well for some students, but not all."

It's much more effective, says Berliner, to explain and model writing skills, and guide students in practicing them. He describes the work of researchers Jill Fitzgerald and Lynda Markham, who found that students learned to write better when they were taught explicit revision skills—additions to text, deletions, substitutions, and rearrangements. The training occurred during four 3-day cycles (one for each skill) of 45-minute lessons and proceeded like this:

On the first day, the teacher taught the revision skill, using charts to model the strategy; talking aloud while demonstrating it; and guiding students through a revision of actual text. After a review on the second day, students worked in pairs to revise some actual text, then write a brief story. They worked individually on the third day to revise another teacher-supplied text, then revise the stories they wrote the day before.

Students who received the direct instruction, when compared with those who had not, made 42 percent more revisions overall. And they scored 79 percent higher on suggesting needed revisions—on seeing discrepancies between what they intended and what they had actually written.

• *Young writers need help with the concept of rough draft.* Clark and Florio-Ruane found that young writers distinguish between their first and final drafts largely on the basis of neatness and correctness. Like those in the study of revision skills, students need to learn that revision is a problem-solving process where one detects discrepancies between what's intended and what's written, decides what to change, and fixes the problems identified.

• *Grammar instruction is most effective when taught as part of writing instruction.* The research evidence indicates that "the memorize-the-rules approach" to grammar instruction does not lead to improved writing. This approach, says author Jean Sealey, can only damage the writer's attitude toward writing and take time away from the real task—putting thoughts on paper. More effective, says Sealey, is to relate grammar to students' own writing and have students apply grammar instruction to their own work.

• *Computers are an important writing tool.* Word processing programs make it much easier to edit and revise written work. This may encourage some students to be more creative and daring.

• *Writing in school works better as a cooperative pursuit than a solitary one.* From brainstorming for writing ideas to editing each other's work to sharing the final product, two or more heads are better than one for learning to write.

• *Writing must be evaluated according to how successfully the writer achieves the purpose.* "We first need to specify what it is we want to know," says Sealey.

— Has the student learned the mechanics of the language—grammar, spelling, sentence structure, syntax, punctuation?

— Can a student take an idea, develop it and create a paragraph, essay, short story, or poem?

— Does a student understand that effective communication has a purpose and is directed to a specific audience?

— Are students able to apply rules and principles to their writing?

There are direct methods and indirect methods of assessing student writing, says Sealey.

Indirect methods, such as paper-and-pencil tests—evaluate students' knowledge of rules and facts, not actual writing ability. They show whether a student has learned grammar, vocabulary, mechanics, sentence structure, and syntax.

But such indirect methods do not offer feedback on the content or organization of the student's writing. "So students' writing does not improve," Sealey notes.

To evaluate actual writing ability, says Sealey, you must look at a student's writing sample. Here your assessment will be much more subjective.

To increase the reliability of teachers' ratings and allow them a means for rating a paper's overall merit, Sealey and colleagues have developed a Dichotomous Scale for

Evaluating Writing (see p. 189). The scale lists a variety of features—style and form, mechanics and technical—and teachers simply decide whether or not each feature appears in the writing sample.

But analyzing and evaluating each piece of writing a student produces will consume a lot of time. That's why you'll need to rely on informal as well as formal evaluations. Observing and conferring with students at each stage of the writing process, asking students to evaluate themselves and each other—these are ways you can informally diagnose students' progress.

• *Writers need constructive criticism.* The experts agree that offering constructive criticism is one of the most difficult aspects of teaching writing.

Author John Collins (his book, *The Effective Writing Teacher,* is described later in this chapter) offers these helpful comments. Instead of saying, "Avoid punctuation mistakes," say, "You have a problem with contractions. See the grammar book, pp. 101 and 102, and do the lesson. If you need an explanation, ask me or another student." Instead of, "Too many run-on sentences," say, "Watch for sentences longer than twenty words. I've indicated where you've made run-on sentence errors."

Peer editing

Peer editing is a technique whereby students read each other's papers, then edit them or offer helpful feedback. Peer editing benefits those who give as well as those who receive. Among the many advantages of this cooperative technique are:

• Writers receive feedback on early drafts—usually more than their teachers could provide.

• Peer editors provide a built-in audience for the writers.

• Using teacher- or student-developed guidelines, peer editors can relieve teachers of much of the work of correcting/commenting on papers.

• Editing teaches students the elements of good writing, which they can then use in their writing.

• Editors have the chance to study others' work.

And there are other benefits. Notes Sealey, "Students will benefit academically, socially, and personally if we increase the opportunities for student-student interactions in cooperative situations. One excellent way to do this is by creating peer editing groups."

Okay, you're convinced. But how can you make peer editing work in your classroom?

Sealey offers these tips:

• Group (or pair) the students. Mix together students of varying ability. And change groupings frequently to let students interact with a wider audience.

• Establish goals for peer editing and discuss them with students.

Sealey suggests the following as important goals:

1. To give each student feedback from other students. Students will then be able to revise their papers before turning them in to the teacher.

Teaching Writing Step by Step

Prewriting activities:

1. Provide opportunities for students to discuss and clarify writing assignments before they begin writing. (A writing assignment is any assignment that requires students to do more than one draft.)
2. Provide opportunities for students to get more information about a topic before they begin writing (brainstorming, reading, discussing, interviewing, etc.)
3. Give writing assignments based on the personal experiences of the student.

Drafting activities:

4. Provide specific information about the criteria you will use to evaluate each assignment.
5. Provide opportunities to write during class time.
6. Give writing assignments a minimum of a paragraph in length.
7. Provide students with specific suggestions for improvement.

Revision and proofreading activities:

8. Provide opportunities for students to review and revise written work completed earlier in the year.

9. Encourage students to edit each other's papers before they are submitted.
10. Teach grammar, usage, and mechanics in relationship to the students' current writing problems.
11. Teach editing skills (sentence-combining, eliminating unnecessary words and phrases, checking for variety of language, organization, etc.).
12. Teach proofreading skills (punctuation, editing, symbols, manuscript form).

Sharing activities:

13. Provide opportunities for students to read their written work out loud to individuals or to small groups of students.
14. Give writing assignments that are meant to be read by readers other than yourself.
15. Display or "publish" examples of high-quality work.
16. Write along with students during class time, on the same writing assignment that they are working on.
17. Write positive comments on students' work.
18. Conduct individual writing conferences with students.

Adapted from *The Effective Writing Teacher* by John Collins. Regional Laboratory for Educational Improvement of the Northeast and Islands. Andover, MA, 1985.

2. To give students editing and proofreading skills that will enable them to read their papers with a more critical eye.
3. To help students develop a greater sense of audience by reading and experiencing other students' papers.

• Develop a way for editors to give feedback to writers.

One way is to establish editing/evaluation criteria. The criteria will change from assignment to assignment, depending on the purpose of each. Suppose, for example, you are teaching children how to develop an idea within a paragraph. The evaluation criteria for related assignments will focus on expressing the main idea, logical progression of ideas, and use of detail to support the main idea. You can list the criteria on the chalkboard or give students checklists.

Another way is to focus on overall effect. Ask editors to respond to such open-ended questions as: *What is the main idea of this paper? How did the author support the main idea? How could this paper be improved?*

• Structure the activity. Research has shown that the most effective way to begin the editing process is to have partners exchange papers and read the papers aloud. It's not a quiet activity, but it allows students to listen for flaws and strengths that are more apparent to the ear than to the eye.

"Your classroom may be a little noisier as students exchange ideas at the pre-writing stage, read their papers aloud, and discuss their comments on other students' papers," says Sealey. "Your classroom may even look less organized as students gather in small groups or pairs. These disruptions are minor, however, when you consider the benefits: less work for you and improved writing skills for your students."

Putting It All Together

Writing is a process of prewriting, drafting, editing, and sharing, says author and former writing teacher John Collins. But too often, teachers ignore the process and focus only on

---

The Critical Six

Think about your approach to writing instruction. Which of these important steps do you tend to ignore? If you're like most teachers, you'll list one or more of the following steps. John Collins calls these the "critical six"—the strategies on which teachers most often rate themselves lowest. Ironically, they also happen to be the six preconditions to a good writing program.

• Provide opportunities for students to discuss and clarify writing assignments before they begin writing.

• Provide opportunities for students to get more information about a topic before they begin writing.

• Provide specific information about the criteria you will use to correct each assignment.

• Provide opportunities for students to review and revise written work completed earlier in the year.

• Encourage students to edit each other's papers before they are handed in.

• Provide opportunities for students to read written work out loud to individuals or to small groups of students.

---

the product. They assign a composition, correct it when completed, and call that writing instruction. Students don't learn how to write, they don't see improvement, and teachers are overwhelmed by reading and correcting all those papers.

There is a better way—a step-by-step approach that Collins has drawn from the best of research and practice. It is organized around 18 strategies. (See box, preceding page.)

There are several special features of this "process approach" to teaching writing.

One is "focus correcting." Teachers focus on correcting two or three writing skills at a time, allowing students to focus on these skills until they are mastered. The focus areas are announced in advance.

"Student writing improves more quickly when the student works to improve a few writing problems at a time," Collins explains. He adds that teachers shouldn't try to teach too many skills at once.

"The main problem of good writing teachers is the irrational yet powerful fear that, 'If I don't cover it, no one else will,'" says Collins. "Writing is not easy to teach, but many teachers make it even more difficult by assuming all the responsibility for producing a competent writer in one year. The attempt to develop too many competencies is almost as bad as doing too little, and the results are about the same—incompetent writers."

Another special feature is storing children's finished compositions at school, rather than sending them home. This gives students the chance to revise them later in the year and see how much their writing skills have improved.

For details on the 18 instructional strategies; specific examples of helpful teacher comments; a continuum of writing competencies grouped into five levels; a detailed monthly plan for producing two completed assignments and offering about five hours of instruction; a letter to parents explaining the program and soliciting their help; and much more, see *The Effective Writing Teacher* (1985), available from The Regional Laboratory for Educational Improvement of the Northeast and Islands.

Solving The Problem With Mathematics

"One of the most serious problems the typical elementary teacher faces today is the effective teaching of mathematics."

That's what mathematics professor Max Sobel believes. Veteran teachers agree. Teaching mathematics is a tough job—for any teacher. It's an area fraught with problems (no pun intended) and challenges. And the greatest challenge of all is teaching kids to be problem solvers.

"Problem solving is the most important skill students can take into the twenty-first century."

"Problem solving is not just another chapter in your math book," says elementary mathematics teacher and author Lola May. "It's the most important skill students can take into the twenty-first century."

Educators concur that problem solving should be the main focus of school mathematics. They recommend shifting emphasis from teaching computational skills to teaching students how to apply these skills in problem situations.

Yet most new elementary teachers come to the classroom with little, if any, training in teaching problem solving—or any other aspect of mathematics, for that matter. And textbooks aren't much help, either.

Further complicating the situation is the "back to basics" movement. Although math is considered a basic subject, mathematics instruction has actually been hindered by the movement. As Sobel explains:

Problem-solving Strategies

Children can approach a problem in a variety of ways. Teach them possibilities, such as

- Look for a pattern.
- Construct a table.
- Make an organized list.
- Guess and check.
- Draw a picture.
- Use objects or act it out.
- Work backwards.
- Write an equation.
- Simplify the problem.
- Change point of view.
- Brainstorm.

"The concern with 'back-to-basics' has succeeded in providing our elementary school students with an excess amount of emphasis on fundamental computational skills to the neglect of other important basic topics, such as problem solving."

Problem-solving Process

Teach children to think of problem solving as a four-stage process, suggests author Jean Sealey.

1. First, teach them to obtain a better understanding of the problem. Have them rephrase the problem in their own words, identify relevant information, determine if additional information is needed, and estimate a reasonable answer.

2. Teach them to devise an appropriate plan of attack. Have them: look for similarities between this problem and others they've solved; draw a picture or diagram; break the problem into parts; simplify the problem, if possible, and solve the simpler problem; organize the information; look for a pattern; and write a mathematical sentence (for example, a + b = __).

3. Teach them to carry out the plan efficiently, and show them how to ensure proper execution. Have them: record what they've done; solve the mathematical sequence; complete the diagram; and fill in the blanks.

4. Teach them to check their work. Have them: check answers, if possible; make sure answers are in appropriate form or units (for example, feet instead of inches, if that's what the question asked for); determine if all the information given in the problem has been used (if not, why?); determine if this is the only possible answer to the question; and use the solution to solve a similar problem.

What are the "basic skills" in mathematics? Here's the list Sobel offers. (Note that computation is only one of the ten.)
- problem solving
- applying mathematics to everyday situations
- alertness to the reasonableness of results
- estimation and approximation
- appropriate computational skills
- geometry
- measurement
- reading, interpreting, and constructing tables, charts, and graphs
- using mathematics to predict
- computer literacy

Problem solving

As mathematics educators Andrea Lash and Gary Tsuruda explain, mathematics is the study of patterns. We use numbers to quantify and examine the relationships involved in patterns. Problem-solving instruction helps students see structure throughout mathematics by drawing from all areas of the curriculum—numbers and operations, geometry, measurement, probability and statistics, functions, and logical thinking.

What is problem solving?

Problem solving is the ability to think, analyze situations, and apply appropriate skills to arrive at a solution. It is the ability to develop, execute, and evaluate a plan of action. When we solve problems, we apply previously learned skills and concepts to new situations.

Problem solving is a process. The methods used to arrive at a solution—the thinking and analysis preceding it—are more important than the solution itself, because frequently there is more than one "right" answer.

Most important for teachers, problem-solving skills can be learned—skills you can help students develop. When you teach kids to solve problems, you teach them to become better thinkers. The problem-solving skills they learn in one class transfer to all areas and facets of their lives.

Teaching problem solving

You can help your students become good thinkers by teaching them thinking strategies and problem-solving skills.

Basically, teachers play four separate roles in teaching kids how to solve problems, according to Sealey. As children progress from novices to experienced problem solvers, the roles change.

• First, you must model successful problem solving for inexperienced students. Read a problem aloud, then tell students what information is relevant and what is extraneous. Reread the problem with only the relevant information. Think aloud as you consider several approaches to solving it. Explain why you selected a certain one. Try to solve the problem, still thinking aloud. Check your work. Ask yourself aloud if your solution answers the question.

Don't correct their mistakes immediately. Instead, ask probing questions.

See the reproducible on pp. 197-198 for ideas on how to present and model problem-solving skills and strategies.

You can also have students model problem solving for each other by assigning problems to pairs or small groups of students and asking them to think aloud as they decide what approach to take.

• After students understand various problem-solving strategies, your role is to help by suggesting which strategies they might try with certain problems. One idea is to provide a checklist of possible approaches. Make sure they actually know how to use the strategies. For example, diagraming might be a great strategy, but not if students don't know how to draw a diagram. Teach them.

• As students gain confidence, your role changes to where you primarily provide problems. You give students opportunities to practice solving a variety of problems. (For tips, see the section which follows on "good problems.")

• Experienced problem solvers need teachers to facilitate and help sustain interest in problem-solving activities. For example, don't correct their mistakes immediately. Instead, ask probing questions such as: "Why did you do it this way? Is this like another problem that might work here? What would happen if you tried another approach?"

Keep three important points in mind as you teach problem solving, advises Lola May:

"Problem-solving activities should start as early as the first grade. This stretching of minds needs to begin that early. Second, convince your students that problem solving is not a clear-cut procedure and solutions are not found instantly. And third, practice . . . practice . . . practice! That is the one sure road to success."

From the very beginning, stress that process is more important than product. That is, make sure students focus on how they solve the problem, rather than the actual solution itself. And teach them that many problems have more than one solution, and more than one way of being solved. This is difficult for students who have been primed to "get the right answer as quickly as possible" since they entered school—or even before. But there are certain characteristics of good problem-solving instruction that will help them learn these important lessons. Among them:

• Students participate daily in problem solving. Tsuruda and Lash recommend that even if you present only one new problem a week, allocate some time during each lesson to discuss the problem.

• There is an atmosphere of success. Work hard to establish a positive climate where students feel safe—safe to take risks, volunteer information and ideas, try alternate methods, and accept that answers aren't always clear-cut.

• Students work together. The research shows that listening to other students discuss problems is one of the best ways for children to learn problem-solving skills. Allow students opportunities to work with their peers in all phases of problem solving—from identifying the pertinent questions to developing a plan of attack, initiating the plan and rechecking the final solution.

• Teachers evaluate all phases of student work, not just their answers. Lash and Tsuruda suggest you develop a point system based on students' understanding of the problem and how they set it up to be solved.

Good problems

Author Jean Sealey says a problem consists of an unrealized goal, an obstacle, and the use of reasoning to overcome the obstacle and reach the goal. This definition implies two important conditions: First, a student must be interested in solving the problem, and second, the solution must not be immediately apparent.

Textbook word problems typically fall short on both accounts, Sealey points out. They're not inherently interesting to students. And they usually don't involve problem solving. For example, word problems requiring multiplication typically appear at the end of the multiplication unit. Also, key words give away the operation required. A problem asking, "How many left?" clues students to subtract, for example.

Good problems go beyond the traditional story problems that have always appeared in math programs. Teachers must design problems in which students need to experiment, search for additional information, discover patterns, make judicious estimates, and more, says Max Sobel.

He offers this example: "Each resident of our state is required to stand on an equal area of the border. If the distance around the state is divided evenly, how much territory will each person have to cover?"

To solve the problem, says Sobel, students will have to find population figures for the state, plus an estimate of the distance around the state's border. (One way would be to use an atlas' scale of miles, but let students figure that out.) Then they must calculate the number of inches, feet, or meters per individual standing on the border.

This problem allows students to focus on something they know about—their state. The answer certainly is not apparent, nor is the process required for solving it.

One of your main roles in problem-solving instruction is to provide students with good problems, says Jean Sealey. To do so, you can:

• Modify textbook word problems to make them real problems and not just exercises. Add extraneous information. Delete information. Offer information without a question and let students come up with the problems. Extend the problem. These simple strategies will allow students to practice important problem-solving skills.

• Search your local newspaper. The sports, weather, and business sections all contain information for creating real-life problems. Have students use advertisements to make comparisons and determine best values.

• Ask students to develop problems from real-life situations—installing new carpet, building a doghouse, choosing car insurance, determining the probability that the football team will win the week's game, and so on. The problems students develop are not only good sources for the rest of the class, they demonstrate that problem solving has a practical place in their lives.

• Look in magazines and professional journals. *The Mathematics Teacher* and *School Science and Mathematics* have regular sections on problems. *Arithmetic Teacher, Instructor,* and *Games* are other possibilities.

One of the best sources of good problems is another teacher. Ask your experienced colleagues to share the problems they've developed or collected over the years. (And offer, of course, to share those you find.)

Veterans Lola May and Barbara Bethel can get you started with the problems they offer. See "Problem solving," pp. 197-198.

Technological problems

Technology in the form of computers and calculators is an important tool for helping us solve problems. Yet few of us take advantage of the technology. We worry that technology causes more problems than it solves—that kids won't learn longhand computations if they rely too much on calculators and computers.

But the main problem with technology is that it's underused, say the experts. Mathematicians, educators and researchers unite in their call for calculators and computers at all levels of mathematics instruction. Why? To free students from tedious calculations so they can concentrate on problem-solving activities and higher forms of mathematics.

Research demonstrates technology's promise. Studies show that computers can diagnose students' misconceptions and learning difficulties, help teach them how to think, allow them to concentrate on concepts, simulate difficult math experiments and dangerous science experiments, guide them through problem solving, supplement teacher instruction, and more.

And consider the merits of the hand-held calculator. This relatively inexpensive tool is readily available to most children. Teachers who use calculators cover more topics and

deal more with concepts than other teachers, the research shows. And calculators keep kids motivated and engaged in their work.

Lash and Tsuruda point out that calculators allow students to solve problems that otherwise would have been impossible, and facilitate problem-solving strategies such as guess-and-check, which are effective with complex problems.

"Calculators should be used for imaginative explorations and discovery in elementary mathematics," says Max Sobel. He offers these examples:

1. Write a three-digit number and then repeat the three digits, such as 375, 375. Now use a calculator to divide this number successively by 7, 11, and 13. What is the result? (375) Can you explain why? (If you multiply 7 times 11 times 13 you get 1001. If you multiply 1001 times any three-digit number you will get the three-digit number repeated, as in 375, 375. When you divide the six-digit number by 7, 11, and 13, you are reversing the process.)

2. Interesting number patterns can be found using a calculator. Find these products:

$$25 \times 25 \ (625)$$
$$35 \times 35 \ (1225)$$
$$45 \times 45 \ (2025)$$
$$55 \times 55 \ (3025)$$

Do you see a pattern? (Hint: compare the increase in these products.) Use the pattern to find these products (then check with the calculator):

$$65 \times 65 \ (4225)$$
$$75 \times 75 \ (5625)$$
$$85 \times 85 \ (7225)$$
$$95 \times 95 \ (9025)$$

Computers, which are becoming almost as accessible as calculators in many schools, also have tremendous potential for increasing student learning in mathematics.

The computer's ability to hold students' attention and engage them in complex problems has been documented by research. Reviewing computer software and studies of higher-order thinking and problem solving,

Janice Patterson and Marshall Smith concluded that computers offer great promise for promoting instruction of higher-order thinking skills.

According to Patterson and Smith, three types of software facilitate higher-order thinking:
- programs to develop knowledge and skill (drill and practice);
- problem-solving simulations (often complex "games");
- problem-solving aids (for example, word processing, information retrieval, and so on.)

Some computer programs are specifically designed to teach problem-solving strategies, for example, fantasy simulations. These programs require little prior knowledge, and they offer increasingly deeper information and more complex problems as kids become more involved.

The researchers describe students with serious reading difficulties who spend extended periods working on adventure games presented in a narrative format. They suggest that the motivation, opportunity to control the environment, and the objectivity of the feedback are powerful teaching devices.

Computers have great capabilities! But there are also problems, not the least of which is software so abundant that teachers don't know which to use. The Northwest Regional Educational Laboratory has developed a software evaluation information system. To find out about it, write to NWREL. (The address is listed on page 298.)

Science Instruction

There's no doubt about it. Students need more—and better—science instruction. National Science Board experts estimate that fewer than 2 percent of students in this country receive a solid science education. In an age of science and technology, students can't afford to be scientifically illiterate. Yet most are.

National Science Board experts estimate that fewer than 2 percent of students receive a solid science education.

What's the problem?

Science, which is not a member of the "3 R's" club, fell victim to the "back-to-basics" movement. Federal funding for science education virtually dried up, and teachers were pressured to spend more time and attention on reading, writing and arithmetic. There was little time to teach science, and even less to prepare and plan for it.

But the thinking, reasoning, and problem-solving skills fostered by science education are "basic" to individual well-being and national survival, we've learned. And that means we must teach science in school—at all levels.

Good science instruction enables children to become good thinkers. In learning scientific process, they learn to look closely at the world around them—observe, take note, solve problems, discover, experiment, guess, keep careful records, make inferences, and draw conclusions. The goal of science instruction, the experts agree, is scientific literacy. (See box.)

Let them be scientists

What constitutes good science instruction? Ask that question of scientists, science educators, and researchers and they say the same thing: The best teaching method for elementary students is a hands-on approach, through which students learn to think like scientists by acting like scientists.

Teach science every day in an active, intensive way, advises Mary Kohlerman of the National Science Foundation. "Hands-on science is the stepping-stone for getting kids to learn how things work—and don't work," says Kohlerman. "It is the critical link in preparing kids for the scientific and technological world they will face in the years to come."

You can't rely only on textbooks. Let kids experiment, observe, and get involved, the experts stress.

By interviewing over 150 teachers, researchers, and science specialists, author Jerome Cramer gathered tips for teaching hands-on science. Here's the advice of the experts he interviewed for *Instructor*'s Spring 1987 Science Supplement:

• *Just begin.* Start by focusing on the scientific aspects of the activities or lessons you already teach—cooking or gardening, for example.

• *Learn from your colleagues.* Collaborate with teachers who love science and teach it well.

• *Teach science at least three times a week.* Veterans who realize the value of science for teaching higher-order thinking skills schedule science daily.

• *Have students do science*—not just read about it. Identifying air currents, feeling magnetic pull, creating electrical currents—activities like these help students learn through experience and discovery. In fact, many educators believe that textbooks are most useful after an experiment or activity, when they help students understand what they've been doing without dulling the thrill of discovery.

Activities should involve students in observing, describing, comparing, classifying,

"If kids touch it, lift it, and manipulate it, they learn whether it is hot or cold, big or little, heavy or light," says **Thomas Fitch of Illinois State University. "And kids then can begin to make estimations, measure, and calculate. That is how science works."**

measuring, using numbers, predicting, graphing, posing questions, recording information, and so on.

• *Organize activities to accomplish a specific purpose.* While science does not require a strict progression of skills, instructional activities must have a goal and help students progress in conceptual knowledge. Most educators recommend a balance among the physical, life, and earth sciences.

• *Emphasize process more than content.* Teach students how science works, and the content learning will follow.

• *Capitalize on the characteristics of your learners.* Kids love to play, explore, ask questions, and satisfy their curiosity. These are all great qualities for future scientists. Hands-on science activities foster these natural tendencies toward experimentation and discovery. And above all, science is fun!

• *Common, everyday objects often make the best science materials.* The experts note that young children are sometimes put off by strange objects. Build activities around everyday items—straws, water, coins, vinegar—and add the exotic ones later. See the reproducibles on pp. 202-206 for simple science activities using materials at hand.

• *Relate science experiences to the real world.* Help children understand how much science is a part of our daily lives. Concepts relating to air and water, for example, can help kids learn about weather and pollution. Concepts of energy and calories relate to the foods they eat.

• *Turn failed experiments or projects into successful learning opportunities.* When an experiment fails—and some will—don't get discouraged. Instead, seize the moment to demonstrate an important aspect of the scientific process: failures become new questions and problems. "Look at what just happened, kids! Why do you think that solution turned out red instead of purple? Let's find out!"

• *Use a variety of methods to evaluate kids' progress.* Measuring learning is perhaps the most difficult aspect of teaching hands-on science. You can see the students love science—they're involved and active, they understand how to approach a problem in a systematic way, and they're discovering scientific principles as they work. But how can you demonstrate that in a paper-and-pencil test?

It's difficult. Many teachers and schools use alternative evaluation techniques, such as teacher observation, or they're developing their own tests. The National Assessment of Educational Progress has published a manual to help teachers create tests for hands-on science. (For information, contact NAEP, (CN6710), Princeton, NJ 08541-6710. Or call toll-free (800) 223-0267.)

"Don't give up on testing," advises Phyllis Marcuccio of the National Science Teachers Association. "And don't stop explaining to parents and policymakers that good science instruction isn't evaluated by a check on the answer worksheet."

Fourth-grade teacher Robert Pringle sees it this way: "The payoff isn't how kids test, it's how they live their lives."

• *The more you teach science, the better you'll become.* You'll learn what works and what doesn't, just as your budding scientists do. Give science instruction a boost by attending workshops and training sessions. School districts, state departments of education, universities, and science museums are likely sources of such training.

The National Science Teachers Association, 1742 Connecticut Ave. N.W., Washington, DC 20009, and its state affiliates offer many different workshops on hands-on science. Summer courses in science teacher training are offered by the National Science Foundation, 1800 6 St. N.W., Washington, DC 20550. The Western Regional Environmental Education Council offers Project WILD—a nationwide program of free training and activity guides for integrating environmental education into the total curriculum. To find the training center nearest you, write to Dr. Cheryl Charles,

Director, Project WILD, Salina Star Route, Boulder, CO 80302.

Computers in science class

Conducting science experiments by computer? It's not only possible, it's a viable option in many schools today. Computers extend hands-on experience for students by allowing them to simulate difficult, dangerous, or expensive experiments. "Measuring the pH levels of liquids used to require a $1,200 piece of equipment," says middle-school science teacher Roberta Barba. "Now we buy simple materials at the local electronics store, worth 39 cents, attach them to the computer, and we are in business."

Barba describes some of the ways her students use computers to learn science:
• *Keying plants.* Students each collect several plants, examine them closely, then type their major characteristics into the computer. The computer, using a data base covering some 500 common plants, generates questions (How many leaves? What kind of root system?)

Integrated Science Instruction

What does integrated science instruction look like? Fourth-grade teacher Robert Pringle, who tries to "relate what we're learning in science to as many activities as possible," offers the following example of a unit he did on sound. During the unit, Pringle had his students:

• Write about sound in their daily journals. To provoke their thinking, he asked such questions as, "What was the last sound you heard before you went to bed last night? What was the first sound you heard when you woke up? What sounds do you like? Why? Not like? Why? What is the difference between sound and noise?"

• Dictate what they wrote into a tape recorder, then listen to what they'd written.

• Listen to a variety of sounds on the playground at recess.

• Discuss how noise can disturb other people.

• Paint with watercolors the sounds they heard while sitting in the grass outside the school. Through this lesson he showed students how art helps us understand the physical world. Students rendered their impressions of cars and trucks roaring, birds singing, the wind blowing, jets screeching, and so on.

• Dramatize the sounds in a story they read during reading class—cats meowing, dogs barking, babies crying, the wind blowing.

• Write a story in which sounds played an important role. Again, they later acted out the sounds.

• Write homonym stories during a spelling lesson.

• Create a "sound map" of the school grounds by first estimating distances sound would travel and guessing which noises they would hear at certain spots, then by recording actual noises and noise levels. "The students were surprised, for example, that certain noises from inside the building could by clearly heard outside on the grounds," Pringle reports. "We noted this on the map and later discussed why and how sound travels."

• Learn about musical pitch and the mathematical relationship of musical notes.

Pringle urges other teachers to try integrating science into their total curriculum. "Kids like science," he stresses. "It's a motivator."

requiring students to further examine the plant and hypothesize to identify it.

• *Making graphs.* Plotting data on a graph helps kids visualize a problem and analyze their findings. But kids often get bogged down in the mechanics of graphing. Graphing software frees them from mechanical problems by generating the graph for them—after they collect data and enter the information into a computer. In one experiment, students compare the energy requirements of movable and fixed pulleys by entering different weights into the computer and graphing the differences.

• *Keeping records.* With computer word-processing packages, students type their hypotheses, reports, and observations, and correct or revise them quickly and efficiently.

• *Experimenting.* Students experiment with kinetic and potential energy by connecting a pendulum to a computer. They measure calories or conduct other heat experiments with a temperature probe connected to a computer. And computers can simulate experiments, too, like the physics experiments developed at the Learning Research and Development Center. Their computers can show objects falling in a vacuum or sliding down frictionless surfaces.

The effectiveness of computer-assisted instruction will depend, of course, on the software you use. But many good programs are already available, and more are being developed. Some of the most exciting examples of computer-assisted science instruction come from the Educational Technology Center at Harvard University.

One ETC project uses a computer to help young children develop the concept of density. Computer analogs—arrays of dots—represent size, weight, and density.

Another ETC experiment uses a computer, a heat pulse generator, and a temperature probe to explore the common misconception that heat always increases temperature. When students press a computer key, the pulse generator delivers dollops of heat to a liquid.

A heat probe that graphs the liquid's temperature is also connected to the computer. Students can monitor temperature changes over time as heat is added.

Integrating science with other subjects

"I don't see science sitting by itself in the early grades. It should be integrated in a practical way."

That's what Thomas Fitch of Illinois State University says. Most educators would agree. Experts claim that the best elementary science instruction is cross-curricular. Although this chapter devotes a whole section to subject matter integration, the strategy deserves special mention where science is concerned.

Multipurpose lessons involving science are a good idea for two reasons. First, they're a way to teach science and emphasize the three R's at the same time. Second, students use many of the same thinking skills in science as they do in the other basics.

Kindergarten teacher Betty Starkey uses hands-on science every day throughout the curriculum. She's found that young children love science, and it motivates them in other academic areas.

Starkey blends many language activities into her science instruction. Kids read poems, stories, or books about what they're studying. They sing or draw what they experience and observe.

Teachers can "use science to reach all kids in all subjects," Starkey claims. She should know. She's trained over 8,000 teachers to use hands-on science.

One way to make science visible all day long is to set up a science center in your classroom, Starkey suggests. The science center, with its good supply of hands-on material, provides a catalyst for many activities. And integrated science lessons should always include specific objectives for teachers and students.

Ranger Rick's NatureScope series provides many good activities integrating science with other subjects. For information, write to the National Wildlife Federation, 1412 Sixteenth St. N.W., Washington, DC 20036-2266.

Another great source of integrated science lessons is Project WILD, an interdisciplinary approach to environmental education. For information on free training and activity guides, write to Project WILD. (The address is listed on p. 181.)

Students' misconceptions

A big part of teaching science is helping students unlearn what they already "know."

That's right. Research shows that students of all ages have explanations for scientific phenomena before they've even studied them. These "explanations"—most often misconceptions—come from what students "know" before they ever come to class.

Most students "know," for example, that:
• Plants get their food from the soil (as opposed to photosynthesis).
• Air is just empty space (rather than a tangible substance exerting pressure).
• We see objects because light illuminates them (rather than light reflects off objects to our eyes).
• Heavier objects (all other things being equal) fall much faster than lighter ones.
• Heat always increases temperature.

Misconceptions or naive theories such as these color the way children see the world. They distort students' thinking. They're resistant to instruction and hinder subsequent learning.

Misconceptions can even distort what students think they observe or experience. For example, when researchers Audrey Champagne and Leopold Klopfer asked students, in a Learning Research and Development Center study, to compare two identically-shaped objects (plastic and aluminum blocks) falling equal distances of about one meter, most reported that they actually observed the heavier object fall faster.

Many teachers don't realize these widespread misconceptions exist, say Charles Anderson and Edward Smith of the Institute for Research on Teaching. The vague or inaccurate language sometimes used during instruction actually fosters these misconceptions, they add.

Textbooks apparently bear much of the blame. Anderson and Smith cite numerous examples of text passages that neither challenge nor contradict student misconceptions. For example, one text refers to the "color of things," reinforcing the misconception that color is a property of objects rather than a property of light.

Misconceptions are a serious problem. You must confront them head-on. Anderson and Smith describe how:
• The first step in effective science instruction is to identify students' misconceptions on a certain topic. Do this by having students predict what will happen in an experiment. Have them explain a scientific concept or natural phenomenon in writing. This record not only reveals students' misconceptions, it preserves them for you to analyze, later.
• After exposing misconceptions, plan instruction to challenge and correct them.
• Make students understand how a correct concept is different from and more adequate than their misconception. Begin a lesson by focusing on a misconception. ("If air is just empty space, how can barometers and siphons work?") Then carefully explain the correct concept and contrast it with the misconception.
• Realize that learning is a process of conceptual change. It's a matter of students changing their initial ideas and adopting new ones, rather than simply acquiring the ideas you hope to teach.

Chapter 5—Read more about it

1. *Teaching Children to Read Through Their Individual Learning Styles*. Rita Dunn, Kenneth Dunn, and Marie Carbo. Englewood Cliffs, NJ: Prentice Hall, 1985.

2. *Teaching Reading Vocabulary*. Dale Johnson and P. David Pearson. New York: Holt, Rinehart, and Winston, 1984.

3. *Reading (Motivation—Teaching Comprehension—Teaching Reading in the Content Areas)*. Jean Sealey. R&D Interpretation Service Bulletins. Charleston, WV: Appalachia Educational Laboratory, 1985.

4. *From Turn Taking to Sense Making: Classroom factors and improved reading achievement* (Occasional Paper No. 59). Gerald Duffy. East Lansing, MI: Institute for Research on Teaching, 1983. Also available in *Journal of Educational Research*, 76, 1983, 134-139.

5. *A Qualitative Analysis of How Various Primary Grade Teachers Employ the Structured Learning Component of the Direct Instructional Model When Teaching Reading* (Research Series No. 80). G. Duffy and L. McIntyre. East Lansing, MI: Institute for Research on Teaching. 1980. Also published as "A Naturalistic Study of Teacher Assistance in Primary Grade Reading." Gerald Duffy and Lonnie McIntyre. *Elementary School Journal*, 83, 1982, 35-40.

6. "Direct Instruction of Comprehension: What Does It Really Mean?" Gerald Duffy and Laura Roehler. *Reading Horizons*, 23, (1982), 35-40.

7. *Effective Teaching of Reading: Research and Practice*. J. Hoffman (ed.). Newark, DE: International Reading Association, 1986.

8. *Improving Classroom Reading Instruction: A Decision Making Approach*. Gerald Duffy and Laura Roehler. New York: Random House, 1986.

9. *Comprehension Instruction: Suggestions and Perspectives*. G. Duffy, L. Roehler, and J. Mason (eds.). New York: Longman, 1984.

10. *Teaching Writing: Some Perennial Questions and Some Possible Answers* (O. P. No. 85). S. Florio-Ruane and S. Dunn. East Lansing, MI: Institute for Research on Teaching, 1985.

11. *Communicating in the Classroom*. L. Cherry-Wilkinson (ed.). New York: Academic Press, 1982.

12. "What's So Hard About Writing? The Issues for Teachers and Students." Susan Florio-Ruane. *Elementary School Journal*, 84, (1983), 93-99.

13. *The Effective Writing Teacher: 18 Strategies*. John Collins. Andover, MA: The Regional Laboratory for Educational Improvement of the Northeast and Islands, 1985.

14. *Oral and Written Communication (Evaluating Writing—Grammar Instruction—Peer Editing Groups)*. Jean Sealey. R&D Interpretation Service Bulletins. Charleston, WV: Appalachia Educational Laboratory, 1985.

15. "Expertise in Mathematics Teaching." Gaea Leinhardt. *Educational Leadership*, 43 (April 1986), 28-33.

16. *Mathematics (Individual Differences—Problem Solving—Remediation)*. Jean Sealey. R&D Interpretation Service Bulletins. Charleston, WV: Appalachia Educational Laboratory, 1985.

17. *Arithmetic Word Problems: Activities to Engage Students in Problem Analysis.* Andrea Lash. San Francisco: Far West Laboratory for Educational Research and Development, 1985. (Includes over 200 problems for classroom use.)

18. *Ideas on Teaching Problem Solving in Intermediate Mathematics.* Gary Tsuruda and Andrea Lash. San Francisco: Far West Laboratory for Educational Research and Development, 1985.

19. *Teaching Problem Solving: What, Why, and How.* R. Charles and F. Lester. Palo Alto, CA: Dale Seymour Publications, 1982.

20. *Science: Instructional Strategies.* Jean Sealey. An R&D Interpretation Service Bulletin. Charleston, WV: Appalachia Educational Laboratory, 1985.

21. "Students' Misconceptions Interfere with Learning: Case Studies of Fifth-Grade Students" (Research Series No. 128). Janet Eaton, Charles Anderson, and Edward Smith. East Lansing, MI: Institute for Research on Teaching, 1983. Also available in *Elementary School Journal*, 84, (1984), 365-379.

22. *Curriculum Materials, Teacher Talk, and Student Learning: Case Studies in Fifth-Grade Science Teaching* (R. S. No. 171). K. Roth, C. Anderson, and E. Smith. East Lansing, MI: Institute for Research on Teaching, 1986.

23. *The Planning and Teaching of Intermediate Science Study: Final Report* (R. S. No. 147). E. Smith and C. Anderson. East Lansing, MI: Institute for Research on Teaching, 1984.

24. *Research Within Reach: Science Education.* David Holdzkom and Pamela Lutz (eds.). R&D Interpretation Service Bulletins. Charleston, WV: Appalachia Educational Laboratory, 1984.

25. *Writing in Elementary School Social Studies.* Barry Beyer and Robert Gilstrap (eds.). Boulder, CO: Social Science Education Consortium and ERIC Clearinghouse, 1982.

26. *Children's World View: The Basis for Learning Activities.* F.N. Lewis and Jane Margold. San Francisco, CA: Far West Laboratory for Educational Research and Development, 1987.

27. *Instructor*'s "Windows on the World" Series.

28. *Hands-On Sience.* Sandra Markle. Cleveland, OH: Instructor Books, 1988.

29. "The Role of Computers in Higher-Order Thinking." Janice H. Patterson and Marshall S. Smith. In *Microcomputers in Education.* 85th Yearbook of the National Society for the Study of Education, Part I. Chicago: University of Chicago Press, 1986.

N O T E S

Dichotomous Scale for Evaluating Writing

Author _____ Reader _____

Paper _____

I. **Style and Form Factors**	YES	NO
A. Author's role consistent?	_____	_____
B. Interesting personal voice?	_____	_____
C. Theme clearly presented?	_____	_____
D. Background rich and supportive?	_____	_____
E. Sequence of events clear?	_____	_____
F. Central figure fully developed?	_____	_____
G. _____	_____	_____
H. _____	_____	_____
I. _____	_____	_____
J. _____	_____	_____
Total "YES"	_____	

II. **Mechanics and Technical Factors**	YES	NO
A. Wording unique and developed?	_____	_____
B. Syntax correct?	_____	_____
C. Syntax varied?	_____	_____
D. Usage errors few?	_____	_____
E. Punctuation errors few?	_____	_____
F. Spelling errors few?	_____	_____
G. _____	_____	_____
H. _____	_____	_____
I. _____	_____	_____
J. _____	_____	_____
Total "NO"		_____

Note areas of strength ("yes")/weakness ("no") here:

_____

_____

_____

_____

Directions for scoring. After reading the paper, the rater responds more or less subjectively to questions in Part I. Total "yes" responses indicate assessment of author's style and elements that are woven into the writing. Part II items can be identified rather quickly and more or less objectively. Total "no" responses indicate an assessment of mechanics and technical factors. Depending on the intent of the writing assignment sample, you may want to give more relative weight to one part than the other.

Developed by the Appalachia Educational Laboratory, Charleston, West Virginia

Improving Reading
Comprehension

The ReQuest Procedure

ReQuest encourages students to develop their own questions about specific reading material and to acquire a questioning attitude. To illustrate how we make assumptions as we read and how questions can be used to clarify our understanding, read the story below.

Going Swimming: Part I

John swallowed the last drops of orange juice and looked at the sky. He turned to his dad and said, "Dad, will you take Sue and me swimming today?"

Mr. Singer started to answer, then paused. After a moment, he replied, "I'd find that enjoyable myself. But first, I'd better keep my promise about today's yard work."

John bounded up from the table with such enthusiasm that he nearly upset it. Starting toward the garage, he shouted, "I'll begin collecting the tools now so we can get started."

Now answer these questions: What is the time of day? What is the weather like? What is the meal? What day of the week is it? What season of the year is it? Who is Sue? Whom had Mr. Singer promised? How old is John? Would they go swimming? Where would they swim? In whose yard would they work? What is Mr. Singer's occupation?

Could you answer all the questions? How certain of each answer are you? For many of the questions you had to draw on your own experience to arrive at tentative answers.

The rest of the story is on the next page. Read it and check your hypotheses.

As we read, we form hypotheses about what the author is saying to us. This is a necessary part of comprehending what we read. Our hypotheses can be plausible but inappropriate. For example, if you thought the meal was breakfast, it was probably because you associate orange juice with breakfast. If you thought Sue was a person—John's friend or sister, perhaps—it was because most Sues you have known were people. Although your hypotheses were entirely reasonable, you had to revise them as you read part 2.

ReQuest shows students how to ask questions. It begins with the teacher asking questions. As originally designed, the teacher works with an individual student.

The teacher and student read a selection from the passage and take turns asking questions. In a classroom, teachers may have difficulty scheduling individual students for ReQuest sessions. There is also the problem of providing activities for the rest of the class. So, we've taken the principles of ReQuest and modified them for use with the whole class.

You will have different ability levels in your class, including some students who are not experiencing difficulty in reading comprehension. However, the ReQuest procedures can be beneficial for these students, too. It makes them aware of strategies they may already be using unconsciously. An awareness of the strategies enables students to use them more effectively and to apply them more consistently.

Prepare Materials

Review the material for its adaptability to ReQuest. ReQuest involves making predictions about what will happen next. Select stories or articles that lend themselves to making predictions.

After you have made the selection, identify breaks in the passage where you can ask students to make predictions. If the passage you select is not in the students' textbooks, have each section of the passage duplicated so each student will have a copy. Or you may wish to have each section put on a transparency if you have access to an overhead projector.

Develop Readiness for ReQuest

Developing readiness includes introducing vocabulary words that may not be familiar to your students. You may also need to provide background information necessary to an understanding of the story. A brief discussion of the title is sometimes helpful in developing readiness.

You can introduce the procedure with:

The exercise we are about to do is intended to help you better understand what you read. We will all read the same passage silently together. When we have all read the passage, we will take turns asking each other questions. I will ask you questions; then you can ask me questions. If you are asking me questions, I will not look at my book. When I am asking you questions, you will answer the best you can without looking at your book. I want you to ask me the kinds of questions that you think I might ask you.

Your instruction will differ depending on how you organize the session. For example, you may want to allow students to ask questions that you will write on the board. When students run out of questions, you could then see how many different answers you get to each question. Or you may wish to take turns with each student—first ask the student a question, then answer the student's question.

Developing Questioning Behaviors

Direct students to the reading passage. Everyone reads silently at the same time. When all students have finished reading, have them turn the paper over or close the book. Ask different types of questions: questions that can be answered from the text, questions that build on the previous question, and questions that require students to draw upon their own experiences.

When the students are asking questions, be sure to reinforce appropriate questioning behaviors. When students are asking questions in a group, it is especially important that their questions not be rejected. If they are made to feel that their questions are "stupid," they will be reluctant to try again. If the other children laugh at or ridicule a student's question, you might say something like, *Well, I never would have thought of that! That shows you're thinking.* If the question is unclear, ask the student to rephrase it. Help the child reword the question, if necessary, to arrive at an appropriate question. *Let me see, John. Are you asking . . . ?* Make sure all students have a chance to ask questions.

Develop Student Predicting Behaviors

When all students have asked questions, you will begin to develop predicting behaviors. Ask the students, *What will happen next?* Record their answers on the board. As each student responds, ask, *Why do you think so?* You may want to ask the student to read the part of the passage that supports the response. After all the responses have been recorded, ask the students to vote on the predictions they think are most likely.

Allow Time for Silent Reading

Tell the students to read the rest of the passage silently. As the students read, observe to see if any students are having difficulty. As you give assistance to those students who need it, try to do so in a way that does not disrupt the other students' reading.

Follow-up Activities

When all students have completed the silent reading, go over the list of predictions you recorded on the board to see which ones were accurate. Were these the ones that had the most student votes? Which predictions were plausible but not accurate? Discuss why they seemed reasonable earlier. Ask the students what happened in the story that made their predictions inaccurate. Ask the students to manipulate the story. *What do you think would have happened if . . . ? Could you write a better ending to this story?*

Summary

ReQuest is a relatively simple procedure to try. Preparation consists of finding appropriate materials and making them available to your students. You also need to introduce unfamiliar vocabulary words and to develop background necessary to an understanding of the story. You don't have to take time away from the class or prepare additional materials for students not participating. All students benefit from hearing the questions, answers, and predictions of other students. ReQuest procedures are flexible, and they're adaptable to all reading levels. For younger students, you may show students a picture and tell them to ask questions about it. For older students, you may ask them to write another ending to the story or to write a similar story in a different setting. You may even make a game of the questioning strategy. One student begins the question, e.g. *Why did . . . ?* and directs it at another student. The second student finishes the question. Using our example, he might say, *(Why did) Mr. Singer and John collect tools?* The student who initiated the question must answer the completed question. These are only a few of the possibilities. Think of others to use.

Going Swimming: Part 2

John loaded the rake, clippers, lawn mower, and sacks into the back of the truck. Mr. Singer emerged with his appointment book, found the entry that said, "Smiths, 101 Cleveland, 1:00 p.m., Wednesday."

John turned the key and checked the rearview mirror. Just then, Mr. Singer shouted, "Wait, we forgot Sue." He jumped out and gave a loud whistle. In a moment, there was Sue, tearing around the corner of the house. She leaped into the back of the truck and began licking the rear window.

Mr. Singer looked at John and chuckled. "I hope Sue won't mind waiting for her swim until we finish the job."

Reprinted with permission from Appalachia Educational Laboratory, R & D Interpretation Service, P.O. Box 1348, Charleston, West Virginia 25325

Forty-five great games to improve
Reading Comprehension

Here are 45 classroom-tested activities by Nicholas Criscuolo
that can help you improve your students' reading comprehension.

Emotional outlet Ask each student to choose a main character from a story and write a list of feelings or emotions expressed by that character. All items on the list must start with the initial letter of the character's first name. When the kids have finished their lists, have them share their choices with classmates, describing the circumstances in the story that led them to select those words.

Hold up the card Give each child a set of cards on which you've printed the names of the central characters in a particular story—one character per card. Then read some descriptive sentences about these characters and their functions in the story. Students are to identify the character being described and hold up the appropriately labeled card.

Quiz bowl Divide your class into small groups and have each present a quiz program based on several different stories found in the reading text. The stories should be divided into categories, such as travel, sports, nature, and so on. The groups may use additional sources of information—almanacs, encyclopedias, and travel brochures—to form questions dealing with designated categories. Then the groups can take turns presenting their quiz programs, with the rest of the class acting as contestants.

Fishbowl fun Have your kids write questions about stories they've read on small slips of paper, making sure to include the title of the story and the author's name. Fasten a paper clip to each slip and place them together in a fishbowl. Then make a "fishing pole" from a pencil, string, and small magnet. Let the kids "fish" for questions and attempt to answer them orally.

Story notebooks Ask each child to keep a small notebook entitled "Stories I Have Read." After they've read a new story, have them answer the following question in their notebooks:
a. What is the name of the story?
b. Who wrote it?
c. Who are the main characters?

d. Which character did you like best and why?
e. What part of the story did you like best? Why did you like this part?
You might also want the kids to illustrate a major scene from each story on the pages opposite their answers.

Secret Identities Have each child write a description of a famous character from literature—making sure not to divulge that character's name. For example:
I am brown and furry.
I love honey.
Christopher Robin is my best friend.
Who am I? (Winnie the Pooh)
The kids should take turns reading their descriptions aloud while the rest of the class tries to guess the characters' identities.

Story rolls Have your children choose their favorite stories and list the main events in sequence. Then let them illustrate the incidents, in order, on long sheets of butcher paper. When the drawings are finished, give each student two cardboard tubes (paper towel or aluminum foil rolls work best) and have each roll his or her illustrations from the first tube to the second and narrate the story for the rest of the class.

How would you feel? You can help your kids recognize tone and feeling with this exercise, which is unrelated to any particular story. Start by listing the following questions on your chalkboard under the heading *Would you feel sad or glad if:*
a. You could solve a mystery?
b. Your bicycle was stolen?
c. Your kite blew away?
Discuss these questions and the feelings they provoke with your class and continue the exercise by changing the initial adjectives to *playful, serious, calm, nervous,* and so on.

Rewrites Have kids choose the final paragraph of a story they've recently read and use it as the starting point for original stories of their own. Or you might want them to rewrite the last few paragraphs of a favorite story to give it a

different ending. Then have the kids share their version with classmates, asking them to supply new titles for the rewritten stories.

True or false? Start by preparing several statements about a particular story, some true and some false. Then give each student two cards—one labeled "true" and the other labeled "false." As you read each statement aloud, instruct the children to hold up the appropriate card.

Mix-up Print the major events of a story on oaktag strips and place the strips in improper order on your chalkledge. Ask students to put the strips in their correct order, according to the sequence of events in the story. Repeat the procedure for several different stories.

Paragraph pickings Divide the class into pairs and have each choose a few paragraphs from a story with a lot of dialogue. They should practice reading the passage orally, then record their reading on cassette tapes. Make sure each pair tapes a summary of the events leading up to that paragraph first. Keep the tapes available for classmates to listen to in leisure time.

Recall sessions Divide the class into small groups and assign each group a different story to read. When everyone has finished reading, ask the kids to position themselves in a circle for this comprehension exercise. Lead off by stating the first main event in the story, then ask the student on your left to state the next, and so on around the circle.

Fortune cookie forecasts Have your kids make "fortune cookies" from folded brown construction paper. Now instruct the children to choose books or stories they've recently read and select one main character to focus on for this activity. Based on the actual events of the story they are to make a prediction that might apply to the chosen character. Let each child put his or her prediction inside a fortune cookie and tape it shut.

Place them all together in a large jar. Students are to take turns picking fortune cookies from the jar and guessing which character and story the prediction refers to. As a follow-up activity, you might also want the kids to write new endings to the stories, based on the predictions they've chosen.

Why did it happen? Print the following sentences on your chalkboard and ask your kids to suggest possible reasons for each event. This exercise will help students improve their ability to make inferences and draw conclusions.

   a. It was a foggy day and a bird flew into the building.
   b. Mark brought a bowl of hot chicken soup over to his friend's house.

Rate it Encourage students to react critically to the stories they read through a numerical rating system. With your guidance, let the kids establish their own criteria for rating stories—from poor to excellent. Then instruct them to make a chart of each story they read, listing the date, title, main character, main idea, and the numerical rating.

Taping sessions Cut out several short stories from discarded basal readers, staple them together, and give one to each child in your class. Ask the kids to read and summarize their stories; then let them record these summaries on cassette tapes along with three comprehension questions that they make up. (Answers to these questions should be printed on an answer key.) Invite students to listen to their classmates' tapes, answer the comprehension questions, and then check their responses against the answer key.

Scrambled sentences Help kids reinforce math and sequence skills with this exercise. Start by writing the following sentences on your chalkboard:

   Anita handed the salesperson $10.
   Anita decided to buy a new pair of shoes.
   Anita went to the large store's shoe department.
   The salesperson said the shoes cost $7.
   Anita selected a pair of black shoes.

Have the children number the sentences in their proper order, rewrite them in paragraph or math-problem form, and compose a comprehension question to accompany it. In this case, the most logical question would be: How much change did Anita receive?

Act it out Isolate particular episodes or events from several stories your class has recently read. Describe these events on small slips of paper and put them together in a jar. The kids should take turns drawing from the jar and acting out, charade-style, the events they pick.

The rest of the class must guess which episode is being acted out and in which story it took place.

Swap shop Ask the children to write descriptive paragraphs about a character or an event appearing in their reading text. Then divide the class into pairs and have the kids read their paragraphs aloud to their partners. The listener must identify the character described and the name of the story in which the character appeared.

People predictions Ask each child to choose a recently read story from the reading text, and to write a sentence predicting a future event in the life of one of its main characters. One by one, have the kids identify their characters for the rest of the class and attempt to convey their predictions, using gestures only.

Marvelous Mobiles Have your kids make decorative hanging mobiles to illustrate major events in stories from their reading texts. They will need wire coat hangers, string, scissors, crayons, and paste. Have them begin by writing the titles and authors of the stories they've chosen on long strips of tagboard. Now each child should punch one hole at the top of this strip and fasten it with string to the bottom of the hanger. Next, have the kids punch several holes along the bottom of the title

(continued)

strip. From these holes, the kids should hang pictures from magazines and newspapers or original drawings that illustrate major events. These pictures should be mounted on construction paper and hung from the title strips in sequential order. The last hanging piece should be labeled with the student's name.

Problem solving for fun Choose student volunteers to form a panel to discuss the problems that major characters in recently read books or stories encounter. Try these questions for starters:

   a. What major problem did the main character or characters face?
   b. How was this problem solved?
   c. Would you have done something different to solve the problem?

Key words Have kids underline the important words in a story paragraph. They should then list these words in order of appearance and orally reconstruct the paragraph for classmates.

What happened next? Write the following statements on your chalkboard:

   a. Sarah was riding very fast on her bike. She did not see the hole in the road. What happened next?
   b. Chuck came home from school early. His head felt hot and his throat hurt. What happened next?

Ask children to explain what they think happened next, making sure they can defend their answers.

Story line Draw a large grid on your chalkboard with the headings *Scene, Characters, Location,* and *Action.* Choose a few stories your kids have recently read and ask for volunteers to fill in the outline you've drawn. This will reinforce your students' sequence skills and ability to summarize events.

Favorite scenes Have kids construct scenes from their favorite books or short stories using papier mache, bits of fabric, colored construction paper, string, or any other materials that would visually enhance the construction. Then let each child share his or her creation with the rest of the class, making sure to describe the events that led up to and followed the chosen scene.

Who said it? To help students infer from a sentence more than is actually stated, write on the board, "It will cost $400 to paint your house." Ask students who said this—a doctor, painter, or salesperson. After doing this with other, similar sentences ("We will be cruising at 35,000 feet"—pilot, baker, or engineer?), have children work in teams to construct their own "Who-said-it?" sentences.

Classified information Have the children select particular situations from stories in their reading texts and use them as starting points for written classified ads. For instance, a story about a man who moves from Alaska to Florida could be the start of an advertisement selling a used snow blower.

Scrambled words Put these scrambled words on the board: *tesak, plpae,* and *oatomt.* Tell kids that all three are things we can eat, and ask them to unscramble each word and write its correct spelling (*steak, apple, tomato*). Then have students write their own scrambled words that belong to a certain category and exchange them with classmates, who will then unscramble them.

Reactions Make sets of cards with a word expressing a feeling, such as *angry, tired, excited,* or *disappointed,* on each card. Give each child a set. Then read a short passage to which one or more of the words on the cards would be a correct response. For example: "Tony spent many hours building a snowman on the front lawn. When he went inside, a big branch broke and fell on the snowman, smashing it to pieces." Ask students, "How would Tony react? Hold up the card or cards that tell me." Encourage children to defend their answers.

Absurd sentences Read sentences such as the following to students and ask them to tell you which word makes each sentence absurd. Then ask them to tell you what word could be substituted.

   1. The room was hot, so Jim decided to open a football.
   2. For our vacation we drove across the country in a wastebasket.
   3. After the first snowfall, Linda ran outside and started to build a meatball.
   4. Bill ate a tank of spaghetti.

Hidden clues Discuss with children the fact that sometimes we have to think about sentences to find their hidden clues or facts. Then read the following sentence: "Mr. Jefferson took the rake from the cellar and walked out to the lawn." Lead students to infer the fact that the statement describes an incident that happened during the fall season. Discuss similar sentences, such as "John came in the house and took off his wet raincoat," from which inferences can be made.

Detect the bias Explain that a biased sentence will express a personal judgment rather than state an observable fact. Then find three advertisements from newspapers or magazines. Put these on the board, along with a non-biased sentence, such as "It is beginning to rain," and have students indicate which three are biased.

Comic strips Collect as many comic strips as you have children in your class, and cut off the last frame in each one. Pass them out to students and have them complete the final frame by drawing a picture of what they think happened, accompanied by an appropriate caption.

Charting new devices To give kids practice in comparing and contrasting information they learn from reading with information learned through watching television, select a current topic such as the energy crisis or inflation. First, have students find articles from newspapers dealing with this topic and ask them to summarize the articles point by point. Then ask them to watch an evening news broadcast on TV and gather any information heard on the same subject. Have them add this information to what they had already learned on a summary chart. Which source was more comprehensive? Were there any discrepancies?

Creating situations Write words expressing feelings or moods, such as *jealousy, silliness, fear,* and so on, on index cards. Divide the class into groups of two or three and have each group pick a card. Each group should then prepare a short play or pantomime that illustrates the specified feeling or mood, with the rest of the class guessing which feeling was portrayed.

Same or different? Explain to children that sometimes two sentences can have similar meanings. Read the following pairs of sentences and tell students that one pair conveys similar meanings while the other doesn't.
  1. Mrs. Donovan, our teacher, went to Spain last year.
     Mrs. Donovan is Spanish.
  2. Louise had a big smile on her face because the dentist told her she had no cavities.
     Louise was happy because she had no cavities.

Ask children to tell you why one pair (the second) conveys similar meanings and the other does not. Then have each child write two sentences with similar meanings and two that use some of the same words but have vastly different meanings.

If it happened Read to students sentences such as the following and ask them to imagine and tell how they would feel if they were in that particular situation.
  1. If I heard a strange sound in the night, I would feel _____ .
  2. If I received something I wanted for my birthday, I would feel _____ .
  3. If I tried and tried to do a new thing and still couldn't, I would feel _____ .

Connected events Select two or three events from each of four stories the children have read recently. Write these events in mixed order on the board. Then read the story titles to kids, one at a time, and ask them to pick the events that took place in that particular story.

What's missing? Select three connected major events from a story recently read by the class. Read paragraphs about the first and third event but not the second. Ask kids to tell you the missing event. For example, you might read about Joe's cat climbing a tree and then about Joe happily hugging his cat again. Students would supply the part where firemen come to rescue the cat.

Irony or sarcasm? Discuss the meaning of *irony* (expecting one thing and getting another) and *sarcasm* (saying one thing and meaning another). Put the following sentences on the board and ask children which quality each one conveys.
  1. On the first day Jill was able to go to the beach, it rained. (irony)
  2. Thanks for the haircut—I always wanted to look like Kojak. (sarcasm)
  3. The man who won the pie-eating contest was the author of a diet book. (irony)
  4. Ted made the sacrifice of giving up a visit to the dentist in order to see *E.T.* (sarcasm)

Sign of the zodiac Gather information about horoscopes and discuss the qualities associated with people born under the different signs. Then have kids list some of their favorite story characters and choose the sign they think each character was born under, based on the qualities the character displayed in the story. This will help kids analyze the characters they read about.

Specific sentences Discuss with children the meaning of the term *specific,* then put these sentences on the board:
  1. There were a few children in the room.
  2. There were ten children in the room.
Ask them to identify the sentence that is specific and tell why the other isn't. Then ask students to orally construct sentences that are nonspecific and change them to sentences that are more specific.

Cause and effect Explain that usually when something happens there is a cause for it. Put this sentence on the board: "After the heavy snowstorm, the roof of the toolshed caved in." Choose a student to come to the board and draw one line under the cause and two lines under the effect. Do the same thing with other cause-and-effect sentences.

If I heard a strange sound in the night . . .

Nicholas Criscuolo is supervisor of reading at the New Haven Public Schools, New Haven, Connecticut.

Analytical Evaluation Factors for Essays

Author _____ Reader _____

Paper _____

Element	Yes	No

Syntax
- Complete sentences _____ ____ ____
- Subject/verb agreement _____ ____ ____
- Pronoun cases _____ ____ ____
- Paragraphing _____ ____ ____

Mechanics
- End punctuation _____ ____ ____
- Interior punctuation _____ ____ ____
- Capitalization _____ ____ ____
- Spelling _____ ____ ____

Language Use
- Blend use of active and passive voice _____ ____ ____
- Verbs are action words _____ ____ ____
- Language is vivid _____ ____ ____
- No unnecessary repetitions _____ ____ ____

Organization
- Clear pattern of organization:
  general to specific _____ ____ ____
  specific to general _____ ____ ____
  chronological _____ ____ ____
- All sentences are "useful"
  (no digressions) _____ ____ ____
- Transitions are smooth _____ ____ ____

Note areas of strength/difficulty here:

_____

_____

_____

_____

_____

Developed by the Appalachia Educational Laboratory, Charleston, West Virginia

Problem Solving

*Math educators Lola May (Winnetka, Ill.) and Barbara Bethel (San Diego) offer the following ideas for presenting and modeling problem-solving skills and strategies. The goal is to have students **think**, not just **compute**.*

1. Identify the question or questions in a problem. Understanding what is being asked in a problem is essential to finding the solution. To help students acquire this skill, first have them read a problem silently, then have it read aloud. For example: *Maria has 3 pencils. Cathy has 2 pencils. How many more pencils does Maria have than Cathy?* and *Tony earned $15.50 mowing lawns. He spent $5.75 on a model airplane. How much money does he have left?*

Wait a few minutes before talking about a problem. Research has shown that if you do so, many of your students will begin to work on a solution among themselves. They will discuss the problem—and they should be allowed to do so.

Then have students restate the problem in their own words, asking them to identify the question that must be answered to solve it. Although the questions may seem obvious to you, not all students will understand them until they are discussed.

Continue this activity with more difficult problems containing two or more questions. For example: *Helena had $75. She spent $13.28 and $26.45. How much money does she have left?* Be sure students understand that questions are often implied rather than asked directly. In the above example, the solution to the question *How much money did Helena spend altogether?* must be found before the question *How much money does she have left?* can be answered.

2. Identify the process or operation needed for solving a problem. If students have trouble with this, try using problems without numbers, such as: *Susie's father earns the same salary each week. How can you find how much he earns for a certain number of days?* (division) *Jose bought a baseball, a bat, and a glove. How can you find how much he spent altogether?* (addition)

3. Help students examine a problem and make a *logical estimate* as to what the answer will be. That way, they'll know when they check their final answer if it makes any sense at all or whether they've gone off in the wrong direction.

4. In going over the estimation process, help students understand that there is not always a single way to solve a problem and that experimentation is essential to good problem solving. Demonstrate that some problems don't have to be solved through computation alone. For example, many can be effectively solved by constructing a picture or diagram of the problem. For instance: *Frank lives 10 miles west of the zoo. Dominik lives seven miles east of the zoo. How far do they live from each other?* This problem can be illustrated with a simple line sketch, with a house drawn in at one end (for Dominik), a zoo further along (marked at 7 miles), and a house at the other end (for Frank, marked 10 miles from the zoo).

5. Problem-solving skills can be sharpened quickly by creating word problems for a number sentence. This activity will help focus attention on the problem situation and process for solution. For example, place a number sentence on the chalkboard, such as $9 + 8 = 17$. Have students tell or write word problems that could be solved by the number sentence. Here are several possibilities: *Vic had 9 pencils. His teacher gave him 8 more. How many does he have altogether?* and *There are 9 rows of chairs on one side of the auditorium and 8 rows on the other side. How many rows of chairs are there in the auditorium?*

6. Identify problems with too much or too little information. Word problems that contain either unnecessary or insufficient information are difficult or impossible for children to solve. The following exercise will improve student ability to weed out unnecessary information and to seek out more when it is needed.

Write problems with too much information on the chalkboard. For example: *Chris bought a shirt for $8.95 and a purse for $5.79. She gave the clerk $20. How much did she spend?* Discuss which information in the problem is needed for the solution. Ask a student to put a line through the unnecessary information. The revised problem should read *Chris bought a shirt for $8.95 and a purse for $5.79. How much did she spend?*

Next, write problems containing too little information on the chalkboard. For example: *The trip to San Diego will take the Andersons five hours. About what time will they arrive?* Discuss the given information, the additional information needed, and methods of rewriting the problem so that it can be solved. Have your students add the necessary facts to the problem and then find the solution. (In this problem, students need to know when the Andersons started the trip.)

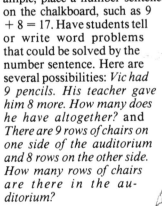

Problem-solving problems

Primary

◆ You're helping your pupils understand the value of coins and how to make change; so you ask them to come up with 50 cents using only six coins (four dimes and two nickels, or maybe five nickels and one quarter). When they are done, ask them why they approached the problem the way they did. And when appropriate, help them to understand that one method was as valid as another.

◆ Tell your students to imagine they are in a bicycle shop where they spot 31 loose wheels leaning against a wall. Ask students how many bicycles and tricycles they could make using all the wheels. Discuss how many correct solutions there are to this problem—1 tricycle and 14 bicycles; 3 tricycles and 11 bicycles; 5 tricycles and 8 bicycles, and so on. Children might approach this problem by using multiples of 3 and 2, by drawing circles to represent the wheels, or in any other way that works for them.

◆ While helping your students learn addition facts, offer them this trial-and-error problem. Using the numerals 1 through 5, have students arrange these numerals so they produce the sum of 7 in three directions. Following is one possible solution.

$$\frac{5}{2}\ 1\ \frac{4}{3}$$

◆ Have your kids write their own problems to exchange with their classmates. For example, start with 25 cents. Erasers cost 3 cents and pencils 8 cents. Using that information, each student is to write five questions and exchange them with a friend, who will work on the problems while the first student works on five received from another friend.

Intermediate

◆ Show your students an illustration of a rectangle with a perimeter of 32 centimeters. Have them draw four more rectangles, each different, that also have perimeters of 32 centimeters (15 cm by 1 cm; 14 by 2; 13 by 3; and so on). The point is to help students learn how to draw pictures or diagrams to help themselves solve problems.

◆ Tell students that during a football game, one team scored 18 points. Ask them to figure out how many different ways the team could have reached that total.

◆ In geometry, students can make tables of various data and then check for patterns to answer questions. Draw a quadrilateral, a pentagon, and a hexagon, for example. Have your students draw all the diagonals in the figures, count them, and make a table of the results. Can they find a pattern in the data? (For one, they might notice that there are three more diagonals in a pentagon than in a quadrilateral, and four more in a hexagon than in a pentagon.) Now, have them determine how many diagonals there are in a seven-sided figure (heptagon), and how many in an eight-sided one (octagon).

Article appeared in Instructor, April 1981.

Do-It-Yourself
Science Labs

Transform a corner of your classroom into a place for super science experiments.
All you need are low-cost, collectible supplies.

Teach science without a science lab? Without a Bunsen burner, flask, or beaker—not even a test tube? That's right! You can set up your own super science lab with no more than a good supply of everyday items. The simple experiments in this article are just ten examples of scientific investigations you can make at low cost. One set of five experiments will teach your students about the physical properties of matter; another set will effectively demonstrate the characteristics of acids and bases. These experiments, and others you will think of, will teach children to make realistic predictions, become good observers, use proper scientific techniques, and draw meaningful conclusions from their observations.

Set up a bright, inviting area in your room for the lab. Inside it, place a table where experiments can be conducted and a shelf or two for supplies. To get kids interested in the lab right away, have them help you collect the supplies through a classwide treasure hunt. Give each child a large paper bag—the treasure bag—with his or her name printed on it. Run off copies of the following list of supplies and tape one list to each bag. Then ask children to find and bring in as many of these items as they can from home:

crayons
food coloring
rocks (different sizes)
notebook paper
empty 3-lb. shortening can
package of yeast
sugar
salt
lemon juice

tea
bleach
uncooked chicken bones
grape juice
ammonia
white vinegar
balloons
glass pop bottles
rubber bands
pennies
baking soda
paper cups and plates
plastic cups
small plastic bowl

Some supplies you will need to gather yourself. These include several glass quart jars, an indoor-outdoor thermometer, a tape measure, a measuring cup, litmus paper, an eyedropper, scissors, matches, and a large plastic tub to work over.

As students bring in their bags, check off the items they were able to collect on their lists. Then have children help you empty the bags, put all like items into groups, and put each group of items into a separate bag. Label each bag with the name of the item it holds and stock the bags alphabetically on the shelf. This will help your young scientists locate supplies quickly and will provide good practice in alphabetizing each time the materials are cleaned up.

When supplies have been assembled, prepare children for experimenting by having them make science "log books." These could have construction-paper covers and should contain a piece of notebook paper for each experiment the child does. Explain to students that they should keep neat, careful records of each experiment so that others can read their results. These log books make it easy for you to

check students' results, and when completed they make nice displays for parents. At this time you might also display books about scientists like Thomas Edison, Louis Pasteur, Marie Curie, Galileo, or Albert Einstein for children to read during free time.

Now put your scientists to work! Make sets of "discovery cards," with one experiment written on each card, and put these in a box in the lab for children to do in any order they wish. You might want to make a big classroom graph for the bulletin board that lists children's names down the side and the experiment name or number across the top; then students can keep track of their progress by coloring in the appropriate squares as they finish experiments.

Here are the first ten discovery cards for your science lab, which direct pupils in exploring the physical properties of matter, and acids and bases.

What is matter?
Does matter take up space?

Matter is everything that we can see, touch, or smell; everything that's either a solid, liquid, or gas. While the objects around us are very different from one another, they all have common properties. Let's see if we can discover what some of these properties are.

Collect a glass jar, a little rock, a bigger rock (one that will fit in the jar), a crayon, and a tape measure. Fill the jar halfway with water and mark the water level with the crayon. Carefully drop the small rock in the water and mark the water level again. Now take out the little rock and carefully drop in the bigger rock; mark the water level

This article, by Sandra Markle, appeared in INSTRUCTOR, February 1984.

now. Use the tape measure to measure how many inches the water went up each time you dropped in a rock. Make a chart that shows these results in your log book.

1. Which rock made the water go up higher? (The bigger rock.)
2. Why did the level of the water change when you put the rocks in the jar? (Rocks take up space.)
3. Does matter take up space? (Yes) How do you know? (The water was pushed up by the rocks.)
4. What do you think would happen if you put both rocks in the water together? (The water would rise to the level of the combined inches of the little-rock level and the big-rock level.) Try it and see if you are right.
5. What does this experiment show about matter? (That matter takes up space.)

How does temperature affect matter?

All matter is made up of atoms. These atoms are constantly moving, even in solids (although these move more slowly). Here's how we can observe how molecules move.

Gather together a thermometer, food coloring, and a quart jar. Fill the jar with hot water and put the thermometer in to check the temperature. Let the thermometer rest against the side of the jar, and watch it to see when the mercury stops rising. How warm is the water? Record the temperature.

Remove the thermometer and add one drop of food coloring. Look at the second hand on the clock. How many seconds does it take for the color to spread completely through the water? (Answers will vary.) Now repeat the test using cold water. How many seconds does it take for the coloring to spread? (Answers will again vary, but the times will be longer.)

1. How could you see that molecules were moving? (From the spreading food coloring.)
2. Which causes molecules to move faster, heating or cooling? (Heating)

How does a physical change affect matter?

Collect a piece of notebook paper, scissors, and a crayon.

1. Think of four ways you can change the paper, using your hands and these supplies. Make these changes.
2. In your log book write down the ways you changed the paper. (Answers will vary, but they can include tearing, poking holes, crumpling, coloring, cutting, folding, writing, and so on.)

What you did changed the physical properties of the paper—its color, shape, or size—but not its *molecular structure*. That means that even though it looks different now, you can still recognize it as paper.

How does a chemical change affect matter?

For this experiment, ask the help of the teacher. (To the teacher: You should do this experiment yourself because it involves burning a piece of paper. You'll need a three-pound can, a piece of notebook paper, and a match. Crumple the paper into a wad and put it in the bottom of the can. Light the match and drop it on the paper. Let the paper burn completely, and allow it to cool 15 minutes before examining the results.)

How did the paper change? (It could be flaky, lighter in weight, black, or have an odor.) A chemical change completely alters matter, so that after the change the matter does not resemble its original form. The chemical change we saw is called *oxidation*. After the oxidation, caused by the burning process, the paper was changed to a residue of chemicals. A slower kind of oxidation takes place when iron rusts.

How can plants cause a chemical change in matter?

For this experiment you'll need a package of yeast, 1 tablespoon sugar, $\frac{1}{3}$ cup of warm water, and a quart jar.

Yeast is a kind of plant known as a *fungus*. Mix together the yeast, sugar, and water in the jar. Stir well and then put the jar in a warm place. Check the results after 15 minutes.

Write down two ways you can tell that a chemical change has taken place. (The liquid will foam and give off an alcohol smell.) This chemical change took place because yeast plants use sugar for food; they break down the sugar into carbon dioxide gas and alcohol, and give off these two substances as they begin to grow. When we put yeast in bread dough, the carbon dioxide bubbles make the bread rise.

Acids and bases
How can you tell an acid from a base?

An acid is a chemical compound. When it is dissolved in water, it has a sour taste. A base is a chemical compound that tastes bitter when dissolved in water. Because tasting some acids and bases may be very harmful, a better and easier way to identify acids and bases is with an indicator. Prepare an indicator solution by mixing one tablespoon grape juice and nine tablespoons water in a bowl. First we'll find out how grape juice indicates a base. Put two tablespoons ammonia (a base) in a paper cup. Use an eyedropper to drip five drops of the

ROCK LEVEL —
WATER LEVEL —

This article by Sandra Markle appeared in INSTRUCTOR, February 1984.

grape juice solution into the ammonia. What color does it change to? (Dark green. If there isn't any change, add more solution.)

Now repeat this test to see how the grape juice solution affects an acid. Put two tablespoons vinegar (an acid) in a paper cup and add five drops of the solution. What color does it turn? (red)

Now test each of these mystery liquids to see whether it is an acid or a base. (To the teacher: Into four lidded jars put baking soda and water [base], lemon juice [acid], strong tea [acid], and bleach [base]. Label the jars, e.g. A, B, C, and D.) Pour a little of each liquid from jars A, B, C, and D into a separate paper cup. After you've added five drops of the grape juice solution to the liquids, note what color the liquid changed to and indicate in your log book whether each one was an acid or a base.

How can you neutralize an acid?

Another way to identify acids and bases is by using a special kind of paper called *litmus paper*, which comes in two colors—pink and blue. Pink litmus paper turns blue in a base, and blue litmus paper turns pink in an acid. If the substance is neutral—neither an acid nor a base—such as saltwater or sugar water, the pink paper stays pink and the blue paper blue.

Prove this by pouring $\frac{1}{4}$ cup vinegar into a paper cup and $\frac{1}{4}$ cup ammonia into another cup. Dip a piece of the pink and blue litmus paper into each sample. The blue turns pink when it touches the vinegar and the pink turns blue when it touches the ammonia. Now use an eyedropper to transfer ammonia, five drops at a time, into the vinegar. After each drop, test the vinegar with blue litmus paper. When the paper no longer turns pink, test the vinegar with pink litmus paper. If that also remains unchanged, you've neutralized the acid. How many drops of the base (ammonia) did it take to neutralize the acid (vinegar)? (Answers will vary depending on the strength of the vinegar and ammonia used.)

What happens when acids and bases react with each other?

Collect a dry glass pop bottle, a balloon whose end will fit over the bottle neck, a rubber band, vinegar, and baking soda. Measure two inches from the bottom of the bottle and mark it with a crayon. Pour vinegar into the bottle up to this mark. Add two tablespoons baking soda. *Quickly* fit the balloon over the bottle and wrap the rubber band around the balloon on the bottle neck to hold it tight. Shake the bottle.
1. What happens to the balloon? (It swells up somewhat.)
2. Why do you think this happens? (When you mix an acid and a base they give off a gas.) The gas given off, which made the balloon swell, is carbon dioxide.
3. How could you make the balloon swell more? (By adding more vinegar and baking soda, or by shaking the bottle harder.)

What effect does acid have on a bone?

For this experiment, you'll need a clean chicken bone, a jar, and vinegar. Put the bone into the jar and pour in enough vinegar to cover the bone. Put the lid on the jar. Every two days pour off and

replace the old vinegar (which, as you remember, is an acid). After one week pour off the vinegar and see how the bone has changed.
1. How is the bone different? (It should be rubbery; if it isn't, continue the test another week.)
2. Calcium is what makes bones hard. What do you think the acid did to this bone's calcium? (It dissolved it.)

How does acid affect metal?

Collect several dirty pennies—the blacker the better—a paper plate or plastic cup, salt, and vinegar. Put the pennies side by side on the plate or in the cup. Cover the pennies with salt. Pour vinegar over the salt and pennies (just enough to cover them). After a few minutes, remove the pennies and rinse them with water.
1. What happened to the pennies when you rinsed them? (They became clean.)
2. How could you tell a reaction was happening? (When the vinegar was poured over them, they bubbled.)
3. Why do you think the pennies were changed? (The acid reacted with the outer coating of dirt.)

After students have had a chance to do most of the experiments, discuss their individual results as a group. Encourage children to draw general conclusions, such as heating makes molecules move faster, and print these on a poster to mount near your lab. Did any other questions about matter or acids and bases come to mind while they were experimenting? If so, write new discovery cards based on these questions for students to try out later.

And they will be eager to find out more. You can get other ideas for low-cost experiments from such books as *Great Ideas of Science* by Isaac Asimov (Houghton Mifflin, 1969), *Experiments with Everyday Objects* by Kevin Goldstein-Jackson (Prentice Hall, 1978) and *Hands-on Science* by Sandra Markle (Instructor Books, 1988). Let simple materials open up scientific worlds to your students.

Super-yet-simple-science

These hands-on science activities developed by Sandra Markle will really get kids involved. Your students will experience sound concepts of science with only simple materials. Use these activities in the classroom or duplicate them to send home so parents can get involved, too.

Investigating water

These activities will help your child think about some of the properties of water: its power to erode soil, its ability to change to a solid (ice), its magnifying qualities, and the way it dries away (evaporates). Start a scrapbook together. Include pictures on water use and conservation.

Magnificent view

Get out a piece of plastic wrap and a sheet of newspaper. Have your child put the plastic wrap on the newspaper and then place a drop of water on top of it. Ask your child how the print looks through the drop of water. Is it different from the areas without water? (S)he'll be surprised to find that looking through the water tends to magnify the letters in the newspaper. Why? The shape of the water drop creates a kind of magnifying lens.

Up, up, and away

Help your child witness the process known as evaporation. Have him or her measure two cups of water into a shallow dish and let it sit uncovered for three days. After that time, have your child carefully measure the water that is left in the dish. Ask whether there is more, less, or the same amount of water in the dish. *(There should be less because air moving over the surface of the water speeds up some of the water molecules until they become fast-moving and spread out. These water molecules mix with the air to become water vapor. This process is called evaporation.)*

Drop it!

Have your child drop water from an eyedropper, first onto loose soil, then onto hard-packed dirt, and finally onto sand. Ask where the drops of water dug the deepest hole. *(On the loose dirt.)* Can your child think of ways to increase the water's force? (No fair using a hose or a squirt gun.) Let your child experiment. He or she will find that dropping the water from a greater height will increase its force. Measure each hole by putting a toothpick in the hole and then laying it on a ruler to measure.

OK, freeze!

Have your child find two small metal or plastic containers. Each container should be the same size and shape. Then he or she can fill one with water and the other with fruit juice. Have your child carefully lay a popsicle stick in each. Put both in the freezer. Check them every 30 minutes. Which freezes first? *(Water.)*

Water use

Have your child collect magazine pictures of the many ways we use water. Don't forget water is used for transportation, recreation, and production. What animals and plants depend on water for their homes? Ask your child to imagine what life would be like without water. Could we survive?

This article by Sandra Markle appeared in INSTRUCTOR, October 1982.

Super-yet-simple-Science
The human body

Children need to understand about their bodies and how they grow. Talk about the importance of good food. Compare the traits of adult relatives. Finally, use the ideas below to make your child aware of his or her senses and physical capabilities.

Fill your plate

Draw lines on paper plates, dividing each plate into four equal parts. Label each part with one of the four main food groups: bread and cereal, meat and egg, fruit and vegetable, and dairy products. Then paste pictures of food on 3'' x 5'' index cards. Be sure to include foods from each of the four groups. Shuffle the stack and place the cards face down. Players take turns drawing and discarding. If the card can be used, it is put on the player's plate. The winner is the first person to have all four food groups on his or her plate.

It's in the bag

Collect five paper bags. Label one for each of the five senses: sight, hearing smell, touch, and taste. Think of things which can be identified mainly by one sense, such as candy (by taste), a skunk (by smell), a bell (by hearing), leather (by touch), and a house (by sight). Write their names or paste pictures of them on index cards and shuffle the cards. Have the child sort the cards into the appropriate bags.

Hands on

Challenge your child to list everything that can be done with his or her hands, such as: slap, wave, pat, rub, draw, scratch, poke, clap, and so on. The child can also try listing everything that can be done with his or her feet, such as run, hop, and skip.

Take inventory

Make a family tree with your child. Show your immediate family, grandparents, aunts, uncles, and cousins. What color hair do most family members have? What color eyes? Are most members of your family tall, short, or medium in height? Make an inventory of family traits and then ask your child to name the traits he or she thinks might be hereditary. Look in books to find out which traits can be hereditary and which traits may not be. For example, weight problems may not be hereditary, but may be simply the results of poor eating habits passed down from generation to generation.

Stand by

Here's an experiment your child will enjoy. Have your child stand up sideways against a wall. Make sure that one foot and one shoulder and one ear are touching the wall. Now challenge your child to lift his or her outside leg to the side without moving away from the wall and without bending his or her knee. Now you try to do it. You'll both find it's impossible. Why? You've changed your center of gravity and can't move without losing your balance.

This article by Sandra Markle appeared in INSTRUCTOR, October 1982.

Super-yet-simple-Science
Sorting and classifying

Sorting and grouping buttons, beans, or other objects may seem like a game, but it is actually a first step in learning to classify. These activities suggest ways to teach your child to sort by color, shape, texture, size, weight, and so on.

What's the texture?

For this game, glue pictures or print the names of objects which are soft, rough, hard, or smooth on 3'' x 5'' index cards. Make at least 10 cards for each category. Deal each player five cards. Place the rest face down in a pile. Players take turns drawing cards and discarding others. Each player keeps just five cards in his or her hand. The first person to collect five cards in any one category wins.

It's a mystery

Cut pieces of construction paper into squares. Use the broad side of a crayon to make rubbings from different objects in your house. Challenge your child to match the rubbings to the mystery objects. For even more fun, let him or her make another set of rubbings to challenge *you*.

Shape up

Cut out lots of paper triangles, circles, and squares. Use a hole-punch to put a hole in each shape. Thread shapes on a long shoestring to form a repeating pattern. Let your child duplicate this pattern on his or her own shoestring. For a tougher challenge, make the pattern consist of both color and shape sequences. Be sure that the child also has an opportunity to initiate pattern sequences for you.

Rock collection

Go for a walk together and collect rocks. Let your child think of ways to sort the rocks: by color, size, texture, or shine, for example. Let your child store and display his or her rock collection in egg cartons. Look in books together to identify and label the different rocks.

Rainbow hunt

Have a *color scavenger hunt* inside or outdoors. Give each player a paper bag. Then challenge the scavengers to find one object for each color of the rainbow. They must find at least one yellow, one orange, one red, one purple, one blue, and one green object. (No fair using paint or crayons!)

People puzzle

Cut out pictures of people from magazines and paste them on index cards. Give the cards to your child and ask him or her to think of different ways to sort them into piles. For example, he or she could sort by hair color, eye color, height, approximate age, and so on.

This article by Sandra Markle appeared in INSTRUCTOR, October 1982.

Super-yet-simple-Science
Shadows

Shadows illustrate the effect of light as it hits an object and lets children see the changes as the light is moved closer or farther away. Shadow stretch will reinforce a study of the earth rotating and revolving around the sun.

Me and my shadow

Shine a bright light at a wall in a dark room. Have the child stand in front of the light. Ask the child to change the size of his or her shadow. *(Do this by moving closer or farther from the light.)* Play music and let your child dance with his or her shadow. Tell a story and take turns making shadow figures with your hands to illustrate the story. Play shadow tag outdoors on a sunny day. This is played like regular tag, but a person is tagged when his or her shadow is stepped on.

Changing shadows

Collect a can, a paper cup, and a wood block. Take these objects into a dark room. Have your child place them on a piece of paper and shine a flashlight at them. Tell him or her to move the flashlight around and to change the position of the objects. Ask, "How many different shadows can you get from each object?" Let the child pick one object and draw each of its different shadows on the piece of paper.

Shadow stretch

Go outside on a sunny morning. Draw an X on a sidewalk or driveway. Have your child stand on that mark while you use chalk to outline his or her shadow. Have the child stand on this same mark at noon and late in the afternoon. Use different colors of chalk to outline each shadow. Let the child compare the shadow shapes. Talk about what caused the shadow to stretch or shrink. *(The angle of the sunlight.)* Would there be a shadow on a cloudy day? *(No.)*

Silhouettes

Make a shadow silhouette of your child. Tape a large piece of paper to the wall and have your child sit or stand in front of it. Shine a light on the child and trace his or her silhouette created on the paper. Let your child color in the silhouette or use it as a pattern to cut out the shape from black paper. The black paper can then be mounted on white paper for a dramatic effect. Let your child create a silhouette of you, too.

Lights! Camera! Action!

Your child will have hours of fun playing with his or her own shadow theater. Just cover a table with a sheet and then hang another sheet above the table. Shine a light behind the top sheet to illuminate the area. Puppeteers sit behind the table and hold their puppets up into the lighted area when their character is on stage. The audience doesn't see the puppets; they see their shadows. The story can be told by a narrator or the play can be simply a mime production accompanied by music.

This article by Sandra Markle appeared in INSTRUCTOR, October 1982.

Super-yet-simple-Science
Plants and animals

Use the ideas here to encourage children to observe plant and animal life. Begin by going on a scavenger hunt. Then create a map to chart the birds and animals that live in your area. The whole family will enjoy the Tree Hotel idea. Watch your tree as it changes with the seasons.

Scavenger hunt

Have your children's friends over and divide them into teams for a scavenger hunt. Or have your child go hunting solo. Hunters should find: a plant growing in a crack in a sidewalk, a hopping insect, a flying insect, a crawling insect, a plant growing on a tree (such as moss, lichen, or fungus), a vine, a flower, a bird feather, a root, and a seed. Score two points for the feather and one point for each of the other items.

Map it

Have your child draw a simple map of your backyard or neighborhood. How many animals and birds can he or she find and mark on the map? Have your child try to name these animals and birds. Do they appear in the same area on other days? Where are their homes? What do they eat? Where do they find water? Work with your child to name the trees and plants on his or her map.

Leaf it to me!

Collect leaves in your neighborhood. Have your child find the trees the leaves came from. Use books to help identify the names. Then pick out a few interesting leaves. Coat the underside of the leaf (the veins stand out more on this side) with water-based printer's ink or acrylic paint. Move the leaf to a clean paper, keeping the ink side up. Lay construction paper over the leaf and press firmly from the stem up. Your child can get several printings from one inking. Each will be slightly lighter.

That's the rub!

Let your child make rubbings of tree bark by putting paper over the bark and stroking across it with the broad side of a crayon. Each type of tree shows a different kind of pattern. Look in books about trees to identify your trees and label the rubbings. These rubbings can be cut into shapes and used to make interesting mosaics.

Tree hotel

A large tree is full of life. Find one, stretch out under it together with your child, and begin to watch and listen. What do you see? What do you hear? If the wind is blowing, the tree may even "talk" to you with its rustling branches. While you're checking out the tree's residents, be sure to peek under loose bark and look on the underside of leaves. A number of insects like such sheltered places. Talk about the residents that you can't see that live in tunnels and burrows beneath the ground around the tree's roots.

This article by Sandra Markle appeared in INSTRUCTOR, October 1982.

Science Resources
(Where to go, whom to ask)

PLACES:

American Association for the
Advancement of Science (AAAS)
1515 Massachusetts Ave. NW
Washington, DC 20005
(202) 326-6400

American Chemical Society
1155 16th St. NW
Washington, DC 20036
(202) 872-4450

Edmund Scientific Co.
Dept. 5556 Edscorp Bldg.
Barrington, NJ 08007
(609) 547-3488

Exploratorium Museum
3601 Lion St.
San Francisco, CA 94123
(415) 563-7337

Franklin Institute Science Museum
20th and Parkway
Philadelphia, PA 19103
(215) 844-1192

Invention Convention and
Science Olympics
Silver, Burdett and Ginn
250 James St.
Morristown, NJ 07960
(201) 285-7700

Lawrence Hall School of Science
University of California at Berkeley
Berkeley, CA 94720
(415) 642-5132

Missouri Botanical Garden
4344 Shaw Ave.
St. Louis, MO 63110
(314) 577-5100

Museum of Science and Industry
5700 S. Lakeshore Dr.
Chicago, IL 60637
(312) 684-1414

NASA Headquarters
Code LE
Washington, DC 20546
(202) 453-8396

National Science Board
Committee on Precollege Education
in Mathematics, Science,
and Technology
National Science Foundation (NSF)
1800 G St. NW
Washington, DC 20550
(202) 357-9859

National Science Foundation (NSF)
1800 G St. NW
Washington, DC 20550
(202) 357-9859

National Science Teachers
Association (NSTA)
1742 Connecticut Ave. NW
Washington, DC 20009
(202) 328-5800

Technical Education Resource
Center (TERC)
1696 Massachusetts Ave.
Cambridge, MA 02135
(617) 547-3890

Triangle Coalition, NSTA
1742 Connecticut Ave. NW
Washington, DC 20009
(202) 328-5800

U.S. Department of Education
Office of Education, Research,
and Improvement (OERI)
555 New Jersey Ave. NW, Room 504
Washington, DC 20208
(202) 245-3192

PUBLICATIONS:

National Geographic World
(ages 8-12; $10.95 per year; 12 issues)
The National Geographic Society
17th and M Streets, NW
Washington, DC 20036
(202) 857-7000

Ranger Rick
(ages 3-5; $14.00 per year; 12
issues) and *Your Big Backyard*
(ages 6-12; $10.00 per year; 12 issues)
National Wildlife Federation
1412 16th St. NW
Washington, DC 20036
(202) 797-6800

Odyssey
(ages 8-14; $16.00 per year; 12 issues)
1027 N. 7th St.
Milwaukee, WI 53202
(414) 272-2060

3-2-1 Contact
(ages 8-14; $8.00; 10 issues)
Children's Television Workshop
One Lincoln Plaza
New York, NY 10023
(212) 595-3456

Science Weekly
(Ages K-6; $3.75 for 18 issues;
$2.60 per semester; 9 issues)
PO Box 70154
Washington, DC 20088-0154
(202) 656-3777

From: INSTRUCTOR, 1987 Science Supplement

PUBLICATIONS FOR TEACHERS:

The Museum of Science and Industry: Basic List of Children's Science Books compiled by Bernice Richter and Duane Wenzel (American Library Association, 50 E. Huron St., Chicago, IL 60611; 1986)

Ranger Rick's NatureScope ($24.00 per year; 4 issues and a calendar) National Wildlife Federation 1412 16th St. NW Washington, DC 20036

The publications listed below are selected from the National Science Teachers Association. (A membership catalogue is also available.) Write:
NSTA
1742 Connecticut Avenue
Washington, DC 20009.

Focus on Excellence series, edited by John E. Penick ($7.00 each; 13 titles: *Elementary Science; Science as Inquiry; Biology; Physical Science; Science/Technology/Society; Physics; Middle School/Junior High Science; Science in Non-School Settings; Earth Science; Energy Education; Chemistry; Teachers in Exemplary Programs; How Do They Compare?; Exemplary Programs in Physics, Chemistry, Biology, and Earth Sciences*)

Science and Children ($33.00 per year; 8 issues) and *Science Scope* ($7.00 per year; 6 issues) *Promoting Science Among Elementary School Principals* series, edited by Kenneth R. Mechling and Donna L. Oliver (NSTA, 1983, $15.25 for set of 4 titles: *Science Teachers Basic Skills; The Principal's Role in Elementary School Science; Characteristics of a Good Elementary Science Program; What Research Says About Elementary School Science*)

PROJECTS:

The projects below are selected from the COSMOS Corporation's *Catalog of Practices in Science and Mathematics Education.*

Activity-Oriented Laboratory Science Program
Washington School District
8610 North 19th Avenue
Phoenix, AZ 85021
Grades 4-6

Awesome Science
Rocky Run Intermediate School
4400 Stringfellow Road
Chantilly, VA 22021
Grades 4-7

Cato-Meridian K-6 Program
Cato-Meridian Middle School
PO Box 100
Cato, NY 13033
Grades K-6

Dahlen Environmental
Education Center
7117 South Jackson Road
Jackson, MI 49201
Grades Pre-K - 5

Coping and Cognitive Skills
Through Science
Northeast Region Education Center
Box 1028
Williamston, NC 27892
Grades 4-7, Special Ed

Einstein's Closet
Carmel Junior High School
300 South Guilford Road
Carmel, IN 46032
Grades 2-5

Elementary School Science
Exploratory Laboratory
John S. Haitema Elementary School
11870 Eldorado Drive
Sterling Heights, MI 48077
Grades 1-6

Fitchburg Area Collaborative for
Excellence in Teaching Science
(FACETS)
Hawthorne Brook Middle School
Brookline and Dudley Roads
PO Box 654
Townsend, MA 01469
Grades K-8

Grandteacher Program
Marlborough Public Schools
Bolton Street
Marlborough, MA 01752
Grades 2-5

Hands-On Experience
Atkinson Elementary School
310 5th Street, S.E.
Barnesville, MN 56514
Grades K-6

Have a Healthy Heart
Model Classrooms, Inc.
4095 173rd Place, S.E.
Bellevue, WA 98008
Grades 4-8

Plan-ahead
social studies

Start creating and collecting materials for these units!

Task cards help to settle the West

Task card activities can enhance the effectiveness of many social studies units. The following cards developed by Kathryn M. Sommers and Kathy Olinger are excellent examples. They form the basis of a middle-grade unit on the pioneer movement westward.

All-Class Motivators

1. Read and dramatize an incident about a famous hero of the westward movement, such as Daniel Boone. Discuss his character; show that hardship, good judgment, and a belief in what he was doing advanced him further than he ever believed.

2. If there is a reconstructed log cabin, pioneer village, or museum exhibit in your community, arrange a visit. See firsthand the challenging life of the people who settled this land.

Language Arts

1. Pretend you are an Indian, watching the white man blaze a trail across your hunting grounds. Describe your feelings.

2. Imagine you are one of the first settlers at Boonesborough. Write a letter to a friend back east urging that person to move to your community. List what he/she can gain by such a decision.

3. Prepare a daily log describing one of the following: Life on the Oregon Trail, The Journey with Lewis and Clark, Cutting the Wilderness Trail.

4. Imagine you are a member of the Lewis and Clark expedition just after the completion of Ft. Clatsop. Write several paragraphs in your diary expressing your pride in having crossed the continent, describing some of the troubles the expedition had.

5. Pretend you are one of the soldiers with Lewis and Clark. Your own pack of belongings may weigh no more than two and one-half pounds. Write what you are taking. Explain choices.

6. Imagine you are a member of the Transylvania Company or the Ohio Company, trying to sell land to prospective buyers. Write about the low prices for land, the fertility of the soil, the ease with which a man may establish a comfortable home, and other advantages of moving West.

7. Think of yourself as a newspaper editor who has just read the census figures of 1790. Write an editorial inspired by the number of people living in Kentucky and Tennessee. Note that most of these people have moved over the Appalachians only recently, and predict that it will not be long until the entire region between those mountains and the Mississippi River will be populated.

8. Write a daily diary of a person making the trip west by Conestoga wagon. Mention any hardships or risks, and describe what life is like as the party advances farther west.

9. Imagine you are living on the frontier. Write a letter to a friend in Pennsylvania. Tell about your new house, your school, or some social gathering you attended. Draw pictures to illustrate your letter.

10. Pretend you are one of the riders for the Pony Express and that you are speaking to a group of school children about your job. Prepare a short speech mentioning your duties, as well as some of the troubles you have encountered.

11. Choose a person from this time in history and read about him or her. Then prepare a report and

Original article appeared in INSTRUCTOR, August, 1978.

record it on tape. Make the report in the first person, and include as many sound effects as you can.

12. Write a puppet play, dramatizing an interview with an applicant for a job with the Pony Express. Ask several friends to work with you in creating the puppets and writing the script.

13. Pretend you were one of the first of what we now call the forty-niners. Tell about your campsite, your mining equipment, the cost of living, and the claims you have discovered.

14. Write a composition praising the early hunters in the United States for their contributions to America. Remember, they created the first trails to the West, discovered passes through the mountains, learned the ways of the Indians, found the best places for settlement, and taught these ideas to people who followed.

15. Ask other class members to help you plan and write the front page of a newspaper for this period. Decide which events and stories are important. You may want to include important business meetings. Perhaps each member of your group could be responsible for writing about one event. Remember to make interesting headlines.

16. Create an original poem telling about life as a pioneer. Is the restless spirit of these pioneers still present in Americans today? Maybe you'll want to write about moving today, compared to pioneer days. Or maybe you want to write about the moving as though you had experienced it. Illustrate your poem if you wish.

Geography and Map Skills

1. Make a pictorial map of the Lewis and Clark Expedition. Include a legend and scale of miles.

2. Prepare a route map of the Lewis and Clark Expedition. Label the Appalachian and Rocky Mountains. Include the major rivers and label them. With colored pencils, show the various routes pioneers used to travel west. Include appropriate pictures along the routes.

3. Suppose you are a farmer living in Missouri in 1830 and want to get your corn to New York. On maps, show the route you might take, and the kinds of transportation you'd use. (This will involve a legend.) Write your material as a report, or prepare overlays to use with the overhead projector.

4. On outline maps, show how much land the following included: The Louisiana Purchase; Texas Annexation of 1845; Oregon Territory, 1846; Mexican Cession, 1848.

5. Using a map of the Louisiana Purchase, draw and color the states eventually formed from this territory.

Math

1. Lewis and Clark and their men traveled well over 5,000 miles in two years and four months. Assuming that during this time they never traveled during a leap year, compute the following:
If their journey began on January 1 and ended two years later on April 30, how many days did their journey last?

2. The Louisiana Purchase added 828,000 square miles of territory to the United States. On October 30, 1803, the U.S. purchased it from Napoleon for $15 million.
How many acres of land did the United States gain? (Note: 1 acre = .0015625 square miles. Round your answer to the nearest acre.)
What was the cost of the land per acre?

3. When the news of gold being discovered in California reached the East Coast, many people headed west in search of their fortunes. As a result, prices soared. For instance, at one time a dozen eggs sold for $10 per carton. How much would just one egg cost? Make up some other inflation prices for food items, and figure the unit pricing.

4. In 1849, $10 million in gold was mined. By the year 1852 the yield peaked at $81 million. What was the percent of increase during the three-year period?

Original article appeared in INSTRUCTOR, August 1978.

Science

1. As the pioneers moved westward, they encountered new difficulties with their crops. It would be interesting to observe various plants and their reactions when placed under new conditions. Experiment with corn, wheat, tobacco, barley, and cotton seeds or plants. Place them in the following situations and record the results: Rocky soil, sand, extreme soaking of the soil, darkness, intense heat, extreme cold. Can you think of other growing conditions to test?

2. If possible, purchase some cream and churn it into butter.

3. Make foods like the pioneers might have cooked. Try this recipe for vinegar pie, a pioneer substitute for lemon pie. Bake one, and share it with the class: 1 c. brown sugar; 2 T. butter; 2 c. water; ½ c. flour; 1 c. vinegar; 1 plain pastry shell (baked) Mix sugar, water, and vinegar together. Heat until the mixture comes to a boil. Make a paste of the flour and a little water. Add the paste to the boiling mixture, stirring constantly until thickened. Stir in butter. Remove from heat and cool. Pour into the baked shell.

4. Pioneer women had few cosmetics, and those they did have were homemade. Make a type of hand lotion pioneer women used. Melt down a cake of soap and stir in ½ cup honey. After cooling, pour lotion into bottles and store for use. Share your lotion with your classmates.

Physical Education

1. Pioneer dances included the Schottische, the Virginia reel, the Quadrille, and square dances. Find directions for dancing one of them and teach it to the class.

2. Some of the games pioneer children played were jumprope, pitching pennies or horseshoes, marbles, blind man's buff, London Bridge, and leapfrog. Learn to play one of these games and teach it to the group.

Music and Drama

1. The settlers' ambitions, needs, and lives are portrayed in pioneer literature. Read one or more of the following poems: "Daniel Boone" and "The Roaring Forties" by James Daugherty; "Effortlessly Democratic" and "Santa Fe Trail" by Martha Baird; "A Peck of Gold" by Robert Frost; "Buffalo Dusk" by Carl Sandburg; "The Wilderness Is Tamed" by Elizabeth Coatsworth; and "Lewis and Clark" and "Western Wagons" by Stephen Vincent Benet. Read one aloud to the class and discuss it.

2. With two or three friends, role-play teen-age Miami Indians, telling their parents about the habits and customs of white settlers who have moved into the area. Let other kids role-play the Miami parents, explaining to their children how the behavior of the white man has created problems.

3. Visit your school's music teacher and borrow records of western songs. Plan a program of songs and describe the story of each song you play.

Art

1. The year is 1818. Create a miniature village in a clearing in the Indian woods, with one or two log cabins. A family, made of matchsticks, pipe cleaners, or even small dolls, could be working at an open fire, making a winter's supply of soap. Show the National Road under construction in the near distance.

2. Construct a small thriving village on the Mississippi River several miles north of St. Louis. The year is about 1825. Keelboats, flatboats, and canoes rest at the shore or float on the river. A blacksmith's shop and a fur-trading company's post are doing business.

3. Develop a Mormon farm where the first crop has been raised in Salt Lake Valley in 1848.

4. Create a mining town on a mountain slope in California in 1849.

5. Draw a picture of a covered wagon "village" at Independence, Missouri, and compare it to the settlement at Boonesborough.

6. Draw a cartoon showing the pioneers overcoming the barrier of the Appalachian Mountains. Maybe the pioneers are going around the mountains by way of the Erie Canal or the Gulf Plains, or through them by way of the National Road.

7. Prepare advertisements attempting to persuade people to join a company to Oregon. What arguments might be effective? The ads could be large enough for a bulletin board display.

8. Picture drawings were often the style of the pioneer artists. Invite several friends to help you make a mural, showing the westward spread of settlers in America. A typical theme might be the ways by which pioneers traveled West.

9. Construct Conestoga wagons from cardboard boxes. Plan what you will take in your wagon. Remember to consider the object's importance, weight, and space it takes up.

10. Make a chalk drawing of a Pony Express rider going from one station to another.

11. Make life-sized forms of people and dress them as you would find the early pioneers dressed. Choose a friend and work together. One person lies down on a large sheet of butcher paper, while the other traces his outline in pencil. Go over the outline with felt pen and paint the costume. When finished, cut out the figure and display.

Large-Group Summing-Up Activities

1. Review the history of the westward movement by pretending you are news reporters for live TV. Interviews, on-the-scene coverage, news flashes, and reports of eyewitnesses are a few of the techniques which would lend themselves well to this type of review. Some music and perhaps a few commercials will add to the program.

2. Plan a pioneer classroom and work in it for an entire day. Incorporate as many aspects of pioneer education as you can. Consult encyclopedias and other books for pictures and descriptions.

Plan-ahead
social studies

Grouping and regrouping small objects, as in a science experiment, can also work in social studies to help pupils visualize concepts. Here, Helen Lambert counts and regroups items to help kids understand population concerns.

Today's students are asking a host of questions about their future, including "What will life be like for me when I am an adult? Will there be enough food and energy? Where will I be likely to live?"

In expressing these concerns, the students are acknowledging that changes in population size—decline, growth, stabilization—and in population distribution have important implications for all of us. The study of these changes and their effects constitutes population education. Many of the following activities are from the *Population Education Resources Kit* (see resources at end of article).

Stork and Grim Reaper
This activity was originally developed by Charles Daniels.
Concepts: Birth rate, death rate, carrying capacity.
Supplies: Large clear container, food coloring, measuring cups of two different sizes, a bucket three-quarters filled with water, a sign reading "Stork" and another "Grim Reaper."

Activity: Color the water in the bucket with food coloring. Ask for a volunteer to be the Stork and one to be the Grim Reaper. Pin or tape the signs on the appropriate volunteer. Tell students that the water in the bucket represents the reservoir of life. The clear container represents our planet. Give the Stork a large measuring cup; it represents our current world birth rate. Give the Grim Reaper a measuring cup half the size of the Stork's cup.
Ask the Stork to populate the Earth by dipping into the reservoir and depositing lots of "people" into the "Earth." Then ask the Grim Reaper to remove some "people" and return them to the bucket. Because of the difference in the size of the measuring cups the "Earth" will soon nearly overflow with "people."
For even the youngest student this exercise demonstrates that the difference between birth and death rates accounts for the world's population growth. Also it suggests the concept that there may be a limit for the moment to the number of people which the Earth can support.

How Big Is The World's Population?
Concept: How much is a billion?
Activity: Tell this story. "Your rich uncle has decided to give you one billion dollars. However, there's a catch. You may not spend the money until you have counted it at

the rate of one dollar per second, eight hours per day. Do you accept? How old would you be when you finished counting?" At first most students will probably say they would accept. But after calculating the number of years required (roughly 95), they reconsider their choice! In the world today, there are *five* billion people, and if present growth rates continue, the sixth billion will arrive before the turn of the century.

The Calendar Riddle
This riddle is paraphrased from a version by Elaine M. Murphy.
Concept: Populations generally grow by ever larger amounts.
Activity: Tell students this riddle: "A father complained to his daughter that her allowance of $5 per month was too much. The daughter replied, 'Dad, why don't you just give me a penny on the first day of the month, two cents on the second, four cents on the third, eight cents on the fourth, and so on, doubling the last amount to arrive at the next amount?' The father, thinking his daughter a little foolish, agreed to the arrangement. Which person was the more clever?" Ask the students to calculate the amount of money the father would owe the daughter after 31 days. (Answer: $21,474,836.47)
Like the allowance, the world's population grows by adding ever larger amounts. Admittedly, the world's

growth rate is roughly two percent, a much smaller figure than the 100 percent by which the daughter's allowance increased each time. Even so, if this seemingly low rate of growth continues, world population will double to eight billion by the year 2012.

The Island Puzzle

Concepts: Earth's limited resources; advantages and disadvantages of community planning.

Supplies: Each student has a drawing of an aerial view of an island with mountains and bodies of water.

Activity: Tell this story: "Some 200 years ago 100 men, women, and children were shipwrecked on an island which had abundant natural resources. Some domestic animals and tools also survived the wreck. Draw your idea of how the island looked 200 years after the shipwreck. What are your assumptions about population change, technology, and government?"

Next, suggest students draw their idea of how the island will look 200 years from today. "What could change your prediction?" This activity is particularly well suited to small groups.

Human Beans

Concept: Average family size plays a major role in determining the size of a population. A slight difference in average family size produces a large difference in the size of the total population, if the average is carried over several generations.

Supplies: Clear plastic sandwich bags, uncooked kidney or pinto beans.

Activity: (developed by Charles Daniels): Distribute to each student six bags and roughly 100 beans, to make some bean families. Into each of two bags they should put two beans, representing the mother and father of the family to come. Then to one of these bags they should add two more beans; this will be a two-child family! To the other bag they should add three beans; this will be a three-child family! Put those two bags to one side.

Now tell them to take two empty bags, recreate the same bean families, and add another generation, assuming the same rates of growth. To one empty bag add two beans for the first mother and father, two beans for their children, and *four* beans for their children's children. (Spouses of bean parents are not included after the original mother and father.)

Into the second empty bag add two beans for the original mother and father, three beans for their children, and *nine* beans for the next generation. Put these two bags to one side.

Kids now take the last two empty bags, recreate these three generations, and add a fourth, continuing to assume these same growth rates. For the two-child average family the next generation numbers eight, yielding a total in this bag of 16. For the three-child average family the next generation numbers 27 giving a new total of 41—a difference of 25 in the sizes of the two families. Hence, a slight difference in average family size, if sustained over several generations, results in a significant difference in population size. The six bags which the students have filled demonstrate visually this mathematical fact.

What Is A Population?

This experiment is from *Population Education Task Cards,* by John Landahl *et al* (Dalphin Enterprises, Seattle, Washington).

Concept: What does the word *population* mean?

Supplies: A bowl for each student; assorted small items such as rubber stoppers, paper clips, seeds, and rubber bands.

Activity: Give each student a bowl which contains an assortment of small items. Ask the student to group the items according to their shapes. Each group is a *population* of those items. For an outdoor experience, ask each student to examine a one-foot square section of lawn. How many plant and insect populations can he find?

These activities and many more have been developed by educators excited by the potential of population studies to help build a sound instructional program. Other teaching resources, in the form of print and audiovisual materials, as well as background readings, are being produced in response to interests.

Population Reference Bureau, Inc., 1337 Connecticut Avenue, NW, Washington, DC 20036. Ask to receive its free newsletter, *Interchange,* which includes a complete teaching module. Although geared chiefly to the secondary grades, much of the publication's content is adaptable to the older elementary grades. Moreover, *Interchange* contains notices of training opportunities around the country.

In addition, the bureau distributes the game *Food for Thought* ($3) which contains many activities as well as background information, and focuses on world distribution of people and resources. It is adaptable to any grade level. You may wish to consider educator membership in the bureau; the $5 fee brings a wealth of materials.

National Science Teachers Association, 1742 Connecticut Avenue, NW, Washington, DC 20009. Ask for *Population Growth: The Human Dilemma* (1977, $3.50). This annotated listing contains the best in nontext materials, including curriculum guides, readings, and audiovisual aids.

An organization actively involved in facilitating population education is the **Sierra Club** (530 Bush Street, San Francisco, CA 94108). It is joined by many educational groups who have conducted or sponsored teacher-training workshops in population education.

Of special note is *Population Education Activities for the Classroom,* selected and developed by Judith M. Schultz and Herbert L. Coon, January 1977 ($4 each; ERIC/SMEAC, Ohio State University, 1200 Chambers Rd., 3rd Floor, Columbus, OH 43212). This compendium of hands-on activities includes 32 lessons suitable to the elementary grades, as well as annotated bibliographies of print and audiovisual materials.

The home-school connection

66 *The more involved parents became, the more they appreciated the dedication and the difficulty of a teacher's job. We also found that children's performance improved as they realized teachers and parents were working for their benefit.* *99*

— *Barbara Birnie*
veteran teacher

eachers, parents, and kids know how important it is for parents to be involved in their children's schooling. Where parents volunteer their time and attention, students achieve more and like school better.

Just think of it! Each year you have potentially 20 or more well-qualified helpers to assist you all year long. Adult helpers! In a class of 20 students, you have at least 20 parents or guardians with a vested interest in what you are trying to accomplish. They can make your job much easier.

At home, they can encourage and help motivate kids, foster a good attitude toward school and work, provide practice and supplemental learning activities, and make sure children get the rest, food, and exercise they need to perform well. In school, parents can volunteer to tutor individual students, read to groups or classes, share special skills or knowledge, help make dittos and photocopies, organize field trips, and so on, giving you more time to teach.

In the community, parents can spearhead

fund-raisers for schools and classes, lobby for better education budgets, promote positive public relations, sponsor school activities, and more.

There are many different ways to involve parents in children's schooling. But there's really only one reason for it: to provide the best possible education for their children. In this respect, you and the parents of your students share a common goal.

But working toward this common goal is another matter. Cooperation doesn't just happen. It requires mutual effort, and good communication and interpersonal skills on your part. No matter how you interact with parents, always treat them as the VIP's they are—Very Important Partners.

Communication and Interpersonal Skills

Every teacher needs to develop special skills for interacting with parents. Good listening techniques, tact, kindness, consideration, empathy, enthusiasm, and an understanding of parent-child relationships are important in communicating effectively.

No matter how you interact with parents— through conferences, telephone conversations, written notes or reports, lobbying or fund-raising efforts, working together in the classroom—good communication and interpersonal skills will send your message home.

How's your attitude?

The first step to good relations is developing the proper attitude and approach. Keep the following guidelines in mind as you communicate with parents, suggests former teacher Oralie McAfee in her *Resource Notebook for Improving School-Home Communications* (a major source of information for this chapter).

• *Recognize that schools and homes have shared goals.*

Both teachers and parents are committed to the nurturing, development, and education of children. "Before any real progress can be made," says McAfee, "teachers must believe that parents have a crucial role in their children's education, and parents and teachers must trust each other." Schools must cultivate that trust, she adds.

• *Respect parents and communicate that respect.*

Tone of voice, word choice, facial expressions, body language, expectations, how long we make people wait—all these communicate respect, or lack of it. Many parents have personal, family, work, health, or

other problems that we know nothing about. Make a special effort to give parents the benefit of the doubt. And, assuring them of confidentiality, gently encourage them to tell you about special circumstances for their child's sake (pending divorce, illness in the family, or other circumstances that affect the child's performance).

• *Acknowledge the changes in the American family.*

"No need to lament that both parents work away from the home—most school people do the same thing!" Whether they are single parents, involved in custody battles, unemployed, wrapped up in their own careers, or have overwhelming personal problems, "most are genuinely concerned about their children," says McAfee.

Single-parent families deserve special mention here. A 1986 U. S. Census Bureau survey showed one child out of four lives in a single-parent home. Yet this common lifestyle is still treated as an aberration by many teachers.

Researcher Joyce Epstein at the Center for Research on Elementary and Middle Schools found that parents' marital status affects teachers' evaluation of students. Some unfairly rate children from single-parent families lower than other children. Single parents often have the best relationships with those teachers who actively initiate parent involvement.

• *Understand the different types of school-family communication and the advantages and limitations of each.*

Communications about individual children include academic progress reports, attendance and tardiness notices, get-acquainted calls or messages, conferences, work samples, telephone calls, and suggestions of how parents can help their children.

"All too often individual messages from school to home or home to school are about problems," says McAfee. "Parents and schools need to hear more about the good things that happen!"

Class or schoolwide communications include newsletters, recorded telephone messages, radio and television messages, handbooks, bulletin boards, announcements, and flyers of all kinds. Whatever the medium, make it a point to project enthusiasm and a positive outlook.

• *Tailor communications to your audience.*

All communications should be clear, expressed in plain language (no technical jargon nor acronyms), short, and to the point. Don't patronize. Find out what types of communication work best with your students' families. (Ask them which they read and prefer.)

• *Be sure to check written material for spelling and grammar.*

• *Get expert help if you need it.*

If your district has school psychologists, social workers, or experts in public relations, communication, graphics, photography, and so on, use them. Their communication skills

Guidelines for Communication

Keep the following guidelines in mind as you communicate with parents.

1. Recognize that schools and homes have shared goals.

2. Respect parents and communicate that respect.

3. Acknowledge the changes in the American family.

4. Understand the different types of school-family communication and the advantages and limitations of each.

5. Tailor communications to your audience.

6. Be sure to check written material for spelling, grammar, and punctuation.

7. Get expert help if you need it.

8. Communication is a two-way street. Invite responses when communicating with parents.

can help you reach parents.

• *Communication is a two-way street.* Invite responses when communicating with parents. Include statements such as:

— For further information call (   ).
— If you have any questions (   ).
— If you want to talk to me, I will be available between 3 and 4 p.m. Or please jot me a note telling me a convenient time to reach you.
— If you have any suggestions or questions, write them in the space below and send them back to school with your child or drop them in the mail. We want your ideas.

Put your school's name, telephone number, street address, and mailing address on written communications. On the first day of school send home a card with that information plus the names of school personnel parents might need to contact—the principal, secretary, resource teacher, and so on.

Plain talk

Auditory memory, visual-motor integration, norms, percentiles, psychological inventories—educational jargon is a good way to throw up a smoke screen. But if honest communication is your goal, take time to speak plainly. Translate your professional shorthand into meaningful words and explanations. Jargon reduces rather than improves your credibility with parents.

(Columnist and parent Erma Bombeck illustrates the point beautifully; see box.)

Stop, look, and listen

When people speak to you, what do you hear? Chances are it's only one-quarter of what they say. Researchers estimate that our listening efficiency is about 25 percent. Maybe that's proof of the adage, "You hear what you want to hear."

But listening is one of the most frequently used aspects of communication—and probably the most important. Good listening

"When my son, Bruce, entered the first grade, his report card said, 'He verbalizes during class and periodically engages in excursions up and down the aisles.'

In the sixth grade, his teacher said, 'What can we do with a child who does not relate to social interaction?' (I ran home and got out my dictionary.)

At the start of his senior year, Bruce's advisor said, 'This year will hopefully open up options for your son so he can realize his potential and aim for tangible goals.'

On my way out, I asked the secretary, 'Do you speak English?' (She nodded.) 'What was she telling me?'

"Bruce is goofing off," the secretary said flatly.

"I don't know if education is helping Bruce or not, but it's certainly improving my vocabulary!"

(from *At Wit's End*, by Erma Bombeck. Copyright 1978, Field Enterprises, Inc.)

skills are essential in home-school relations. They are the difference between talking *to* parents and talking *with* them.

Many factors can inhibit our ability to listen:
• distractions, such as 25 children about to let loose while you speak with a parent who has dropped by unexpectedly;
• tension, when you may be defensive and trying to think of what to say next, instead of paying attention;
• an environment that may be too noisy, too crowded, too uncomfortable;
• impatience, when you think what's being said is unimportant;
• time, if you are in a hurry;
• preoccupation;
• impressions of the way a speaker looks, acts, or talks.

Listening skills can be improved; it takes practice, a few simple strategies, and most important, the proper mindset.

First of all, you must genuinely want to listen to what someone says, advises home-school specialist Edward Gotts of the

Friendly partners

Establishing good rapport with parents is just one of those many intangible qualities about good teaching—one that pays big dividends in home-school relations. To be a friendly partner:

• Meet parents in a nonauthoritarian way.

• Sympathize and empathize.

• Try to see the child from the parents' view.

• Help parents feel good about themselves and their child.

• Be positive and enthusiastic.

• Let parents know you are interested in their child as an individual—one who has strengths, weaknesses, and his or her own way of learning.

• Don't compare one child with another.

• Avoid getting too personal. If problems at home affect the child's behavior at school, report the behavior and ask parents if they have any ideas about the cause. But don't press.

• Respond to parents as individuals, realizing each has a unique personality and set of concerns.

• Don't interrogate. Parents will be more open if you don't put them on the defensive.

• Discuss, but never argue. And don't criticize.

• If parents need help with a problem, suggest ways they might solve it.

• In general, treat parents with the same regard for their self-esteem as you would students.

Appalachia Educational Laboratory. Be mentally and emotionally receptive and responsive. And give your total attention to trying to understand. How?

• Maintain eye contact.
• Face the speaker and lean forward slightly.
• Nod or give other non-interrupting acknowledgments.
• When the speaker pauses, allow him or her to continue without interrupting.
• Ignore distractions.
• Wait to add your comments until the speaker is finished.
• Ask for clarification when necessary.
• Check your understanding by summarizing the essential aspects of what the speaker tried to say or the feelings he or she tried to convey.

The parent interview

Here's an activity that can give you double—even triple—duty. By actually interviewing your students' parents, you can practice listening skills, demonstrate that you are genuinely interested in involving them, and acquire useful information in the process.

The interview is especially helpful if conducted during the first half of the school

Learning to listen

Here are some teacher tips for learning how to listen—and strengthening the home-school connection in the process.

• Ask parents to tell you about children's interests, habits, chores and responsibilities.

• Be alert for visual cues, body language, and other nonverbal signs. Pay attention even to offhand comments that may give insight to personalities and family situations.

• Find out what parents know about what goes on in school and in your classroom. If their academic or social expectations are too high or too low, explain what you think are realistic expectations. But first try paraphrasing what they have said to make sure you understand.

year. And it makes a good "get-acquainted" exercise. Conduct it in person during a parent conference. Or use the telephone (but send a note home first to say you'll be calling and why). And don't forget to use those important communication and interpersonal skills! Use the information presented in the box on this page as guidelines in developing your own parent interview questions.

Parent Conferences

The parent-teacher conference is touted by expert elementary teachers as the best way to communicate with parents. Parents of grade-school children report that they want regular conferences with their children's teachers.

Most people prefer to express themselves verbally in a personal, one-on-one situation. Yet these face-to-face encounters can become emotionally charged, too, as teachers and parents size each other up.

The skillful directing of parent conferences is a lot to expect of the beginner—or any teacher, for that matter. It is somewhat analagous to the accountant's task of sitting down with tax clients. Sometimes they are happy with their returns, sometimes not.

Part accountant, diplomat, psychologist, friend—but totally a professional. These are the roles you play when you meet students' parents.

Part accountant, part diplomat, part psychologist, part friend—but totally a professional. These are the roles you play when you meet with the parents of your students. Your challenge is to make parents feel comfortable, show them how to get involved with their child's learning, and establish a working partnership.

The basic purpose of a conference is to inform parents of their children's progress and school performance. They get to ask questions, and you gain valuable insights into a student's home life. And what better time to ask parents

---

The parent interview: Points to consider

1. Please tell me about your child—his/her likes and dislikes, strengths and weaknesses, whatever you think is important.

2. What are your expectations from me and the school?

3. How do you think you can help your child learn?

4. Are there any unique situations or problems you want to share to help me understand your child better?

5. What kinds of communication do you like to receive from teachers—notes, newsletters, phone calls? How often would you prefer them?

6. What is a good time to call you?

7. What are some special hobbies or skills you can share with students?

---

to volunteer some time in school?

No two teachers conduct conferences the same way. That's because no two teachers are the same. Like teaching, conducting a conference includes elements of personal style. This section offers tips, ideas, and activities from a large sampling of professionals.

Planning the conference

Here are some important steps for planning a successful conference:
• Prepare a send-home that invites parents to meet with you, states the purpose of the conference, and lists potential times. (Schedule some evening slots to accommodate working parents, and invite both to attend. Have parents call you or send a return note to reserve a time.)
• Decide upon goals for the conference: put "A warm, friendly exchange" at the top of the list.
• Prepare an agenda that you share with parents before the conference. Include such topics as your general impression of the child,

his or her progress in each academic area, standardized test scores, your goals for the child in each content area, and the strategies you will use to meet goals.

• Plan questions to ask, points to make, and suggestions to offer.

• Ask parents to do their homework. Have them bring to the conference a list of their child's strengths and needs as they perceive them. (Include the reproducible on p. 247 in the send-home packet for this purpose.)

• Collect samples of the student's work to display.

• Prepare to explain your goals and teaching strategies.

• Schedule enough time for questions and discussion.

• Pull together necessary materials such as a daily schedule of classroom activities, a checklist of skill areas and notes on student progress, sample work, test scores, and reports from other school personnel where

The Conference:

Do:

1. Select one or two major goals for the conference.
2. Be on time.
3. Prepare in advance.
4. Remember that you are talking to another adult, not a child.
5. Keep the discussion simple and straightforward.
6. Watch body language and voice tone.
7. Provide support when appropriate.
8. Abandon the situation and yell for help when necessary (see p. 224 for suggestions on dealing with parents who think you're wrong).
9. Share information with the child in advance, when possible.
10. Share some positive information with all parents.
11. Keep information confidential.
12. Give parents time to share their perceptions.
13. Keep a notepad handy to jot down questions you'll need to address.
14. Keep a small clock in sight so you can stay on task and on time.

Don't:

1. Minimize problems.
2. Use jargon.
3. Make promises that can't be kept.
4. Be afraid to interrupt.
5. Share personal experiences.
6. Say anything you wouldn't want the child to know.
7. Argue.
8. Take things personally.
9. Cover too much information.
10. Drag the conference out too long (15-30 minutes is usually sufficient).
11. Write things on the conference form that you might not want placed in a cumulative folder.

In addition to the above suggestions compiled by the Appalachia Educational Laboratory, *do* start the conference on a positive note (that is, with a positive comment about the child) and *don't* ever compare students.

appropriate (the resource teacher, for example).

The setting

To put parents at ease, make the conference area as comfortable as possible. Are adult-size chairs available? Teacher Doris Dillon suggests playing soft music to relax both of you. Greet parents at the door, and sit with them at a table or in-facing chairs. Provide paper and pens. Provide refreshments, if possible. And make sure you have a few activities for younger siblings that come along.

Hang a "Conference in Progress" sign on your door to prevent interruptions, advises David Hunt. Hunt also suggests setting a table of materials parents can take home: curriculum plans; homework and grading policies; newsletters; suggestions for how parents can help—either at home with their child or in school; a directory of school personnel and parent-group representatives; and invitations to school activities or parent-group meetings. Doris Dillon posts a list of all conferences for the day, to keep everyone on schedule.

Conducting the conference

At the beginning, review the agenda you have prepared. Then communicate the specific information you have gathered about the child. Listen carefully to parents' responses, answer their questions, explain each point, and ask them if they can confirm your impressions. Set goals together for the child's future progress.

Conclude each conference by recommending specific steps parents can take to help improve their child's education. You might hand out a list of general suggestions for parents, such as the one on p. 240. Thank them for their interest, and tell them how nice it is to work with parents who care about their children. Invite them to call, send a note, or stop by after school if they want to talk about their child or ask questions. Assure them that you wish to keep the communication channels open all year.

The aftermath

After each conference, take a few minutes to jot down the gist of what was said. (Note-taking during the conference generally is not a good idea, because it makes many people uncomfortable. The exception is writing specific questions that parents want an answer to.) And list any commitments made by either you or the parents. Make follow-up calls or send notes, where necessary.

Finally, take time to evaluate your own performance. Were you well-prepared? Was the atmosphere informal and friendly? Did you use time well? Did you begin on a positive note? Did you encourage parents to talk and offer suggestions? How could the conference have been improved? When it's all over, ask yourself what you have learned that will help you teach the child.

One teacher's experience

Parent conferences are usually pleasant, productive encounters. But on those few occasions when they're not, try to learn from your experiences. Thirteen-year veteran Judy Smith, shares an incident that taught her some valuable lessons. Here's what happened:

Smith had decided that one of her students should be retained, so she scheduled a conference with his parents. The only time they could meet her was before school. They arrived late, leaving Smith only 10 minutes to explain why she thought the child should be retained.

"So I hit them with the facts right away," she recalls. "They became very angry and left angry. The bell had already rung, and the kids were waiting to get into the classroom. I was upset from the conference, but I had to control myself and have a nice day.

"I blew it," Smith continues. "It was my worst conference and my worst day of teaching ever!" What has she learned?
1. Never schedule a conference that important under time pressure.
2. A before-school conference can ruin the whole day. Avoid them if you anticipate problems.

3. Build up to telling parents you think their child should be retained—don't blurt it out all at once.

"Now, we come to the conclusion together," says Smith, explaining how she first shows parents the evidence and talks about how difficult the next year will be for the child.

Based on her personal experiences, Smith has six good pointers for parent conferences:

1. Start by saying something positive about the child.
2. Have parents sit next to you at a table, instead of across from you with the table as a barrier.
3. Remember that as a teacher, you are in control of the conference. Make them comfortable, and they will better accept what you have to say.
4. Take cues from parents and try to sense which direction they want a conference to take. "Be tuned in to what parents want to know—what they're most concerned about," Smith advises. She cites the example of a father who didn't want to hear about his child's academic and social progress, but instead wanted to know the teacher's philosophy of teaching and what she believed about certain things.

During another conference, a mother brought a clipboard to take notes, and the father was very anxious to talk academics. So that's what they did first. Afterwards, Smith reports, they relaxed, and the mother wanted to know all about the child's social development—did she have friends, did she play with other kids on the playground.

Parent Conference Advice

Parent-teacher conferences are fraught with potential pitfalls. To avoid them:

- Be sympathetic.
- Realize that your evaluations and impressions of their children affect the feelings of self-worth of the parents themselves.
- Think carefully about inviting children to conferences with their parents.
- Conferences are not the time for surprises.
- Time your conferences to accommodate parents' work schedules.
- Recognize the pervasive changes in family structure.
- Interpreting test scores can be a delicate situation.
- Proceed cautiously.
- Help parents understand achievement test results.
- Explain to parents how policies help you determine grades.

Earlier, when Smith had taught an older child of theirs, these same parents were most interested in social development and the problems that child was having on the playground.

"Keep in mind that it's different for each parent and for each time a parent comes about a particular child," Smith stresses. "You must be flexible."

5. Let parents unwind first if they're concerned about something. "If parents come to the conference needing to talk, I let them talk first or they won't hear a thing I say," Smith notes. "For example, if they're late because their car broke down, they may need to tell you about it. It's all a part of making them comfortable."

6. "Always leave room for hope." Never make a terminal statement or judgment about a child. Offer your professional opinion and even a personal one ("If this were my child . . .") when appropriate.

Cautions and considerations

Parent-teacher conferences are fraught with potential pitfalls. To avoid them, heed this advice from experts.

- Be sympathetic in the face of mistrust or open hostility. Understand the fundamental fear most people have about placing their children in a "stranger's" hands for such extended periods of time. Without realizing it, many parents may resent giving up their children to school.
- Realize that your evaluations and impressions of their children affect many parents' own sense of self-worth.
- Think carefully about inviting children to conferences with their parents. Some teachers think a child's presence inhibits a conference, others think it enhances the encounter. At any rate, do involve children somehow. Tell them the kinds of topics you will discuss during conferences. Meet individually to ask each child what he or she thinks you should discuss. Together, select work samples that illustrate progress and problems.
- Conferences are not the time for surprises. Don't wait until you meet with parents or send home a report card to alert them to a problem. Use the telephone, send informal letters, and send classwork home regularly to let parents know how their children are progressing.
- Time your conferences to accommodate parents' work schedules. Early morning, lunch time, late afternoon, and early evening are alternatives to the traditional after-school conference. Working parents—both of them—have just as much right to be involved as any other parent.
- Recognize the pervasive changes in family structure. Try to involve non-custody parents. Invite them to meet with you individually, if they prefer.

• Interpreting test scores can be a delicate situation. Avoid labels such as "retarded," "gifted," "perceptually handicapped," and so on. Instead, describe the child's actual behavior as revealed by tests. Parents are entitled to see all the information in their child's cumulative folder. And they have a right to a clear explanation of what it means. But confer with your principal or school psychologist before presenting potentially damaging material.

• Also proceed cautiously in presenting to parents the information collected by psychologists, social workers, nurses, and other professionals. Always report who actually gathered the information.

• To help parents understand achievement test results, explain that a child's scores only make sense when compared with his or her daily performance in school or at home. Achievement tests are only one measure of performance. Their purpose is to guide instruction, not evaluate students or teachers.

• You will undoubtedly be questioned about your grading policies. If district and school policies influence how you assign grades, explain to parents how these policies help you determine grades. What does a grade in a certain subject mean? Does an "A" mean that the child is working above grade level? Or does it mean the student is completing all work perfectly, even if that work is below grade level?

When parents think you're wrong

There will always be some parent conferences you wish you could avoid. Given the wide range of personalities and situations you'll deal with, occasional problems are inevitable.

How can you defuse an explosive situation? Charles Edwards, in *The Parent-Teacher Conference*, offers this advice:

1. Include the principal when you expect parents to be hostile.
2. Remain as calm and unemotional as possible. Your mood is contagious.
3. Ask parents to be seated.
4. Let them talk first and find out exactly what they are unhappy about.
5. Be open-minded. Don't assume they are wrong.
6. When they are finished, give your side of the story.

Group conference variations

Other variations on the group conference include:

• A hands-on workshop for parents, in which they became active classroom participants. To see for themselves the value of varied learning activities, parents work with different multisensory materials with accompanying activities and a list of learning objectives. (Contributed by Marie Carbo, Valley Stream, N.Y.)

• "Parents Together Night," a two-hour evening session without children. Here, parents take time to get to know one another and the teacher. Then the teacher discusses his/her role and the parent role, expectations for academic performance, student responsibility, social skills, and so on. Afterwards parents ask questions; sign up for an individual conference; sign up to volunteer; review texts and materials; look at learning centers; and chat. (Contributed by Jim Bellanca, Arlington Heights, Ill.)

• Group meetings centering on questions teachers ask parents to think about ahead of time. For example:

What amount of time do you expect a teacher to devote to children who need extra individual help?

Without naming names, what are some of the most satisfying and frustrating experiences you have had with teachers?

(Remember, never discuss individual children in a group setting.)

7. If you were wrong, admit it. Don't try to defend an indefensible position.

8. The tone that should prevail in such discussions is one of cooperation between teacher and parent for the good of the child, not teacher versus parent.

9. Usually the two of you will agree when all the facts are known.

10. When you don't agree, remind the parent that even when you don't agree, both of you are interested in doing what is best for the child.

11. Make certain parents understand your position on the issue and won't be surprised by any future action you take. If they are demanding something you are not willing to do, be certain they understand this.

12. Don't expect that everyone will agree with you and be happy about the outcome of the conference.

Group Conferences

"With so much to do in so little time, I tried a group parent conference. Its design allowed for talks with individual parents while the others took part in class activities. It was so successful I'm going to do it again next year."

Like Eva Schmidler of Los Angeles, many teachers have discovered the efficiency and effectiveness of group conferences. Bringing parents together in one large group accomplishes several purposes.

First, it saves time. Only once will you have to describe the direction and scope of your class activities, talk about individual learning styles, explain your strategies and goals for the year, talk about materials, and so on.

Second, the group conference makes many of the more reluctant parents feel at home in school. And an *esprit de corps* can develop among parents of classmates.

Group conferences are also a great time to describe how parents can help in school and then solicit volunteers. Adults are susceptible to peer pressure too.

Sometimes, in conferences handled the way Schmidler handles hers, parents can experience a regular school day. One group conference she had occurred this way:

When parents arrived for the two-hour conference, she introduced them to students. First they observed a language lesson and examined textbooks and supplementary materials. Then, while students attended physical education class, she talked to parents about children's special needs, overall academic goals, and how she hopes to instill in each child feelings of belonging and individual importance, and of functioning as a class unit.

After students returned to the classroom and had a snack with their parents, Schmidler began brief individual conferences. These miniconferences gave her a chance to show parents their child's work samples and parents the chance to ask questions in private. During the conferences, students and parents participated in math, social studies, and reading activities that were led by an aide.

As Schmidler discovered, the individual conferences were more meaningful than they had ever been.

"Perhaps many of their questions were answered in the group conference," she speculates. "Or perhaps the parents were relaxed after being in the classroom and had lost some of their anxieties. Whatever the reasons, the questions were brief and realistic and the parents gave me the feeling that they were satisfied and confident that their children were receiving a good education."

You can't beat that!

Walk a Mile in My Shoes: Parents in the Classroom

Seeing is believing. If you really want parents to know what a great place your classroom is, how well their children are learning, or how much you want and need their involvement, invite them to school. Once there, they can casually observe, participate in activities, or help you run the show. The changes in attitude that can occur from such visits are amazing. *Walk a mile in my shoes . . .*

The open-door policy

The first step is getting parents in the door. All parents should be encouraged to visit their child's classroom. But you must establish guidelines. While some teachers welcome an unannounced visit, others feel it is too disruptive.

One strategy is to explain to parents that valuable teaching time is lost when unannounced visits break students' concentration and your tight schedule. Instead, suggest they call first or come during a specially designated time. One teacher writes this note to parents:

> "We have set aside Wednesday morning as a special time for parents to visit. We will have some adult-sized chairs for you at the back of the room. Feel free to come in. A rough weekly schedule and some observation guidelines will be placed next to the chairs. If you have any specific questions please make an appointment with me because I will continue working with the children throughout the morning. We look forward to sharing our school day with you. Hope to see you at school."

Group visits might make some parents feel more at ease. Also, you will be more comfortable—and so will parents—if you give them written guidelines on what you expect. Do you want them to wander around the room and interact with students? Or would you prefer for them to be as unobtrusive as possible? Can you give them information that will make their observations more meaningful? How about providing copies of textbooks or materials so they can follow along with your lesson?

Classroom visits are not likely to become an abused privilege, given the busy schedule of most parents. So even if they occasionally drop in unexpectedly, make them feel at home.

Honor thy parents

Enthusiasm is contagious. When parents do visit, make sure they know how glad you are they came. Make a special name tag or a badge that reads, "Honorary Assistant Teacher of the Day."

Invite your visitors to get into the swing of things. They can read stories to the class, dictate words for a spelling test, assist on an art project, or referee games on the playground.

Special events

An open-door policy sets a good tone for home-school relations. But unless you issue a specific invitation, few parents will actually visit. Here are a few ideas that will have them beating down the doors:

Try a Parents' Visitation Day. Send letters home inviting parents to class on a specific day. (Make sure you have the principal's support on this.) Tell them this day will be a window on their child's world at school. Send home a schedule of activities so parents can plan to visit all or only part of the day. Encourage parents to write or call with comments or questions after their visit—anything to keep the communication channels open.

This day will be a window on their child's world at school.

Make lunch dates with parents. Even those who work will often be able to spend a lunch hour at school. They won't see much of classroom activities, but just the chance to be greeted by you and to sit and talk with their children in a lively dining hall should give them a warm feeling of belonging.

You might invite parents to school for special classroom events. Are your students performing a play based on a history unit they've just completed? Will they be presenting the science reports they spent two weeks preparing? Ask parents to share the moment. This gives them a chance to witness their child's accomplishments, and gives students an audience for their performances.

Schoolwide events are another time to invite parents. Ask them to meet your class at the room, then join you as you go to the auditorium for a special assembly or program.

Parent volunteers

You can do more than evoke good feelings by bringing parents to school. You can recruit volunteers. Once parents start coming to the classroom, many become interested in actually helping out.

Parents can be:

• Tutors. With individuals or small groups, parents can listen to children read, give spelling words, play math games, read aloud, or help out at learning centers.

• Aides. Parents can supervise individual reading time, project time, or other independent work periods.

• Field trip assistants. Let parents organize some of your field trips as well as going along to help with the children.

• Room mothers and fathers. Have parents help with special parties and school activities.

• Lunchtime and playtime supervisors.

• Clerical helpers. They can photocopy materials, make teaching aids, help type or edit class newsletters, correct papers, and help with your record-keeping. (Parents shouldn't have access to confidential information about other children, however.)

• Room coordinators. With an active volunteer program, you'll need someone to juggle schedules, make assignments, and find last-minute replacements when necessary.

Obviously, most working parents will not be able to volunteer in classrooms. But that doesn't mean they can't be involved. Far from it! Ask working parents to help at home by making learning games and teaching aids, sewing puppets or costumes, or baking for parties and special events. Make sure their efforts are noted in class so their children receive the same satisfaction and recognition as other children whose parents help in school.

There are many roles parents can play at school. No matter how you involve them, though, be sure to brief them on your teaching goals and strategies, the type of classroom climate you are trying to create, and your expectations for them.

Also, show them the ropes. Is there a special place to park? Can they use the teachers' lounge? Do they check in at the office? Should they call if they'll be late?

Finally, develop an all-purpose Parent Recognition Certificate (or use the one on p. 249) to show your appreciation to parents who help out in any way. A volunteers' tea is another nice way to show you're glad they're involved. Or have the children plan a special activity to honor volunteers.

Tapping all that talent

Your students' parents have a wealth of information, ideas, special skills and hobbies to share. Tap some of that talent in minicourses and enrichment classes taught by them.

The first step is to find out what parents' occupations are, and what special interests they have. Use the parent interview you develop from the guidelines on p. 219. Or send a survey home explaining your purpose and asking for ideas. You may want to create a language skills unit based on the students interviewing and writing feature stories about their parents.

You'll probably discover a parent who can teach your class about tropical fish and setting up an aquarium. Or someone who can help the children learn macramé or the techniques of bird-watching. Ask parents to describe their occupations: they can explain what it's like to be an engineer, police officer, auto mechanic, or writer. Are there parents who could help students understand different cultures and customs? Don't let these valuable resources go untapped; use every opportunity to enrich your students' education.

Some teachers set aside one day a month as minicourse day, organizing the day around various parent instructors who come to share their hobbies, talents, and skills. Other teachers find that occasional Friday afternoons are a good time to offer these enrichment activities.

Phone Home!

Telephone calls are almost as good as being there. They are an effective tool for home-school communications.

Telephone calls offer several advantages over notes, newsletters, and other written communications:
• You can establish personal contact.
• Messages are more immediate.
• You are certain your message reached parents.
• Phones allow an exchange of ideas and information. You can find out things you wouldn't learn from notes.
• You can clarify any portions of your message parents don't understand.
• Oral communication is familiar and comfortable for most people.

But there are disadvantages, too. Most can be overcome if you are aware of them.
• It may be difficult to find parents at home.
• You risk interrupting a family's dinner or favorite television show.
• Telephoning every parent takes a lot of time.
• Many of your calls will have to be made at home on your time.
• It may be difficult or awkward to discuss certain topics.
• You can't interpret nonverbal language over the telephone.

But most teachers agree that the advantages of telephoning parents far outweigh the disadvantages. So pick up the phone and put communication technology to work for you.

Sunshine calls

The most frequent and effective way teachers use telephones is to report on student progress or behavior—and not just poor progress or misbehavior! Get in the habit of calling at least one parent a week to relay good news. Keep track of these sunshine calls on a copy of your class roster. And make sure each family receives one at least once every two or three months.

These telephoning tips from the experts will make your calls easy, effective, and well-received:
• Before calling, make notes about what you want to say.
• Make sure you know the parent's name. It may not be the same as the child's.
• Introduce and identify yourself—"Hello, I'm Rob Carter, Cheryl's third-grade teacher."
• Ask if this is a good time to talk for five or ten minutes.
• Begin with a positive comment.
• Speak clearly and avoid jargon.
• Keep your message short, simple, and straightforward.
• Listen carefully and use "I-messages."
• Conclude on a positive note, and invite response. ("I'm glad we've had this chance to talk. If you need to call or see me about anything . . .")

When there's a problem . . .

When you do call parents about a problem, think of it in terms of soliciting an ally's aid. Use the following strategies in addition to the guidelines listed above:
• Report objective information.
• Be specific.
• Call as soon as possible after the problem arises.
• Avoid labels.
• Don't blame the parent or child.
• Talk about the problem as a shared one.
• Ask parents if they've noticed problems at home.
• Listen for facts and feelings.
• Ask parents to participate in solutions and offer suggestions.

Telephone tidbits

• Before school begins or very early in the year, send parents a form (or index card) to list their telephone numbers, emergency numbers, and the best times for you to call. (Or get this information from emergency cards in the office, if possible.)

• Keep students' telephone numbers handy. Many teachers find that an index file with a card for each child works best.

• Keep track of all calls made. Note the date, nature of the call, parents' responses, and outcomes. Again, the index card file works well. Or use the Telephone Record on p. 238.

• Make your first call to any home a positive one. You can accomplish this with welcoming calls before the school starts. Talk to both the child and the parent. Such calls go a long way toward smooth relationships with parents.

• Even problem calls should begin on a positive note.

• Call parents who don't respond to a written invitation for a conference. A call lets them know you're interested, and it could encourage those who are hesitant.

• Always invite a response. Ask parents to call back, write, or meet with you.

Dial-a-teacher

In an era of telephone answering machines, many schools are relying on recorded messages. Parents can use school answering machines for early morning call-ins, to get general information when no one is there, or as hot lines when they have problems or complaints.

Individual teachers who have access to answering machines use them to record homework assignments, list the weekly spelling words, make suggestions for developing or supplementing a curriculum unit, and so on.

Keep several ideas in mind when using recorded messages for your class:

• Messages are for a general audience.

• Make them short and to the point.

• Change messages regularly.

• Make them available at a regular time each day or week.

• Messages pertaining to children's work should include suggestions for how parents can help.

The Written Word

Happy Grams, newsletters, monthly calendars, informal letters or notes, and interim reports are ways teachers write to parents. In fact, writing is the most frequent form of communication between home and school.

Basically, there are two types of written messages sent home: messages for the whole class (newsletters, class calendars, open letters to parents) and messages about individual children (notes, recognition awards, interim reports).

Newsletters

Surveys of parents show that they read school newsletters and consider them a useful source of information. Parents indicate that classroom newsletters would be even more helpful.

You are limited only by your imagination in what a class newsletter can include. Here are some ideas to get you started:

• Lists of items parents could collect or save for class projects.

• Reminders.

• Announcements of upcoming events.

• Invitations to class activities.

• Thank-you's to parents who help out.

• Descriptions of study units and suggestions of ways parents can supplement the units.

• Reprints of articles you think are important.

• Explanations of grading policies, standardized testing, and other means for assessing and evaluating performance.

• Highlights of community resources, such as a children's museum or a good television show.

• Writing or artwork produced by children.

• Spelling words.

• Class averages on certain tests.

You must also decide on a format to use for your newsletter. One idea is to place a one-page newsletter on the back of a monthly school calendar. (You'll need a copying machine that can make back-to-back copies.)

More common is the multiple-page newsletter stapled together (by students or volunteers) and printed under a logo (or banner in newspaper lingo). Use a consistent format each time so the newspaper becomes instantly recognizable. Keep the format clean and uncluttered. Headings make it easier to locate different topics and articles, simple graphics help to summarize main points, capture attention, and so on. (Don't forget to number or date issues.)

Newsletters should be brief and to the point, with main ideas presented at the beginning of each section. Keep the tone informal and friendly, but not sticky-sweet.

Newsletters project an image of you and your class. How do you want to come across to parents? Dignified and serious? Whimsical and playful? Humorous? Proud and full of school spirit? Child-oriented? Solid as a rock? Caring and responsive? These and other images are created by the way a newsletter looks in content, format, logo, and neatness.

Newsletters communicate before parents read the first word. A sloppily dittoed newsletter full of typos communicates a strong message to parents—but not the one you want!

What about the frequency of your newsletter? Many teachers send a weekly update; for others, once a month is enough. A quarterly publication—four times a year— allows more time to do a better job. But the tradeoff is timeliness. The information might be too little and too late to do anyone much good.

Frequency should depend on what you are trying to accomplish. If your main purpose is to suggest supplemental activities for a study unit, a weekly or bimonthly newsletter might be your best bet. If you are trying to showcase student work and highlight achievements or contributions, a less frequent newsletter would suffice.

However frequently you issue the newsletter, try to send it home on a certain day each time so parents can be looking for it. Let your parents know, for example, that they can expect a newsletter on the first Monday of each month.

Open letters to parents

Start the school year with an open letter to parents. This letter can cover nitty-gritty details you wouldn't want to include in a personal welcoming call to each family (information about regulations and student supplies, for example). See p. 18 in Chapter 1 for ideas about what to include in your letter.

Send other letters throughout the year to make special announcements, explain a new policy, ask for volunteers, and so on. These brief letters can supplement the information

Classroom handbook

Linda Farr of San Jose takes the beginning-of-the-year letter to parents one step further with a classroom handbook she developed. She sends the handbook to parents within the first month of school, along with a sheet they can sign to show they've read the handbook. The handbook includes (among other things):

— her teaching philosophy

— a homework policy

— behavior standards and consequences for misbehavior

— schedules for spelling and math tests

— description of her VIP program that features a different student each week

— explanation of her assertive discipline program

— discussion of her policies on work quality (for example, she makes no corrections in creative writing)

— reminder to watch for notes in the daily folder students bring home

— explanation of her correction marks

— list of necessary supplies and also what not to bring to school

— a library schedule

— birthday policies (no sending treats, please)

you include in a regular newsletter.

The reproducibles on p. 249-253 are various formats you can use for your letters. Again, your format will project a certain image, so choose one that best sends your message home.

Personal notes

Don't wait for problems before contacting individual parents. Make your first personal note home a positive one. This way, you can gain parents' trust and confidence before you have to enlist their help if a problem should develop.

Take the time to share good news about individual children with their parents. Like the sunshine call, these warm touches on paper can cultivate good rapport with parents (not to mention your relationships with students).

Has a child accomplished an academic goal? Helped you or someone else? Finished his or her work on time? Tutored a younger child? Led a group? Let parents in on the good news. Good-news notes allow you to recognize and reward the efforts of individual children.

> Dear Mr. and Mrs. Jones:
> I thought you would be pleased to know how well Amanda is doing in reading. Her work improves every day, and her cheerful attitude brightens the whole classroom.
> Sincerely, Ms. Howard.

The Happy Gram is one common format. The good news is written on preprinted paper patterned after a telegram form. Many schools now have available pads of these preprinted forms. If yours doesn't, use the reproducible on p. 249, or develop a form of your own.

The good news can also be a brief handwritten note or a certificate or award of some kind. (See the reproducibles on pp. 251-253 for examples of different types.)

Two words of caution. Keep track of the good news notes you send out so every student occasionally receives one. (Some teachers routinely write several a week.) And never distribute the notes in masses. They're not special if everyone gets one.

Unfortunately, not all your personal notes will be good news. Problems do arise. Perhaps you've noticed that a child seems sick or constantly tired. Another is having difficulty in math and risks a failing grade. A shy child seems to be withdrawing more every day.

You need to tell parents. But if you have already contacted them on a positive note, chances are they'll be more responsive now to problems. Always let them know you share the problem.

One personal communication concerning academic problems is the interim report. This is an academic deficiency notice sent home between regular grading periods. It gives parents and students time to correct a problem before a poor grade becomes part of the child's permanent record.

"Parents who have received such a notice or have heard about the practice tend to view this special effort at personal communications as helpful and useful," reports Edward Gotts of the Appalachia Educational Laboratory. Gotts adds that parents' attitudes are very positive toward this practice and toward the schools that implement it.

More important, most parents who receive an interim report take corrective action. These actions are most effective when teachers provide some type of academic guidance sheet or suggestions for how the parents can help.

No matter what the nature of your personal note, always invite a response. Urge parents to call you, schedule an appointment to talk, or write back. If they don't, call them. Show them that you care.

Homework

As its name implies, homework includes those tasks and assignments students usually complete at home. Homework is a way to extend learning and practice time and encourage student responsibility. It's a means of assessing how well students have learned what you tried to teach. And it certainly affects home-school relations.

Homework is the most visible proof parents have of their child's learning and your teaching. It is the most common link between home and school life. And it can be a way for parents to actively participate in their children's learning, as you will see in the ideas and activities presented here.

Homework has become a highly charged national issue. Some school boards now regulate the types and amounts of homework teachers can or must assign.

Relations with parents can get touchy where homework is concerned. Perhaps you can remember family fights and arguments over homework during your days as a student. Even if parents philosophically acknowledge the benefits of homework (and most do!), they resent having to struggle with a child frustrated by assignments that are too difficult.

Homework should be an opportunity to practice newly learned skills that you have taught and students have practiced in class.

Many teachers with the right intentions assign homework for all the wrong reasons. Consider the list of *should-nots* generated from practice and research on this page.

No wonder kids have a bad attitude about homework. Under the conditions it's presented, they realize you'd have to be dumb, slow, or naughty to have any.

For example, using homework to make students teach themselves is a mistake many beginners make. Researcher Gaea Leinhardt of the Learning Research and Development Center in Pittsburgh found that novices often used homework to finish an incomplete math lesson. This made the homework more difficult to do (and thus more punishing) and it decreased the likelihood the children would complete it.

Okay, you know what homework should *not* be. But what *should* it be? An opportunity to practice newly learned skills—skills you have taught and students have practiced in class, under your guidance.

This guided practice is very important. It means working and talking through examples of the types of problems you will assign. Suppose, for example, you taught a lesson on diagraming sentences. You might have some students diagram a sentence on the board while the rest worked on the same sentence at their seats. You would continue to discuss strategies and errors as the students worked.

Research has documented striking differences between novice and expert teachers. Gaea Leinhardt found that experts regularly assigned math homework, but only after at least two rehearsals in class where they guided and monitored student efforts. Novices, on the other hand, rarely guided the class in practicing new skills. Instead, they jumped from presentation to assigning independent practice.

Homework contracts

The strategies above increase the odds that students will successfully complete their homework. But they don't guarantee 100 percent compliance. What about those who consistently "forget" or "can't do it" despite your best intentions? A contract might be the answer.

Homework contracts should involve parents

Homework can work

Here's some advice to help you see that it does.

- Assign tasks and activities that allow students to practice skills they've already learned.

- Guide students through sample homework problems.

- Explain the specific purpose of every assignment and why it's important to complete it.

- Make sure everyone understands the assignment. Don't assume that because no one asks questions there are none.

- Praise children's efforts in completing homework and encourage parents to do the same.

- Encourage parents to create an atmosphere conducive to homework. (The sofa in front of a blaring television is not a good place!) See p. 240 for a list of suggestions to send home.

- Show parents that you take homework seriously and send home a weekly folder of completed work. (This could include in-school assignments, too.)

- Don't grade homework. Remember, it's intended as practice, not a test.

- Do collect, check, discuss, or in some way show that you value children's efforts and that it's worth their while to complete homework assignments. Some school districts have specific policies. Some schools require teachers to review homework assignments in school and return them home again with students.

- Be sensitive to problems or frustrations students express about their homework.

- Keep in mind that the important question is, "Has the student learned?"

as well as you and the student. To negotiate one:

- Bring parents and child together in a conference. Discuss the situation in a straightforward, friendly manner.
- Set realistic goals.
- List the contract's objective, the follow-up actions you or the parents will take (signatures, phone calls), and the consequences for not meeting the contract's terms.
- Include awards for contracts completed. (Perhaps you should emphasize awards at home. Special privileges in school may not seem fair to other children who faithfully complete their homework.)

An example of a homework contract you can copy for your own use is found on p. 114.

Other ideas

- *Assignment logs.* You can also develop contracts around a weekly assignment log you use with the whole class. Assignment logs are a good idea for many reasons. Students have a complete and accurate listing of all assignments. The logs document student work and provide a simple record-keeping system for you. They demand active parent participation. (Parents sign the assignments completed.) And they help organize work to be sent home to parents. The reproducible on p. 248 is one example.

- *Enrichment activities.* Enrich your students' experiences and extend their individual interests by assigning creative homework. Enrichment assignments, often optional, give students choices and let them express individuality. Often they involve the whole family. Try the ideas on p. 239. Or use them as guidelines for developing your own ideas.

You can also suggest learning activities for summer fun. See the ideas on pp. 258-263.

- *Personal skill cards.* With pencil and ruler, divide a sheet of paper into 20 squares. Make multiple copies of this sheet and have children fill the squares with questions or problems they need to work on. (This can be used in any subject area.) Then have them write the answers on the back of each corresponding square (with your help, usually). Children can cut the squares apart to form personal sets of skill cards. Shared at home with parents, these skill cards can be used as flash cards or adapted to games of bingo or Concentration. (Idea by Patricia S. Koppman)

• *Bulletin board bingo.* Keep track of who completes homework each day by having students place a daily marker on a special homework bulletin board. To students who complete a full week, award a bingo prize.

• *Marking math homework.* Design math worksheets that have a column on the right side for answers. After working the problems, students place the answers in the right column. When correcting the homework, place your answer key right next to the column and mark the paper much more rapidly. (Idea by Barbara Gruber)

• *Standardized homework.* Simplify your planning by standardizing some homework assignments for certain nights. Every Tuesday, for example, students alphabetize the weekly spelling list and on Thursday they write a sentence for each spelling word. (Contributed by Barbara Gruber)

• *Give homework a home.* Give each child a 9 x 12-inch envelope for carrying homework to and from school. This doubles as a carrying case for notes sent to parents, and for papers and assignments sent home each week.

Chapter 6: Read more about it

1. *A Resource Notebook for Improving School-Home Communications.* Oralie McAfee. Charleston, WV: Appalachia Educational Laboratory, 1984.

2. "Parents and Schools." *Resources and Practice*, 5, 2 (April 1987). San Francisco: Ca: Far West Laboratory for Educational Research and Development.

3. *TARGET: An Examination of Parallel School and Family Structures that Promote Student Motivation and Achievement.* (Rep. No. 6, Jan. 1987). Joyce L. Epstein. Baltimore, MD: Center for Research on Elementary and Middle Schools, The Johns Hopkins University.

4. *Mind Movers: Creative Homework Assignments—Grades 3-6.* Diane Hart and Margaret Rechif. Menlo Park, CA: Addison-Wesley, 1986.

5. "Homework's Powerful Effects on Learning." Herbert Walberg, Rosanne Paschal, and Thomas Weinstein. *Educational Leadership*, 42 (April 1985), 76-79.

NOTES

NOTES

School-Family Telephone Record

Teacher _____

Student _____

Parent _____

Telephone number called: _____

You may wish to use this same record for calls from the family to you. Simply record "H" in the Response column.

	Day/Date	Time	Response*	Comments
1.				
2.				
3.				
4.				
5.				
6.				
7.				
8.				

Additional Comments/Record: _____

_____

_____

*Response List   A. Spoke with parent
B. Busy signal
C. No answer
D. Disconnected telephone
E. Scheduled call back _____
F. No adult home
G. Declined to speak
H. Family initiated call
I. Other: _____

_____

_____

HOMEWORK
Giving yourself and the kids a break!

Thirteen homework ideas by Jean Gatch—adaptable to various areas of the curriculum

1. Make a map of somewhere you would like to go or somewhere you have been. Put your map up on the bulletin board.

2. Visit the zoo (or an art gallery, or a factory, or a museum, or a concert). Tell the class at least five interesting things about your visit.

3. Learn a new poem and say it for the class.

4. Spend an hour watching a dog, a bird, a worm, or any other animal or insect. Write down four things you discovered.

5. Make up a menu for one entire day's meals for your family. Go to the grocery store, and find the food items you need. Figure out what it would cost to make the meals.

6. Think of something you can do that others in the class may not be able to do—or learn something new. Plan how you would teach it to the class when you are ready.

7. Make a puzzle. Bring it to class so everyone can work it.

8. Go to work with your father or mother or some other adult and find out what that person does. Write down all the reasons you would like to do the person's job and all the reasons you wouldn't like to.

9. Choose a country you are interested in and make a scrapbook about the country with clippings, brochures, and pictures. Write a letter to the ambassador from that country asking him or her to send material for your scrapbook.

10. Build something or make something. Bring it to show the class. Be prepared to show the class how you made it.

11. Make up a new game. Make all the pieces you need to play it. Bring it to class and teach everyone how to play.

12. Take a pet census in your building or on your block. Go to the library and find what species each animal is. Report to the class.

13. Read a book about a famous person. Make a hat or part of a costume he or she would wear. Wear the costume part to school and tell everyone about the book.

Reprinted with permission from *Elementary Learning*, October 1977

Helping your child at home

Here are some suggestions for how you can help your child become a better learner and show that you care.

- Encourage your child and express your pride in his or her efforts and accomplishments.

- Make sure your child gets eight or nine hours of sleep each night.

- Keep your child healthy by providing:
    1. regular medical checkups and booster shots;
    2. a balanced diet;
    3. regular exercise;
    4. clean hair and fresh clothes.

- Please notify me of any medical problems.

- Make sure your child has a good attendance record. Missing school means children fall behind in their work. They become anxious and frustrated when they can't keep up.

- Establish a time and place for studying. Give your child a quiet corner to read and do homework.

- Discuss homework assignments and discreetly monitor the child's progress. Offer praise or help when appropriate.

- Your child will regularly bring home completed papers and assignments for you to review. Ask to see these graded papers.

- Read to your child, and encourage him or her to read to you. Let your child see you reading. Remember: the best way to communicate the importance and value of reading is to read. Be a reading role model.

- Be an effective reading tutor by asking your child to find specific details in a passage, paraphrase a paragraph, or describe a character.

- Please stay in touch with me. I am happy to discuss any problems your child is having. Let's talk, and together we can try to find solutions.

I suggest the following enriching books and activities:

_____

_____

_____

_____

_____

_____

_____

_____
Teacher signature

Thank you for your interest and concern. I appreciate your support!

Creating the
Homework Habit

*Family situations—each one unique—undoubtedly influence
a child's approach to homework and learning. Parents can help children
develop good working habits. Please show your child that homework
is an important priority and you value its worth
by offering the following kinds of support:*

1. Sit down with your child and together schedule a time for completing homework assignments. Homework habits are more easily formed if children work the same time each day.

2. Help your child choose an appropriate study location—a quiet corner, a desk, a comfortable chair. The location can vary with the assignment. (Papers must be written at a desk or table, but books can be read in a recliner.)

3. Provide your child with good lighting and necessary materials (pencils and paper, a dictionary, etc.)

4. Ask your child to describe the assignment before beginning, and later show you the completed work or summarize what he or she learned.

5. Encourage your child to work on his or her own, but say that you are available for help.

6. If your child does need help, look over the material before you begin so you are familiar with the assignment.

7. Be a resource and consultant for your child, but don't hover over him or her with constant advice. Remember that sometimes the best help is a hug, a smile, or a word of approval.

8. If your child becomes frustrated, put away the assignment for a while.

9. Please be available to check work and check whether the assignment has been completed.

10. Praise your child for completing homework.

11. When possible, help your child relate homework assignments to everyday life and skills.

12. In general, be encouraging and supportive. Your attitudes are contagious.

Helping your child

For parent who receives report that student's work "Needs Improvement" (N).

This sheet is to help you decide how to help your child do better. Please study the list of *Reasons* below on the left. Ask yourself if one or more of them apply to your child. If you think a given *reason* applies, study and try the *action* to the right of it. For example, if Reason #1, "Poor attendance or tardiness," applies, then try Action #1, "See that makeup work is done." You can ask the school for more help if you need it.

Reasons	**Actions**
Possible reasons for poor work	*Here's what to try:*
1. Poor attendance or tardiness.	1. See that makeup work is done.
2. Seems tired all the time or easily loses control.	2. Get child to bed on time and be sure child eats good breakfast and lunch. Get medical checkup.
3. Does not know what the teacher said to do or cannot remember.	3. Teach child to write down what the teacher says.
4. Lack of attention in class or too much daydreaming.	4. Talk with teacher and child about what distracts or holds child's attention.
5. Daily class work or homework is not done or turned in.	5. Ask teacher to send work home; then have a quiet place and a time for study.
6. Is not putting out enough effort or easily discouraged.	6. Encourage your child; use rewards, if necessary.
7. Works on homework but forgets to do part of it.	7. Have child list all homework to be done before starting.
8. Daily work is fine but student does not do well on tests or child is nervous and restless.	8. Teach your child to try relaxing while you ask questions from the lesson.
9. Dreads going to school; shyness.	9. Be firm about going to school; take the child to school if necessary.
10. Is bothered in class by another student.	10. Ask student to sit someplace else.
11. Tries but cannot seem to catch on or keep up; acts helpless.	11. Tutor your child or get a tutor. Ask the teacher if the child needs to be in a different class.
12. Seeks a lot of attention.	12. Tell child which behaviors will get positive attention; then give that attention as promised.
13. Is stubborn and always wants to have own way.	13. Try to go along with the child's way, as long as the job gets done.

Try talking things over with your child and your child's teacher. That will help you decide which of the reasons explain why your child is not doing well. If you still cannot decide what is wrong, talk with the principal or counselor. Please keep this sheet to refer to.

Source: Applachia Educational Laboratory, Charleston, West Virginia

HOT OFF THE PRESSES

The latest news from our class:

Calendar Activities

Run off copies of these activities
and paste them on the calendars.

Primary

For June

1 List 10 things you want to do this summer.

2 Start a list to keep track of every book you read this summer.

4 Start a stamp collection. Cut the stamp off any envelope that will be thrown away. Look for different ones every day.

5 World Environment Day

6 Write a letter to your teacher. Thank him or her for helping you this year.

8 Be an architect today and build yourself a secret hideaway.

10 Draw a picture of the main character of the book you're reading.

12 Take a walk and look for animal tracks. Compare them to the size of your feet. Try to identify them.

13 Make an original flag and fly it tomorrow on Flag Day.

14 Flag Day. Count the flags you see flying today.

15 Make a Father's Day gift by drawing a picture of your dad.

19 Father's Day

21 Summer solstice--the longest day of the year. What time does the sun set tonight?

22 Find out on what day of the week you were born. That's your lucky day!

23 Draw a picture of your favorite animal. Give it a name.

24 Poet John Ciardi was born this day in 1916. Read some poems from his book *I Met a Man.*

25 Stand in the sunlight and see how small you can make your shadow.

27 Start a leaf collection. Press leaves between the pages of an old book.

28 Write a letter to your favorite author. Send it to the book's publisher.

For July

1 What if ET invited you to a party on his planet? Draw a picture of what the party would look like.

3 Decorate your bicycle for the Fourth of July.

4 Independence Day

6 Read a book by Beatrix Potter to celebrate her birthday.

7 Read from the tale of Pinocchio, first published this day in 1891.

8 The Liberty Bell cracked on this day in 1835. Draw a picture of the bell.

9 Ask your parents to help you make a family tree.

10 Today begins National Ice Cream Week.

11 Celebrate author E.B. White's birthday by reading from *Stuart Little.*

12 Look at yourself in the mirror. Draw what you see.

13 Write a letter to your teacher telling what you've been doing this summer.

14 Bastille Day. France's independence day. Draw the French flag.

15 Read your favorite poem to your parents.

18 Pull 15 weeds in your lawn.

20 First landing on the moon in 1969. Look at Erich Fuch's book *Journey to the Moon.*

21 Write a letter to a friend you haven't seen since the end of school.

22 Tell a story to a friend and make up a new ending.

23 Interview your parents about what you were like as a baby.

25 Draw a map of your house.

26 Make a sandwich and cut it into fourths.

27 What flower grows between the nose and the chin? *Tulips!* Make up your own riddle.

29 Give a name to an imaginary planet and draw a picture of the planet's surface.

30 Stand in the sunlight and make your shadow's arms disappear.

For August

1 Sing ''The Star-Spangled Banner'' in honor of Francis Scott Key's birthday.

3 Crickets, ladybugs and spiders can bring good luck. Can you find any of these bugs?

4 Write a letter to a relative you haven't seen this summer.

6 Make a funny hat from newspaper or a paper bag.

7 National Family Day

8 Collect a pile of stones, twigs and leaves. Arrange them on newspaper to make an animal portrait.

9 Write out the alphabet. After each letter write an item of food that begins with that letter.

10 Draw a picture of your home from the outside.

11 Measure your brother, sister, or a friend.

13 Hold a rope-skipping contest today. Run a skipping relay race and skipping marathon.

15 Balance on one foot. Try it with your eyes closed. Have a one-footed race with your friends.

16 Guess how many windows are in your home. Count them. How close were you?

17 Read some of Ogden Nash's funny poems in honor of his birthday.

19 Design your own bumper sticker.

21 Play a game of basketball in honor of Wilt Chamberlain's birthday.

22 Read your favorite comic strip to someone.

23 Write out your first name. Under each letter write all the names you can think of that begin with that letter.

25 Have a picnic with friends.

26 Hold some beach ball races. Try running with the ball between your knees or ankles.

29 Make a collage of pictures cut from old magazines.

30 Stand in the sunlight with three friends and make the biggest shadow you can.

31 Make a list of things you hope to do in school this year.

Intermediate

For June

1 Start a list to keep track of every book you read this summer.

2 Start a summer diary. Write or draw a message in it every day.

4 Write 10 things you want to do this summer.

5 World Environment Day

6 Write a letter to your teacher. Thank him or her for helping you this year.

8 Celebrate Gwendolyn Brooks's birthday by reading from *Bronzeville Boys and Girls.*

9 Make up two word problems and ask someone to solve them.

10 Design your own bumper sticker.

11 Start a stamp collection. Look for a different stamp on a used envelope every day.

13 Make an original flag and fly it tomorrow on Flag Day.

14 Flag Day

15 Today in 1752, Ben Franklin proved that lightning is a form of electricity. Read a biography of Franklin.

Make a Father's Day gift by drawing a picture of your dad.

21 Summer solstice--the longest day of the year. What time does the sun set tonight?

22 Read a newspaper article. Write five facts that you learned.

23 Draw a picture of your favorite animal.

24 Poet John Ciardi born today in 1916. Read from his book *John J. Plenty and Fiddler Dan.*

25 Meet with two friends. How much do you weigh together?

27 Helen Keller born in 1880. Read about her life in *The Helen Keller Story* by Catherine Owens Peare.

28 Find out on what day of the week your were born. That's your lucky day!

30 Draw a picture of the main character of the book you're reading.

For July

1 Start a leaf collection. Press leaves between the pages of an old book.

3 Decorate your bicycle for the Fourth of July.

4 Independence Day

6 Draw a picture of yourself doing your favorite summer activity.

7 Compare the amounts of vitamins and minerals listed on two different breakfast cereal boxes.

8 The Liberty Bell cracked on this day in 1835. What does the inscription on the bell say?

9 Draw a picture of your home from the outside.

10 Today begins National Ice Cream Week.

Learning Calendar

Research indicates that children achieve better in school when parents get involved. *How do you get parents involved?*
In the elementary school the teacher can use a "Calendar of Learning" that gives a suggested activity for the parent to do with the child each day. The activity takes a brief amount of time, but lets the child know that the parent is interested in the child's work. A sample for the months of March and April 1990 is printed below.

MARCH

SUNDAY	MONDAY	TUESDAY	WEDNESDAY	THURSDAY	FRIDAY	SATURDAY
Memo:				**1** Study spelling and reading words.	**2** Ask your child to tell you what time it is several times today.	**3** Let your child invite a friend to come and play.
4 National Peanut Month. Roast peanuts with your child.	**5** Give your child a catalog. Ask him or her to cut out four pictures of tools, toys, shoes, etc.	**6** Read part of a story to your child. Let him or her tell you how he/she thinks the story will end.	**7** Read the whole story to your child. Talk about the difference in the way the story ended.	**8** Let your child write the names of common household things. Example: sofa, chair.	**9** Draw a clock face for your child. Have some of the numbers missing. Let him or her fill in the missing numbers.	**10** Take your child to the library to check out a book.
11 Have your child clip "cents-off" coupons from the newspaper and count the savings.	**12** Cut a comic strip apart. Have your child put it in the right order.	**13** Write 10 math problems for your child to work.	**14** Write five compound words. Example: bedroom / bed room, housetop / house top.	**15** Listen to your child say his or her address, zip code, and phone number.	**16** Praise your child for something he or she has done well in school.	**17** Read to your child about St. Patrick's Day.
18 Spring begins this week. Take a walk with your child and look for signs of spring.	**19** Write four sentences about spring with your child.	**20** Ask your child's teacher if you can help him or her in any way.	**21** Read a book about animals to your child.	**22** Have your child write five sentences using words from his or her spelling or word cards.	**23** Let your child make up 10 math problems. You work them and have your child check your answers to see if you got them right.	**24** Fly a kite with your child.
25 Tell your child you love him or her today.	**26** Start a seed collection with your child.	**27** Help your child look up three words in the dictionary.	**28** Listen to your child read a story aloud.	**29** Continue to make word cards from your child's reading list.	**30** Watch a TV program with your child and talk about it.	**31** Have your child help fix and serve lunch.

APRIL

SUNDAY	MONDAY	TUESDAY	WEDNESDAY	THURSDAY	FRIDAY	SATURDAY
1 Praise your child for everything he or she does well at home and at school.	**2** Make math cards with your child.	**3** Have your child write five word pairs that are opposite in meaning. Example: left/right.	**4** Have your child draw two clocks, one showing the time he or she gets up and one showing the time he or she goes to bed.	**5** Study your spelling and reading words.	**6** Have your child look at a cereal box. Circle the words that tell what is in the cereal.	**7** Have your child help plan Sunday dinner.
8 See that your child gets a good night's sleep.	**9** Help your child make a list of the things he or she needs to do each morning. Hang this on the wall.	**10** Have your child follow these directions: (1) Draw a house. (2) Draw a tree next to it. (3) Draw a kitten next to the tree.	**11** Discuss the value of coins with your child. Example: dime/10 cents, quarter/25 cents.	**12** Help your child circle the short vowel sounds in his or her spelling or reading words.	**13** Help your child add the high and low temperature for today. Use the radio, TV, or newspaper weather report.	**14** The Easter Bunny colored 25 eggs. During the night he ate eight. How many does he have left?
15 Let your child help prepare Easter dinner.	**16** Give your child a ruler. Have him/her draw a rabbit with ears four inches long.	**17** Pretend you are an animal. Write a story about what you like to do.	**18** Have your child draw four carrots. Write a root word on the root and an ending on the top of the carrot.	**19** Write spelling words in ABC order.	**20** Read a nature book with your child.	**21** Pick some wild flowers with your child.
22 Help your child plant a flower or a vegetable.	**23** Read a poem to your child. Have him or her name the rhyming words.	**24** Help your child think of words that sound alike but have different meanings. Example: by/buy, sea/see.	**25** After watching a TV program, have your child tell the main event of the program.	**26** Play word games with your child. Say a word and have him or her say a word that begins with the same letter.	**27** Write five math problems with mistakes in two of them. Have your child choose the two that are wrong and correct them.	**28** Take your child to the grocery store. Help him or her add the cost of two or more things.
29 Don't forget to set your clocks forward one hour. Let your child help.	**30** Have your child select five comic strips or books. Put the titles in ABC order.			**Memo:**		

This information was excerpted from the *Community Education Parenting Resource Guide*, Alabama State Department of Education, Community Education Section, State Office Building, Montgomery, Alabama 36130.

Sample Teacher Form for School Conference

Name _____   Grade _____

Date _____   Teacher _____

School _____

✓ **Student Strengths Observed by Teacher:**

✓ **Student Needs Observed by Teacher:**

✓ **Suggestions for Action:** (To be completed at time of conference)

Home Setting:

School Setting:

Teacher: Complete form prior to scheduled conference.

The Parent-Teacher Conference; Charles W. Edwards, College of Education, East Tennessee State University, Tennessee Department of Education.

Sample Parent Form for School Conference

Name of Child _____

Parents _____

Date _____ Grade _____

✓ **Student Strengths Observed at Home by Parent:**

✓ **Student Needs Observed at Home by Parent:**

✓ **Suggestions for Action:** (To be completed at time of conference)

Home Setting:

School Setting:

Please complete form prior to scheduled conference. Bring to conference. (Optional)

The Parent-Teacher Conference; Charles W. Edwards, College of Education, East Tennessee State University, Tennessee Department of Education.

Student Work Folder For

_____

Date	Parent Signature	Comments

Success-o-gram

_____

_____

_____

_____

_____

_____

_____

_____

_____

Certificate of Achievement

Strike up the band for

_____

who is doing excellent work in

_____

_____
signature   date

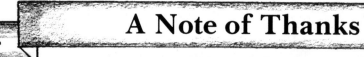

A Note of Thanks

In appreciation for what you have done!

Merci!Thanks!Danke!Gracias!Merci!Thanks!Danke!Gracias!Merci!Thanks!Danke!

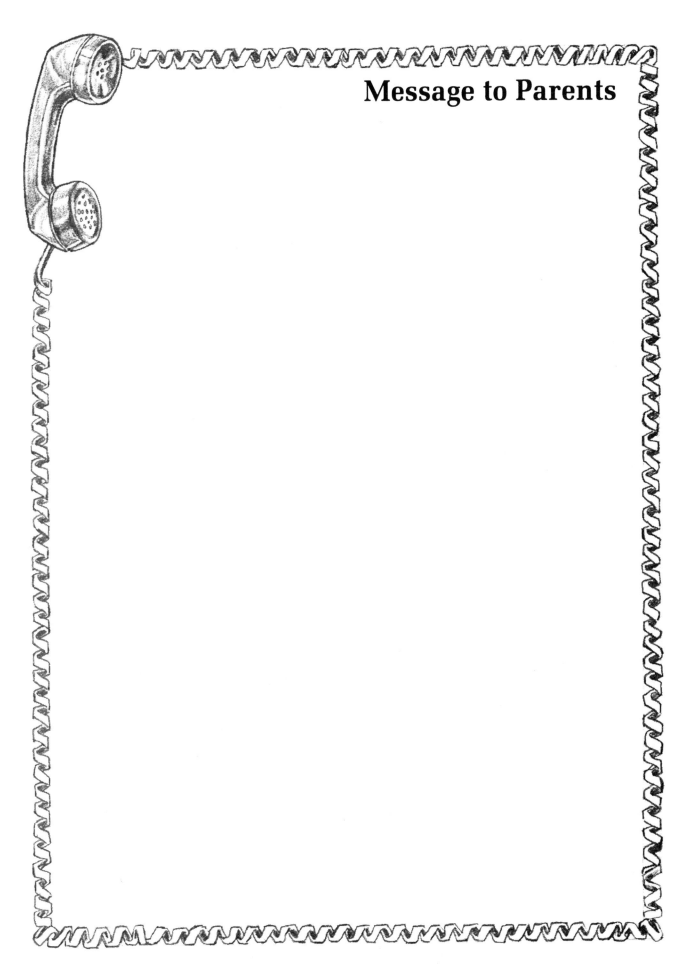

Message to Parents

Just-A-Note

Dear Parents,

This is just a note to tell you that _____

_____

_____

_____

_____

_____

_____
Signature   Date

Parent, Can you lend a hand?

Dear _____ ,

Our class is planning _____

_____

And we need your help! _____

_____

_____
Signature   Date

Dear _____ ,

Don't forget! This is important!

_____

_____

_____

_____

_____

_____
Signature   Date

A reminder to parents

Extra! Extra!

Read all about it!

Dear _____
name of person or organization

We've got good news at _____
name of school

And we'd like to tell you all about it! _____

_____

_____

_____

Please call us for more information.

_____
signature   date

_____
phone

253

Send-Home Sheet

Dear Parent:

Television has become another member of your family and mine; we eat meals near it, learn from it, and spend more time with it than with any single individual. Unfortunately, television is central in our children's lives—as tutor, babysitter, teacher, entertainer, and salesperson, all rolled into one.

Has television grown so powerful we can no longer control it? No. But it very well might unless we act now to harness its influence and channel its awesome power. Television, like a potent drug, can either enhance or cripple a person's life. What can a parent do? Follow these guidelines—they will make a difference!

What can you do at home?

Start now. Many children are already habitual TV viewers by the age of two. Harmful viewing habits can be changed only by substituting new habits. Do a little at a time—some each day.

Put the TV in a little-used room. With the TV in an area away from the living room, family room, and other places where heavy family activity occurs, children will watch less and plan more what they want to watch.

Plan to have one night a week with the TV off. Meet as a family and pick a no-TV night. Decide whether you want to do things together or have time alone.

Avoid using the TV as a babysitter. You would not leave your child alone in the care of a stranger. A television cannot respond to a cry for help, nor can it tell when a child is frightened.

Plan ahead what to watch. With a TV viewing guide, decide what you and your kids will watch each night. Don't just turn on the set to see what's on.

Seek out programs made for kids. Help your children plan to watch programs designed for their ages, interests, and maturity.

Watch TV with your children. View their programs with them and help them evaluate what they're watching in light of your family's values and traditions.

Help kids distinguish between make-believe and real life on TV. Explain that terror and violence on TV shows is only acting and is not like real-life violence.

Discuss TV commercials selling junk food. Help young children see that ads are trying to persuade them to spend money by developing buying habits which could be unhealthy. Let your children help select nutritious family foods and snacks.

Use TV to start family activities. Make a list of TV-advertised products, and see how many you have in the house. Watch different news programs the same night, and see if all use the same lead stories. Play along with your favorite game show as a family or play your own version with the TV set off. Do a TV commercial product test and compare your results with theirs. Reinforce nonsexist programs by discussing them with your kids.

Find leisure activities besides TV. Watching TV is relaxing, but so is a good crossword puzzle or game of cards. If you break the TV habit, your child will have a better chance of avoiding an addiction. Buy a puzzle book to work on together, or a model rocket to build together.

Read to your child. Start at an early age to help your child discover the magic in reading. Children of all ages enjoy being read to by their parents.

No need to try all these ideas at once. Start small by picking one you want to try and doing it. Post this list on your refrigerator and choose as a group one idea to try each week.

What you and school can do

Work with teacher and principal. Support use of quality educational television programs in school.

Acknowledge that appropriate TV viewing is a skill that can be learned. Bring in speakers fom the PTA and local TV stations.

Let your feelings be known. Write newspapers, TV stations, networks, the FCC, and advertisers; tell them what you like and don't like.

Teacher signature

These ideas come from the Illinois State Board of Education and appeared in INSTRUCTOR, March 1978.

Send-Home Sheet

Dear Parent:

The best way to become a better reader is to read, and then discuss what you've read with others. Summer is the perfect time to help your child read. How to help depends on your child's attitude toward reading.

You can measure his or her attitude by completing this simple checklist. Answer each question with one of three words: seldom, sometimes, or often.

1. My child spends time looking at or reading books. _____
2. He/she asks to have stories read. _____
3. He/she tells me about stories heard or read. _____
4. He/she writes down thoughts on paper. _____
5. He/she wants to be heard reading aloud. _____
6. He/she asks to own magazines or books. _____
7. He/she reads aloud words on signs, television, and other places. _____
8. He/she chooses to read books or magazines when other choices are available (playing with a friend, television, baseball). _____
9. He/she finishes books that are started. _____
10. He/she asks to go or be taken to the library. _____

Score as follows: one point for each answer marked *seldom*; two points for each *sometimes*; and three points for each *often*. If the score is in the twenties (30 points is the highest score), your child probably likes to read. You can help most by making reading matter and time available (for example, offer a ride to the library).

If the score is in the teens or below, you probably have a reluctant reader in your family. Here are some ways you can help.

Let your child see you reading

A young child will form lasting impressions at home about reading. If your child sees you reading, notices books and magazines around the house, and senses that you enjoy the activity, he or she will copy you and be much more likely to enjoy reading. Subscribe to a magazine or two you enjoy. Spend some time at home talking about what you're reading. And let your child see you doing these things. He or she will read more too!

Spend time reading with your child

A child of any age likes to be read to. Read to your child often. Let him or her choose a story, and you choose one that you enjoy.

Keep children's reading matter around the house

There are many excellent books and magazines designed specifically for the young child. Magazines such as *Highlights for Children*, *Jack and Jill*, *Humpty Dumpty*, and *Cricket* are available through subscription. The public library is bursting with books, magazines, and other publications for children. Your local department stores sell inexpensive comic books and workbooks. Flea markets and garage sales are gold mines of good books for little money. Find some books, let your child choose some, and replenish your home supply every few months. If books are around, they'll be read.

Help your child write (then read) about him- or herself

Everyone likes to read about him- or herself. By helping your child translate experiences and feelings into writing, you will be creating a product that will get read with great interest. Ways to do this: Keep a diary on a family trip. Take pictures and arrange them in a scrapbook with child-created captions. Help your child write letters to friends and relatives; have copies made so you can reread them together. Each week, help your child write a short story about his/her favorite event or activity, and read it together.

Reward your child for reading

For the child who likes to read, reading is its own reward. But for the reluctant reader, praise and encouragement increases confidence and makes reading more fun. To do this: Keep a chart of the books or comics your child reads and give a star or treat when he or she reads a certain amount or for a certain length of time. Praise your child for reading.

Explore your public library

Libraries have changed. Many have records and tapes, newspapers, microfilms, story hours for kids, a special children's librarian, puppet shows, filmstrips, and even field trips. Explore these with your child.

_____
Teacher signature

The reading attitude checklist appeared in INSTRUCTOR, May 1978, sent by Alvin Granowsky, director of reading for Dallas schools. Suggestions come from Tom Bernagozzi of Clarkson Elementary, Bay Shore, NY.

A bagful of summer

Ever wish you could help students bridge the learning gap between June and September? It's easy. Send them home when school closes with bags full of summer learning activities!

Create the bags in class during May and June by following these steps. Have each student get a large, heavy-paper shopping bag with handles, and label it with his name. Then you and the class make and put a different item into each bag every day or two until school is out. Explain that these are fun things to do during the summer, and that nothing is to be taken out of a bag until school is over and the bag has been taken home.

Use the ideas below or ones you make up. As you or the students place an item into a bag, attach a length of yarn, thread it through a hole punched in the top of the bag, then tie on a tag telling the student when to open that item.

◆ Assign a student to gather scrap cloth material, the right size and shape to make a flag. Let each child select one piece of scrap he/she likes. Put it into the bag with written instructions to design a flag for family, fort, or vacation spot. Explain symbolism in the instructions and encourage youngsters to incorporate meaningful personal symbols into the flag's design.

◆ Have students make a booklet with 20 or 30 pages of blank, 8 ½" by 11" paper and a construction-paper cover. Collect them and print "My Sketch Book" on each cover. On the back paste instructions that suggest where to sketch and possibly show several geometric shapes which are basic to all drawing. Then put sketch books into the bags without students knowing what they are used for.

◆ Make a birthday card for each child having a birthday in the summer, mark the tags with when-to-open dates, and place in bags when students are not around.

◆ As a class, make a list of points of interest in your area that your students might like to visit during the summer. Assign a different student to write each of these places and request brochures for each class member. Have a secret assistant help you divide this material into surprise baggies.

◆ Have each student bring one favorite summertime recipe from home. Duplicate on one sheet and have a committee paste the sheet onto card-

board to hang on a refrigerator. These recipes can then be secretly placed into each bag with a tag saying: "Open when you're very hungry."

◆ Challenge students to research what special events will take place locally during the summer. Include such things as fairs, library programs, swimming schedules, carnivals, and parades. After students put this events calendar onto a spirit master, run it off and paste a copy on the back of each bag.

◆ Ask a volunteer to secretly skim the *Guiness Book of World Records* and make a list of those records a youngster could challenge. Duplicate the list, paste copies on tagboard, and tape a hanger on the back. Any student who wants the list can put a copy in his or her bag, along with instructions from the book as to witnesses, rules, and guidelines a challenger must follow. At home the child posts the list in his or her bedroom and refers to it through the summer to establish a new record.

◆ Hold a letter-writing party, where each student writes a letter to another student, so everyone gets a letter. Letters are sealed in envelopes and put into bags with *don't-open-till* dates on each tag. Letters could be written as if students were already on vacation; could describe proposed summer plans; or could even contain secret information.

◆ Collect Popsicle sticks as a class project or buy a box of them at a craft store. Stretch your students' creative powers by brainstorming what summer games could be played with Popsicle sticks. Could they be used as the basis for a swimming pool math game? Could they be used like miniature boards to build something? Can they be made into a musical instrument? Divide up the sticks, and put into bags wrapped in a page with your list of ideas.

◆ Fourth of July picnics are occasions for fun and frivolity, when we toast our debut as a nation. Duplicate one or two of each student's favorite jokes and put them into each bag with an open-and-share-with-friends-on-July-4 tag.

◆ Conduct a used-book drive. Parents, students, local bookstores, staff members, and possibly local libraries or school districts can donate unwanted books. After screening them for appropriateness, select for each student's bag a book that you think he/she would enjoy reading during the summer. Give remaining books to a student who is willing to set up a summer loan library at home and have the student create a checkout card file. Include in each student's bag a student-designed borrower's card and a description of the books.

◆ Help youngsters become teachers themselves during the summertime. Write your students a letter, saying that just as teachers often become students in the summer, students can become teachers. Then list several suggestions: set up a learning center in your home, and rotate the responsibility among family members for keeping it stocked with activities and displays. Set up a school in the yard or playroom, and teach friends or relatives how to read, tie flies for fishing, or do some interesting craft. Offer to tutor a younger student in reading or math. Choose a topic that fascinates you, learn all about it, and share your growing knowledge with interested friends. Volunteer to teach a summer class at your local recreation area in something you're particularly good at— macrame, origami, or perhaps skateboarding.

◆ Encourage students to record special summer events in art. Students first draw or trace a large simple line drawing on white art paper or butcher paper. Put the unfinished art project plus directions into each bag. Directions tell each student to invite parents, relatives, friends, and other guests to each complete a portion of the picture with felt pens, watercolors, or crayon, as the summer progresses. By fall, the result will be a framable record of summer experiences.

◆ Prepare a Summer Danger poster. As a May art project, have students cut out and decorate a larger-than-life poster in the shape of a skull and crossbones or some other design which means *danger* to them. Duplicate a sheet titled "Beware! Here are the six hazards most likely to take you out of circulation this summer!" Include this list from the National Safety Council:

1. *Drowning.* Swim with a buddy and have an adult nearby.
2. *Cars.* Look before you enter a street, and use those seatbelts!
3. *Fires.* Campfires can kill. Summer fires often spread faster than you can run. One match can murder people, so beware of all fires.
4. *Poison ivy, poison plants, and poison berries.* Wear long pants in the woods. And eat only what you're sure is safe.
5. *The sun.* Sunburn can sneak up on you. Wear lotion, and take direct sun a little at a time.
6. *Guns.* Summer is a favorite time to explore. Leave guns and ammunition alone!

Tape list onto front of each danger poster and put in bags, with tags saying to open, read, and post at home as soon as school closes.

◆ Encourage students to create new looks for their vacation fun. Use materials, papers, found objects. Cut two-sided tape to form huge sideburns, mustaches, and eyebrows; then have kids stick on the hair to create realistic disguises. These go in envelopes and into the bags for use at summer events.

◆ Encourage your students to participate in local, county, or state fair. Send for information on how youngsters can become involved (as entrants or volunteers) and place this information in each bag.

◆ Help students launch a summer business. Send for or check out the book *Good Cents* (Houghton Mifflin), which describes many excellent money-making projects for youngsters. Then establish a student task force to make up a list of the businesses they think are most likely to succeed, along with brief instructions. These ideas can be rolled into a "summer gold mine" scroll and placed in bags.

◆ Summer is a perfect time to start a collection, or build one already started. Create a list of possible collections and put into bags with a tag saying to open on a rainy day or when the student is looking for something fun to do. Some unusual collectibles include fingerprints, leafprints, idiomatic expressions, labels from canned goods, bloopers and misspellings in newspapers, types of headwear, business cards, matchbooks, car parts, and recordings of voices.

◆ Combine the initials of a person's name for a stylish monogram. Ask students to choose colors, and produce a finished drawing of their personal monogram. Duplicate suggestions for embroidering or painting the design on towels, swimsuits, camping gear, and other summer items. Staple design and instruction sheets together and place in bags with tag saying to open two days before first swimming or camping trip.

◆ If you spend a little time on this project every few days, and involve the students while still keeping them in suspense, you'll have an end-of-school product that will make the last school days more productive and will turn summer into a time for learning for every youngster.

A KID'S *GUIDE TO SUMMER*

Summer vacation—it's just around the corner! Special teacher that you are, you'll want to give your students a special summer send-off.

On the pages that follow, you'll find *A Kid's Guide to Summer* to help you do that.

Think of these reproducible pages as a starter kit for your own tailor-made super summer send-home. You might use them as a core for a summer booklet to make in class. Encourage kids to design their own covers and make notes of things they won't want to forget during vacations, such as the hours that school recreation facilities are open, day camp schedules, and the like.

The Kid's Guide can even be the first item to put into a Bagful of Summer, a decorated envelope to which students might add one thing every day until vacation. Provide something personal for each child to insert: a motivator, a puzzle, a joke, a birthday wish, a note, or a message that will remind kids of something that they learned this year.

Because some of the summer projects recommended here require adult supervision, add a note for parents. Explain that how children choose to spend their summer vacations can make a big difference, not just in the quality of their vacation, but in the kinds of time-use habits they form. Point out to parents that *A Kid's Guide* is packed full of constructive ways for kids to spend their time—there are freebies to write for, noodle-doodles to solve, summer celebrations to plan, projects and recipes to try. Encourage parental involvement.

Another good way to extend the *Guide's* usefulness is to organize a schoolwide Summertime Fair with booths, where community resource people can tell students about available summertime activities. One booth might have summer first-aid and health tips. Another might provide a way for kids to meet others with the same interests. Included in the guide is a chart—*If I could, I would . . .*—that can serve as a starting point for your fair. Set up a special booth where these charts can be filled in.

Use the guide to send students off to a safe, fun, productive summer. And to you, teachers, good wishes for a refreshing, renewing vacation.

Happy Summer!

A KID'S GUIDE TO SUMMER

Nothing's better than summer vacation, but nothing's worse than being bored. If you could do anything this summer, what would it be? Chances are some things will be beyond your reach right now, but who's to say you can't do them in the future? Start by investigating different activities.

For instance: Name three things that you and your friends would most like to do? What are you good at? What would you like to be better at? How would you like to change the way you use your time? The chart below is packed with ideas to help you think of new ways to spend your summer. With your parents, friends, or by yourself, check the ones that sound interesting to you. Add your own ideas, too!

And there's even more! Your guide comes to you packed with noodle-doodles, contests, games, projects, and even relaxation tips. You can begin some of the activities before school is out and brainstorm still more with your classmates. *A Kid's Guide to Summer* will help make this summer a terrific one!

If I could, I would . . .

TRY:

Aerobics

Baking

Birdwatching

Camping

Card tricks

Carpentry

Cartoon drawing

Ceramics

Clown lessons

Community theater

Decoupage

Designing and making posters

Doll-making and dollhouse-making

Dough art

Entomology (the study of insects)

Face-painting

Filmmaking

Fishing

Freehand drawing

Gardening

Hiking

Horseback riding

Jogging

Kite-making

Knitting

Magic tricks

Mask-making

Mathematical art

Meditation

Mime

Mountain climbing

Mural painting

Music lessons

Needlepoint

Oil painting

Origami

Photography

Pottery

Printmaking

Puppet-making

Sand-sculpting

Sculpting

Sign language

Silkscreening

Snorkeling

Songwriting

Surfing

Tennis

Track and field

Train spotting

Ventriloquism

Voice lessons

Weaving

Whale watching

Whittling and woodworking

Windsurfing

LEARN:

African dance

Archery

Badminton

Ballet

Batik

Baton twirling

Belly dancing

Bowling

Breakdancing

Cake decorating

Calligraphy

Canoeing

Creative movement

Darts

Fencing

Field hockey

Folk dancing

Golf

Gymnastics

Irish dancing

Jazz dance

Judo

Juggling

Karate

Modern dance

Quilting

Racquetball

Rug making

Square dancing

Squash

Tai chi

Tap dancing

Yoga

EXPLORE:

Archaeology

Astrology

Astronomy

Aviation

Cars—old and new

C.B. radios

Chemistry

Classical music

Computers

Cooking

Genealogy

Geology

History

A KID'S GUIDE TO SUMMER

Languages

Making instruments

Model car racing

Navigation

Opera

Shell collecting

Writing my town's history

VISIT:

An airport

Aquarium

Bakery

Ballet recital

Bird sanctuary

Book publisher

Botanical garden

Bottling company

Candle factory

Car manufacturing plant

Cereal factory

Circus

Computer company or store

Concert

Courthouse

Farmers' market

Greenhouse

Historical sites

Modeling school

Museum

Newspaper

Parents' places of work

Planetarium

Printing company

Radio or TV station

Telephone company

Toy manufacturer

Travel Bureau

Zoo

BE A PART OF:

American National Red
   Cross programs

Audubon Society

Big Brother/Big Sister

Coin Collectors' Club

Community newspaper

Historical Society

Hobby clubs

Horticulture or garden club

Humane Society

Library and reading clubs

Sports fitness organizations

Stamp collectors' club

Student letter-exchange program

ENJOY:

Daydreaming

Family time

Listening to music

Long walks

Old movies

Skipping stones

Sky-watching

Training a pet

Volunteer programs

When you just can't think of anything to do . . .

OUTDOOR FUN!

Bucket brigade

Summer's a time to be outdoors, and a wet relay is just the thing for a hot, sunny day! Fill a bucket with water for each team and place it about 15 feet from the starting line. Place an empty bucket in front of each team, and give the first player on each a sponge and a plastic cup. At the start, each lead person runs up to the filled bucket, soaks the sponge with water, and wrings it into the cup. Leaving the sponge in the bucket, this same player runs back to his or her team, empties the water from the cup into the empty bucket, and passes the cup to the next player. After everyone has finished, the team with the most water in its once-empty bucket is the winner!

Horsin' around!

You can make your own horseshoe game by using a piece of rope 18 inches long. Fray the ends and interweave them to form a ring. Bind the intersection together with heavy string. Use a piece of wood for the stake, hammer it into the ground, and mark the ground at one-foot intervals as far as you'd like. If your "horseshoe" lands all the way over the stake, your score equals the number of feet you threw it. A great game for a neighborhood tournament!

For sale!

Raise some extra money by holding a summer garage sale. Start by checking to see if you need a special permit; choose a location that's easy to find, and make sure you've advertised in advance (get those flyers out). Sell your old toys; ask neighbors to donate, too. Broken items can be sold as special bargains! If yours is a group sale, use different-colored price tags to make it easier to keep track of who sold what. Donate any unsold merchandise to a charitable organization.

READ AND RELAX

Here are some great books to read (especially under a shady tree). Check for them at the library!

Ramona Forever is all about Ramona in third grade. She meets Howie's rich uncle. There's a surprise wedding, and more. It's by Beverly Cleary (Morrow, 1984).

Children of the Wild West shows how the west really was in real-life photos. This book is by Russell Freedman (Clarion, 1983).

Saint George and the Dragon describes the deeds of a daring knight as he goes into combat with his enemy. It's by Margaret Hodges (Little, Brown, 1984).

Like Jake and Me is the story of Alex, his seemingly unkind stepfather, and a spider. It's by Mavis Jukes (Knopf, 1984).

In the Year of the Boar and Jackie Robinson takes place in 1947, when Shirley Temple Wong, age 10, comes to the U.S. and discovers baseball. This book is by Bette Bao Lord (Harper, 1984).

One-Eyed Cat watches what happens to an 11-year-old when he shoots a cat. The author is Paula Fox (Bradbury, 1984).

SUMMER COOLDOWNS

Whew! It's hot outside! How can you stay cool when the temperature soars?

Drink, drink, drink some more! Do you seem to sweat more in the summer? That's your body's natural way of cooling off. To feel good, you need to put back that fluid; and that means drinking eight to nine glasses of liquid each day. Make half of those water, and the other half juice.

Be cool in cool clothes. What you wear in summer makes a difference in how comfortable you feel. Light-colored clothes reflect the sun's rays. Light fabrics like cotton let air circulate through the weave.

Be sun smart. Whether you tan, burn, or freckle, be careful when you're in the sun. Too much sun can cause a painful sunburn, and it can also cause skin problems that won't show up until you're an adult. Protect your skin by using tanning lotion that screens out harmful rays. It's the safe, sensible, healthy way to get a tan!

BE A SUPER SNOOPER

You can find out a lot about people and nature if you only keep your eyes open, your ears tuned in, and your nose in good shape. Here's how you can investigate all sorts of things this summer:

Have you ever wondered how far away a bolt of lightning is? During your first summer storm, notice exactly when lightning appears. Then count the seconds that go by from the time you see the flash until you hear the thunder. For every five seconds you count, the lightning is one mile away. (That's because it takes five seconds more for sound to go one mile than it takes light.)

Want some more summer detective work? Tell the temperature with the help of insects. Next time you hear some crickets beginning to rub their wings together, take out your watch and start counting. The number of chirps you hear in 15 seconds is your first clue. Then add 39. The number you get equals the temperature in Fahrenheit. (This is the rate for the common green tree cricket. It chirps faster as the temperature rises.)

Some detective work you can do with friends involves food. Try this super-snooper test using an apple, potato, and onion. You'll need a grater, a blindfold, nose clips (the kind used for swimming), and some forks.

Peel and rinse the food, and grate it so it's very fine. Blindfold a friend. Are the nose clips on? Now put a quarter teaspoonful of one of the grated foods in his or her mouth. Tell your friend not to chew, but just to roll it around on the tongue. Which of the three foods does your friend think it is? Have him or her spit it out. After rinsing with water, it's time for the next samples. How does not being able to smell affect the results?

Vacation Creations

JUST YOUR SIZE!
Make a pal that's just your size. For this project you'll need a discarded bed sheet. First double it, then lie down on it, and have someone trace around you with a felt-tip marker, keeping the line a few inches from your body. Don't worry about small details like fingers and toes. Carefully use straight pins to pin the halves smoothly in place and then cut the figure out with sharp scissors (your cutting line should be a few inches outside your outline). With a needle and thread carefully stitch on the outline, leaving an open space somewhere for stuffing. Remove the

pins, turn the doll inside out, and stuff with rags or foam. (Don't use newspaper for stuffing; it is very flammable.) If you keep your stuffing pieces small, your doll won't be as lumpy. When it's all stuffed, sew the opening together. Decorate the doll any way you'd like: use markers, dress it in your clothes, or embroider features on it. You can even make a whole family with pets!

REMEMBER SUMMER
Keep a record of your summer right from the beginning of the vacation. Use a purchased scrapbook or sketchbook, or make one of your own with heavy manila paper. Punch three holes along the side and tie together with colored yarn or metal fasteners or rings. This is a good project to begin before school is out. The *If I could, I would . . .* chart could be your first page. Add other notes about what you hope the summer will bring. Save menus, postcards, letters, and other kinds of mementos, and don't forget to write about what the summer brought you and how you changed. Your summer record can be Volume One: 19 _ _ . Next summer can bring another volume, or perhaps you'd like to make a book for the school year.

POP POP! FIZZ FIZZ!
Make your own soda pop! Just fill about two-thirds of a glass with fruit drink or juice. Add 1/4 teaspoon baking soda and 1/2 teaspoon cream of tartar. You may need to add a little sugar. Stir for a few seconds until the mixture gets bubbly. You have to drink quickly to get the fuzz!

ADD COLOR TO YOUR LIGHT
See-through window designs can brighten any room in your house. Draw a design on scrap paper. Smooth a piece of plastic wrap over the paper very carefully, and trace the design onto the plastic with black marker. Overlap small pieces of colored tissue paper, using rubber cement to glue them within the outline of your design. When you've finished, smooth another sheet of

plastic wrap over the tissue design; be careful not to leave any air bubbles. Lift it from the scrap paper and retrace the black lines on both sides of the plastic. Tape to a sunny window!

GOURMET ART
Silly sandwiches are fun to think about. Try creating your own as a work of art. Imagine you are looking at the cross-section of your giant sandwich. To begin to construct it, you'll need two pieces of bread (draw two slices or cut them out, one for the top and one for the bottom); choose rolls, bagels, even French bread for a submarine sandwich. Glue these onto a background of a brown paper bag. Be sure to leave plenty of space in between. Remember you're imagining this view of a sandwich after it's been cut in half. Now look for what you want to put in between the bread. If you like marshmallows and hot dogs, cut them out! Stack all the ingredients so each one can be seen. Glue everything between your slices of bread (the sky's the limit), and don't forget to give your creation a name!

BUTTER UP!
With your spare time this summer, you might want to try baking your own bread and even making your own butter to go along with it. It's not hard to make your own butter churn, too. You'll need a coffee can with a tight-fitting plastic lid, a one-quarter-inch dowel, and the plastic top of a small margarine tub. Punch a hole in the center of the margarine top just big enough for the dowel to fit through. (It's very important that this be a tight fit!) Punch another hole in the center of the plastic coffee can lid and slip the other end of the dowel through it so that it sticks up at least two inches. Fit the coffee can over the bottom of the dasher (the margarine top), and snap on the lid. Your butter churn is ready for action!

To make butter, let whipping cream or heavy cream stand at room temperature for several hours. Now pour it into the churn until it's about half full. Beat the dasher up and down. You can take turns with a friend. Keep churning, and after about 20 minutes, you'll get lumps that float to the top. These are your butter curds. Continue churning; when no more curds seem to be forming, take off the lid and scoop them out. You can put the buttermilk that is left into the refrigerator.

Rinse the curds in a bowl under cold running water to remove any milk that is left. Chill the butter ball in the refrigerator for a few hours. The butter can now be shaped and tasted. If it's sweeter than you're used to, add a little salt.

Butter can also be made by using a wide-mouth glass jar and the same procedure, but this time shake the jar vigorously up and back for at least 20 minutes. Then follow the procedure above.

STRANGE EFFECTS

Want to try a project where the product looks more complicated than the procedure? First look through old magazines for a large photograph of a person's face or a scene that's interesting to you.

You'll need a ruler to draw straight lines at any angle across the picture, making it into strips of about the same width. Cut these strips apart and reassemble the picture on a colored background, leaving space for the background to show between the strips. By experimenting, you can get all sorts of odd effects. Try drawing curved lines on the picture. Cut part of the picture into strips that go up and down and part of it into strips that go across. You'll be surprised at the many different effects you can achieve!

DYE AWAY

Try folding and dipping light-colored paper into food colorings diluted with water. Afterwards, use black crayon or marker and draw a simple design on your new colorfully dyed background. It goes well with birds, dragons, flowers, and any interesting silhouettes. Experiment with the food coloring to mix new colors.

SUMMER CELEBRATIONS

You can have a holiday all summer long. Here are some days to celebrate.

Garfield, the lasagna-loving cat who was "born" in 1978, celebrates his birthday on June 19. But Garfield won't mind if you celebrate the day before. After all, it's International Picnic Day on June 18, a day for rejoicing by fat-cat standards. (Did you know June is Adopt-a-Cat Month?)

Summer begins on or around June 21 (varies from year to year). It's the longest day (and shortest night) of the year. Have a sunrise breakfast. Make your parents some sun-tea. (Fill a quart jar with water and add four teabags. Four hours in the sun, then lemon, honey, and ice, and it's ready.)

Boom! It's JULY, National Hot Dog, Peach, Blueberry, and Ice Cream month. Ask an adult to help you make your very own pint of vanilla:

Mix 1/3 cup sugar, one tablespoon of flour, a dash of salt, and a cup of milk in a pot. Heat this mix-

ture at medium-low heat until it thickens. Stir occasionally.

Beat an egg and add it in. Keep cooking and stirring one more minute. Turn off the heat. After the mix has cooled for 10 minutes, add one cup of cream and one tablespoon of vanilla. Stir.

Put a layer of crushed ice in a pail and sprinkle with salt. Pour the ice cream mixture into a coffee can (2/3 full) and put it in the pail.

Stir! Use a wooden spoon. It will take 1/2 hour. Add ice to the pail as it melts.

When the ice cream is very thick, cover the can and freeze it for two hours. Eat!

Each July the International Cherry Pit Spitting Contest is held.. Whose pit goes the farthest in your neighborhood?

July 11 is National Cheer Up the Lonely Day. Make a gift and bring it to someone who might be lonely.

In mid-July is National Space Week. Launch a rocket with the help of *The Alpha Book of Model Rocketry*. Send $1.10 to Estes Industries, Dept. 103, 1295 H St., Penrose, CO 81240.

Swoosh . . . it's August. Eat watermelon. Run through sprinklers and cool off.

During the first week of August celebrate National Clown Week. Try some face paints.

Also in August is the annual Popcorn Festival. Pop! Send 25 cents to Jolly Time Popcorn Recipes, Box 178, Sioux City, IA 51102.

Put your feet up on National Relaxation Day, August 15. And make a point of celebrating the new moon this August. Make a moon bone. Carve each night's moon onto a bone or stick just the way it looks in the sky. For more lunar ideas, see *The Night Sky Book* by Jamie Jobb (Little, Brown, 1977).

"A Kid's Guide to Summer" appeared in the May 1985 issue of INSTRUCTOR magazine.

Special thanks to Joan Bergstrom, author of *School's Out—Now What?* (Ten Speed Press, 1984); Allan Yeager for "Read and relax"; The Fernbank Science Center in Atlanta, "Be a super snooper"; Jean Stangl, "Summer cool-downs"; Katherine Bartow, Regina Cabral, Amy DeMarco, Margaret Kolak, Carolyn Martin, Ireene Robbins, Nancy Sliker, Helen Kratcha Thomas, and Lila Wainer, "Vacation creations."

C H A P T E R 7

Teachers helping teachers

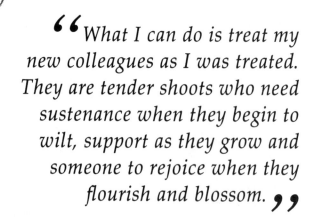

"What I can do is treat my new colleagues as I was treated. They are tender shoots who need sustenance when they begin to wilt, support as they grow and someone to rejoice when they flourish and blossom."

— *Susan Audap*
Teacher advisor

> **" *Approach people with a blend of confidence and openness. You are new and willing to grow, but you are also a very capable person.* "**
>
> — *Jane Bluestein*
> *Author*

Here you are, suddenly in charge of 28 kids, and sometimes you can't help feeling isolated and overwhelmed. For most of the day, there's not another adult in sight. Those you do see in the teachers' lounge (when you don't have lunch or playground duty) have their own concerns. You can't ask them for help. They're busy, and besides, they'll think you're incompetent!

Or will they?

Your colleagues are your best bet for surviving that difficult first year. They remember their own shaky starts. Susan Audap, who now directs the Park Avenue Teachers' Center in Los Angeles, describes her early teaching experience: "What got me through my first year was an advisor who came to my classroom once a week for an hour or two. On a scale of one to ten, my classroom control was a two, and this was not a rough school. When my advisor worked with my kids they were wonderful. With me they were a mess. What I learned from her was that the kids were not the problem. I was."

That first year was tough for Audap. But it was also a time for growing, sharing, and learning.

"Sometimes I needed soothing, sometimes I wanted to share triumphs, sometimes I needed to be invigorated," Audap remembers. "I met these needs by talking and working with other teachers, advisors and parents of my students. I cannot overstate the importance of these relationships. We shared a vision of how wonderful classrooms could be, and we shared the work of making them that way. It didn't happen overnight."

Think of the collective wisdom and practical knowledge your school's veterans have. The faculty in a single elementary school with 15 or more teachers represents hundreds of years of classroom experience with thousands of students. That's a great source for a lot of helpful information! Consider these colleagues your allies.

Teachers—all teachers—need formal and informal networks for tapping and sharing this information. Teachers helping teachers and learning from each other. Everyone benefits, especially the students. As researchers Judith Warren Little and Tom Bird of the Far West Laboratory for Educational Research and Development have observed in the Lab's *Resources and Practice*: "[Teachers] accumulate such skills and wisdom as they can by themselves and then take their inventions with them when they leave. Superb teachers leave their marks on all of us, but they leave no marks on teaching."

This chapter describes some of the ways teachers can leave their mark on teaching. Teachers can work together to improve teaching—from the first years on.

The Buddy System

Who do we go to most often for help and advice? A friend. A trusted colleague. Someone whose opinion we value. Ever since schools have grown larger than one room, teachers have sought the companionship of like-minded colleagues.

In many districts today, teachers are assigned mentors, advisors, or helping teachers in addition to those they might choose. These mentors are not TORmentors sent to spy upon or evaluate newcomers.

Rather, they are experienced teachers recognized for their effective teaching and their willingness to help others—experienced professionals supervising and overseeing the efforts of their inexperienced colleagues. Doctors do it. Lawyers do it. So do other professionals. They'd never abandon novices to learn by trial and error.

But in teaching, the internship portion of professional training is conspicuously absent. Teacher mentor programs are one way to address this need. And there are others surfacing across the country, each one involving teachers helping teachers.

Whatever name they go by—mentors, lead teachers, helping teachers, coaches, advisors, friends—these experienced professionals have a lot to offer. And whether your relationship is formal or informal, relish this chance to work together.

The roles mentors play

Companionship, support, technical feedback, opportunities to observe different models of teaching or reflect and analyze practice—such are the rewards of a good mentor/mentee relationship.

Judith Shulman and Joel Colbert, editors of *The Mentor Teacher Casebook*, identify five important ways mentors can assist:
• informing beginners about attendance and grading procedures and other school policies (if they teach at the same school) or helping them find out;
• providing opportunities to observe other teachers using different teaching models;
• sharing their knowledge about new materials, unit planning, curriculum development, and teaching methods;
• assisting with classroom management and discipline;
• encouraging beginners to reflect on their teaching practices and helping them adapt new strategies for their classrooms.

"The first four types help teachers survive," say Shulman and Colbert, "but the last one represents the key to continuous learning."

Mentors offer these types of assistance by:
• individually consulting with the new teacher;
• observing and coaching in the beginner's classroom;
• modeling teaching strategies in their own classrooms.

The mentoring process succeeds through close contact and continuing support. And confidentiality is critical. Mentors and mentees must develop a bond of trust. Mentors do *not* evaluate new teachers; they help and support them. "One of my early successes was with a teacher who had absolutely no idea how to plan lessons around a particular unit," recalls one Los Angeles mentor quoted in *The Mentor Teacher Casebook*. "Although her lessons were extremely creative,

> **"I'll never forget the look on her face. It was as if I had shown her the most marvelous thing in the world."**

they were just a hodgepodge of activities. We sat down with several textbooks and the instructional guide, and I showed her how to plan a unit around a list of objectives. I'll never forget the look on her face when we had finished. It was as if I had shown her the most marvelous thing in the world. You can imagine how good I felt when this teacher put together the next unit, completely on her own."

Mentors can also play an important role just by showing the ropes to their charges. Susan Audap tries to buffer her advisees from the bureaucracy in schools.

"I cut the red tape. It is mundane, but especially important in a large bureaucracy to have someone who understands the system. I am a go-fer: I inquire about credentials and requirements; fetch transcripts and forms; arrange special bus trips and speakers; ferret out resources, books and funds; and inform about the union contract provisions and grievable acts and commissions. I want to guard the teachers' energies. They will learn soon enough which questions to ask where, and how to pin down the meaning of the latest memo. But for now, whatever reserves of energy they have need to go toward teaching."

And there's the emotional side to mentoring, too. Even the best of beginners need a shoulder to lean on now and again. One California mentor recalls:

"When the kids were noisy and the day had fallen flat, then I would listen, comfort, console, and bolster. Such emotional support brought a special closeness, and we became personal friends during this time. This greatly enhanced our work professionally."

Making it happen

Productive encounters between beginners and veterans don't just occur spontaneously. Both parties must work hard to make good things happen. What can you do?

Most important is to keep an open mind.

"Be willing to look at more than one way of doing things," advises veteran Cathey Graham. "A mentor can give you a different perspective. If you start your career by always looking for new ideas, you will continue to do this and not become stale or stagnant."

"If I knew then what I know now, I wouldn't have been afraid to ask for help or materials."

Whether you've been assigned a mentor (this term will be used to mean any helping teacher) or just choose to work with a willing colleague, remember several important steps in setting the stage for a healthy relationship:

• *Overcome your initial reluctance.* Sure you feel vulnerable. It's only natural. To have someone watching, discussing, analyzing your teaching is scary to any teacher. But try to push your self-doubt aside and concentrate on how much you stand to gain.

• *Try to get along.* Ideally, your most suitable mentor would be one teaching the same grade, subject, or type of students in the same building—with a personality complementing

---

The picture of success

In a study of how teachers can best help each other, Judith Warren Little of the Far West Lab identified six major features of successful relationships between advisors and the teachers they advise:

1. A common language to describe, understand, and refine teaching. (When discussing engaged time or direct teaching, for example, both parties must make sure they're talking about the same thing.)

2. A focus on one or two key issues or problems at a time.

3. Emphasis on the hard evidence revealed by classroom observation and records. (For example, an advisor's recorded observations that your transitions between lessons average eight minutes is more valuable than a subjective opinion that "your transition times are too long.")

4. Skillful interaction during conferences together.

5. Predictability based on trust in each other's intentions.

6. Reciprocity: acknowledging each other's skills and knowledge, and giving their work a full measure of energy, thought, and attention.

---

your own. But reality is something different. In formal programs, where mentors are typically assigned, you probably won't have a choice. If you do, try for a close match. Either way, remember that even if your mentor seems very different from you, your working relationship can still be a good one. Explore your differences and try to understand different points of view.

• *Ask for help when you need it.* Professionals admit they have a problem and know when to ask for help. Your experienced colleagues are ready and waiting to help, but they don't want to intrude. You may have to take the first step.

"If I knew then what I know now, I wouldn't have been afraid to ask for help or materials," says 10-year teacher Sandra Tatum, San Jose, of her first year.

Tatum speaks for most veterans when she urges new teachers to seek necessary help from their colleagues. After thirty years, Ruth Donnelly still recalls her experience: "One [colleague] made all the difference in what happened for me. She told me, 'Honey, you are going to be a great teacher. I can see that. Be careful how you part your lips. Do a lot of observing, active listening, and careful thinking about what you are about. You come with new ideas and enthusiasm and you also need to learn the wisdom and experience of others. And come to me whenever you want or feel the need. I will be there for you.' She was correct, and I share her words with all new staff at my site."

So you see, your experienced colleagues really do want to help. They benefit as well. Helping others is a wonderful learning process. And it's emotionally and professionally satisfying, too. As mentor Doris Dillon admits, "It really gives me great pleasure to train the new generation."

• *Communicate effectively.* Perhaps you don't understand how a mentor can be useful. Ask questions. Voice your concerns. If something about the mentoring process bothers you, speak up. And try not to become defensive. Mentors want to help, so let them know how they can. Here's how one mentor describes the communication between herself and her mentees: "Feedback is a two-way street, and my mentees have been very responsive with me. They have helped me with how I am doing and whether or not I am meeting their needs. Most of the input has been positive. When it has been negative, I have tried to be a good listener and adjust to their suggestions, whenever possible and appropriate . . . Mentees have conveyed fears, frustrations, tears, successes, and lots of laughter to me. It

has allowed me to get to know these special individuals personally as well as professionally."

• *Consider the mentor's perspective.* It's difficult being a beginner, but helping a beginner is no easy task, either! Especially if the help is not asked for or even unwanted, as sometimes happens in formal mentor programs. If mentors are too assertive or forthright, they may come across as pushy and domineering. But if they aren't assertive enough, they may be ineffective. If you understand these difficult demands, perhaps you'll be more inclined to focus on good intentions and overlook minor faults.

Below, teachers describe what it's like to be a mentor.

Classroom observations

An expert wants to come into your classroom to observe what it is you're doing, and you're not even sure yourself! Is this what you've been dreading?

The classroom observation is probably the most frightening—yet potentially the most beneficial—aspect of veterans helping new teachers: frightening because it exposes your classroom behavior to careful scrutiny; beneficial because it is a window on teaching—a way to analyze real teaching of real kids. Observations offer a means for reflecting on practice. And reflection helps us grow.

Ideally, it works like this: The mentor and the new teacher sit down together and agree to focus on a specific problem or concern. With that concern in mind, the mentor then observes a lesson, recording specific behaviors, comments, interactions, and other classroom happenings. Afterwards, the mentor presents his or her observations to the teacher. Together, they reflect on what happened and try to develop strategies for improvement.

Suppose, for example, you wanted to help with classroom discipline. There are no severe behavior problems in your class, but the noise level and general rowdiness sometimes get out of hand. You express your concerns to a helping colleague and ask her to watch you teach a science lesson to help you figure out what's going wrong.

After the observation, you sit down together and go over her detailed notes. She has recorded how many minutes were spent on each of the three experiments the students did, and how much time elapsed between the end of one experiment and the beginning of another.

These transition times were much longer than you realized. And you can see from the observation notes that here was where most of the misbehavior occurred. When you paused to reprimand those misbehaving, you delayed the experiments even further, inviting more misbehavior.

The solution here is obvious. Keep students busily engaged and on task by reducing dangerous transition times and stepping up the pace. Your colleague shares some of her strategies. And she also suggests that some

minor misbehavior is better ignored so as not to disrupt the lesson.

You resolve to make these changes. And you ask your mentor to observe once more, just to help you assess the new strategies.

This is a simple example. But it illustrates the concrete results and immediate usefulness of a technique custom-tailored to each teacher. This technique is one form of peer coaching. In its truest form, peer coaching is a reciprocal relationship where two colleagues take turns observing each other as they implement new teaching strategies. See the corresponding section on p. 272.

In *The Mentor Teacher Casebook*, Shulman and Colbert state that successful classroom observations depend on several conditions:
• conferring beforehand to agree on the purpose for the observation;
• analysis based on credible and concrete evidence (a written record, for example);
• discussion and problem solving in pre- and post-observation conferences;
• an atmosphere of mutual respect and trust;
• an assurance of confidentiality.

Knowing someone is watching you do your job can be very stressful, especially for beginners full of self-doubt. But remember you *are* a beginner, and your colleagues know it. They've all been there. If you're lucky enough to have a colleague who's willing to observe and coach, seize the opportunity. Like a doctor, you're asking a colleague for expert opinions and advice. That's just good professional practice.

And don't forget that the observation process works two ways. Ask to observe your mentor or arrange observations in other teachers' classrooms. Most will be happy to demonstrate a technique you are interested in, or connect you with someone who can. Mentors and other experienced teachers can model teaching styles and demonstrate the strategies you'd like to learn.

The collegial process of experienced teachers helping inexperienced ones benefits all involved. Two teachers—one veteran and one beginner—describe their mentoring experiences.

"We began to exchange lesson plans and reading materials. Now we observe each other whenever we use a new approach or special activity. We also meet regularly, during lunch or conference periods. Jeff and I have become professional buddies. We share ideas, jokes, learning theories, rooms, books, teaching strategies, and our real concern about effective teaching. I started out to help Jeff, but I ended up becoming his teammate."

—Veteran Teacher,
The Mentor Teacher Casebook

"It gives you a secure feeling to have someone there for you—someone to lean on, someone who's such a good resource. You know you're not alone."

—Phyllis Young,
Beginning teacher,
San Jose

Working and Growing Together

As team teachers, peer coaches, members of professional associations, colleagues meeting at a teachers' center, or friends sharing some other professional activity, we're usually at our best when working together.

What options are available to you? How can you develop a working relationship with

colleagues? It's well worth the trouble to find out.

Sometimes it helps just to talk

That advice certainly applies well to teaching. Talking about teaching with other teachers helps you reflect on your own practice. One on one, in informal support groups, or as members of organized networks, teachers talking together share ideas, experiences, problems, and solutions.

What's the result of all this talk? Improved practice, increased collegiality, professional growth, and decreased isolation, frustration, or burnout.

As a new teacher, Susan Audap remembers being so obsessed with teaching that she used to "eat, drink, and sleep teaching." She'd seek out other beginners to talk about lessons and kids and instructional strategies and anything else pertaining to classroom life. As an advisor to new teachers, she saw the same needs in her advisees.

Make it a point to meet the other new teachers in your building or district. Organize or join a beginners' support group that meets informally once a week or so. Express your joys and concerns, share your horror stories, give each other a sympathetic ear and some moral support.

Camaraderie is not the only payoff of support groups. Barbara Diamond, a 17-year veteran who now teaches other teachers at Eastern Michigan University, says that exchanging ideas with colleagues is one way teachers gain the self-confidence to make decisions about what is best for their students.

"Beginning teachers must include time for fueling the knowledge base from which instructional decisions should flow. Initially, this could be informal meetings with other beginning teachers in the building, or in the district. Gradually, these meetings could become more focused and formalized.

"I know this doesn't happen often, because of the myriad duties teachers have. However, I feel that this is also a responsibility and makes a real difference between teachers who enjoy their jobs and feel that they're effective and contributing, and those who become frustrated and burned out."

Support groups aren't just for beginners. Experienced teachers, who are just as isolated in their classrooms, also benefit from meeting and talking with their peers. Frequently, veterans form support groups organized around a particular curriculum area or teaching strategy. Or they tap into networks of teachers with similar interests.

At the Park Avenue Teachers' Center in Los Angeles, primary teachers have formed an Early Years Network. A core group of teachers comes together regularly to share information and insights about teaching very young children. When teachers express interests in early education, the Center "acts as broker," putting them in touch with teachers in the network.

Network members are even developing their own resources, such as videotapes of classroom block work and funds so that teachers can be released to come to the center and create specific materials to complement their teaching.

Grassroots groups initiated by one or two teachers are common. One of them involved teachers who wanted more literature and fewer worksheets in reading instruction. Together they shared a vision and worked to make it happen.

One district hosted periodic curriculum parties, where each teacher brought 100 copies of one idea to share with colleagues. Teachers could initiate curriculum-sharing parties on any level or scale.

Support groups and networks put teachers in touch with others who share their interests and concerns. And it's not all just talk. Talking stimulates thinking and reflecting on what it is you do in the classroom. And above all, teachers must be thinkers—not technicians applying a prescribed curriculum or strategy, but professionals whose expertise, judgments, and decisions guide the classroom.

Peer coaching

Teachers are their own best resource.

That's the idea behind a technique called peer coaching. In peer coaching, two colleagues take turns observing each other as they both attempt to implement new teaching strategies. They analyze evidence from their observations and plan ways to change. It's a way to make significant improvements—with a little help from a friend.

Learning new teaching strategies is difficult and demanding. It's easy to make mistakes and get discouraged. Coaching provides much-needed support.

In fact, research shows that without sustained feedback and support of the type offered by peer coaching, teachers never really learn to use all those new strategies they hear about in workshops and inservices.

Teachers in many schools around the

Peer coaching

To try peer coaching, keep these general tips in mind:

- Pick your own partner. Coaching should be a comfortable, nonthreatening experience involving someone with whom you share a mutual trust and commitment to help.

- Seek training, if it's available. Coaching is a skill that must be learned, like any other. Many districts now offer coaching partners training in factual data gathering, constructive feedback, and analysis of teaching. And local teachers' centers also frequently offer such training.

- Focus on a specific problem or strategy. Sit down with your coaching partner during lunch, after school, or any time the students are absent to discuss what types of observations to record. Identify your concerns and map out strategies for working together.

- Coaches should conduct systematic observations, keeping thorough and appropriate records. In the programs Showers developed, coaches use Clinical Assessment Forms to record the presence or absence of specific behaviors and how thoroughly they are performed. The Checklist for Observing Teaching on p. 281 is an observation instrument you can adapt to your own needs. Or develop your own observation instruments with your partner's

help. Instruments might help you record what each student is doing during a lesson (on-task behavior), or how teacher and students are interacting, for example. Or you and your partner could just agree on a systematic process of note-taking. Data-gathering procedures could also include audio- or videotaping, anecdotal record-keeping, seating charts indicating student interaction, and on-task behavior—whatever lends itself to the specific focus of the coaching.

- Follow up on each observation with a conference for offering technical feedback. Technical feedback is specific information on how a teacher uses certain skills or strategies, not an evaluation of general teaching ability. Coaching conferences should be collaborative problem-solving sessions; they often result in the partners jointly planning a lesson with which to experiment. The teacher experiments with a new lesson while the coach observes, and the process continues with a new cycle of analysis, problem solving, and experimenting.

- Try to implement the changes suggested and schedule another (or several) follow-up observation. There's always room for improvement. With peer coaching, professional teachers engage in the continuous study of teaching.

country use peer coaching based on an inservice program developed by Beverly Showers and her colleagues at the University of Oregon. Here, peer coaching is an alternative to traditional inservices, giving teachers long-term support and encouragement, not just one-shot training. The coaching focuses on implementing specific models of teaching.

"Peer coaching needs to be centered around something people are trying to master, no matter what it is," Showers emphasizes.

Teachers in the Oak Grove District of San Jose, California, for example, coach each other to learn to use expectations and behaviors that improve student achievement. It's all part of the Teacher Expectations, Student Achievement (TESA) program, reports TESA instructor Judy Smith.

Here's how one teacher sums up her peer coaching experience: "As one of the *oldies-but-goodies* soon to leave the classroom, how truly wondrous to have had the opportunity to end it all on such a high note. I've had to sharpen my skills, pay more attention to techniques, check those lesson plans, and work harder to be a good educator. When a teacher has earned respect from his or her peers and can share concerns with fellow teachers; can sit and listen/watch/record in another classroom for a specific reason; and can truly affect the teaching of others, then one can smile a lot."

—anonymous,
Continuing to Learn

Teachers' centers

"Wish I had some better ideas for motivating my students."

"If only I had some hands-on materials to bring this history unit to life."

"I wonder how other teachers are mainstreaming students in their classrooms?"

For practical answers to teaching's daily challenges and problems, a teachers' center is a sure bet. A teachers' center is a place to call your own—a place to go for companionship and support. No two centers look or function alike, but the best share certain characteristics.

• *Most important, a teachers' center focuses on teachers' individual and continuing needs,* with local, practical solutions to specific problems. A teacher who comes looking for help with a history unit, for example, might learn he or she can tap into a whole network of local resources, both human and material. There may be books, films, teaching aids, educational materials, and even local experts who can talk to his or her class. The center director might suggest a field trip to a local museum.

To tap community resources, the staff of the Pittsford Teacher Center in New York sent surveys to all Pittsford residents asking them to share their personal expertise. The surveys yielded a wide response in many different fields and subjects. Help and information was there for the asking.

• *Practical make-and-take programs are another prominent feature.* Using center supplies and equipment, teachers can make many types of classroom materials—from a customized worksheet to activities and manipulatives for a learning center.

• *Teachers' centers also feature teachers teaching teachers.* Teachers with expertise in a certain area might demonstrate teaching techniques. Or they might help colleagues develop and plan a curriculum unit. The center director is often a resident mentor or advisor who, upon request, will coach teachers in their classroom, demonstrate strategies, and even help teach lessons. Some set up informal networks of teachers sharing common interests and concerns.

Center directors and staff also arrange or conduct workshops and professional development activities. In fact, so many professional development activities take place in teachers' centers that many are now officially called teacher development centers. Teachers can often take in-service courses at the center rather than being sent to universities. Or they can design their own course of study.

At the Park Avenue Teachers' Center in Los Angeles, staff members make in-class videotapes of teachers for other teachers to watch and study. One involves very young children doing block work. Another features a teacher demonstrating art techniques, and a third shows a teacher helping his junior high school students set up individual and group projects.

The opportunities for professional development are many and varied. During just one month at the Park Avenue Teachers' Center, for example, teachers could participate in a seminar for teaching and learning social studies, a four-part Appleworks computer class, a language arts conference, or informal conversations about the early years (pre-K through third grade). All but the early years conversations involved in-service credit.

• *Personal growth is encouraged, too.* The Pittsford Teacher Center has offered courses ranging from disco dancing to investment counseling. Other centers urge teachers to get to know their colleagues by meeting informally and chatting over coffee.

• *Prevailing over all is a warm, friendly atmosphere and a spirit of collegiality.*

Sound inviting? Teachers' centers can be fantastic places and fun. Companionship, moral support, expert guidance, help with curriculum or teaching methods, new ideas and perspectives, time to think and reflect, a place to unwind, professional development, resources beyond traditional textbooks and worksheets are some of the considerable benefits that centers offer. Check your center out!

Today's team teaching

Linda Farr of San Jose and two of her primary teacher colleagues had a great idea. They would each plan and develop a super science unit and teach it to each other's students. They wouldn't simply rotate classes, but they would divide all the students into three groups composed of kids from each class.

Pooling time and talents

Here are some of the ways Linda Farr and other teachers pool their time and talents:

• Teachers with combination classes exchange some students to combine kids of one grade. From two classes of second/third grade combinations, for example, one teacher takes the second graders and the other takes the third graders for certain lessons or subjects.

• Periodically exchanging classes to take advantage of teachers' academic specialties. A teacher who is very strong in social studies might exchange classes with another who's strong in science. One teaches social studies to two classes and another teaches science.

• Sharing classes, as some resource teachers do; or teaching under split contracts.

• "Cross-grouping" for reading or math—grouping students by ability from two or more classes.

• Teaming to teach different units, as Farr and her colleagues did in the example above. After planning one extensive unit or lesson, each teacher presents the unit to several classes or exchanges lesson plans and materials to teach different units to their own classes.

• Combining classes for lessons or units. One teacher teaches while the other is released to observe, catch up on record-keeping, plan other lessons, and so on.

• Two teachers and their respective classes share a double classroom, combining for some lessons and separating for others.

The idea worked, and the payoffs were tremendous. The students completed two very good science units. And in the mixed groups, they got to know and work with children from the other classes. The teachers used their time and energy more efficiently by concentrating on one unit each and doing it very well.

Linda Farr is a team player. In 26 years of teaching primary grades, she has teamed with colleagues to teach lessons in a variety of ways. (See box, preceding page.)

There are countless combinations. The nature and frequency of teaming largely depends on the individuals involved. Teachers in many districts are free to initiate team teaching, usually with administrators' blessings.

How do you choose a teammate? Farr advises teaming with colleagues who have the same philosophical leanings and similar classroom management strategies. On the other hand, you might profit by joining forces with someone quite different. Exposure to different teaching styles and strategies stimulates both beginning and experienced teachers. In whatever shape or form, team teaching has a lot to offer:
• opportunities to brainstorm and share ideas;
• more efficient use of time and lesson preparations;
• capitalizing on teachers' strengths and expertise;
• peer coaching opportunities and chances to observe other teachers in action;
• students benefiting from different personalities and teaching styles and the chance to work with other kids;
• shared resources.

"Teaming is just a better use of personnel," Farr concludes.

And the resulting companionship is nice, too.

"When you're working with kids day in and day out, it's nice to be able to speak to an adult sometimes," says Farr.

Team teachers report higher job satisfaction than those who don't team-teach.

In IRT's *Communication Quarterly*, Michigan teacher Kathleen Juntunen explains team teaching this way:

"My experience in team teaching, where there is constant communication with other staff members, paid off in increased creativity in the classroom and almost total absence of boredom. Interaction among colleagues can lead to improved perspective in problem situations, often making them more manageable. You have the opportunity to observe the behavior of other teachers, reflecting on your own in the process. Along with many other benefits, interaction with colleagues leads to a high level of morale."

Professional development— team style

Teachers team up outside the classroom, too. One way is through joint professional improvement projects.

Doris Dillon and two colleagues, for example, developed a state-funded program on language arts and literature. They brought authors and booksellers to their school to talk to students, acquired supplies for kids to make their own books, and developed specialized activities which involved every grade in the school.

Linda Farr and Cathey Graham are putting their heads together to create ways of featuring animals in the language arts curriculum. "I'm the detail person. I'm better at doing the library work, and Cathey handles the creative side," Farr says of their complementary working relationship.

"Sharing ideas and materials makes them more permanent and accessible," Farr continues. She recalls the time she lost her notes on an activity she had shared with Graham. "If I had not shared it, it would have been lost forever."

On a larger scale, professional knowledge is lost every time a teacher leaves teaching. Teachers need a way to document and share the expertise they acquire. For Doris Dillon, that means cataloguing the work of colleagues in the San Jose School District.

For 13 years Dillon has served on a committee to review and authorize district-funded professional improvement projects. The projects become district property available to all teachers, but they are not indexed or readily accessible.

"After being on the committee so long and seeing all these great things coming in, I felt there should be some way for other teachers to find out about them," explains Dillon. She's undertaken her own professional improvement project to catalogue and describe what's available.

Dillon's work is one important step toward documenting good practice and sharing it with other professionals.

Professional associations

Another way to grow is to interact with colleagues through professional associations. See p. 280 for a list of some of the more prominent ones.

Chapter 7: Read more about it

1. *The Mentor Teacher Casebook.* Judith Shulman and Joel Colbert (eds.). San Francisco: Far West Laboratory, 1986.

2. *Continuing to Learn: A Guidebook for Teacher Development.* Susan Loucks-Horsley et al. The Regional Laboratory for Educational Improvement of the Northeast and Islands and the National Staff Development Council, 1987.

3. "The Coaching of Teaching." Bruce Joyce and Beverly Showers. *Educational Leadership*, 40, 1, (Oct. 1982), 4-11.

4. "Teachers Coaching Teachers." Beverly Showers. *Educational Leadership*, 42, 7 (April 1985), 43-49.

5. *Essays on Teachers' Centers.* K. Devaney (ed.). San Francisco: Far West Laboratory for Educational Research and Development, 1977.

6. *Building a Teachers' Center.* Kathleen Devaney. San Francisco: Far West Laboratory for Educational Research and Development, 1979.

7. "So You Want to Start a Teacher Center." Wanda Ward. *Instructor*, (April 1980), 68-70.

8. "Professionalism." *R&D Notes*, 1, (1985), 1. Aurora, CO: Mid-continent Regional Educational Laboratory, 1985.

NOTES

NOTES

Professional Associations

Through professional organizations, teachers can meet others sharing their particular interests. These organizations host professional meetings and offer professional development opportunities in all fields of teaching. Many of their journals and magazines routinely include research synthesis articles.

National Council of Teachers of English (NCTE)
1111 Kenyon Road
Urbana, IL 61801
(217) 328-3870
— *English Journal*
— *Language Arts*

International Reading Association (IRA)
800 Barksdale Road
Newark, DE 19711
(302) 731-1600
— *Journal of Reading*
— *The Reading Teacher*
— *Reading Research Quarterly*

National Science Teachers Association (NSTA)
1742 Connecticut Avenue, Northwest
Washington, DC 20009
(202) 328-5800
— *Science and Children*
— *The Science Teacher*

National Council of Teachers of Mathematics (NCTM)
1906 Association Drive
Reston, VA 22091
(703) 620-9840
— *Arithmetic Teacher*
— *Mathematics Teachers*
— *Journal of Research in Mathematics*

School Science and Mathematics Association (SSMA)
126 Life Sciences Building
Bowling Green State University
Bowling Green, OH 43403
(419) 372-2531
— *School Science and Mathematics*

National Art Education Association
1916 Association Drive
Reston, VA 22091
(703) 860-8000
— *The Art Education Journal*

Music Teachers National Association
617 Vine Street, Suite 1432
Cincinnati, OH 45202
(513) 421-1420
— *American Music Teacher*

Phi Delta Kappa
(professional association in education)
Eighth and Union
P.O. Box 789
Bloomington, IN 47402
(812) 339-1156
— *Phi Delta Kappan*
— *Fastbacks*

American Educational Research Association (AERA)
1230 17th Street NW
Washington, DC 20036
(202) 223-9485
— *American Educational Research Journal*
— *Journal of Educational Statistics*

American Federation of Teachers (AFT)
555 New Jersey Avenue NW
Washington, DC 20001
(202) 879-4400
— *The American Teacher*
— *On Campus*

National Staff Development Council
P.O. Box 240
Oxford, OH 45056
(513) 523-6029
— *The Developer*
— *Journal of Staff Development*

National Council for the Social Studies
3501 Newark Street NW
Washington, DC 20016
(202) 966-7840
— *Social Education*

National Education Association
Division of Instruction and Professional Development
1201 16th Street NW
Washington, DC 20036
(202) 822-7370
— *NEA Today*

Association for Supervision and Curriculum Development (ASCD)
125 Northwest Street
Alexandria, VA 22314
(703) 549-9110
— *Educational Leadership*

Guidelines for
Observing Teaching

Here are some guidelines to use when observing a colleague in action.
Focus your observations and comments on these important dimensions of teaching.
(Chapters 2, 3, and 4 provide detailed discussions of these dimensions.)
Decide with your colleague ahead of time which dimensions you'll focus on.
And add those you value but don't find included here.

Classroom Management

- Efficient classroom routines
- Time management (allocated time, instructional time, engaged time)
- Physical environment conducive to teaching and learning
- Seating and grouping arrangements that minimize racial and sexual segregation and enhance cooperation
- Necessary material readily at hand
- Well-organized lessons
- Smooth transitions between activities
- Learning centers, independent activities
- Handling paperwork, checking assignments
- Delegating routine tasks
- Use of peer and cross-age tutors
- Use of cooperative activities
- Classroom rules firmly and fairly enforced
- Discipline strategies

Active Teaching and Instructional Techniques

- Assess how much students already know on a topic
- Explain a lesson's purpose and relevance
- Explicit instructions
- Task focus
- Lesson presentation
- Pacing
- Periodically checking for understanding
- Providing examples, asking questions
- Guided practice
- Independent practice
- Review
- Subject matter integration
- Appropriate difficulty of material
- Ability grouping (tailoring instruction and curriculum to needs and abilities of students)
- Opportunities for "hands-on" learning
- Capitalizing on "teachable" moments

Teacher-Student Interaction

- Treat students with courtesy and respect
- Provide leadership
- Enforce rules and discipline equally
- Encourage responsibility and independence
- Motivational techniques
- Questioning techniques
- Make direct eye contact
- Boost students' self-esteem
- Model positive behavior
- Offer specific, appropriate praise
- Allow all students opportunities to respond in class
- Solicit ideas from students
- Communicate high expectations

CHAPTER 8

> **"** *Learning to teach is a bigger job than universities, schools, experience, or personal disposition alone can accomplish.* **"**
>
> — *Sharon Feiman-Nemser*
> *Institute for Research on Teaching*

Still so much to learn!

> *The best teachers I know are always actively involved in the process of becoming better teachers.*
>
> — *Eliot Wigginton*
> *Teacher, author, and creator of the Foxfire series*

By now, it should be obvious that learning to teach is not just for beginnners. It's a process that continues well after your first, third, or even twentieth year of teaching. But that's what keeps teaching interesting.

Author and educator David Hawkins recalls hearing a 35-year veteran tell a student teacher that what held her to teaching after all those years was that there was still so much to be learned.

"So much to be learned." Why not adopt that as a personal motto to guide your professional teaching career? So much to learn . . . so much to explore . . . so many exciting challenges and opportunities. The hallmark of professionalism is a constant striving to refine and improve practice. And that's what this chapter is all about.

Professional development. Without it, we stagnate, wilt, burn out. Teachers at the Institute for Research on Teaching and elsewhere claim that professional development and expanded career opportunities mean more to teachers than increased salaries or improved working conditions!

Professional development is the responsibility of professional teachers. And what does it mean to be a professional? A professional is someone who makes informed judgments in complex environments, supported by solid, research-based knowledge.

The first step toward professional development is recognizing that classrooms are places where both students and teachers learn. Once you understand that, there should be no stopping you!

The peer coaching, mentoring, networks and support groups, team teaching, and teacher centers discussed in Chapter 7 are all professional development activities, and alternatives to the traditional one-shot workshop or inservice. This chapter explores these other approaches.

You probably won't have time to pursue many of these professional development activities during your first years of teaching. But you can still make the commitment to lifelong learning and professional excellence. After all, the very qualities that probably brought you to teaching—your own excitement and zest for life, learning, and a desire to help young people develop into productive, whole, and happy persons—will keep you striving for excellence. And there is a path, as you'll see here.

Reflective Teaching—Think About It

"In teaching, it's the thought that counts."

That idea doesn't mean that intentions are more important than actions. It means that teachers must be thinkers and decision makers who take full responsibility for their classrooms and students, as opposed to technicians merely applying a prescribed practice.

We often tell students, "Think about what you're doing!" The same advice applies to us. Reflecting on what one does in the classroom is the key to professional growth.

Many of the things teachers simply don't realize they are doing or not doing become obvious when they just stop and think. And realizing a problem is half the battle of correcting it.

But systematic reflection is not as simple as it sounds. It takes time and concentrated effort—two things always in short supply.

Here are some strategies to help you stop and think.

Keeping a journal

In their studies of planning, researchers Christopher Clark and Robert Yinger asked teachers to describe their thinking and planning in a daily journal or diary.

"The process of journal-keeping was a powerful experience for the teachers who undertook it," the researchers noted. "They reported that they learned a great deal about their thinking and teaching. Until asked to keep a detailed report of their planning, they did not realize how much thought and energy they put into planning for instruction. In a sense, they were newly appreciating themselves as professionals."

"Two things happened to the teachers who kept journals—their morale seemed to improve and they became researchers investigating their own teaching."

Two things happened to the teachers keeping journals.

"Their morale seemed to improve," the researchers continue. "But more importantly, these teachers became researchers on their own teaching—alert to the many opportunities teachers have to take responsibility for their own continued professional development—and to gradually and systematically improve the effectiveness of their teaching and the quality of life in their classrooms."

Pen your thoughts to share

When you're writing for an audience, the reflective process is much the same, because writing in any form requires a large measure of thought. There are many outlets for articles on your experiences, ideas, or innovations.

Test your wings (or pen) by developing your own class newsletter (see p. 229 in Chapter 6). Parents are a captive audience who will enjoy the extra effort you put forth. Go beyond explanations of the rules and regulations in your classroom and tell them about your general goals or teaching philosophy. Describe the challenge of teaching fractions to your fourth graders or the joy of witnessing the students work out a problem on their own. Let them know what teachers and teaching are all about. Give them some insight into the complex job you undertake every single day. Invite them to share their insights and responses to your articles. Their comments will stimulate your thinking even further.

Share your written thoughts with other teachers, too. How? Writing for a teacher's publication is a great way. *Instructor* regularly features articles written by practicing educators. The magazine also has two monthly columns, "One Teacher's Story" and "Speak Out!," that are forums for teachers' thoughts. Teachers' ideas for activities or curricula appear throughout the magazine.

Some teachers publish the results of original research in education journals (see the listing on p. 296). General interest magazines also frequently carry articles by teachers about teaching.

Write to the editors of the magazines or journals that interest you and ask for a copy of their writers' guidelines. You can find a publication's address on its masthead or listed in the sourcebook *Writer's Market*.

Lights, camera, action

Reflection is a way of seeing. And nothing helps you see yourself more accurately than watching a videotape of your classroom. Readily available in most schools, videotape allows you to look at the classroom as an outsider, analyze yourself in action, and see things in a new way.

For example, a tape might show when students are confused because you've failed to communicate the intent of a lesson or activity. Or it might reveal that when students gather in a circle, they tend to sit in the same circle each time, leading you to consider whether you can improve the lesson or eliminate behavior problems by adjusting the seating arrangements.

Just by seeing yourself in action, you can spot some easily-remedied problems. Another plus of videotaping is the chance it affords to watch individual kids—responding to a lesson, interacting with you or peers, and so on.

Teacher educator and former teacher Barbara Diamond gives the example of one child who persistently asked questions. After

---

Tips on Journal-keeping

Journal-keeping can be eye-opening, cathartic, and instructive. To make the experience as beneficial as possible, keep these tips in mind:

- Make regular entries. Get into the habit of writing often—every day, if possible.

- Keep a permanent record by writing in something durable—a bound notebook, datebook, calendar, or diary.

- Set aside a certain time each day for journal-writing. You might have your students keep daily journals, too, and work on yours at the same time. You'd be offering them a valuable experience, providing an effective model, and writing—all at the same time. Of course, don't deny yourself the chance to write uninterrupted and in private sometimes.

- Anything goes. If all you can do at first is complain about how terrible everything is going, fine. Once that's off your chest you'll be able to write more objectively and analyze what's going wrong. You'll probably even start noticing that a lot is going right.

- Record your growth and look for those small successes. "Take the time, every day, to pat yourself on the back for the risks you have dared to take and all the things you are learning to do well," suggests teacher and author Jane Bluestein. She offers these examples of entries made by beginners recording their growth each week:

    "My self-control seems to be improving. I kept my cool through a tough situation."

"I don't cry every day."
"I'm remembering to get each child's attention before talking."
"I'm smiling more."
"I am feeling comfortable with the faculty at my school. The teachers have become so supportive, and I am becoming more confident as a teacher."

- Occasionally try to target different aspects of your teaching to study in detail. Are you interested in offering equal time and attention to all students? Then keep track of your personal interactions each day. Make a list of the students you enjoy being around and those you don't. What are the characteristics you like or dislike? Write about it. Get it down in black and white where you can see it. Then try to assess where you can change.

- Daily journals are a good way to keep track of your time allocations—both academic and nonacademic (see p. 141 in Chapter 4).

- Reread your journal entries occasionally. It's instructive, sometimes amusing, and usually encouraging to see how your concerns have changed over time.

- Store your journal in a safe place. Your thoughts are private, and you need to be completely candid with yourself. Unintentional readers may misinterpret.

---

carefully studying him on videotape, she recognized two patterns to his questions. Some he asked to gain information, but others he asked to gain control.

Patterns and habits in speech, body language, interactions—all things teachers don't have time to analyze in classrooms—reveal a lot when they're analyzed on videotape.

So take advantage of the video equipment in your school and get those cameras rolling. For an excellent resource on using videotape to study teaching, see *Sights and Sounds of Life in Schools*, by Fredrick Erickson and Jan Wilson.

Stimulating thoughts

Whether you keep a journal, analyze videotapes of your teaching, or just occasionally cogitate, you can stimulate your thinking with the classroom observation instrument found on p. 281. This instrument helps a classroom observer focus observations on several critical areas of teaching.

Used alone, the instrument can help you organize your thoughts around the same teaching areas. Use this instrument as a starting point to develop *your own* areas of concentration along the way.

Another way to focus your thoughts is to

rate your teaching by responding to quizzes or questionnaires such as the one a group of elementary teachers developed to describe superior teaching (see pp. 150-151). The quiz can boost your confidence or show areas where you need to improve. Individual quiz items can also direct your thinking and reflection. The teacher-manager quiz on p. 149 is another example.

These strategies demonstrate the power of reflection. Solutions to problems and the means to improvements often become obvious after one has had a chance to analyze the situation.

Think about it.

The Search for Knowledge

"A professional, by virtue of a long period of education, training, and experience, is capable of autonomous decision making and can justify his/her decisions with specialized knowledge that goes beyond common sense."
　　　　　　—Michigan teacher Nancy Brubaker.
To grow professionally, teachers need information about teaching. And there's a lot of it out there. Just as lawyers or doctors need to keep current with what's happening in their professions, teachers must keep pace with new knowledge about teaching—or create their own.

Read, read, read

There is extensive professional literature on teaching. It ranges from the practical to the scholarly, with books and publications focusing on every aspect of teaching and all subject matter.

Practical publications offer ideas and activities teachers can implement immediately in the classroom. The more scholarly works— research reports and education journals— inform your thinking and provide information to help you make decisions. Professional teachers need a healthy measure of both.

The reproducible on p. 296 lists many of the major publications devoted to teaching and/or subject matter. Find these magazines in your

school library or teachers' center, or write to the publishers for sample copies.

The National Education Association, the American Federation of Teachers, and their state affiliates have their own offerings of newsletters, publications, and curriculum materials. Write for information.

The Educational Resources Information Center (ERIC) is another valuable source. Sponsored by the Department of Education, ERIC operates clearinghouses that catalogue and classify vast amounts of information on various education topics. For a fee, you can request a search on a particular topic and receive a listing of relevant papers and publications. The clearinghouses also analyze and synthesize information to produce research reviews on particular topics. Included on p. 299 are the names and addresses of the ERIC clearinghouses which pertain to elementary-school teaching.

Educational laboratories and research centers

Get to know the educational laboratories and research centers located around the nation (see p. 298 for their names and addresses). These institutions study teaching and actively interpret and disseminate research results to teachers. Most are federally funded and offer information free or at a nominal cost.

Most of the labs and centers publish at least one free newsletter or periodical. These publications highlight research results; offer practical suggestions for implementing research findings; announce conferences, workshops, and inservices; discuss national educational issues; and describe other products available from the lab or center— books, pamphlets, curriculum materials, and so on.

Write and ask to be placed on the newsletter mailing list. And request a free publication/ products catalog. Still one of the best-kept secrets in the profession, these labs and centers offer teachers a wealth of information and services.

Take the Appalachia Educational Laboratory (AEL), for example. Among its many offerings to educators is the lab's *Research Within Reach* series. "We are committed to helping teachers find research-based answers to classroom questions," is the claim made in an AEL bulletin.

In creating the *Research Within Reach* series, lab staff members survey teachers and administrators for questions about teaching. A panel of educators and researchers then selects the most representative questions to include in the series. Answers to each question include a summary of relevant research, a discussion of classroom implications, and suggestions for classroom use.

Not only do teachers determine the series content in the first place, they help review drafts of each document. In this way, the series is user-validated.

To date, the series includes books and bulletins on mathematics instruction, oral and written communication, reading, and science.

AEL also has a free newsletter and catalogue. Other labs and research centers have equally useful products and services.

Alternative inservices

You're lucky. Teacher inservices have come a long way since the days when your more experienced colleagues suffered through long lectures where university "experts" told them what was wrong with their teaching and how they should correct it.

Today, the trend is for teachers to shape their own inservices. Focusing on common problems, teachers share their experiences and work toward solutions—together. The source of new information might be an outside expert, but it doesn't need to be. More and more frequently, professionals right in the school or district share their expertise with colleagues. Look for these features in the inservices you choose:
• opportunities to interact with your colleagues—to discuss teaching and learning and share classroom experiences;

• encouragement to adapt new teaching strategies to individual classrooms and situations and allowance for professional judgment calls;
• opportunities to plan together for improved instruction.
• the use of peer coaching to provide support and assistance when learning new teaching techniques;
• sustained training, rather than one-shot inservices (except where the goal is to increase subject matter knowledge).

This section only scratches the surface of the possibilities. There are virtually unlimited resources available to teachers searching for knowledge. The important thing is to get started and keep at it.

Researching Teaching

When researchers asked Michigan teacher Rhoda Maxwell to join a research team to study the teaching of writing in school, she was delighted. She had previously been a research subject, but participating as a researcher was a whole new professional opportunity.

"It was an odd experience to be on the other side, Maxwell writes. "Although I had little knowledge of research methods when I began, I had an advantage over my university colleagues by knowing about schools."

Knowing about schools is what makes teachers indispensable research partners. Swelling the ranks of researchers these days are regular classroom teachers on temporary or part-time leave to study teaching, like those at Michigan State University's Institute for Research on Teaching, for example. The Institute employs teachers part-time to participate in all phases of research—from planning a study to collecting and analyzing data and disseminating findings.

"Taking a sabbatical from the classroom, I became a full-time member of the research team," explains Maxwell, who worked at the Institute. "As a researcher, I brought a teacher's perspective to the collecting of data, the analysis and interpretation of results, and the writing of the final research report," says Maxwell.

As a researcher, Maxwell studied the teaching of a colleague.

"When I first began interviewing Mary, I was hesitant about asking questions, afraid she would misunderstand them as judgmental," Maxwell reports. "However, I found that, just as I had been, Mary was delighted to find someone interested in what she did and why. She told me that she really looked forward to these talks because they were the high point of the week."

Professional growth, rewarding relationships with school and university colleagues, time to think and reflect on teaching, improved practice, intellectual stimulation, increased self-esteem—do these sound good to you? They are some of the benefits of doing research. As an opportunity for professional development, research collaboration is hard to beat.

"Being able to step back and carefully study teaching as a researcher has helped me tremendously," says Maxwell. "I now look at my teaching through new eyes."

Daisy Thomas, another teacher collaborating on IRT research, tells what it feels like to work with researchers who "seemed to be genuinely interested in how we taught children."

Rejuvenating!

Rejuvenate where and when you can. Extended vacations to tropical hideaways might be nice, but there are many ways to renew yourself much closer to home. Here are some renewal strategies:

- Redecorate your classroom. Create a fresh teaching environment and revive your spirits by having students rearrange their desks and moving yours.

- Don't forget to smell the flowers. Bring a breath of fresh air into the classroom with plants. The cheery effect of a blooming plant perched atop your desk is hard to beat.

- Talk it out. When life has gotten you down, talk to another teacher, your spouse, a friend—someone you can trust. Don't keep feelings and emotions pent up.

- Get outside. There's something healing and rejuvenating about fresh air and sunshine, so plan outside activities when the weather is nice.

- Laugh a lot. A sense of humor can be your best friend or secret weapon.

- Focus on the positive. Acknowledge a job well done. At the end of a particularly grueling week, try listing everything that went well during that time. (The list will be longer than you imagined!) Save all those special notes you received from parents and students and reread them when you're feeling down. You'll soon feel re-energized.

- Publish and flourish. Type up those teaching ideas, amusing or inspirational anecdotes, or thoughtful essays and submit them to education publications (see listing on pp. 296-297). You'll find that sharing your ideas with other teachers will renew your enthusiasm.

- Don't play "Super Teacher." Nobody's perfect, so don't try to be. Teach and manage your classroom to the best of your ability, and don't judge yourself too harshly if things don't always turn out the way you had hoped. Remember, tomorrow's another day—and another opportunity to do well.

"My intellectual ego soared," Thomas writes in a program report. "This was the first time in my teaching career that I had consistently discussed teaching with colleagues over an extended period of time."

But Thomas also refers to the hard work and trust it takes to build collaborative relationships. Teachers and researchers come from two different environments, she notes. She had to adjust to language differences, the slower pace of research (compared to teaching), differences in tasks and daily routines, and changes in her relationship with teacher colleagues as a result of her research collaboration.

Is it worth it? Maxwell thinks so:

"I value teaching more now than I did before," she admits. "Looking at someone else made it possible for me to see how complicated a task teaching is. No wonder teachers become frustrated and tired. After a year of documenting what one teacher accomplished, my enthusiasm has been renewed. We cannot solve all the problems,

Give yourself some credit

In striving for excellence, teachers are frequently too hard on themselves. They lose sight of the many small successes achieved daily and become mired in frustrations and anxieties over problems frequently beyond their control. Too many focus on the negative. And sometimes, they even question their self-worth.

It's an easy trap to fall into, warns editor Jane Schall, a former teacher who now writes about teaching. "Teachers, isolated in separate classrooms, don't receive enough pats on the back from colleagues observing their work," Schall says. "Often administrators, school boards, and even whole communities are busy examining 'the problems,' and the problems are what teachers hear about."

No wonder teachers get the "blues."

"In a profession where it is often up to us to remind ourselves that the day wasn't so bleak, that we've given a child something lasting and special, and that teaching is really worth it, believing in ourselves is essential," Schall stresses.

Jack Ahern of the University of Toledo teaches classes in self-awareness. He says that to feel emotionally satisfied, we need to identify with others, feel control over our lives, consider ourselves worthy of dignity, and associate with those who provide positive role models. Ahern suggests you:

- Let your friends, family and colleagues know when they've hurt your feelings. Tell them specifically what hurts.

- Ask a respected colleague to evaluate you and help you see the positive aspects of your work. Do the same for that colleague or someone else.

- Stay home and take care of yourself when you don't feel well. Poor health lowers your emotional as well as physical stamina.

- Write angry letters, but don't send them. Just the process of writing the letter can release tension.

- Be big enough to admit when you need help and get it! You teach your kids that they can't be superhuman, but do you have trouble heeding your own advice?

Denis Waitley, author of *The Winner's Edge: The Critical Attitude of Success*, endorses "positive self-talk as a way to build a stronger belief in yourself. As Waitley explains, repeatedly telling yourself things like "I can," "I look forward to," or "Next time I'll do better" improves your self-image and builds more confidence. The result is a stronger, more positive you.

So don't wait for others to pat you on the back for a job well done. Do it yourself!

but we have many more successes than I had ever imagined. Teaching has again become, for me, intrinsically enjoyable."

Research collaboration benefits all teachers, not just those directly involved—and students, too. The end product of collaboration is practical knowledge that all teachers can use to improve their teaching.

How can you become a researcher of teaching? Opportunities are more widespread than you might think. You may not get leave to work at a research institute like Rhoda Maxwell did. But you can collaborate as a research subject in your classroom. You'll have similar chances to "talk teaching" and interact with others. Search for opportunities by contacting:
• friends and colleagues;
• a teachers' center;
• the district research office (if there is one) of a central office administrator, where researchers frequently go to request teacher participation;
• the regional educational laboratory or research center nearest you;
• the college or department of education in a nearby university.

Getting Personal

While working to improve your professional life, don't forget about the personal side. Here's how some teachers rejuvenate when teaching seems too tough. Their tips will help you make sure the "personal you" is nourished so the "professional you" can flourish.

Take time for you

It's very important to acknowledge your personal life apart from teaching. Take time for you by eating right, exercising, getting enough sleep, and pursuing personal interests.

Summer is an especially good time for rejuvenation. After your first year of teaching (and every summer thereafter), try these ideas suggested by Elvin Warfel.
• Seek out a long-lost friend. The hectic school year sometimes separates us from persons we enjoy and those who can provide emotional support, says Warfel. "Summer's the time to pick up the phone and make contact with one of those friends you've been meaning to call for ages."
• Participate in a service organization. Work closely with other adults, make new friends, participate in a cause you believe in, explore a new environment, or develop new skills by doing community or volunteer work.
• Read novels or books that have nothing to do with education.
• Redecorate. Create a fresh living environment.

During the school year you need to take time for you as well. For example:
• Bring your personal skills and interests to the classroom. Try teaching kids a subject you find personally intriguing or would like to know more about. Why not set aside your regular textbooks for two weeks and make the new subject a multidisciplinary unit? During the Winter Olympics of 1988, Doris Dillon focused instruction on the host country, Canada. Or create an exciting yearly project that totally absorbs you and students. New York teacher Robert Bauer had one class build a puppet stage and another build a giant chessboard.
• Plan something unexpected and new. The set schedules and routines of teaching can make you feel stale after a while. Tom Bernagozzi of Bay Shore, New York, suggests these ways to freshen up: Hold a class contest. Have a theme party. (Nutrition is a good one.) Plan a theme week which focuses on something the kids want to know more about. Host a younger class for a special event; a play or music hour, for example.
• Expand your horizons. Pursue a special interest outside of school, take a night course, meet new people, and ask your colleagues what they do for relaxation and renewal.
• Choose one or two afternoons or evenings a week to do something just for you. Colleagues in one school in San Jose devote each Wednesday evening to forgetting about teaching for a little while and just enjoying each other's company.

• Take time off. When you're really in a slump, take a day of vacation or sick leave. Think of it as a personal "mental health day," advises Sister M. Kathleen Glavich and Judith Roper Marrou. Sleep late, fix yourself an elegant brunch, watch television, read, go for a long walk, buy yourself a special present. You'll likely go back to school feeling physically and emotionally rested.

Handling stress

Your personal well-being depends on how successfully you handle that inevitable job-related stress. Larry Clarke of the University of Arkansas offers these tips:
• Schedule your day to include some fun.
• Set realistic goals for yourself, just as you do for students. Take smaller steps and savor the successful completion of each one.
• Support your support system. Encourage your colleagues to share their ups and downs. And let others share yours.
• Retreat and regroup—behind closed doors, alone after school. The rest will leave you fresher to make better decisions.
• Examine your perspective. Do you waste time worrying about the little things? Don't.
• Be at least as tolerant, encouraging, and nonjudgmental of yourself as you are of students and colleagues. You have the most control over the stress you place on yourself.
• Unwind from school before facing your responsibilities at home. Take a walk, talk to a friend, or spend a few minutes alone.

Avoid burnout

Committed, caring teachers sometimes run the risk of "burning out." It's a condition resulting from too much effort with too little return.

We all need regular recharging. In his book *Sometimes a Shining Moment*, teacher Eliot Wigginton describes teachers who have managed to avoid burnout and how they've done it. Here's his advice:
• Build relationships with colleagues—both professional and personal. By playing and working together, you can fight the isolation that surrounds those who teach and work in separate classrooms.
• Become involved in your students' community—participating in community functions, holding summer jobs, developing friendships outside of school.
• Welcome situations in which you can continue growing—as a person and as a teacher. Teachers who avoid burnout recognize that adults are not finished products, says Wigginton. "They enjoy the sensation of mental exercise and the surprise and amazement that always come as one masters a new skill or becomes acquainted with a new philosophy or idea. It is in this role that the best often have so much fun with their own students, for together, they trek out into the unknown, exclaiming together over what they find."
• Share responsibilities with others. You can decrease your workload and increase your effectiveness, for example, by realizing how much students have to offer each other. "[Energized teachers] see a new class of thirty-seven youngsters, for example, not as thirty-seven albatrosses but as thirty-seven potential teachers," says Wigginton.
• Keep the proper perspective on those temporary setbacks, disappointments, and frustrations. And have enough fun with what you're doing so that the setbacks and frustrations don't matter so much.

Personal and professional growth are complementary processes. Neglect one, and the other will suffer. But by concentrating on both, you're assuring yourself of a healthy and happy teaching career.

Chapter 8—Read more about it

1. "Learning to Teach" (Occasional Paper No. 64). Sharon Feiman-Nemser. East Lansing, MI: Institute for Research on Teaching, 1983. Also in *Handbook on Teaching and Policy*. L. Shulman and G. Sykes (eds.). New York: Longman, 1983.

2. *School Teacher: A Sociological Study*. Daniel C. Lortie. Chicago: University of Chicago Press, 1975.

3. "Essentials of Professional Growth." T.U. Wildman and J. A. Niles. *Educational Leadership*, 44, 5, (Feb. 1987), 410.

4. *Sometimes a Shining Moment*. Eliot Wigginton. Garden City, NY: Anchor Press/ Doubleday, 1986.

5. "What It Means to Teach." David Hawkins. *Teachers College Record*, 1973, 75, 1, 7-16.

6. "Using Observation to Improve Your Teaching" (Occasional Paper No. 21). Jere Brophy. East Lansing, MI: Institute for Research on Teaching, 1979. Also in *Childhood Education*, 55, (1979), 313-317.

7. *Beyond Surface Curriculum: An Interview Study of Teachers' Understandings*. A. Bussis, E. Chittendon, and M. Amaral. Boulder, CO: Westview Press, 1976.

8. *A Teacher's Guide to Classroom Research*. D. A. Hopkins. Philadelphia: Open University Press, 1985.

9. "Collaborative Research on Teaching." W. Tikunoff and B. Ward. *The Elementary School Journal*, 83, (1983), 4, 453-468.

10. *Writer's Market*. (Published Annually.) Cincinnati, OH: Writer's Digest Books.

11. "Sights and Sounds of Life in Schools" Frederick Erickson and Jan Wilson. East Lansing, MI: Institute for Research Teaching, (R.S. No. 125). Michigan State University, 1984.

12. *The Winner's Edge: The Critical Attitude of Success*. Denis Waitley. New York: Times Books, 1980.

NOTES

NOTES

Journals and Other Publications for Educators

ACEHI Journal (Association of Canadian Educators of the Hearing Impaired
Administrators Notebook
Adult Education Quarterly
AEDS Journal (Association for Educational Data Systems)
Alliance Update
American Biology Teacher
American Journal of Education
American Scholar
American School and University
American School Board Journal
American Speech
American Teacher
Arithmetic Teacher
Audio-Visual Communications
Audio-Visual Journal
AV Guide Newsletter
AV Guide: The Learning Media Magazine
Biology Digest
The Book Report
British Journal of Guidance and Counseling
Cahiers De Lexicologie
Cahiers Pedagogiques
Canadian Journal of Economics
Canadian Journal of Education
Canadian Journal of Educational Communication
Career World—Real World
Cartoonist Profiles
Change: The Magazine of Higher Learning
Children Today
Chronicle of Higher Education
Classical Journal
Classical World
Classmate
Classroom Computer Learning
Clearing House
College Board Review
College Composition and Communication
College English

College Teaching
Communication Education
Community/Junior College Quarterly of Research and Practice
Counselor Education and Supervision
Crafts 'n Things
Creative Child and Adult Quarterly
Current Health
Curriculum Review
Down East Magazine
Educateur
Education
Education Canada
Education Daily
Education Digest
Education Enfantine
Education Permanente
Education Three-Thirteen
Education Times
Education & Training of the Mentally Retarded
Educational Communication & Technology Journal
Educational Digest
Educational Forum
EITV (Educational & Industrial Television)
Educational Leadership
Educational Media International
Educational & Psychological Measurement
Educational Record
Educational Research
Educational Review
Elementary School Guidance and Counseling
Elementary School Journal
Elementary Teacher's Ideas & Materials Workshop
ELT Documents
English Journal
English Literary Renaissance
Et Cetera: A Review of General Semantics

Exceptional Children
Executive Educator
Focus on Exceptional Children
Forecast for Home Economics
Foreign Language Annals
French Review
German Quarterly
Germanic Review
Graphis
Harvard Educational Review
Health Education
High School Journal
Highlights Magazine for Children
History and Social Science Teacher
History Teacher
Ideas Para Su Hogar
IEEE Potentials (Institute of Electrical & Electronics Engineers, Inc.)
Illinois Teacher of Home Economics
Innovative Higher Education
Instructor
Instrumentalist
Interracial Books for Children Bulletin
It Starts in the Classroom
Journal of Architectural Education
Journal of Chemical Education
Journal of College Science Teaching
Journal of Counseling and Development
Journal of Counseling Psychology
Journal of Curriculum Studies
Journal of Education
Journal of Educational Psychology
Journal of Educational Research
Journal of Employment Counseling
Journal of Environmental Education
Journal of Experimental Education
Journal of Health, Physical Education & Recreation
Journal of Higher Education
Journal of Home Economics
Journal of Learning Disabilities
Journal of Negro Education

Journal of Physical Education,
   Recreation and Dance
Journal of Reading
Journal of Recreational
   Mathematics
Journal of Research and
   Development in Education
Journal of School Health
Journal of School Psychology
Journal of Speech and Hearing
   Disorders
Journal of Teacher Education
Junior Education
Junior Scholastic (Teacher Edition)
Language Learning
Learning
Let's Find Out
Library Imagination Paper
Lifelong Learning
Lovejoy's Guidance Digest
Master Teacher
Mathematics Teacher
Measurement and Evaluation in
   Counseling and Development
Media Review
Mental Retardation
Midstream
Modern Language Journal
My Weekly Reader (Editions for
   Grades 1-6)
Principal (National Association of
   Elementary School Principals
   membership)
Nation's Schools Report
New Jersey Parent Teacher
New Jersey School Boards
   Association Leader
NSTA Technical Journal (National
   Science & Technology Authority)

Observer
Ontario Education
Orbit
Peabody Journal of Education
Phi Delta Kappan
Physical Educator
Physics Teacher
Pre K Today
Psychology in the Schools
Psychology Today
Quarterly Journal of Speech
Reading Abstracts
Reading Research Quarterly
Reading Teacher
Reading Today (Membership)
Rehabilitation Counseling Bulletin
Religion Teachers Journal
Reprints From the Soviet Press
Report on Education Research
Research in Higher Education
Research Quarterly for Exercise
   and Sport
Resources in Education
Review of Educational Research
Revue Belge De Psychologie et de
   Pedagogie
Russian Literature Triquarterly
Saturday Review
Scholastic Action
Scholastic Editors Trend
Scholastic Math
Scholastic News: News Citizen
   (Teacher Edition)
Scholastic News: News Explorer
   (Teacher Edition)
Scholastic News: News Pilot
   (Teacher Edition)
Scholastic News: News Ranger

Scholastic News: News Trails
   (Teacher Edition)
Scholastic Sprint
School Counselor
School Law News
School Library Media Quarterly
School Microcomputing Bulletin
School Musician, Director, and
   Teacher
School Science and Mathematics
School Shop
Schuss
Science and Children
Science Education
Science Teacher
Scienceland
Sentinel
Sesame Street
Shining Star
Social Education
Social Studies
Teaching and Computers
Teaching English to the Deaf and
   Second Language Students
Teaching Exceptional Children
The Technology Teacher
Theory Into Practice
This Magazine
Thresholds in Education
Tips and Topics in Home
   Economics
Urban Education
Voice
Voice of Youth Advocates
Volta Review
Wee Wisdom
Wellness Newsletter
What's New in Home Economics
World Newsmap of the Week

Educational Laboratories & Research Centers

Educational Laboratories

Appalachia Educational Laboratory, Inc.
P.O. Box 1348
Charleston, WV 25325
(304) 347-0400

Far West Laboratory for Educational
Research and Development
1855 Folsom Street
San Francisco, CA 94103
(415) 565-3000/3125/3115

Mid-continent Regional Educational
Laboratory
12500 East Iliff, Suite 201
Aurora, CO 80014
(303) 337-0990

North Central Regional Educational
Laboratory
295 Emroy Avenue
Elmhurst, IL 60126
(312) 941-7677

Northwest Regional Educational
Laboratory
101 S.W. Main Avenue, Suite 500
Portland, OR 97204
(503) 275-9500; (800) 547-6339

Regional Laboratory for Educational
Improvement of the Northeast and
Islands
290 South Main Street
Andover, MA 01810
(617) 470-0098

Research for Better Schools
444 North Third Street
Philadelphia, PA 19123
(215) 574-9300

Southeastern Educational Improvement
Laboratory
P.O. Box 12746
200 Park Avenue, Suite 204
Research Triangle Park, NC 27709
(919) 549-8216

Southwest Educational Development
Laboratory
211 East Seventh Street
Austin, TX 78701
(512) 476-6861

Southwest Regional Laboratory for
Educational Research and Development
4665 Lampson Avenue
Los Alamitos, CA 90720
(213) 598-7661; (714) 821-7790

Research Centers

Center for Bilingual Research and
Secondary Language Education
University of California
   at Los Angeles
1100 Glendon Avenue, Suite 1740
Los Angeles, CA 90024
(213) 825-8886

Center for Effective Elementary and
Middle Schools
The Johns Hopkins University
3505 North Charles Street
Baltimore, MD 21218
(301) 338-7570

Center for Policy Research in Education
Rutgers, The State University
   of New Jersey
The Eagleton Institute of Politics
Wood Lawn—Neilson Campus
New Brunswick, NJ 08901
(201) 828-2210

Center for Research on Evaluation,
Standards, and Student Testing
Center for the Study of Evaluation
UCLA Graduate School of Education
145 Moore Hall
Los Angeles, CA 90024
(213) 825-4711

Center for the Study of Reading
University of Illinois
   at Urbana-Champaign
174 Children's Research Center
51 Gerty Drive
Champaign, IL 61820
(217) 333-2552

Center for the Study of Writing
University of California at Berkeley
School of Education
Berkeley, CA 94720
(415) 642-0746

Educational Technology Center
Harvard Graduate Center
337 Gutman Library
6 Appian Way
Cambridge, MA 02138
(617) 495-9373

Institute for Education and Employment
Teachers College, Columbia University
525 W. 120th Street/Box 174
New York, NY 10027
(212) 678-3091

Institute for Research on Teaching
Erickson Hall
Michigan State University
East Lansing, MI 48824-1034
(517) 353-6413

Learning Research and Development
Center
University of Pittsburgh
3939 O'Hara Street
Pittsburgh, PA 15260
(412) 624-7020

National Center on Effective Secondary
Schools
University of Wisconsin
School of Education
1025 W. Johnson Street
Madison, WI 53706
(608) 263-7575

National Center on Postsecondary
Governance and Finance
University of Maryland
6525 Belcrest Road, Suite 430
Hyattsville, MD 20873
(301) 454-1568

National Center for Research to Improve
Postsecondary Teaching and Learning
University of Michigan
School of Education, Suite 2400
Ann Arbor, MI 48109-1259
(313) 764-9472

National Center for Research in
Vocational Education
The Ohio State University
1960 Kenny Road
Columbus, OH 43210
(614) 486-3655; (800) 848-4815

Research and Development Center on
Teacher Education
Erickson Hall
Michigan State University
East Lansing, MI 48824-1034
(517) 355-1716

Educational Resources Information Center

The Educational Resources Information Center (ERIC)
is an information system sponsored by the U.S. Department of Education.
Here are the names and addresses of eight pertaining
most directly to K-8 education.

The ERIC Clearinghouse for Science, Mathematics, and Environmental Education
The Ohio State University
1200 Chambers Road, Third Floor
Columbus, OH 43212-1792
(614) 422-6717

The ERIC Clearinghouse for Information Resources
Syracuse University
School of Education
130 Huntington Hall
Syracuse, NY 13244-2340
(315) 423-3640

The ERIC Clearinghouse for Elementary and Early Childhood
University of Illinois
805 West Pennsylvania Avenue
Urbana, IL 61801-4897
(217) 333-1386

The ERIC Clearinghouse for Educational Management
University of Oregon
1787 Agate Street
Eugene, OR 97403-5207
(503) 686-5043

The ERIC Clearinghouse for Languages and Linguistics
Center for Applied Linguistics
1118 22nd Street NW
Washington, DC 20037-0037
(202) 429-9292

The ERIC Clearinghouse for Social Studies/ Social Science Education
Social Studies Development Center
Indiana University
2805 East 10th Street, Suite 120
Bloomington, IN 47408-2373
(812) 335-3838

The ERIC Clearinghouse for Tests, Measurement, and Evaluation
The American Institute for Research
3333 K Street NW
Washington, DC 20007
(202) 342-5060

The ERIC Clearinghouse for Reading and Communication Skills
Indiana University
Smith Research Center
2805 East 10th Street
Bloomington, IN 47408-2373
(812) 335-1236

CONCLUSION

Learning to teach is not just for beginners. It's a challenge that stimulates professionals throughout their careers. The best teachers are those who are always trying to become better.

Successful teaching is not a hit-or-miss proposition dependent on the right bag of tricks. There's a real "science of teaching" to guide your actions and decisions and a growing knowledge base gleaned from the practical wisdom of your experienced colleagues. We do know many of the factors contributing to effective practice. We can say that some practices are more effective than others in certain situations with certain students.

Yet there are no recipes for effective teaching. It boils down to individual teachers making individual decisions for individual students. Teaching, as other professions, relies on the judgments of its individual practitioners. Therein lies the "art of teaching."

You really matter! You are the most important factor in school learning. Your teaching is a unique product—the result of your unique endeavor. Protect it, nourish it, give it room to grow.

Best wishes, teacher. And may your journey toward professional excellence be rewarding and filled with happy times.

INDEX OF CHARTS

INDEX OF REPRODUCIBLES

Instructor Books

7500 OLD OAK BOULEVARD, CLEVELAND, OH 44130

INSTRUCTOR RESOURCE SERIES

Big Idea Book — 750 best classroom do-its and use-its from Instructor magazine. **IB401.**

Big Basics Book — 55 master plans for teaching the basics, with over 100 reproducibles. **IB402.**

Big Holiday Book — Seasonal songs, stories, poems, plays, and art, plus an activities calendar. **IB403.**

Big Seasonal Arts & Crafts Book — Over 300 projects for special days and seasons. **IB404.**

Big Language Arts Book for Primary Grades — 136 reading and language skills reproducibles. **IB405.**

Big Math Book for Primary Grades — 135 reproducibles on number concepts and processes. **IB406.**

Big Book of Teacher Savers — Class lists, letters to parents, record-keeping forms, calendars, maps, writing forms, and more. **IB407.**

Synonyms, Sentences, and Spelling Bees: Language Skills Book A — 140 reproducibles. **IB408.**

Periods, Paragraphs, and Prepositions: Language Skills Book B — Over 140 reproducibles. **IB409.**

Big Book of Reading Ideas — Teacher-tested reading ideas for use with any reading system. **IB410.**

Teacher's Activity Calendar — Red letter days, ideas, units for the school year. **IB411.**

Early Education Almanac — Hundreds of activities for kindergarten and beyond. **IB412.**

Paper, Pen, and Think — Ideas galore for developing a sequential writing program. **IB413.**

Beating the Bulletin Board Blues — Step-by-step ways to bulletin board learning centers. **IB414.**

Success with Sticky Subjects — Books A and B together offer over 240 reproducible worksheets for classroom drill in problem areas of the curriculum. **Book A—IB415. Book B—IB416.**

Foolproof, Failsafe Seasonal Science — Units, experiments, and quick activities. **IB417.**

Poetry Place Anthology — 605 favorite poems from Instructor, organized for instant access. **IB418.**

Big Book of Plays — 82 original, reproducible plays for all occasions and levels. **IB419.**

Artfully Easy! — "How-to" workshops on teaching art basics, group projects, and more! **IB420.**

Big Book of Study Skills — Techniques and activities for the basic subject areas. **IB421.**

Big Book of Study Skills Reproducibles — Over 125 classroom-tested worksheets for all levels. **IB422.**

Big Book of Computer Activities — A hands-on guide for using computers in every subject. **IB423.**

Read-Aloud Anthology — 98 stories for all grades and all occasions. **IB424.**

Page-a-Day Pursuits — Over 300 reproducibles on famous days, birthdays, and events. **IB425.**

Big Book of Holiday Word Puzzles — 400 skill-builders for 130 year 'round celebrations. **IB426.**

Big Book of Health and Safety — Reproducible activities to shape up the health curriculum. **IB427.**

Teacher Savers Two — Reproducible awards, contracts, letters, sanity-keepers galore. **IB428.**

Celebrate America — Over 200 reproducible activities about the symbols, the land, the people of the U.S.A. Maps, graphs, timelines, folklore, and more. Eight pull-out posters. **IB429.**

Big Book of Absolutely Everything — 1001 ideas to take you through the school year. **IB430.**

Language Unlimited — 160 reproducibles sharpen reading, writing, speaking, listening skills. **IB431.**

Children and Media — Activities help kids learn from TV, radio, film, videotape, print. **IB432.**

Blockbuster Bulletin Boards — 366 teacher originals for all grades, subjects, and seasons. **IB433.**

Hey Gang! Let's Put On A Show — 50 original skits, choral readings, plays for all ages. **IB434.**

Puzzle Pals — Mazes, decoders, wordsearches, hidden objects and more. **IB435.**

Hands-On Science — Jam-packed with facts and activities to develop young scientists, K-8. **IB436.**

21st Century Discipline — Practical strategies to teach students responsibility and self-control. **IB437.**

Learning to Teach — A blend of research on teaching with the practical insights of experienced teachers. **IB438.**

Teaching Kids to Care — 156 activities to help young children cooperate, share, and learn together. **IB250.**

Games, Giggles, and Giant Steps - 250 games for children ages 2-8; no equipment needed. **IB251**

Everybody Sing and Dance - 80 hands-on, shoes-off song, dance, rhythm, and creative movement experiences. **IB252**